The Shaping of Tuscany

To its many tourists and visitors, the Tuscan landscape evokes a sense of timelessness and harmony. Yet, the upheavals of the twentieth century profoundly reshaped rural Tuscany. Uncovering the experiences of ordinary people, Professor Gaggio traces the history of Tuscany to show how the region's modern conflicts and aspirations have contributed to forging its modern-day beauty. We learn how the rise of fascism was particularly violent in rural Tuscany, and how struggles between Communist sharecroppers and their landlords raged long after the end of the dictatorship. The flight from the farms in the 1950s and 1960s disorientated many Tuscans, prompting ambitious development projects; and in more recent decades the emergence of the heritage industry has raised the spectre of commodification. The book tells the story of how many Tuscans themselves have become tourists in their own land – forced to adapt to rapid change and reinvent their landscape in the process.

Dario Gaggio was born and raised in the outskirts of Florence, Tuscany, before moving to the United States for graduate school. He holds a PhD in History from Northwestern University and is Professor at the University of Michigan in Ann Arbor. He is the author of *In Gold We Trust: Social Capital and Economic Change in the Italian Jewelry Towns* (2007). His research has pioneered the integration of cultural change and political economy from an interdisciplinary perspective, combining historical methodologies with the theoretical insights of sociology, anthropology, and human geography.

The Shaping of Tuscany

Landscape and Society between Tradition and Modernity

Dario Gaggio

University of Michigan, Ann Arbor

CAMBRIDGE
UNIVERSITY PRESS

CAMBRIDGE
UNIVERSITY PRESS

University Printing House, Cambridge CB2 8BS, United Kingdom

Cambridge University Press is part of the University of Cambridge.

It furthers the University's mission by disseminating knowledge in the pursuit of education, learning, and research at the highest international levels of excellence.

www.cambridge.org
Information on this title: www.cambridge.org/9781107127777

First published 2017

Printed in the United Kingdom by Clays, St Ives plc

A catalogue record for this publication is available from the British Library.

Library of Congress Cataloging-in-Publication Data
Names: Gaggio, Dario, 1966– author.
Title: The shaping of Tuscany : landscape and society between tradition and modernity / Dario Gaggio.
Description: Cambridge, United Kingdom : Cambridge University Press, 2016.
Identifiers: LCCN 2016023881 | ISBN 9781107127777 (hardback)
Subjects: LCSH: Rural development – Italy – Tuscany – History. |
Land use, Rural – Italy – Tuscany – History. |
Cultural landscapes – Italy – Tuscany – History. |
Tuscany (Italy) – Civilization. | Tuscany (Italy) – History – 1945–
Classification: LCC HN488.T84 G34 2016 |
DDC 306.0945/5–dc23
LC record available at https://lccn.loc.gov/2016023881

ISBN 978-1-107-12777-7 Hardback

Contents

Acknowledgments

I started working on this book almost a decade ago with a very personal agenda, having grown up at the outskirts of Florence in the 1970s and 1980s. The town where I lived was neither city nor countryside, and it was surrounded (perhaps also haunted) by the vestiges of a rapidly disappearing "peasant civilization." Many years and detours later, after moving to the United States, I confronted my own longing and many Americans' romantic admiration for Tuscany, a place both they and I "knew" so little about. The first people I want to acknowledge are therefore my friends and colleagues who, on American soil, helped me look at my native land with fresh eyes, at once soberly and empathetically. I am deeply grateful for the conversations I had with my fellow historians at the University of Michigan over the years. They make a blissfully long list: Paulina Alberto, Kathryn Babayan, Pamela Ballinger, Howard Brick, Charlie Bright, Kathleen Canning, John Carson, Rita Chin, Joshua Cole, Jay Cook, Geoff Eley, Will Glover, Dena Goodman, David Hancock, Gabrielle Hecht, Nancy Hunt, Kali Israel, Paul Johnson, Val Kivelson, Matthew Lassiter, Farina Mir, Anthony Mora, Gina Morantz-Sanchez, Rachel Neis, Doug Northrop, Brian Porter-Szücs, Helmut Puff, Rebecca Scott, Perrin Selcer, Minnie Sinha, Scott Spector, Paolo Squatriti, Ron Suny, Melanie Tanielian, Tomi Tonomura, and Jeff Veidlinger.

Working at a famously interdisciplinary institution, I also took advantage of the wit and wisdom of many other colleagues in departments nearby and farther afield. They include Kerstin Barndt, Giorgio Bertellini, Vincenzo Binetti, Alison Cornish, Susan Crowell, Amal Fadlalla, Megan Holmes, Stuart Kirsch, Alaina Lemon, Mike McGovern, Karla Mallette, Elizabeth Sears, Andrew Shryock, Peggy Somers, Lydia Soo, George Steinmetz, and Geneviève Zubrzycki. I also learned a great deal from former and current graduate students, especially Trevor Kilgore, Davide Orsini, Roberta Pergher, Lissy Reiman, and Joseph Viscomi. Many scholars and friends on both sides of the Ocean shared with me their insights and advice. I am especially grateful to Ken Alder, Karl Appuhn,

Wallace Best, Vicky de Grazia, Giulio Giovannoni, Tracey Heatherington, Silvia Ross, and Fred Wherry. A heartfelt thank-you goes to the Program in Agrarian Studies at Yale University, which provided me with much-needed time off teaching. I learned a great deal from the Program's leaders, Peter Perdue, James Scott, and Kalyanakrishnan Sivaramakrishnan, as well as from the other fellows, Arupjyoti Saikia, Roseann Cohen, and Ling Zhang.

What started as a somewhat romantic attempt at deromanticizing rural Tuscany morphed into a more subtle exploration of the ways in which a variety of actors have invested (or divested) value in place by telling stories, shaping the land, and readjusting their stories accordingly, in a cycle that is at once a powerful historical process in its own right and a process of history-making, sometimes bordering on (self-) deception. I owe whatever subtlety I have managed to convey in this book to a group of diverse but equally insightful "local informants," who have shared with me their aspirations, achievements, and disappointments. Their Tuscany is now mine as well. They include Alessandro Andreini, Giuliano Cannata, Pietro Clemente, Paola Falini, Antonio Franchetti, Martino Manetti, Gianfranco Molteni, Benedetta Origo, Pietro Piussi, Paolo Pellizzari, Rino Pecci, and several others who desire to remain nameless or only shared with me their first names in short but engaging exchanges. Finally, like all historians, I owe a great deal to many archivists and librarians who were patient enough to indulge my curiosity, often keeping venues open just for me. Again, there are many more benefactors than I can acknowledge here, but a special thank-you goes to Roberta Cortonesi, Elisa Costa, Calogero Governali, and Loretta Veri. I also wish to thank Danielle LaVaque-Manty for helping me with my prose and Rachel Trudell for designing the maps.

Perhaps we should all try to look at (but also listen to, and smell) landscape the way children do, ready to be surprised and willing to believe the stories places tell. Some children grow up to become historians, and they learn to approach places with the kind of jaded skepticism the profession demands. Hopefully, I have managed to retain a bit of the magic that pervades rural Tuscany – the magic of sharing stories and making a coherent tale out of them. In the end, I owe the most to the thousands of people I met as a child, as I ran wild in the woods and backyards of postrural Tuscany.

Introduction

In her best-selling memoir, *Under the Tuscan Sun,* Frances Mayes imagines heaven as a maze of gravel roads lacing the Tuscan countryside, each leading to a villa or church to be explored with the thrilling sensation of having gotten lost.[1] One visits rural Tuscany, like many other iconic places in the world, in the hope of feeling the intoxicating combination of recognition and disorientation that Mayes calls her heaven. The Tuscan countryside, like other rural places, seems to invite the visitor to dwell for a while, perhaps even buy an old house and try to become one with the place and its history: "The language, history, art, places in Italy are endless – two lifetimes wouldn't be enough. And, ah, the foreign self. The new life might shape itself to the contours of the house, which already is at home in the landscape, and to the rhythms around it."[2] A sojourn in Tuscany promises a new self, at once at home in the landscape and foreign to it, in a perpetual tension that keeps taunting the "residential tourist" with the power of one hundred renovation projects. The perfect home, at once true to the land and to oneself, is as elusive as it is tantalizing.

The residential tourist, Mayes' aspirational self, is a perfected local, one who learns from an old peasant to forage for herbs and call them by their Tuscan names but refuses to join so many other locals in shopping at the mall down in the valley, by the autostrada. In a similar vein, for many Italians, Tuscany has become Italy perfected. Marco Tullio Giordana's filmic saga, *The Best of Youth* (2003), follows a family through the violent conflicts of post–World War II Italy until everyone who has survived the storm can be gathered safely in a nicely restructured house somewhere in the Tuscan countryside at the dawn of the new millennium. After all, by the time the series aired on TV and was released in the theaters, every Italian had been exposed for years to Gavino Sanna's 1980s commercials for Barilla's line of baked goods, named after a Sienese white mill

[1] F. Mayes, *Under the Tuscan Sun: At Home in Italy* (New York: Broadway Books, 1996): 4.
[2] Ibid.: 12.

1

(the Mulino Bianco). Appearing after a long season of political strife, those commercials promised a newly pacified and prosperous society the wholesome authenticity that only a Tuscan rural setting could evoke. The brick-and-mortar mill soon became a tourist destination in its own right, a symbol of harmony worth a detour, perhaps as a family outing to one's own family ideal.

These experiences of the Tuscan countryside rely on highly selective senses of place and time, capable of producing coherent and legible images. They are also exquisitely modern. According to sociologist Dean MacCannell, tourism should be understood as the search for an experience of coherence and totality, contrasted with the fractured and relatively meaningless character of the tourist's perception of modernity.[3] In a modern form of pilgrimage, the tourist collects experiences of authenticity in the ongoing attempt to make herself whole and share this wholeness, or meaningfulness, with others. A central argument of this book is that in a fundamental sense everyone in rural Tuscany has been a tourist over the past century. Even the "locals" have struggled to be "at home in Tuscany," to paraphrase the subtitle of Mayes' book. Over the past century, the Tuscan countryside has changed radically in its social and spatial features. Generations of locals and strangers have witnessed these changes with a mix of disorientation and exhilaration, even as they contributed to shaping them, trying to make sense of them and construct coherent narratives. This search for coherence and totality has been particularly successful in Tuscany, making it the setting for countless clichés. But Tuscany has also been the setting of countless stories of conflict and misrecognition. Many of those stories have been forgotten, but often not without leaving traces that have shaped what Tuscany is today. This book attempts to retrieve some of those stories and traces.

Not only are the experiences to be had in Tuscany exquisitely modern, the very landscape people come to see and feel is the complex and contradictory product of modern processes and sensibilities. Rural Tuscany is today above all an iconic landscape, represented and recognized all over the world. It is a landscape that projects an aura of immutability and yet also one that has changed radically and rapidly over the past century. In celebrating the Tuscan lifestyle, another residential tourist and memoirist, Ferenc Máté, detects a distinctive resonance between people and landscape in rural Tuscany: "Perhaps part of a Tuscan's calm comes from the ancient hamlets and towns around him, where houses, churches, and art have stood firm for centuries; and from a countryside that, for the

---

[3] D. MacCannell, *The Tourist: A New Theory of the Leisure Class* (Berkeley: University of California Press, 1976).

most part, has changed little over time. There are olive groves whose trees are hundreds of years old, and vineyards that have been vineyards since Etruscan times."[4] Calm is far more present in Máté's perception than in the historical record. Rural Tuscany was one of the areas where the rise of fascism in the early 1920s was most violent; where the struggle between Communist sharecropping peasants and conservative landlords raged for years after the end of World War II; where the flight from the farms in the 1950s and 1960s was widely lived as a threat and a trauma; where the influx of Sardinians and other immigrants raised specters of decay and barbarization; and where leftist administrators nurtured for decades dreams of regeneration through massive infrastructural investments. And it is also a place where olive and vine growing have changed a great deal. The vineyards and olive groves Máté sees (and owns) look very different and are cultivated very differently from those of half a century ago, and of course they are often tended to by people like himself, rather than by sharecroppers. Indeed, there are no sharecroppers left in rural Tuscany.

A beautiful landscape is one that resonates with its inhabitants and visitors.[5] This is not only a personal and subjective experience but also one with a collective dimension. Some societies are perceived to be at odds with the landscape they inhabit, others as perfectly adjusted to it. Of course these perceptions are selective and problematic insofar as no landscape conveys a simple and unitary message, but they can also be powerful and persuasive. This book understands landscape not as simple topography or scenery, but as a complex and evolving set of relationships between place, in its multiple meanings, and society, with its tensions and fractures. From this perspective, landscapes are of course about senses of place.[6] They look and feel in distinctive ways to those who experience them. This book, however, contends that landscapes are also about senses of time, about the stories that a place tells (or is made to tell) and those that are left untold or get forgotten. Writing the history of a landscape means to follow at least some of those stories over time, tracing the origins of the stories a place tells today, but also retrieving those that have been silenced, all the while trying to understand how and why that silencing "took place." Doing so means to challenge the

---

[4] F. Máté, *The Hills of Tuscany: A New Life in an Old Land* (New York: Flamingo, 1999): 29.
[5] This notion of beauty as resonance (*stimmung*) was theorized by Friedrich Schiller and the German romantics. See Chenxi Tang, *The Geographic Imagination of Modernity: Geography, Literature, and Philosophy in German Romanticism* (Stanford: Stanford University Press, 2008): 77–81.
[6] Steven Feld and Keith Basso (eds.), *Senses of Place* (Santa Fe: School of American Research Press, 1996).

sense of coherence and totality some landscapes project. Historians are often cruel storytellers, eager to dispel myths and comfortable tales, but a good historian must also take those myths seriously, understand their appeal, and account for their emergence. Thus, this book is about the incongruities as well as the clichés that have made up one of the world's most celebrated landscapes.

Like any other landscape, but perhaps with uncommon poignancy, rural Tuscany bears the incongruous signs of a myriad of stories and trajectories. Sly sharecroppers, even slyer real estate agents, rebellious rural Communists, pragmatic politicians, immigrant Sardinian shepherds, concerned preservationists, and millionaire celebrities have all left traces and told stories about the hills of Tuscany. Indeed, as recently as the late 1970s, rural Tuscany appeared as a cacophony of voices and perspectives. Some of the farmhouses that had been abandoned by the peasants lay as decaying ruins; others were being restructured for tasteful relaxation; some others were surrounded by large herds of Sardinian sheep; and yet others concealed kidnapping victims. Yet, today few landscapes in the world appear as unitary, coherent, and seemingly legible as the Tuscan hills. Their beauty depends on such legibility, nor is the coherence simply an illusion. The Tuscan landscape may well be the most painstakingly regulated countryside in the world, and such regulatory efforts are themselves the product of complex and conflicting senses of place and time, not to mention massive amounts of physical and cultural work. There is no denying that the Tuscan landscape today "resonates" more than many others in the world, but this resonance has been the outcome of complex and contingent historical processes, full of twists and turns. Thus, this book is in part about the ways in which societies, sometimes, "come together" and manage to create a coherent sense of themselves and of the spaces they inhabit, malgré tout, just to see such coherence come under ongoing and forever increasing threat. After all, resonance between society and place produces both beauty and vulnerability.

Many of the memoirs written by people who grew up in rural Tuscany share the mix of familiarity and disorientation evoked by Mayes in her version of heaven, although their attention focuses on different objects and events. Ivo Guerri, for example, was born in 1945 to a family of small-scale farmers in the Orcia valley, at the southern edge of the province of Siena. Like many of his generation, he did not follow in his parents' footsteps but became a construction worker instead, eventually specializing in the restructuring of old farmhouses for the tourists' enjoyment. He also developed a passion for biking and storytelling. His memoir opens with the tale of a bicycle ride on a spring morning: "As my legs pedaled calmly and effortlessly, my mind and my eyes were attracted to the land-scape, which I knew so well." There was Mount Amiata, the extinguished volcano that "seemed to have been put there by someone, as guardian of the valley." There were the odd clay formations, similar to upside-down udders. And there were the smells of spring. But then Guerri switches from a spatial to a temporal tale, marveling at how much the valley has changed in his lifetime. What used to be a hostile and barren landscape is now a paragon of harmony and gentility. But who created all that? "The Fanfani Plan [a major land reform of the early 1950s], the Reclamation Consortium, the new earth-moving machines that were made available to the new farmers, and their entrepreneurial initiative have contrib-uted to the radical transformation of this land, giving it that harmonious aspect we admire today."[7] For Guerri, the Orcia valley, which UNESCO has listed as a World Heritage Site largely for being recognizable from the paintings of the fourteenth-century Sienese Primitives, is a landscape where modernity has redeemed itself. Harmony and gentility have come with the roar of the tractor.

Guerri is far from alone in telling the recent history of the Orcia val-ley (and of rural Tuscany in general) as a story of ruptures.[8] The sense of historic continuity evoked by some residential tourists contrasts with more fractured senses of time, punctuated by the succession of distinct generations. The first rupture was World War II and the anti-Fascist and anti-Nazi Resistance of 1943–1944. In the wake of these events the sharecroppers of Tuscany, and of north-central Italy more generally, organized by the Communist Party, rose up against their landlords. As former sharecropper Rino Pecci told me in an interview, "from the foundation of sharecropping in the 1400s until 1943 nothing had changed. After that everything has changed. But it was not inevitable. All of that could have lasted another one hundred years. Some people do not realize that." The second rupture was the "rural exodus" of the late 1950s and 1960s, when Tuscan agriculture shed two-thirds of its workforce and thousands of farms were abandoned. Then came a third rupture in the late 1970s and 1980s, when a new kind of agriculture, based on the recapitalization of a few crops (above all the newly estab-lished vineyards), and novel kinds of cultural valorization and tour-ism ushered in some welcome, albeit always fragile and contentious, prosperity.

[7] I. Guerri, *Val d'Orcia: Mattino di Primavera: Ricordi di un Ragazzo di Campagna* (San Quirico: Donchisciotte, 2008).
[8] Federico Scarpelli, *La Memoria del Territorio: Patrimonio Culturale e Nostalgia a Pienza* (Ospedaletto: Pacini, 2007).

These ruptures are part of the senses of place and time that have made the Tuscan hills, and, on one level, this is a book about transitions in political economy and the ways these transitions have reshaped both land and society. The book's narrative arc charts a path from tradition to modernity, and finally to postmodernity, setting these shifts in the unlikely setting of an iconic place that now projects an aura of permanence and immutability. Since the early twentieth century, if not earlier, Tuscans of all stripes have debated the categories or "regimes" of tradition and modernity, and today's reliance on intangibles such as landscape beauty is often interpreted by Tuscans themselves as the hallmark of a postmodern or postproductive economy. Each of these regimes produced specific spatial configurations, or landscapes, and they all shaped distinctive senses of time and place. In space we read time, as Karl Schlögel has put it, and in Tuscany tradition, modernity, and postmodernity could indeed be read in space – in the present, retroactively, and as aspirations for the future.[9]

The landscape of tradition in Tuscany was that of sharecropping, which forged both land and society for centuries. This regime, however, felt more coherent in retrospect, after its disappearance, than when it ruled the land. Arguably, sharecropping had been in flux for decades before its collapse in the 1960s, and the Fascist regime had been instrumental in both buttressing and transforming it. By the same token, rural Tuscans, especially a restless and militant peasantry, had anticipated the landscape of modernity for decades, only to find its realized features surprisingly hard to decipher. The Communist Party, by far the most popular political force in the region after World War II, struggled to articulate a coherent message, promoting "modern" ways of life and bemoaning many of their consequences. Finally, the postmodern or postproductive landscape is shot through with the melancholic quest for elusive sources of authenticity, a quest that leads people to harken back to imagined pasts that are made to matter in the present.

This complexity of perspectives suggests that the language of transition is ill equipped to make sense of the nonlinear ways people perceive and engage with their surroundings and make sense of change. Historians can tell the history of landscape along one trajectory, shaped by macroscopic changes through which societies go when understood as systems, albeit at different times and speeds. In an economic vein, for example, it would be possible to argue that Tuscany remained traditionally rural longer than, say, Lombardy or the English Midlands; transitioned to

---

[9] K. Schlögel, *Im Raumen Lesen Wir die Zeit: Über Zivilisazionsgeschichte und Geopolitik* (Munich: Carl Hanser Verlag, 2003).

modern forms of agriculture in the 1960s and 1970s; and then partook of the rise of the heritage industry, perhaps even pioneering some of its "postmodern" features. In a political vein, we could argue that the authoritarian paternalism of fascism gave way to class struggle after the war; then a period of uneasy pacification followed, presided over by the Communist Party and allowed by the subsidies the latter managed to funnel from Rome and Brussels; and finally Tuscany reached some kind of postideological stage after the end of the Cold War. Each of those transitions shaped the land as a source of livelihood and a stage for political negotiations. Stated this way, landscape changes in historical time writ large, the one that undergirds the temporality of "history in general," to use Reinhardt Koselleck's expression.[10]

People, however, do not only live in "History." They also live in their own multiple and overlapping times. Mayes was by no means unique in experiencing different senses of time, or temporalities, when travelling between San Francisco and Cortona, Tuscany. Those senses were for her simultaneously deeply personal and meaningfully collective. Indeed, that is why she was able to write a best-selling book about them. But those senses were not linear and mutually exclusive; they coexisted in complex ways. When in Tuscany, Mayes brought with her some of San Francisco, with its sense of time, and vice versa. That is indeed how she came to experience and interpret the two places. But it is not at all necessary to move across oceans to live in more than one time. Post–World War II Tuscan peasants, for example, became "modern" while still on farms, and their sense of modernity was tinged with the seemingly incompatible utopias of consumerism and Communism. They struggled to make sense of the places they inhabited – that is, of their landscape – on the basis of those temporal experiences. Arguably, they had a farther distance to travel than Mayes could ever imagine. Some of them partook of the unprecedented possibilities of the "economic miracle" and became entrepreneurs in the complex networks of proprietary capitalism typical of the Italian industrial districts.[11] Many more came to be employed in the booming construction and manufacturing industries, in trajectories that to them seemed no less entrepreneurial than those of their new bosses. Yet others were "left behind" in a countryside that for a while changed too fast to become a legible landscape.

[10] R. Koselleck, *Futures Past: On the Semantics of Historical Time* (New York: Columbia University Press, 2004). See also Niklas Olsen, *History in the Plural: An Introduction to the Work of Reinhart Koselleck* (New York: Berghahn Books, 2012).

[11] I have written about the Italian industrial districts of small-scale forms and their complex relationships with mezzadria in *In Gold We Trust: Social Capital and Economic Change in the Italian Jewelry Towns* (Princeton: Princeton University Press, 2007).

In a beautifully worded passage, geographer Doreen Massey urges us to imagine space as "a simultaneity of stories-so-far."[12] When we tell the history of society only over "historical time," the temporality of history in general, we are bound to ignore this coexistence of multiple stories, with the senses of time and place in which they are embedded. By contrast, when we tell the history of society over space as well, we are more likely to attend to the mundane but crucial fact that Cortona was made up of Mayes' stories, of those of the old peasant who may have taught her how to forage for herbs, and of those of the locals who shopped at the mall down by the motorway. In slightly more abstract language, thus, the notion of transition cannot do justice to the phenomenology of place, with its plurality of stories and experiences pointing in different directions and embedding different paths. Thus, this is also a book about the opposite of transition. It is a book that attempts to write a "spatial history" capable of attending to the co-presence of different senses of place and time, as well as to the losses societies incur in thinking of themselves as positioned within one trajectory, when the very spaces they inhabit speak of the simultaneity of conflicting paths and experiences. In Tuscany, coherence and totality did not simply emerge (or survive); they came at a cost, and after a fair amount of conflict.

Nostalgia has been the wage of change, its emotional cost. Rural Tuscany is a landscape saturated with nostalgia, an emotion that stems from the awareness of rapid change over space and time.[13] Both "foreigners" and "locals" wax nostalgic on the Tuscan hills, although the foreigners tend to see Tuscany as a stage where they can connect to a more authentic self and way of life that has been lost to their version of modernity, whereas the locals are more aware of the temporal changes that Tuscany has experienced in recent decades. To simplify matters, the foreigners' form of nostalgia is more spatial and the one felt by the locals more temporal in character, with the caveats that Tuscany has produced many kinds of "local nostalgia" and that a "nostalgic local" is perhaps something of an oxymoron (the nostalgic self is never at home).

The following chapters show that these emotional investments are by no means recent. Nostalgia already informed the relationship between rural Tuscany and the Fascist regime, for example. Indeed, almost all the personal and collective trajectories that have intersected in the Tuscan countryside (all those "stories-so-far") have produced their

---

[12] D. Massey, *For Space* (London: SAGE, 2005): 9.

[13] See Frederick Jameson, *Postmodernism, or, the Cultural Logic of Late Capitalism* (Durham, NC: Duke University Press, 1989), and especially the chapter "Nostalgia for the Present" (279–296), in which Jameson theorizes historicity as a perception of the present as history.

own distinctive form of nostalgia. The Fascists in the 1930s fought to "restore" an imagined peasantry that was simultaneously locally rooted and fervently national; the Communists of the 1950s imagined as their mission the completion of the post–World War I peasant struggles, forcibly interrupted by the Black Shirts; the leftists of the 1970s looked at the post–World War II unrest as a missed opportunity to usher in a truly dignified form of modernity; the environmentalists of the 1980s and 1990s argued for the necessity to "preserve" vulnerable relations between people and land; and so on. In some ways (and this is by no means unique to Tuscany), the rural society that mattered in the present was the one that was always already gone.

We owe cultural critic Raymond Williams the fundamental insight that the paradoxes of modernity truly stand out in the countryside and in its relationships with the city. Indeed, the previous paragraph can be interpreted as a version of the "escalator" effect Williams detected in generations of English writers' search for a Golden Age of rural bliss. Tradition, and thus the modernity to which it is contrasted, is a constantly moving target. This book, however, does not look at these cultural perceptions primarily from the vantage point of literature or art, but from the perspectives of "ordinary" people in their engagements with the places they lived in. Williams argued that "a working country is hardly ever a landscape. The very idea of landscape implies separation and observation."[14] In other words, a particular countryside becomes a landscape when the material conditions of its production are ignored. It was the leisured classes that invented landscape as a source of enjoyment and an object of control. Ordinary people do not have "landscapes"; elites do. Geographer Denis Cosgrove has influentially argued that in early modern Europe a particular "way of seeing" gave rise to landscape as abstract space to be dominated and/or artistically enjoyed.[15] Geographers themselves, together with other scientists, have measured, observed, and otherwise acted in such a way as to create landscape categories founded on particular representations of nature-and-society interactions.[16]

---

[14] R. Williams, *The Country and the City* (Oxford: Oxford University Press, 1973): 120.

[15] Denis Cosgrove, *Social Formation and Symbolic Landscape* (Madison: University of Wisconsin Press, 1984). See also Denis Cosgrove and Stephen Daniels (eds.), *The Iconography of Landscape: Essays on the Symbolic Representation, Design, and Use of Past Environments* (Cambridge: Cambridge University Press, 1988). The large body of literature on the relationship between landscape and imperialism also approaches the issue in a similar manner. See, for example, W. J. Thomas Mitchell (ed.), *Landscape and Power* (Chicago: University of Chicago Press, 1994).

[16] In the United States, this conception of landscape as the result of the interaction between a particular natural area and a particular culture was codified by Carl Sauer in the 1920s and 1930s. This conception, and the associated methodology, then became

I do not question the validity of these claims, but I aim to broaden (and perhaps also rescue) the experience of landscape from this elite genealogy, however influential it has been, and consider not only the gazes, but also more generally the senses, of "ordinary" people in their engagements with the places they inhabited and the stories those places told. The elite ideology of landscape, based on the separation of consumption and production, on the distinction between practicality and esthetic pleasure, and on the entire ideological apparatus of emerging capitalism, silenced and removed from consideration other perceptions, sensibilities, and "structures of feeling" that belonged to the subaltern classes.[17] But by attending to people's senses of their landscape, those structures may become accessible again. Capitalism itself has been a structure of feeling in rural Tuscany – a material process that could be experienced not only shaping the land and society, but also the terrain of affect and emotional engagement. Capitalism was a looming threat for some, a set of aspirations for others, and perhaps a combination of the two for most. Tuscans could never agree on when (or even whether) their region had "joined" capitalist modernity. Was traditional sharecropping converging toward a form of rural capitalism even before the rise of fascism? Was the exodus from the farms in the 1960s to be accepted as a sign of progress, or countered as the consequence of social decay? Were the new specialized vineyards a symbol of capitalist restructuring? Were the new shepherds "rural capitalists"? Was rural tourism a form of debasing speculation or a practice of resistance against the homogenizing power of consumerism? Tuscans confronted and debated these questions both as abstract propositions and as emplaced, even embodied, processes, negotiating the distance between the "tide of history" and the personal stories that made up their lives.

In line with recent anthropological thinking, this book argues that landscape is not only scenery to be represented artistically or territory to be investigated scientifically. It is also a set of concrete experiences that connects people and place, informing particular ways of being in the world. In the words of anthropologist Tim Ingold, we should adopt a "'dwelling perspective,' according to which the landscape is constituted as an enduring record of – and testimony to – the lives and works of the past generations who have dwelt within it, and in doing so, have left something there of themselves."[18] From this perspective, landscape

---

canonical in geographical studies. See the collection of essays, Carl Sauer, *Land and Life* (Berkeley: University of California Press, 1963).

[17] Williams was of course aware of this. In his own words, "We can be certain that many more men than writers have looked with intense interest at all the features and movements of the natural world," R. Williams, *The Country and the City*: 120.

[18] T. Ingold, *The Perception of the Environment: Essays on Livelihood, Dwelling and Skill* (London: Routledge, 2000): 189.

is not about distance and observation, but about engagement and even embodiment. Indeed, this book attempts to show that the very people who worked the land also felt nostalgia, exhilaration, and all kinds of other complex emotions about it. Peasants "felt" landscape as well, and those perceptions mattered both to their personal stories and to history writ large. Again, the category of "place" is not sufficient to capture these experiences, for these perceptions are also about time.[19] "Landscape," by contrast, is inclusive enough a category to encompass them.

This approach to landscape as dwelling, as ordinary people's experience, leads to a paradox of sorts. In order to attend to the senses of ordinary people, this book adopts a category and a whole language that many ordinary people did not use to make sense of their lives. Indeed, in Tuscany the language of landscape only became widespread in the 1970s and 1980s, when it came to be deployed as a coherent system of "civilizational" signs in the context of the heritage industry and preservationist movements. The Fascist landlords intent on modernizing agriculture in the 1930s, or the Communist peasants of the early 1950s, or the immigrant Sardinian shepherds of the 1970s, did not speak of landscape as such. But they all perceived and tried to make sense of their surroundings. A vineyard, a herd of sheep, or a farmhouse is not simply an object to be investigated from a distance, but a site of engagement capable of telling different and contradictory stories in its relationships with people and other sites. As deployed in this book, landscape is an analytical category that promises to go beyond representation, separation, and observation, in such a way as to capture some of those experiential senses. I can only hope that this inevitable paradox is a productive one.

This broader understanding of landscape as dwelling also presents obvious challenges for the historian. At least until quite recently, ordinary people did not leave behind many traces of the ways they perceived and engaged with their surroundings. This is indeed one of the main reasons this book limits its scope to the last century, a period for which documentary sources "from below" are abundant and can be integrated with interviews and ethnographic observation. Until the post–World War

---

[19] Ingold's conception of landscape contrasts with that of many cultural geographers, who prefer to limit the scope of landscape to a strictly visual and synchronic experience. In his introduction to the category of place, for example, Tim Creswell expressly states: "We do not live in landscapes – we look at them," *Place: A Short Introduction* (London: Blackwell, 2004): 11. My understanding of landscape, by contrast, is close to John Agnew's theorization of place as a site of political engagement in his *Place and Politics: The Geographical Mediation of State and Society* (London: Allen & Unwin, 1987). I prefer "landscape" to "place" because the former explicitly underscores the interaction of the "objective" and "subjective" dimensions of place (a main feature of phenomenological approaches), and because landscape has a temporal dimension that remains implicit in most conceptions of place.

II period, the perceptual world of Tuscan peasants, for example, was only written about by their landlords and other members of the upper classes. Those utterances were both contradictory and problematic. According to one set of tropes, peasants performed tasks in the landscape that were deliberately aimed at creating beauty. In the late 1930s, Ranuccio Bianchi-Bandinelli, an influential archeologist and aristocratic landlord from the outskirts of Siena who became a Communist after the war, wrote eloquently of the innate aesthetic sense of Tuscan peasants:

The pruning of the olives and vines and the bending and binding of the latter is an art, quite different from merely sitting on a tractor and traveling around in circles or throwing seed potatoes into drilled holes. Every cut has to be carefully considered, or not so much considered – that would make it a science, which is just what it is not – as "felt" intuitively. And the result must satisfy the eye as [well as] fill the pocket at harvest time. Intuition is the impulse behind art, which delights the eye as a result. Bello or brutto, beautiful or ugly: these two words recur incessantly in the conversation of the man in the street; they are filled with ethical content.[20]

According to another set of tropes, peasants were too materialistic and self-interested to aesthetically appreciate their surroundings. After all, aesthetic judgment could only emerge after achieving freedom from instrumental rationality.[21] In the mid-1920s another Tuscan landlord commented in striking terms on the narrowness of the peasants' perceptual world:

The peasant has never had any interest outside of his farm. He never feels the desire to know the names of the mountains that year after year he sees on the horizon, and in fact he ignores them. Ask him which direction the sea is, and he almost always will point to the opposite direction, even though he knows well all the winds that affect his cultivations.[22]

In other words, peasants were part of the landscape but could only perceive it in an immediate and unreflective way. These tropes, whose genealogies went back generations, testify to the paternalistic intimacy Tuscan landlords felt for their peasants. They spoke of and for "their" peasants with ease and relish. It was only after World War II, as we will

---

[20] R. Bianchi-Bandinelli, "Introduction," in Arnold Von Borsig, *Tuscany: 200 Photographs by Arnold von Borsig* (New York: Thomas Crowell, 1955): 7. The Italian edition was published in 1938.

[21] This contrast between an instrumental and esthetic approach to the environment has a very long genealogy in Western culture. Art historian Joachim Ritter traced it back to Petrarch's climbing of Mount Ventoux in Provence in "Le Paysage," *Argile* 16 (1978): 27–58. But this distinction was also theorized in Georg Simmel, "The Philosophy of Landscape," *Theory, Culture and Society* 24 (2007): 20–29, originally published in 1913. For a useful overview of these themes in Italian, see Paolo D'Angelo, *Filosofia del Paesaggio* (Rome: Quodlibet, 2010).

[22] Gino Incontri, *Il Contadino Toscano* (Florence: Vallecchi, 1925): 26–27.

see, that peasants began to speak publicly for themselves and about their changing ways of being in the world.

What holds for peasants can be extended to other social groups as well. Even the experiences of tourists turn out to be more complex and diverse than some clichés would suggest, if we attend to the tourists' evolving perceptual worlds as they themselves articulate them. People have always pursued different kinds of beauty in Tuscany. For all its dominance, the beauty that undergirds the practices and endeavors of the "heritage industry" is only one of the many forms of beauty to be appreciated in the Tuscan hills.[23] In Tuscany, like everywhere else, beauty is about legibility, but it is also about fragility and vulnerability. The landscape has become the subject of both admiration and exploitation, and Tuscans have spent a remarkable amount of energy in framing and containing the threats of "capitalist speculation," never fully agreeing on the exact features of that ravenous monster.

The tension between esthetic appreciation and instrumental rationality is particularly poignant in Tuscany, since over the last few decades one of the region's most lucrative activities has been the placing of its beauty in an increasingly competitive international market. Tuscans, like many other people around the world, are caught between the lure of selling their culture, landscape, and historical artifacts, and the necessity and desire to remain "true to themselves." Perhaps not unlike the peasants of a century ago, contemporary Tuscans make a living on and off the land, dwelling on the land but also distancing themselves from it in order to make it pay. This long-standing tension suggests that all landscapes are both dwelt in and represented, and that a remarkable amount of work is implicated in both activities. In the words of geographer Don Mitchell, "the connection between local morphology and the representations through which those morphologies are ordered and sent around into circulation is, simply, labor."[24] Over a remarkably short period, rural Tuscany appears to have changed from a place of backbreaking work to a venue for leisure and relaxation, but it is important to notice first of all that the two coexisted for generations, peasants' work constituting the condition of possibility for the leisure of others; and second, that the representation and selling of place also rely on the exertion of labor of

---

[23] The most influential study of "heritage" in its relationships with history and memory is arguably David Lowenthal, *Possessed by the Past: The Heritage Crusade and the Spoils of History* (New York: Free Press, 1996). As will become clearer in later chapters, but can perhaps already be gleaned from my approach in this introduction, I am less interested in contrasting these categories than in showing how they define each other in interaction in the actors' complex and changing senses of place and time.

[24] D. Mitchell, *The Lie of the Land: Migrant Workers and the California Landscape* (Minneapolis: Minnesota University Press, 1996): 29.

many different kinds. Contemporary Tuscans have not "preserved" their landscape; they have actively reinvented it through an array of often-conflicting practices, and even the illusion of preservation has relied on a remarkable amount of work. Thus, this book is also about the material and cultural production of a "postproductive" landscape.[25]

Focusing on the last century allows me not only to go beyond elite representations, but also to combine different kinds of sources and methods. I carried out research at a dozen archives in Tuscany and elsewhere, but archival sources, perhaps ironically, are more common for the earlier periods than for the last few decades. Thus, I combined archival and other kinds of documentary sources with interviews and even some participant observation. Inevitably, my own senses of place and time have shaped the ways I perceived rural Tuscany, the questions I asked of my "informants," and what I heard them saying. But more traditional historical sources do not speak for themselves either, of course. Especially in the last two chapters, I rely extensively on ethnographic engagement and observation to explore the complexities and contradictions of the contemporary understanding of Tuscany as patrimony (or heritage). I believe that this methodological eclecticism is a fitting approach to the historical study of landscape as defined in this book.

Like any other place, rural Tuscany is both a geographical expression and a set of concrete experiences and processes. This tension between abstraction and concreteness is at the very core of this book. There are countless "landscapes" within the regional boundaries of modern Tuscany. The focus here is on the part of the Tuscan countryside that was once shaped by the sharecropping system of land tenure. It extends from the outskirts of Florence in the north to Mount Amiata and the beginning of the Maremma to the south. Two ill-defined areas within this broader region will provide the bulk of the examples and stories I discuss – the Chianti in central Tuscany and the Orcia valley in the southern portion of the region (Map). These are now iconic places and major tourist destinations. Today, they look and feel very different from each other. The Chianti is dominated by vineyards, olive groves, and oak forests, while in the Orcia valley wheat fields stretch for miles on gently rolling hills. These two areas looked somewhat more similar when sharecropping ruled the land, but I focus on them precisely because they exemplify some of Tuscany's social and spatial diversity. In some ways, however, this is also an arbitrary choice. This is a book that deals with

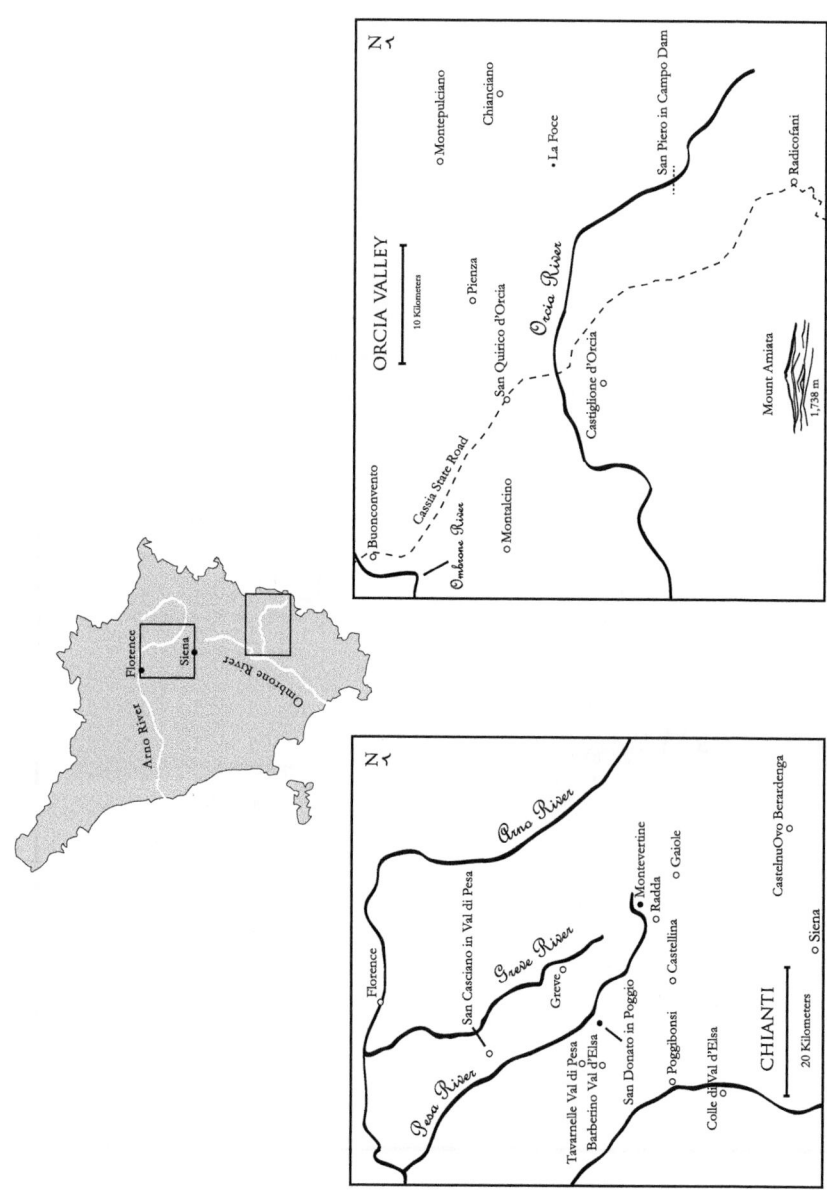

ORCIA VALLEY

o Buonconvento

Cassia State Road

o Montalcino

Ombrone River

San Quirico d'Orcia
o

o Pienza

o Montepulciano

Chianciano
o

• La Foce

Castiglione d'Orcia
o

Orcia River

San Piero in Campo Dam

Radicofani
o

Mount Amiata
1,738 m

10 Kilometers

CHIANTI

Florence

Arno River

San Casciano in Val di Pesa
o

Greve
o

Grave River

Pesa River

Tavarnelle Val di Pesa
o
Barberino Val d'Elsa
•
San Donato in Poggio

o Poggibonsi

Colle di Val d'Elsa
o

• Montevertine
o Radda
o Castellina
o Gaiole

Castelnu'Ovo Berardenga
o

o Siena

20 Kilometers

Florence
•
Siena
•

Arno River

Ombrone River

16

concrete perceptions and aspirations. Therefore, it was important to locate stories and processes as precisely as possible. Undoubtedly, different areas would have yielded somewhat different stories. Like any place, Tuscany is large; it contains multitudes.

The narrative arc followed here begins in the early twentieth century, when the sharecropping system, though under a variety of global and local pressures, still dominated the land and social relations as it had done for centuries. The book examines the efforts of the Fascist regime to save this social and spatial system through modernization schemes, the failure of those efforts, and the rebellion of the sharecroppers after World War II. It then follows the exodus from the farms and charts its spatial and social consequences, including a variety of aborted schemes to counter depopulation that have left important traces on the land. It finally charts the rise of a patrimonial sensibility increasingly focused on the search for beauty and authenticity, as well as the sources of support and resistance this sensibility has generated in recent years.

Chapter 1 provides the reader with a general introduction to the "traditional" features of rural Tuscany, focusing then on the Fascist period, when the regime set out to "reclaim" (*bonificare*) the Tuscan hills and their population through a series of contradictory practices. The Fascist regime extolled sharecropping and the hierarchical relations on which it was based, and attempted to rescue it through massive injections of public money. It was in this period, for example, that some large-scale landlords tried to transform large portions of territory responding to the "wheat battle" willed by Mussolini. In many ways, Tuscany was the regime's "model region," because of its supposedly pliant peasants organized in large patriarchal families and its long-lived myths of class collaboration. As would be common for the remainder of the twentieth century, such fantasies belied the simmering tensions that threatened to transform Tuscany into a site of open rebellion. In its typically paradoxical way, the regime dreamed of preserving traditional hierarchical and paternalistic relations while modernizing the spaces where these relations unfolded. Places would change, so that people could remain true to their imposed nature and destiny.

I examine the decade after the war in Chapter 2. In the mid-1940s, simmering tensions exploded into overt rebellion. Tuscan sharecroppers revolted en masse, organized by the social and political organizations of the Communist Party. In this chapter I show how spatial practices were crucial to the Communists' mobilizing success in the name of a more humane and dignified modernity, even in the face of the peasant movement's ultimate defeat. By relying on memoirs and archival sources, the chapter looks at the ways peasants renegotiated the boundaries between city and countryside, which were very stark and hierarchical in Tuscany.

Part of that renegotiation involved the peasants' increasing fascination with the trappings of modernity – anything from machinery and scooters to plumbing and "hygiene." Finally, I examine the peasants' growing awareness of their place in global narratives of progress and their attachment to the Soviet Union by reconstructing the ways in which they staked out their territory by engaging in bold rituals of defiance, eliciting the ire of their landlords and the police.

Chapter 3 examines the "death" of the Tuscan peasantry and the peasants' "exodus" from the farms to the peripheries of the Tuscan cities and towns. Here I look at two spatial implications of the exodus. First, I examine the spread of vine monocropping in the Chianti region, which replaced the mixed agriculture of sharecropping. These highly capitalized vineyards were established largely with public funds, coming both from national and supranational sources, and they largely benefited aristocratic landlords or their more "capitalist"-minded successors. Thus, they elicited strong anxieties and heated debates among the rural Tuscans who had been left behind, as they searched for a workable narrative capable of making sense of the spatial features of an increasingly empty territory. Second, I look at the anxieties created by depopulation, which elicited a variety of schemes for development and repopulation. Some landlords promoted the settlement of peasants from the south and the former Italian colonies, believed to be more pliant than the restless extant sharecroppers. Former peasants and their leftist representatives, by contrast, lobbied for public funds to restructure agriculture and promote animal farming, as the landscape kept losing much of its coherence and legibility.

Chapter 4 continues threads from the previous chapter by examining other attempts to "solve" the problems posed by the allegedly impoverished environment left behind by the exodus. Many observers in the late 1960s and through the 1970s feared that the Tuscan countryside would degenerate into a disordered patchwork of ravines, woods, and abandoned houses. This chapter reconstructs the contradictory perceptions and experiences produced in this period of great disorientation. I tell this story as a contrast between two animals – the cow and the sheep. Especially in the southern provinces, many Tuscans, including the newly empowered Communist administrators, pushed for the spread of cattle rearing on irrigated land, which led to the building of dams and slaughterhouses. Many of these structures are now haunting rural ruins. As the number of cows kept dwindling, sheep multiplied, thanks to the arrival of thousands of Sardinian shepherds. When a few of these shepherds engaged in a slew of kidnappings, facilitated by the emptiness the peasants had left behind, the attention of the entire region focused on the destiny of the countryside, infusing it with new senses of loss and the urgency of renewal.

In Chapter 5 I examine the ways in which rural Tuscany has come to be understood primarily as heritage, or patrimony, in the wake of the failure of the modernization schemes discussed in the previous chapters. A variety of social actors have inscribed rural Tuscany in a patrimonial lineage that focuses on temporal continuities and spatial homogeneity, smoothing over many of the specificities of an increasingly removed recent history replete with conflict. But this process also elicited enduring forms of resistance. In this chapter, I rely on a combination of oral and documentary evidence and focus on two sites. First, I look at the wide-ranging debate on the fate of Tuscany's rural houses, which became the target both of economic ventures, meant to attract the money of residential tourists, and of conservation practices, meant to thwart the threat of speculation. In this section I also gage the diversity of the tourist gazes that began to scan and reshape increasing portions of territory, and I chart the spread of agro-tourism (*agriturismo*), a highly regulated practice meant to counter the threat of unrestrained commodification. Second, I discuss the establishment of museums of peasant culture, complex institutions that combine nostalgia and radical critiques of the present. By collecting the artifacts expelled from the farmhouses, these sparsely visited museums commemorate the ruptures of modernity, which are such a crucial part of the local sense of place, and admonish an increasingly distracted society over its impending loss of meaning. These two sites exemplify very different, and yet connected, approaches to patrimony.

In Chapter 6 I document the rise of "landscape" as a hegemonic discourse and set of practices capable of making sense of rural Tuscany's complex and contradictory past. The lived experience of generations of artists and travelers came to fruition in a context of rapidly expanding mobility to transform the Tuscan landscape into an icon, a representational space that could be simultaneously idealized and sold in the international market. In this chapter, I reconstruct the intellectual and legal debate on landscape and its protection, both at the national and the regional levels. Over time, the legal concept of landscape has become more diffused, morphing from a particular monumental vista into a system of spatial rules of development. At least in Tuscany, landscape beauty is above all about the imputation of coherence and legibility. Yet, the shared rules of development from which such legibility supposedly stems are as elusive as ever, which has turned the landscape into a site of ongoing litigation. In that vein, I tell the surprising story of how the Orcia valley, in the province of Siena, has become a UNESCO World Heritage Site and a prime example of debasement at the same time. I focus on the story of a housing development near a castle town that has surged to the status of a symbol of degradation. I retell this story as one in which the paradoxes and contradictions of patrimony come into full relief. Finally, I go back to the Chianti to look at the ongoing debates on olive and vine cultivation, which straddle economic and esthetic considerations. Vineyards and olive groves have changed so much in the last half century that it is difficult to agree on the rules of development on which they rest and that need to be preserved.

With all their twists and turns, the stories in this book will hopefully spice up the bland clichés that have stuck to Tuscany in recent years. My main thrust, however, is not simply to dispel those clichés and replace them with a more truthful narrative, nor is this book about the simple oppositions of locality and globality, authenticity and commodification, or (true) history and (fabricated) heritage. My hope is to demonstrate that rural Tuscany is a good case to think with about the ways modern societies produce "landscapes" in their ongoing attempts to read themselves in the spaces they inhabit. These attempts are always problematic and contentious, because they involve the very stuff of social life: power, meaning, and sources of livelihood. Above all, the quest for a coherent and legible landscape reflects the tension between the irreducible plurality of perspectives and perceptions that make up any modern polity and the search for a common sense of purpose and direction.

In this book, landscape is thus a meeting place (but also a conflicting place) that is produced at the intersection of different perceptions and narrations. Landscape is simultaneously personal and collective, "flat" like a painting or a photograph, and "deep" like a tale or a myth. But of course landscape is not just a product, the passive outcome of processes that take place "elsewhere." Landscape is also an actor in its own right; and perhaps nowhere more forcefully than in Tuscany, landscape is also an actor that shapes, refines, and educates people's senses, guiding them to perceive and narrate certain things while ignoring others. It is the main contention of this book that only by attending to this phenomenology of landscape perception can we write histories that are truly open and nonteleological. A "spatial history" is necessarily also a history of plural and overlapping senses of time.

1   Land, Nation, Race: Reclaiming Tuscany's Hill Country under Fascism (1929–1944)

Located at the edge of the Orcia River valley, in the southern portion of the province of Siena, La Foce is today one of the most visited and celebrated corners of the Tuscan countryside. It is a villa with a unique garden, a working agricultural estate, a country hotel where people can hold their weddings and conferences, an "agriturismo" where tourists can stay in tastefully restructured farmhouses, the site of an international classical music festival, and much more.[1] It was also the labor of love of an aristocratic couple, Marquis Antonio Origo and his Anglo-American wife, Iris Cutting, who purchased the estate in 1924 and turned it into something of a model community, relying both on Iris's considerable wealth and on government funds. Iris Origo became a brilliant biographer and memoirist. She featured her rural Tuscan retreat in her writings several times, most notably in a successful journal of the dramatic events of 1943 and 1944, thereby greatly adding to the estate's aura.[2] Despite its unique charm, however, La Foce was only one of many Tuscan *tenute* (estates) to be extensively restructured and "modernized" between the world wars, with a combination of private and public funds. By the late 1930s, these estates were touted as self-contained and self-reliant communities, with elementary schools for the children of the peasants, medical facilities where simple procedures could be performed and from which the principles of hygiene could spread, spaces for leisure activities, and so on.

In the spring of 2011 I drove up to La Foce to interview one of its current owners, Benedetta Origo, a promoter, with her sister Donata, of another major restructuring project that they undertook after their parents' death. The sisters, too, relied on a combination of private and public funds to restructure the estate after its decline in the 1960s and 1970s, when most of the peasants left and many of the buildings began to

---

[1] For a history of the villa and a description of the gardens, see Benedetta Origo, *La Foce: A Garden and Landscape in Tuscany* (Philadelphia: University of Pennsylvania Press, 2001). See also the estate's website: www.lafoce.com.

[2] I. Origo, *War in Val d'Orcia. A Diary* (London: J. Cape, 1947).

decay. But in spite of their personal achievements, as soon as we sat down and before I could ask any questions, Benedetta Origo felt compelled to begin the conversation with her assessment of the interwar period:

La Foce between the wars is an example of educational, economic, and agricultural progress that is very interesting. The schools that were developed, the reclamation of the wetlands, the various reforms.... It was not just La Foce, but an Italian phenomenon between the wars of great social, educational, and public health renewal.... After all, it is in this spirit that my parents set out on their reform.

In light of these words, it may come as no surprise that their venture at La Foce, a restaurant on the premises of the old leisure center for the estate's sharecroppers and employees, has regained the name it was given in the 1930s, Dopolavoro La Foce. No matter that the original name referred to one of the Fascist regime's largest mass organizations, the Opera Nazionale Dopolavoro (OND), in charge of coordinating the leisure-related activities of thousands of institutions across the peninsula. As Victoria de Grazia has shown, in interwar Europe the aspiration to harness the power of leisure by direct government intervention for the organization of consensus was a distinctly Fascist endeavor.[3]

Neither the restaurant's name nor Benedetta Origo's assessment of the interwar decades stem from nostalgia for the Fascist dictatorship. On the contrary, the point is that these signs, memories, and experiences no longer register as Fascist at all. Precisely because, in some important ways, modern Tuscany began to take shape in the Fascist period, some of the features of that era have become part of the landscape. They have been naturalized. It was under Mussolini's dictatorship that considerable financial and political resources were invested in "reclaiming" (*bonificare*) the countryside, in Tuscany and elsewhere. By the mid-1930s, roughly a quarter of the region's agricultural territory, subdivided into thirty-three districts (*comprensori di bonifica*), was subjected to some form of reclamation project, together with the people who lived there.[4] The regime's propaganda was never tired of pointing out that, at its core, fascism was both rural and "ruralizing" (*ruralizzatore*). At least at the ideological level, the regime subjected the countryside to ongoing attention, simultaneously extolling its authenticity and arguing for the necessity of its redemption.

As D. Medina Lasansky has argued, the Fascist regime, represented at the local level by a small army of architects, writers, and administrators, promoted the reinvention of countless buildings and public festivals

---

[3] V. de Grazia, *The Culture of Consent: Mass Organization of Leisure in Fascist Italy* (Cambridge: Cambridge University Press, 1981).

[4] Franco Scaramuzzi and Paolo Nanni, "L'Agricoltura," in Luigi Lotti (ed.), *Storia della Civiltà Toscana, Volume VI* (Florence: Le Monnier, 2006): 135–182.

across Tuscany, all informed by the search for a "usable" Medieval and Renaissance esthetic.[5] These artifacts and rituals have lost their association with fascism over time, even though they were conceived with unmistakably Fascist social and political goals. This chapter makes a similar argument about Tuscany's rural landscape. The Fascist regime developed a complex relationship with rural Italy, and with Tuscany in particular. It simultaneously transformed the countryside and idealized its conservation; it sought to redeem and preserve it at once. As we will see in Chapter 5, this contradictory attitude is still at the core of the appreciation of rural life as heritage. The Fascist approach to the countryside as patrimony, with its paradoxes and contradictions, is the first reason for beginning this book with the interwar period. Those paradoxes and contradictions are still with us. As Benedetta Origo's words suggest, fascism was as much about modernization as about nostalgia and heritage, and although the tension between transformation and preservation is still alive, the regime combined these practices and discourses in distinctive ways.[6]

The second reason for beginning this book with Mussolini's regime is that fascism intervened in the material and institutional makeup of the countryside in partly novel ways. Many of those institutions long survived the end of the regime. In Tuscany, government agencies engaged in a few spectacular drainage campaigns, notably at Alberese in the Maremma, south of Grosseto. But perhaps more relevant were countless smaller-scale interventions of road construction, water regimentation, slope reduction, irrigation, forestation, deforestation, and so on, carried out in many parts of the region by consortia of landowners, with a combination of public and private funds. These interventions also targeted the rural population, but in strikingly (and stridently) conservative and paternalistic ways. The landscape was to change so that the social order could remain fundamentally stable. And the social order in rural Tuscany had been founded for centuries on the sharecropping system of land tenure, a contract that the regime touted as a model to be imitated across Italy and the Empire but was stretched to the limits of its social and spatial sustainability. The dramatic social struggles and drastic transformations of the immediate post–World War II period would be incomprehensible without an understanding of fascism's "reactionary modernism."[7]

---

[5] D. Medina Lasansky, *The Renaissance Perfected: Architecture, Spectacle, and Tourism in Fascist Italy* (University Park: Pennsylvania University Press, 2004).

[6] For a discussion of the relationships between Italian Fascism and modernity in the realm of culture, see Ruth Ben-Ghiat, *Fascist Modernities: Italy 1922–1945* (Berkeley: University of California Press, 2001).

[7] I borrow this term from Jeffrey Hert, *Reactionary Modernism: Technology, Culture and Politics in Weimar and the Third Reich* (Cambridge: Cambridge University Press, 1984).

This chapter will offer first an overview of the regime's ruralization policies, especially of "integral reclamation" (*bonifica integrale*), a set of measures coordinated by the state, but rooted in local societies, that targeted specific areas with the goal of "redeeming" them both agriculturally and socially. At least in theory, no place or social relation would go unexamined and unimproved. Redemption would start with roads, canals, and other works of infrastructure and end with the very consciousness of the settlers. A whole way of life, founded on a holistic understanding of the rural landscape, was at stake. This grandiose vision had to come to terms with a treacherous terrain of deception and petty interests. The ability and willingness to compromise was very much a part of Italian fascism, too. Next, I will show how these general guidelines were applied and received in Tuscany, a region that figured prominently in the imaginings of the regime and that already had a long and problematic history of social and scientific reflection on rural matters. Tuscany had also been one of the regions where the rise of fascism in the aftermath of World War I had been particularly violent. Finally, I will zero in on two areas of Tuscany, the Orcia valley and the Chianti, to illustrate the blandishments and forms of coercion the regime and its local supporters inscribed in society and the landscape.

Integral Compromises: The Paradoxes of Fascist Ruralism

Founded in Milan in 1919, the Fascist movement rose to prominence over the following two years in the countryside of northern and central Italy, fighting an unprecedented wave of peasant unrest, itself the product of the horrors and promises of the Great War. As Adrian Lyttelton and others have documented, it was in the countryside that the Black Shirts morphed from a marginal example of veteran resentment into a mass movement, funded and organized by landowners eager to reestablish threatened social boundaries and economic privileges.[8] Veterans' resentment interacted with the sense of beleaguerment felt by the rural middle and upper classes, igniting something of a civil war to which Mussolini presented himself as the solution with the "March on Rome" in late October 1922. Thus, even though it was born as an urban movement and mobilized around the repression of urban unrest as well, fascism came of age in the countryside and remained cognizant of its rural roots until its demise.

---

[8] A. Lyttelton, *The Seizure of Power: Fascism in Italy 1919–1929* (London: Widenfeld and Nicolson, 1973). For a more recent appraisal, see Donald Sassoon, *Mussolini and the Rise of Fascism* (London: Harper Press, 2007).

Like other instances of radical right-wing populism in interwar Europe, Italian fascism extolled the virtues of rural life. Unlike other similar movements, however, the Italian Black Shirts had violently confronted the landless laborers of the Po Plain and Puglia, as well as the sharecroppers of Tuscany and other central regions, many of whom had rallied to Socialist and Catholic organizations.[9] Fascism did win over sections of northern Italy's "middle farmers," but the regime never forgot that some of the most serious challenges to its rise to power had come from the countryside. As a consequence, the regime's commitment to rural communities came to be founded on an imagined countryside, one that had supposedly been corrupted by extraneous forces and that needed to be fully redeemed to the national community. In other words, Fascist ruralism bore the signs of both nostalgia and utopianism. It is this complex attitude that distinguished fascism's relationship with rural communities and the spaces they inhabited. Italians had drained marshes and canalized rivers for centuries, but no previous regime had committed its very legacy to the destiny of rural societies.

The argument for increasing government intervention in agricultural and rural matters had been mounting for decades when Mussolini was appointed president of the Council of Ministers in 1922. The experience of the war and the wave of social unrest that followed it convinced various interested parties of the urgency of wide-ranging reforms and of the need to prod otherwise reluctant landowners, especially in southern Italy. At the forefront of this movement were several prominent agricultural scientists and technicians, who saw in the new regime an opportunity for enhancing their influence and making a difference on the ground. Prominent among them was Arrigo Serpieri, an agricultural economist from Bologna who had written extensively on land reclamation and held important academic positions.[10] A former reformist socialist and admirer of Vilfredo Pareto, Serpieri believed that the sound modernization of Italian society could only develop on the strong foundations provided by a self-reliant and highly productive agriculture, which would have created contented rural classes embodying the healthy and collectively beneficial social values the national community needed for further progress. This process of regeneration had to be gradual and mindful of local conditions, but it also needed the strong and decisive intervention of the state, so as to win over the resistance and inertia of entrenched private

---

[9] For a comparative analysis of the role of rural–urban politics in interwar Europe, see Gregory Luebbert, "Social Foundations of the Political Order in Interwar Europe," *World Politics* 39 (1987): 449–478.

[10] Lea D'Antone, "Politica e Cultura Agraria: Arrigo Serpieri," *Studi Storici* 20 (1979): 609–642.

interests. It was with this ambitious and yet coolly realistic mind-set that in 1923 Serpieri became undersecretary for Agriculture in the Ministry of the National Economy.

Over the next few months, Serpieri set out to reorganize the legislation on agricultural reclamation (*bonifica*), dating back to the late nineteenth century, with the intention of extending its scope beyond its traditional bounds – mostly works of drainage and water regulation in the alluvial plains of northern Italy. With two decrees, in December 1923 and in May 1924, Serpieri redefined the ultimate goals of *bonifica* as the agricultural development and settlement of previously abandoned or underutilized land, and set the guidelines for the cooperation between public and private actors in areas whose reclamation was "of relevant public interest."[11] The state would provide funds for infrastructures that straddled different properties, but individual landlords would be required to improve their own land with the organizational resources and technical expertise provided by consortia of fellow landowners and their employees. Private companies could step in and carry out the works of improvement if individual landlords were unable or unwilling to perform their duties. In some cases, these companies could even take over the ownership of the neglected land. The organizations of southern large-scale landlords strongly objected to the possibility of expropriation and to the reliance of (presumably northern) companies, waging a campaign that led to the revision of the decrees and ultimately to Serpieri's resignation in July 1924.

These initial, and only partly successful, forays carried out during the early "liberal" phase of fascism gave way to a period of profound and complex transformations of the regime's economic policies. The 1925 protectionist turn, accompanied by a much-trumpeted campaign to make Italy independent of grain imports (the so-called Battle for Wheat), inaugurated a more distinctively nationalist policy meant to shelter the Italian economy from international competition and promote import substitution in a variety of basic industries. The revaluation of the lira in 1926 (the so-called Quota 90, after the new exchange rate with the British Pound) damaged the interests of specialized producers of export goods, many of whom were in agriculture, and signaled a point of no return toward a more hierarchically managed national economy.[12] It was in this context of reduced revenues, falling prices and wages,

---

[11] These were Royal Decrees 3256, issued on December 20, 1923; and 753, issued on May 18, 1924.

[12] For an introduction to the Italian economy in the Fascist period, see Gianni Toniolo, *L'Economia dell'Italia Fascista* (Bari: Laterza, 1980).

and flailing private investments that a new round of legislative measures tackled the issue of agricultural reclamation with renewed vigor.

The centerpiece of this effort was a major law for the *bonifica integrale* issued in December 1928 that reiterated the notion that the state should finance works of agricultural transformation when such works were in the national interest.[13] Arguably the most important aspect of the law was the time horizon it covered, an anticipated fourteen years for the completion of the works, and the amount of funds it committed, almost 10 billion lire, comprehensive of the interest to be paid for funds put up by private agents and disbursed by the state over thirty years. In the areas that belonged to a first category of urgency and public interest, major infrastructural work would be funded entirely by the state, but, as a rule, public funds would match private contributions to different extents, depending on the character of the projects. The consortium of landlords, understood as an institution of public interest, was the preferred organization for identifying and carrying out the necessary work, under the supervision of several public agencies. Membership in these consortia would be mandatory in the targeted areas, and landlords who did not contribute their share could have their lands expropriated. These measures were framed in the language of corporativism, according to which ownership came with collective responsibilities to the national community. This, however, was bound to be a moderate form of corporativism, one that did not envisage the possibility of radical class transformations and relied on the cooperation (and even preeminence) of large-scale landowners, since decisional power in the consortia was proportional to the amount of land owned.

In September 1929 the regime instituted a ministry specifically dedicated to agriculture, under economist Giacomo Acerbo, and Serpieri became undersecretary for land reclamation (Sottosegretario alla Bonifica Integrale). The emphasis on the landowners' consortia, rather than on government agencies, was in line with Serpieri's mind-set, as was the stated goal of simultaneously increasing the capitalization of agriculture, rural settlement, and the kind of "middling" farmers that had a direct stake in the land, as owners or as prosperous tenants or as sharecroppers. It is therefore ironic that the most famous and successful example of land reclamation in these years, the drainage of the Agro Pontino just south of Rome, and the foundation of several new towns on the reclaimed land (then called Littoria, Sabaudia, Aprilia, Pomezia, and Pontinia) was carried out by a government agency (the Opera Nazionale

---

[13] This was Law 197, issued on December 2, 1928.

Combattenti) and relied on the labor of thousands of transient workers.[14] Nevertheless, two-thirds of the more than 1,000 reclamation consortia operating in 1932 had been founded after the 1928 law. Altogether, by the mid-1930s, this process had affected 4.5 million hectares, or one-sixth of the entire country, albeit to widely different degrees. The data publicized by the regime were indeed staggering. Within five years, the *bonifica integrale* led to the construction of 12,200 kilometers of drainage canals; 3,600 kilometers of embankments; almost 6,000 kilometers of country roads; 1,400 kilometers of irrigation canals; 16,300 bridges; and to the drainage of 662,000 hectares of wetlands. The regime boasted that in the late 1920s and early 1930s the state had spent fifteen times more per year on works of agricultural improvement and rural settlement than the yearly average of the previous five decades – that is, since Italy's unification.[15]

As these claims show, the project of "ruralizing" Italian society was deeply embedded in the self-representation of fascism. Especially in the late 1920s and early 1930s, the regime became invested in promoting an image of itself that made fascism almost coextensive with a return to the land and its "redemption." The 1928 law that funded the *bonifica integrale* was immediately named after the Duce himself, supposedly by acclamation of the members of parliament. This was to be known simply as *la Legge Mussolini* (the Mussolini Law). The Duce repeatedly argued that the package of measures that made up the Fascist ruralization program would constitute the regime's most enduring and glorious legacy. In the best-known version of this claim, pronounced in September 1929 in front of an audience of party officials, Mussolini proclaimed that "everywhere an effort is being made that can fill a people with pride and create an eternal title of glory for the Fascist regime. Land is redeemed (*riscattata*); with the land, men; and with men, the race." Serpieri echoed the Duce in 1935 by arguing that this effort "will stay for centuries as a testament to the power and spiritual value of the Fascist Revolution."[16] At the rhetorical level, but also on the basis of the very long time horizon envisaged by the project, fascism was definitely taking a stake in the future.

---

[14] For some recent studies on the reclamation of Agro Pontino and its historical context, see Mauro Stampacchia, *"Ruralizzare l'Italia!" Agricoltura e Bonifiche tra Mussolini e Serpieri* (Milan: Franco Angeli, 2000); Elisabetta Novello, *La Bonifica in Italia: Legislazione, Credito e Lotta alla Malaria dall'Unità al Fascismo* (Milan: Franco Angeli, 2003); Federica Letizia Cavallo, *Terre, Acque, Macchine: Geografia della Bonifica in Italia tra Ottocento e Novecento* (Reggio Emilia: Diabasis, 2011).

[15] Data from A. Serpieri and N. Mazzocchi Alemanni, *Lo Stato Fascista e i Rurali* (Milan: Mondadori, 1935).

[16] Serpieri and Alemanni, *Lo Stato Fascista e i Rurali*: 121.

The centrality of ruralism in the ideological apparatus of Italian fascism lay above all in the regime's self-understanding as a movement heroically fighting against the tide of history.[17] A seemingly uninterrupted thread linked the "Battle for Wheat" (*battaglia del grano*), announced in 1925 to replace the importation of wheat by increasing productivity and protecting the internal market; the "Battle for Births" (*battaglia delle nascite*), proclaimed in May 1927 to boost the nation's demographic vigor; the antiurbanization campaign, launched in December 1928 to stem the migration of rural folks to the cities; and the Mussolini Law of the same month. Rurality stood for self-reliance, population growth, industriousness, and staunch support for Italy's imperial destiny.[18] The coherence of this ambitious project relied on both the "protection" and the mobilization of Italy's rural masses. As Mussolini himself put it in 1928, "the historic merit of fascism, a merit of truly exceptional value, is to have ushered vast masses of rural folks into the living body of our History."[19] Whereas the old liberal elites had given up on battling history's degenerative trends – such as urbanization, industrial strife, demographic decline, and so on – fascism would take charge of the course of history, make it its own, and restore the rural way of life as the healthy core of the nation.

It would be naïve to take the regime's utopian rhetoric for granted, and many scholars have persuasively demonstrated not only that ruralization and its associated policies were unsuccessful (Italian society did not become less urban, more prolific, or even more obedient), but also that the regime's ideological apparatus itself was far more diverse and less coherent than the Duce's self-congratulatory slogans would suggest. As Mauro Stampacchia has argued, behind the façade of Fascist ruralism lay a variety of projects and claims, some of which long predated the regime. The ruralism of Serpieri and other technocrats was of a moderately modernizing kind, aiming at "regulating the transition from an agricultural-industrial society to an industrial-agricultural one," thereby avoiding the conflicts and disruptions that had taken place in more "advanced" countries.[20] The literary and artistic ruralism of Mino Maccari and his motley crew of "Strapaese" collaborators, by contrast, was distinctly localistic and antimodern, and it aimed at preserving the imagined purity and

---

[17] Claudio Fogu, *The Historic Imaginary: Politics of History in Fascist Italy* (Toronto: University of Toronto Press, 2003).

[18] On the connection between ruralization and demographic growth, see Carl Ipsen, *Dictating Demography: The Problem of Population in Fascist Italy* (Cambridge: Cambridge University Press, 1996).

[19] Quoted in Stampacchia, *"Ruralizzare l'Italia!"*: 397. See also Perry Wilson, *Peasant Women and Politics in Fascist Italy. The Massaie Rurali* (London: Routledge, 2002).

[20] Stampacchia, *"Ruralizzare l'Italia!"*: 9.

isolation of Italian rural communities.[21] In the 1920s Maccari's magazine, *Il Selvaggio*, even came out against the prospect of exposing Italian peasants to radio broadcasts, a policy in which the regime will purposefully engage a decade later.[22]

The complex ways in which ruralism was received and negotiated on the ground match this diversity of ideological views. The 1928 antiurbanization law, for example, devolved to the prefects (the government representatives at the provincial level) the task of working out the details of how to discourage and even punish unauthorized migration to the cities. Some prefects followed through more zealously than others, but generally Italians ignored the measure altogether, albeit not without costs and inconveniences.[23] Even the "integral reclamation" of agricultural land came to rely on ongoing negotiations with the diverse local elites of rural Italy, who vied for public funds and the attention of the government for reasons that had very little to do with rural utopias. Guile and corruption lurked just beneath the surface, as did the foot-dragging of landlords well versed in the manipulation of public policy. Serpieri's technocratic rationality ultimately had to come to terms with these organized interests, and land reclamation slowed down drastically after January 1935, when Serpieri himself lost his position after another row over the possibility of expropriation of recalcitrant landlords' holdings by the consortia. Funding for the *bonifica* also felt the brunt of the aggression against Ethiopia and the intervention in the Spanish Civil War. To paraphrase the regime's rhetoric, when the sword began to sway, the plow had to slow down. The internal contradictions of the project, however, were at least as important.

Scholars have also questioned the very foundations (as well as the sincerity) of Fascist ruralism. Domenico Preti and other economic historians, for example, have argued that the Battle for Wheat and the regime's settlement policies were intended to repressively pacify the countryside and keep rural Italians fed at the lowest possible cost, so as to release resources for industrial growth.[24] This form of primitive accumulation

---

[21] On Maccari and Il Selvaggio, see Donatella Capresi and Barbara Cinelli, *Mino Maccari: L'Avventura de "Il Selvaggio": Artisti da Colle a Roma 1924–1943* (Florence: Masolino & Maschietto, 1998); Michele Dau, *Mussolini l'Anticittadino. Città, Società e Fascismo* (Rome: Castelvecchi, 2012). See also Ben-Ghiat, *Fascist Modernities*.

[22] Gianni Isola, *L'Ha Scritto la Radio: Storia e Testi della Radio durante il Fascismo (1924–44)* (Milan: Mondadori, 1998).

[23] Dau, *Mussolini l'Anticittadino*: 40–111.

[24] Massimo Legnani, Domenico Preti, and Giorgio Rochat (eds.), *Le Campagne Emiliane in Periodo Fascista: Materiali e Ricerche sulla Battaglia del Grano* (Bologna: CLUEB, 1982). See also Paul Corner, "Fascist Agrarian Policy and the Italian Economy in the Inter-War Years," in John Davis (ed.), *Gramsci and Italy's Passive Revolution* (London: Croom Helm, 1979): 239–274.

also directly served the interests of large-scale capitalists by providing a protected market for industrial products, such as artificial fertilizers and machinery. Serpieri himself may have had a more sanguine vision of the relationships between agriculture and industry in the 1920s, but the onset of the Great Depression and the decline in prices and revenues that accompanied it meant that his rationalizing and productivist project became in practice increasingly "conservative." The dynamic self-reliance that Serpieri imagined for Italy's rural classes, founded on the reinvestment of self-generated savings, never materialized, as the Italian countryside became the site of ever higher degrees of exploitation (or self-exploitation) and near-subsistence consumption levels.

This gap between bombastic rhetoric and deeply compromised reality is familiar to anyone with any knowledge of Italian fascism. Nevertheless, it would be a mistake to simply dismiss Fascist ruralism as empty rhetoric, and this for at least two major reasons. First, this is a context in which fascism's paradoxical relationships with modernity truly stand out. The regime imagined rural spaces that needed to be transformed and politicized to preserve them in their pristine and prepolitical state. The authenticity of rural life had to be constructed so that it could be perceived to always have been there. Even Serpieri, with his seemingly dispassionate and technocratic mind-set, shared in these visions. For him it was a whole way of life that needed to be "preserved" because of its collective virtues and benefits, and this way of life was made up of "a sentiment of ownership, of family, of religion, the worshipping of tradition, the force of habitual norms, the recognition of hierarchies, the love for saving ... the tenacious attachment to the land and the native town, first root of the attachment to the Fatherland."[25] This paradoxical vision held sway beyond the rhetorical level. In important ways, even economic calculations were to yield to visions that integrated reaction and utopianism.

Second, Fascist ruralism should be taken seriously because of its legacy. The Fascists were right in predicting that land reclamation would become the regime's most enduring and admired achievement, and this is not only in the most spectacular contexts, such as the drainage of the Agro Pontino, but also in more mundane sites, such as Tuscany's hill country, where the Fascist origins of certain visions and practices have all but been forgotten or have come to be viewed as positive achievements of an otherwise deplorable regime. But the redemption of rural territory, as it was carried out in the interwar decades, was profoundly (and not just

---

[25] A. Serpieri, *La Politica Agraria in Italia e i Recenti Provvedimenti Legislativi* (Piacenza: Federazione Italiana dei Consorzi Agrari, 1925): 61.

coincidentally) Fascist, both because it relied on a profoundly hierarchical and paternalistic approach toward the lower classes and because it was shaped by ongoing negotiations and compromises with the powerful. As we will see, these experiences came to constitute Tuscany's complex senses of place and time, setting the stage for massive transformations after the demise of the regime.

A Genealogy of Tuscan Ruralism

Tuscany played a prominent role in the rural imaginings of the Fascist regime but, as is often the case with things Fascist, continuities were as relevant as revolutionary and utopian claims. We can define ruralism as a set of material and ideological practices predicated on the notion that rural life offers a distinctive and desirable alternative to industrial (or otherwise normative) forms of modernity. In that vein, Tuscan elites could be perceived to have been ruralist long before the March on Rome. The entire economic history of Tuscany in the early modern period could be read as an example of cautious progress founded on the primacy of agriculture and rural life. The region's urban elites, once at the cutting edge of capitalist innovation, shied away from commerce and finance in the sixteenth century, as the baton of economic prowess moved across the Alps and over the Atlantic Ocean. These mostly aristocratic elites began to invest their capital in the organization of farms, choosing (or being forced to choose) agricultural rent over commercial or financial profit.[26] The foundation in 1753 of the Accademia dei Georgofili, one of Europe's earliest Academies for the systematic study and debate of rural matters, sealed this process of "enlightened retrenchment." Based in Florence and organized primarily by aristocratic landowners, this Academy exerted its influence over the entire peninsula, making the "Tuscan model" the frame of reference for rural matters in other regions.

Crucial to this model and seductively linear narrative of cautious progress was the cornerstone of Tuscany's rural economy and landscape, classical sharecropping (*mezzadria classica*), a form of land tenure that

---

[26] For the Medieval period, see Giuliano Pinto, *La Toscana nel Tardo Medio Evo: Ambiente, Economia Rurale, Società* (Florence: Sansoni, 1983); Giovanni Cherubini, *Scritti Toscani: L'Urbanesimo Medievale e la Mezzadria* (Florence: Salimbeni, 1991). For the nineteenth century, see Carlo Pazzagli, *La Terra delle Città. Le Campagne Toscane dell'Ottocento* (Florence: Ponte alle Grazie, 1992). For an overview, see Gabriella Piccinni, "Mezzadria e Potere Politico. Suggestioni dell'Età Moderna e Contemporanea e Realtà Medievale," *Studi Storici* 46 (2005): 923–943.

originated in the Middle Ages and became normative for the central portion of the region in the following centuries.[27] Classical mezzadria was imagined for generations as a partnership between a landlord, who provided most of the fixed capital necessary for agriculture, including the farmhouse, and the head of a peasant family, who contributed his labor and that of his relatives. Peasants lived in households of varying size, often in relatively large multigenerational or extended families. Sharecroppers were to share with their landlords both half of the ongoing expenses and half of the revenue of their toil. Peasant families used the revenue mostly for subsistence, whereas the landlords sold it to pay their middlemen and buy the many things that urban life offered, since most Tuscan landlords had their permanent residences in the towns. On the larger estates, the landlord had a villa where he spent some pleasant times hunting and entertaining (the so-called *villeggiatura*). In proximity to the villa stood the *fattoria*, where the produce was collected and stored, the wine and oil were produced, and the accounting books, which documented who owed what to whom, were kept. Most large-scale Tuscan landowners did not participate directly in the daily management of their farms, for which they hired middlemen (the *fattori*), who kept a close eye on the peasants and their work.

Mezzadria shaped the physical layout of the Tuscan landscape primarily in two related ways. The farming unit was the *podere*, a plot of land with a farmhouse placed roughly at its center. The first national census reported that 56 percent of all Tuscans lived scattered in farmhouses in 1861. Some landlords owned only one or two farms (poderi), but central Tuscany was dominated by large estates (*tenute* or *fattorie*). In the early twentieth century in the province of Siena, for example, two thirds of the agricultural land was organized in estates with multiple farms. The average estate had approximately ten farms, but the largest ones included more than fifty. The size of the poderi varied from less than 10 hectares in the more capitalized and commercially oriented areas of north-central Tuscany to more than 100 hectares in the southern portion of the region. Scattered settlement in the countryside contrasted with the density of the hill towns, usually grown around castles built in the early Middle Ages. In the least desirable parts of these towns lived the landless laborers (*braccianti* or *pigionali*), the poorest members of Tuscan rural society, who depended almost entirely on the sharecropping economy and eked

---

[27] On the history of central Italian sharecropping, see Giorgio Giorgetti, *Contadini e Proprietari nell'Italia Moderna* (Turin: Einaudi, 1974); Elisa Bianchi, *Il Tramonto della Mezzadria e i Suoi Riflessi Geografici* (Milan: UNICOPLI, 1983); Cristina Papa, *Dove Sono Molte Braccia E' Molto Pane* (Perugia: Editoriale Umbra, 1985).

out a living by providing various kinds of agricultural and construction work. Unlike in the Po Plain, laborers always remained a minority in rural Tuscany. Indeed, in the late nineteenth and early twentieth centuries conservatives trumpeted the limited size of the "rural proletariat" as the main social achievement of mezzadria.

Scattered settlement dovetailed with the other crucial spatial feature of mezzadria, mixed agriculture (*agricoltura promiscua*). The podere was to provide the peasant family with most of what it needed. Thus, rows of vines and olive trees lay interspersed with large stripes of land that were worked by ox-drawn plows to grow grassy crops in simple rotations of grains and fodder. These mixed crops also provided the landlord with a diversified, and thus relatively safe, rent (Illustration 1). This type of agriculture relied on the strict coordination of family labor. The authority of the pater familias, the *capoccia*, was supposed to go unquestioned in the fields, while his wife (or another older woman), the *massaia*, ruled over the other women who worked predominantly in the house and its immediate outskirts (in the vegetable garden and the poultry pen). Since

Illustration #1 Grape harvest in the Chianti in the late 1940s. The vines are hanging from olive trees, and a wide stripe of arable land separates the vine rows. This was the landscape of mixed agriculture.

the balance between people and land was key in this labor-intensive type of agriculture, the size of these families was strictly monitored. Peasants had to ask the capoccia and landlord permission to get married, for example, and eviction of "mismatched" families was a constant possibility. In sum, mezzadria fostered a chain of patriarchal and paternalistic social relationships. The members of the sharecropping family were to recognize the authority of the male head of the household, while all peasants had to engage in rituals of submission to the landlords, who were in turn held to the expectations of noblesse oblige, in the form of charity and patronage of many kinds.

By the eighteenth century, mezzadria had grown into a "system" that regulated the relationships between social classes, generations, and genders, as well as the ways human beings dwelt on the hilly territory they inhabited and drew sustenance from. Perhaps more than any other form of land tenure in Italy, Tuscan sharecropping invited perceptions of systemic coherence and immobility. At the turn of the nineteenth century, Swiss political economist Jean-Claude de Sismondi, who had sought refuge from the Jacobin Terror by purchasing an estate in northern Tuscany, argued that the Tuscan countryside hung in the balance between immobility and revolution.[28] It was difficult to imagine the possibility of substantial change from within a system that had evolved organically in the course of centuries. Sismondi noticed that even the peasants, despite their poverty, accepted their lot with fatalism and resignation. Social stability was deeply embedded in a harmonious landscape, but such immobility and low productivity seemed out of step with the rapid changes taking place in the age of revolution.

The irony of Sismondi's remarks is that at the time of his Tuscan sojourn enlightened landlords and practitioners were busy trying to improve the productivity of Tuscan sharecropping, and thus the longevity of the social order that relied on it, by reshaping the physical layout of the landscape. The Fascist "redeemers" of the 1930s drew a direct genealogy between themselves and these earlier reformers, who counted on the Georgofili Academy as their platform and on the availability of private investment capital in the larger estates. These earlier reformers also pioneered some of the knowledge and practices that the Fascists attempted to implement systematically a century later.[29] Three figures

[28] Jean-Claude Léonard Sismonde de Sismondi, *Tableau de l'Agriculture Toscane* (Geneva: J. J. Paschoud, 1801): 215–9.
[29] See, for example, Francesco Lami, *La Bonifica della Collina Tipica Toscana da G.B. Landeschi a C. Ridolfi* (Florence: Barbera, 1938).

dominate this genealogy of reformers, who were primarily preoccupied with regulating the water flow and reducing soil erosion in hilly areas.

The first figure was Giovan Battista Landeschi, a priest living on a small estate near San Miniato a Monte, west of Florence, who published an influential collection of essays in 1775.[30] Written in the voice of a humble and ingenious empiricist, always on the lookout for small improvements and innovations, these essays were above all a call to arms against the practice of plowing *a rittochino* – that is, straight down the hillsides and along the slope lines. Landeschi recommended instead a method called *a tagliapoggio* (literally, hill cutting), which he saw as fit above all for sandy soils all over Tuscany and beyond. This method called for the segmentation of the hills according to the direction of their slopes, the construction of banks (*ciglioni*), which would have to be at least six-meters wide to accommodate mixed cultivations, and the digging of horizontal drainage ditches that would lead to a main vertical one at the intersection of the segments or fields. This way, plowing and the installation of vines could take place across the slope lines, on top of very gently sloping banks.

Even more ambitious were the recommendations of the other two reformers. In the course of the 1820s and 1830s, Marquis Cosimo Ridolfi and his agent (fattore) Agostino Testaferrata turned the Meleto estate, just a few miles south of Landeschi's farm in the Elsa River valley, into a model for hillside agriculture, visited by landlords and practitioners from all over Italy and beyond.[31] As a young man Ridolfi, who later led the Georgofili Academy for more than twenty years, learned from Testaferrata to harness erosion to remodel the hills like clay sculptures. By digging deep ditches from the hilltops down the slopes and building small dams and embankments in the gullies at the base of the hills, the shifting silt could be directed in such a way that the hills became in the span of a few years rounder, more gently sloping, and more regular. After this process of remodeling, called *colmata di monte*, the newly gentle hills would be subdivided into roughly rectangular fields, opening up or closing down as they extended from the top ridge, depending on the shape of the hill. Of course plowing would be carried out across the slope lines, and a complex system of drainage ditches made sure that soil erosion and replenishment would be balanced. This arrangement, called *a spina*, had the additional advantage of doing away with banks, which wasted potentially fruitful land. Meleto was also the site of the first agricultural

---

[30] G. B. Landeschi, *Saggi di Agricoltura di un Parroco Samminiatese* (Florence: Gaetano Gambiagi, 1775).

[31] Cosimo Ridolfi, *Lezioni Orali di Agraria* (Florence: Cellini, 1862). About Ridolfi's rural legacy see Luigi Ridolfi, *L'Opera Agraria di Cosimo Ridolfi Esposta dal Figlio Luigi* (Florence: Civelli, 1903).

college in Italy, founded in 1834 and relocated to Pisa with the support of the Grand Duke a few years later. In 1859, on the eve of Italy's unification, a similar institution was established in Florence's Cascine Park. Generations of Tuscan landlords sent their sons to these schools in the following decades.

The cost and complexity of Ridolfi's reforms militated against their wide adoption, at least in their most ambitious form. Nevertheless, the practices associated with the reformers of the late eighteenth and early nineteenth centuries, who undoubtedly built on generations of local and informal knowledge, succeeded in all but eradicating the practice of cultivating *a rittochino*, or down the slope lines – a practice that was resurrected with a vengeance in the 1960s and 1970s (see Chapter 3). At a minimum, all self-respecting and well educated Tuscan landlords began to have their hilly lands plowed across the slope lines and carved with horizontal drainage ditches, in a simpler arrangements known as *a girapoggio* (literally, around the hill) or a *cavalcapoggio* (over the hill) (Illustration 2). As Emilio Sereni argued, even these simpler arrangements were founded not only on the centralization of capital and management power that had been accruing in the large estates, but also

Illustration #2 Landscape near Radda in Chianti in 1896. Cultivations are arranged horizontally, across the slope lines, to hinder erosion.

on the assumptions that land would be more intensely cultivated, the poderi would become smaller, and the more densely settled sharecroppers would provide the labor necessary to maintain the systematizations, if not carry them out in the first place. All of these interventions would have increased the surplus accruing to the enterprising landlords, eager to take advantage of the expanding commercial opportunities offered by the domestic and international markets.[32]

The same processes that made these reforms appealing (population growth, the increasing international integration of Tuscan agriculture, the spread of nonsubsistence crops, and burgeoning mechanization) also exerted increasing pressures on mezzadria from the 1870s on, as the landlords attempted to shift the costs of the innovations onto the peasants. Nevertheless, at the level of political rhetoric, mezzadria kept being extolled by most Tuscan landlords and political leaders as an admirable example of class harmony and as an antidote to the tensions of modernity. Of course this system also had its critics, who never tired of pointing out that the peasants' obligation to share in the cultivation expenses, the absence of the landlords from day-to-day management decisions, and the lack of agricultural specialization were all features that militated against the spread of technical innovations and more highly capitalized farming methods.[33] The production of surplus depended above all on the near-limitless provision of manual labor by the peasant family – labor that often remained invisible and unpaid. These critiques, however, rang hollow in the face of the seeming peacefulness of rural society and the orderliness of a landscape in which every object seemed to have found its proper place and every task its necessary function.

Tuscan large-scale landlords received an indication that this perception of harmony might be deceptive and self-serving at the very beginning of the twentieth century, when a few strikes stirred the areas of the region, such as the Val di Chiana and sections of the lower Arno valley, where the demographic pressure on the land and the spread of commercial crops such as tobacco and sugar beets were particularly advanced.[34] Cows were taken to Chianciano, a main urban center in the Val di Chiana, and left mooing in pain for days on end, as their udders filled with milk. Socialist slogans were shouted and printed in the local press. These episodes of unrest, however, failed to cohere into a movement. After all, the

---

[32] E. Sereni, *Storia del Paesaggio Agrario Italiano* (Bari: Laterza, 1961), chapters 71, 72, and 75.

[33] For this debate, see *La Mezzadria negli Scritti dei Georgofili, 1874–1929* (Bologna: Edizioni Agricole, 1935).

[34] Vittorio Meoni, *Gli Scioperi del 1902 in Val di Chiana: Le Lotte Contadine di Chanciano, Chiusi e Sarteano* (Montepulciano: Le Balze, 2002).

very layout of the sharecropping landscape, with its scattered settlement, seemed to have been devised to discourage communication among peasants and their coordination.

The experience of the Great War brought the tensions mounting in rural Italy to the boiling point. This was not so much the consequence of hardship, for the countryside fared better than the cities even in the most brutal phases of the conflict. Rather, the war brought with it the general awareness that social relations and political institutions could be renegotiated; it changed ordinary people's horizon of expectations. Italian peasants began to feel that they could participate in "historical change." In Tuscany, however, this awareness confronted one of the most deeply entrenched social orders in the peninsula. Suffice it to say that, while at the national level small-scale land ownership increased by a million hectares as a consequence of inflation, in the immediate postwar years Tuscan small-scale farmers increased their holdings only by 30,000 hectares, the smallest growth of any region. The absolute hegemony of aristocratic large-scale ownership in central Tuscany survived World War I and its aftermath almost unscathed. As late as the mid-1940s, Tuscany's large estates (those with more than 100 hectares) made up slightly more than half of the privately held agricultural land, the highest percentage in all of Italy. Commenting on these data, Domenico Preti has argued that fascism, "in terms of land ownership distribution, stopped the clock of history for more than twenty years."[35]

This relative immobility was not the outcome of peasant passivity, but of a victorious and brutal backlash against the peasant movement. For the first time in local memory, after the end of the war Tuscan sharecroppers gained a forefront position in a national movement for radical reform. They came to be organized mostly by socialist leaders, who strategically downplayed the collectivization program their party touted in other contexts. As Frank Snowden has shown, Tuscan mezzadri participated eagerly in strikes and demonstrations through 1919 and 1920.[36] In the summer of 1920, more than two thirds of the region's sharecroppers were reportedly on strike. They also participated in the political process, voting overwhelmingly for the Left (universal male suffrage had been granted in 1913). The local elections of 1919 brought the socialists into positions of power in most of the region's municipal governments. All but 6 of the 36 towns in the province of Siena, for example, found themselves in socialist hands.

---

[35] Domenico Preti, "L'Economia Toscana nel Periodo Fascista," in Giorgio Mori (ed.), *Storia d'Italia: Le Regioni dall'Unità a Oggi. La Toscana* (Turin: Einaudi, 1986): 611.

[36] F. Snowden, *The Fascist Revolution in Tuscany, 1919–1922* (Cambridge: Cambridge University Press, 1989).

The demands of Tuscan sharecroppers were diverse and far-reaching. They fought for the right to unionize; to assign burdensome cultivation expenses entirely to the landlords; to limit evictions drastically; to increase their managerial role in the farms; and to do away with the traditional additional pacts (*patti aggiuntivi*) that forced peasants to provide the landlord with unpaid labor services and specific products at certain times of the year. In 1920 a regional agreement accorded some of these requests to the sharecroppers. In the meantime, however, the landlords had already begun to organize their backlash, funding and even staffing the squads of Black Shirts that terrorized the countryside by punishing the movement's leaders and destroying the buildings where the peasants gathered, all with the complacency (and sometimes outright complicity) of the army and the police. The landlords also established Fascist unions, which over time gained a monopoly of the local labor markets. In Snowden's words, "fascism intended not only to prevent revolution but also to establish a whole new regime in the countryside, a new moral and economic order in which the foundations of a decaying mezzadria system were to be buttressed by the institutions of an ongoing repression."[37] By 1922, this carrot-and-stick strategy had effected the intended results. All the conquests of the peasant movement were rolled back and social hierarchies were firmly restored. In sum, as Snowden has put it, "in many respects Tuscan fascism evolved as an anti-mezzadro crusade."[38] That Tuscan sharecroppers could be simultaneously understood as class enemies to be redeemed and models of class deference to be imitated throughout the peninsula and beyond was one of the most strident and yet consequential paradoxes of Italian fascism.

It is beyond my abilities to give a sense of how Tuscan peasants perceived the Fascist restoration. Their reactions can perhaps only be retrieved retrospectively, as memories relayed after the end of the dictatorship, and the next chapter will attend to some of those recollections and aspirations. Much easier is to retrieve the narratives developed by Tuscan landowners as they made sense of the dramatic events they had just witnessed and participated in. Two kinds of narratives were particularly common among the Tuscan rural elite. In the first, Tuscan peasants had never genuinely embraced socialism and "subversive" attitudes; they were simply trying to take advantage of a very volatile situation, as peasants the world over were prone to doing. In the second narrative, peasants had been corrupted by outside agitators, but then they had realized the importance of the bonds of loyalty that tied them to their landlords

[37] Ibid.: 63.
[38] Ibid.: 82.

and mended their ways under the firm hand of a regenerated national government.

Common to both narratives was the perception that the war had nearly undone centuries of harmonious collaboration between social classes, and that certain lures of modernity constituted a threat to be kept a bay. Marquis Gino Incontri, who owned a large estate not far from Meleto, believed that Tuscan peasants had flirted with insurrection out of sheer opportunism. After all, he wrote six years after the end of the war, they had made opportunistic soldiers, too, as he himself had verified while serving as an officer at the front. But he also perceived that "tradition" was shaky at best on his cherished hills:

The naïveté, the child-like curiosity, have all but disappeared, as was inevitable; today the peasant approaches more people than in the past. The bicycle has had an influence that I would call almost nefarious. Not to mention the other means of rapid transportation – the buses, trains, sidecars – that right after the war have changed our countryside and upset its patriarchal peace! During the war all the farmhouses saw the circulation of newspapers for the first time; and the veterans, having been enchanted by cinematography, could no longer live without.[39]

As we will see, Tuscan elites harbored similar sentiments after the end of World War II as well, when they confronted a newly insurgent peasant movement that they could no longer beat into submission. The irony was that Incontri also thought of himself as an innovative and modernizing gentleman farmer, facing diffident peasants bound to their old ways.

Similar contradictions are evident in another memoir, written a few years later by Giuseppe Dini, who owned a 450-hectare estate with ten farms not far from Siena. Upon being decorated by the government for his contribution to the Battle for Wheat, Dini remarked that he had been an "agricultural modernizer" (*bonificatore*) long before the March on Rome. Wheat yields on his land had risen dramatically in the ten years before the war. He had even begun to rear with success some beautiful Simmenthal cows that he had selected and purchased in Switzerland. All of those efforts came to naught in the face of "Bolshevik insanity" after the war. He included a table with seven columns, showing how wheat yields had risen from 700 kilograms per hectare in 1904 to 1,750 in 1929, with a deep trough between 1917 and 1922. The seventh column recorded the main changes that had intervened over the years. In 1906, innovative rotations were introduced; in 1909 he started mechanical sowing; in 1914 there was hail; then the war, and more hail in 1917; Bolshevism struck in 1918, enduring until 1922; in 1922, noted in bold

[39] G. Incontri, *Il Contadino Toscano*: 25.

letters, the Fascist Era dawned: "Since the beginning of the Fascist Regime total production has exceeded that of 1922 by an average of 29,400 kilograms. Order and discipline! That is all it takes!"[40] The final photographs are of Simmenthal cows and their human attendants. The cows' names and destinies are dutifully noted (most of them had died in the years of "Bolshevism"). Not a word is spent for the men by their side.

These elite perceptions, rooted in widespread interpretations of recent history and the senses of place and time they elicited, help us appreciate the complex and contradictory relationship the Fascist regime entertained with the social and spatial features of rural Tuscany. On the one hand, the Tuscany of classical sharecropping constituted a model to be imitated in other contexts of novel settlement. The reclamation of the Agro Pontino, for example, was meant to attract farmers with a "sharecropping mind-set" (*mentalità mezzadrile*), ready to combine the attachment to the land and the loyalty to the landowner (in this case, a state agency) that was supposedly distinctive of central Italian rural communities. As Roberta Pergher has showed, similar guidelines informed the Libyan settlement plans of the late 1930s.[41] On the other hand, Fascist agricultural reformers were fully aware of the fact that actual (as opposed to imagined) sharecroppers had been at the forefront of the peasant movement in the postwar years. They also realized that the spatial and social makeup of sharecropping hindered agricultural changes. For example, as we will see later in the chapter, mixed agriculture raised exponentially the costs of reimplantation of the vines that had been infested by the phylloxera aphid. It also made the mechanization of grain cultivation difficult at best. In other words, mezzadria severely limited the degree to which land and social reclamation could be "integral." The contradiction between the desire for modernization and the forced preservation of the social order could not be easily bridged.

Serpieri was aware of these contradictions and tried to address them during his tenure as the country's top rural reformer in the late 1920s and early 1930s. He was very close to the social world of the Tuscan landlords. He had taught their sons at the University of Florence, and he remained president of the Georgofili Academy from 1926 to the end of the regime. But he also tried to push through reforms that would have increased the managerial role of the sharecroppers while limiting their exposure to undue risks through insurance schemes jointly paid with

[40] G. Dini, *Agli Avamposti per la Battaglia del Grano e Bonifica Integrale sulla Montagnola Senese: San Chimento e Paurano 1892–1929* (Florence: Poll, 1931): 7.
[41] R. Pergher, *A Tale of Two Borders: Settlement and National Transformation in Libya and South Tyrol under Fascism* (PhD diss., University of Michigan, 2007).

the landlords. He envisioned sharecroppers on the move towards a more productive and self-reliant future. In this case, too, he was defeated, and the 1933 Sharecropping Charter (Carta della Mezzadria) set national guidelines that did not enshrine any of his reforms.[42] After Serpieri's dismissal in 1935, Tuscan landlords managed to enshrine instead one of the most controversial features of traditional mezzadria, the so-called *patti di fossa* (literally, digging agreements), by which peasants had to incur half of the expenses for works of irrigation and drainage maintenance. The costs of Fascist reclamation would thus be shared more "equitably" between social classes.

The only major change to the Tuscan sharecropping contract made under fascism came in October 1938, when the regime decided, against the will of the landlords, to extend to Tuscany some of the rules that were customary in other regions. In particular, Tuscan sharecroppers would now own half of the cattle and share half of the revenue generated by it, like their colleagues in Emilia-Romagna and the Marche. Potentially, this was an important change that could have increased the peasants' managerial role. In practice, however, the main upshot of the reform was to increase overnight the sharecroppers' level of indebtedness to their landlords. There is no evidence in the peasants' recollections that they welcomed this reform or that it improved their lot, but it did become a bone of contention after the war, when inflation decreased the value of peasant debt and raised the revenue the landlords were to share. Whether and how to "index" the value of the cattle became a major terrain of confrontation in the context of renewed peasant militancy.

Fascist Redemption in Practice: The Orcia Valley

October 28 was a date for obligatory celebrations in 1930s Italy. On that day in 1922 the March on Rome had taken place, leading to Mussolini's appointment as President of the Council of Ministers. As the Fascists consolidated their power and restructured the country's institutions, October 28 also became the last day of the new Fascist calendar, to be noted in Roman numerals next to the Christian date. As a marker of accomplished ends and new beginnings, the date of October 28 was a natural choice for the 1934 inauguration of the reclamation works that had been carried out in the remote valley of the Orcia River since the

---

[42] Domenico Preti, "La Carta della Mezzadria tra Politica Agraria e Organizzazione dello Stato Corporativo," in Giorgio Giorgetti (ed.), *Contadini e Proprietari nella Toscana Moderna: Atti del Convegno di Studi in Onore di Giorgio Giorgetti* (Florence: Olschki, 1979): 257–284.

passing of the Mussolini Law in December 1928. For the first time in anyone's memory, the valley was dressed in national clothes: "The tricolor, which had never graced the valley's scattered houses, waved everywhere and decorated with simplicity new and old farmhouses, trees and vineyards, agricultural machines and rural carts, hedges and haystacks. Along the newly built roads stood green arches, portrayals of the Duce, banners with slogans, and an abundance of the national colors."[43]

The day started with some speeches delivered in San Quirico's main piazza, under a large banner depicting Mussolini on a thresher at Littoria, the largest new town built in the Agro Pontino. Antonio Origo, the President of the landlords' consortium in charge of the valley's reclamation works, declared to the Prefect, ready to cut the ribbon leading up to a newly built road, that "today marks the end of a centuries-old past which bore the signs of squalor and desolation. With the gesture that Your Excellency will make in the name of the Fascist Government, a new Era will dawn, an Era of redemption, new settlement, and valorization of our land."[44] With that, the Prefect cut the ribbon, the Bishop blessed the road, and a motorcade got on its way, preceded by two young Fascists on motorbikes. The sharecroppers' families had come out too, with their decorated oxen, sporting their Sunday best. The population of the valley's municipalities gathered in designated areas along the road, ready to give the Fascist salute as the motorcade passed by. The authorities stopped several times to admire the consortium's accomplishments. Particularly impressive were the demonstrations with explosives at Torre Tarugi, where forty mines went off to round out the clay hilltops. Among the people waiting along the road were the staff of the new rural schools, as well as that of the health center, named after Gianni Origo, the recently and tragically deceased son of Antonio and Iris. The three-hour tour ended festively with a reception at the Origos' villa at La Foce.

That day of celebration and pageantry was inscribed in the Fascist Era, but in the eyes of its most vocal participants it also marked the end (or at least the beginning of the end) of trajectories begun in mythical temporalities that straddled the geological and the political, the natural and the historical. The works taking place in the Orcia valley were part of a more general project, sponsored by the regime, meant to reclaim the eroded clay formations (or "badlands") of central Italy. These *bonifiche di monte* (mountain reclamations) constituted the starkest departure from the more traditional forms of agricultural redemption, aimed at

---

[43] Antonio Origo, "Opere del Quinquennio dall'Anno VIII all'anno XII," *Bollettino del Consorzio di Trasformazione Fondiaria della Val d'Orcia* 5 (50, December 1934): 2.

[44] Ibid.: 4.

draining alluvial plains and creating highly fertile areas for intensive cultivation. There was no guarantee, or even expectation, that the clay hills of Emilia-Romagna, Tuscany, and the Marche would ever become prime agricultural land. But the effort to reclaim these previously neglected areas testified to the "integral" character of Fascist policies.[45] At stake was not merely economic profitability, but the reshaping of whole landscapes and settlement patterns with an eye towards the creation of a new rural civilization. On a more prosaic note, it was only state intervention and the promise of long-term public subsidies that made these undertakings possible.

At the deepest level, the Fascist reclamation of the valley seemed to break with a path begun in the early Pleistocene, three to four million years before, when the foot of the Appennines mountain range, the "backbone" of the Italian peninsula, was occupied by shrinking and expanding shallow seas. The Orcia valley then lay at the bottom of one of these seas, where fine sediments originating from the surrounding mountains had been depositing for millennia, producing a layer of almost impermeable clay. But this was also a highly volcanic region, dominated by then-active Mount Amiata. Volcanic activity had twisted and stretched these layered formations, creating a corrugated topography dotted with visually stunning domes of clay resembling resplendent elephant backs (or, in a more recent formulation, giant pieces of popcorn), the so-called *biancane*, from the Italian word for white (Illustration 3).[46] Many observers compared the valley to a stormy sea that had been frozen in place, a scene that filled them with horror. The dream of the Fascist modernizers was to make the landscape smoother, so as to resemble a gently wavy lake instead.[47] These watery visions were perhaps encouraged by the specimens of fossilized marine fauna that lay strewn all around, as relics of a remote aquatic past.

Less certain than its geological origins was whether the valley, barren as it was in recent centuries, had ever been densely forested. At least since the late nineteenth century, some scholars have believed in the possibility that the valley, like many other regions in Mediterranean Europe, was once covered with oak trees, and that extensive deforestation took

[45] Arrigo Serpieri, "Le Leggi della Bonifica Integrale," *Bollettino del Consorzio di Trasformazione Fondiaria della Val d'Orcia* 3 (18, March 1932): 1–5; Vittorio Montanari, "Come si Trasformano le Crete Senesi," *L'Agricoltura Senese* 70 (July 1934): 593–601.

[46] For an introduction to the geological history of the area, see C. P. Phillips, "The Badlands of Italy: A Vanishing Landscape?" *Applied Geography* 18 (1998): 243–257.

[47] Giuseppe Andriulli, "Si Redime la Terra Desolata in Val d'Orcia," *Bollettino del Consorzio di Trasformazione Fondiaria della Val d'Orcia* 5 (48, October 1934): 1–3. The article was originally published in the daily *Il Messaggero*.

Illustration #3 Clay formations in the Orcia valley in the 1920s, before the reclamation.

place in prehistoric times. Deprived of this protection, the upper layer of organic soil eroded quickly, washed out by the typically violent late summer storms, leaving behind bare clay that dried out in the summer sun. On the most exposed formations, such as the biancane, chemical dispersion produced a top layer of very hard mud that very few plants could penetrate, and even those only for parts of the year. Eroded particles had also accumulated at the bottom of the valley, producing a flat river bed over which water moved slowly for much of the year and ruinously in the aftermath of major storms. It should be noted that most contemporary scientists no longer believe that the badlands of Mediterranean Europe, including those of southern Tuscany, are the result of human activity.[48]

In the Orcia valley, this deep tale of geomorphological declension set in motion by prehistoric deforestation coexisted with narratives of political decline staged in more recent centuries. Hard evidence was (and is) lacking for all of these stories, which retained their persuasive and evocative power nonetheless. In these temporally closer tales, despite (or perhaps

---

[48] Alfred Thomas Grove and Oliver Rackham, *The Nature of Mediterranean Europe: An Ecological History* (New Haven: Yale University Press, 2001): 271–87.

because of) deforestation, the valley had once been an agriculturally productive and prosperous region, far more densely populated than in recent memory. It had provided ancient Rome with grains and meat, for example. In one version, decline had taken place in the early Middle Ages on account of ongoing rivalries and warfare between local lords, whose isolation allowed them to act with relative impunity. The valley had also been the last bastion of Sienese power to fall to Florentine domination in 1559, four years after Siena itself had capitulated to the Medicis and their Spanish allies.[49] Thus, in another story, warfare between Florence and Siena, followed by Florentine domination and neglect, had led to agricultural decline and depopulation. Nested somewhere between these tales was the famous story of Pope Pius II, born in the valley as Enea Silvio Piccolomini, who had built Pienza in the 1460s as his ideal city, but who had also planned to dam the Orcia River somewhere between Montalcino and San Quirico, sentencing much of the valley to a new watery destiny. Only his death prevented him from pursuing this project. Commentators in the 1930s remarked that Pius would not have dreamt this up, had the valley been truly densely populated and cultivated. Whatever the case, the Fascist reclamation plans found their niche in the complex senses of place and time produced by these narratives.[50]

The promoters of Fascist reclamation could also point to more recent experiments with the redemption of Tuscany's clay areas. As early as 1911 Count Ghigi-Saracini had used combinations of explosives and more traditional methods on his estate near Castelnuovo Berardenga, obtaining wheat yields as high as 2,300 kilograms per hectare. In the Orcia River valley, Gino Verdiani-Bandi had undertaken similar works immediately after the war, and at first without public subsidies.[51] The estates of the Sienese clay areas had long been understood as transitional agricultural and social formations, nested between the intensively cultivated and more densely populated countryside of classical sharecropping to the north, and the latifundia of the Roman Campagna to the south. Agronomist and landowner Vittorio Racah had called the Sienese clay estates *latifondi a colonia*, roughly translatable as sharecropped latifundia.[52] Similarly to

[49] Giorgio Giorgetti, *Le Crete Senesi in Età Moderna: Studi e Ricerche di Storia Rurale* (Florence: Olschki, 1983).

[50] Alberto Luchini, "Bonifica Integrale in Toscana. La Trasformazione Fondiaria della Val d'Orcia," *Bollettino del Consorzio di Trasformazione Fondiaria della Val d'Orcia* 4 (29, March 1933): 2–3; Vera Baccinetti, *L'Opera di Bonifica nel Territorio Senese* (Siena: Stabilimento Tipografico Ex-Combattenti, 1936).

[51] Giorgio Garavini, "Lavori Agricoli con Esplosivi: Concorso Nazionale per Esplosivi Agricoli," *Agricoltura Senese* 64 (February-March 1928): 29–32.

[52] Luigi Bologna, "Una Singolare Zona Toscana di Monte da Bonificare: La Val d'Orcia," *Italia Agricola* 64 (January 1927): 4–14.

the southern latifundia, the structure of property in the Orcia valley was highly concentrated: 75 percent of the land was occupied by estates larger than 400 hectares in the late 1920s. The average sharecropping family had eleven members, four more than the provincial average, and some of these families resided on farms larger than 100 hectares. Given the low quality of the soil and the relative aridity, low-yield wheat cultivation prevailed. Almost half of the agricultural area was made up of arable land without woody plants (that is, without olive trees or vineyards), and 60 percent of the revenue of a typical farm came from grain cultivation.[53] Thus, the dream of the large-scale aristocratic landlords who dominated the valley was to increase the settlement density of their extensively cultivated estates by reducing the average size of the farms (poderi), with the expectation that the large sharecropper families could be split into smaller units. Grain cultivation would have remained dominant, albeit now deploying the new high-yield wheat varietals developed by Nazareno Strampelli. Nevertheless, the rules of mezzadria required that vineyards and olive groves would remain a feature of the landscape, as staples necessary to the peasant family's subsistence.

These projects of modernization, calling for recapitalization buttressed by more intensive exploitation of peasant labor, predated the Fascist regime and should be set in the context of the general crisis that had been affecting the sharecropping economy since the late nineteenth century. Nevertheless, the new regime offered a series of opportunities and incentives that promised to bring the reclamation of the clay areas to a whole new level of coordination and organization. This was nowhere more evident than in the Orcia valley. Serpieri's early decrees of 1923 and 1924 alerted the valley's large-scale landlords to the possibility of harnessing state intervention to carry out more systematically the kinds of works of improvement that a few of them had started independently. The inauguration of the Battle for Wheat in 1925 gave even more impetus to these reforming ambitions. When the director of the provincial agricultural extension (Cattedra Ambulante), Sergio Garavini, declared his willingness to draft a reclamation plan for the valley, a group of landlords, including Origo and Verdiani-Bandi, met in June 1926 to form a committee that began to lobby the other landlords and the public authorities for the creation of a consortium. They opened a line of credit with Monte dei Paschi, Siena's largest bank, guaranteed by the Federal Agricultural Credit Institute for Tuscany, a public agency, and in 1927 the national government officially declared the Orcia valley a reclamation

---

[53] Data from Viscardo Montanari, *Agricoltura Senese*: 64–65.

area of public interest. Two years later, in the wake of the Mussolini Law, the consortium was established and recognized.[54]

The area managed by the consortium at the time of its establishment covered approximately 35,000 hectares (135 square miles), divided between eight municipalities, with a population of roughly 17,000. Given the obligatory character of the consortium, virtually all of the valley's landlords became members, at least nominally. By 1931, it enrolled 1,746 estates, 77 percent of which were smaller than 5 hectares. The majority of these small-scale units were located high up on the northern slope of Mount Amiata.[55] The largest seventy members (corresponding to less than 5 percent of the local owners) controlled almost three quarters of the land. Decisional power was proportionate to the amount of land owned. The meetings of the consortium's assembly were only valid if at least 20 percent of the votes were represented. This quota was not always reached, and sometimes more members had to be called in. In practice, the typical meeting included fewer than fifty people, and usually the representatives of the largest five estates had enough votes to make any decision.[56]

The original reclamation plan for the valley was quite ambitious, even for a project whose time horizon stretched for several decades. The plan called for 250 kilometers of new roads; 90 kilometers of water conduits; 18,000 hectares of new forests; 16,000 hectares of new agricultural land; and 350 new houses (and farms), as well as the restructuring of 250 old ones. The density of cattle would increase eight-fold, until reaching eight head per hectare of agricultural land. Eventually, six thousand more people would live in the valley, almost all of them sharecroppers and their families.[57] The infrastructural work, such as the major new roads, would be funded entirely by the government, whereas the landowners would cover two thirds of most works of agricultural improvement. More modest plans that limited themselves to the reforestation of the most vulnerable portions of the territory were only considered in passing, since they would

---

[54] For the history of the consortium, see Maria Mangiavacchi (ed.), *Archivio del Consorzio di Bonifica della Val d'Orcia, Immagini Fotografiche per la Lettura del Territorio* (Florence: Aska Edizioni, 2004).

[55] Archivio del Consorzio di Bonifica della Val d'Orcia, Folder 1818, Piano Definitivo di Massima.

[56] The largest estate belonged to Count Piccolomini, with 1,351 hectares and 68 votes, followed by Cavaliere (Knight) Angheben, with 1,291 hectares and 65 votes, Enrichetta Mieli, with 1,188 and 60 votes, Count Adimari Morelli, with 942 hectares and 48 votes, and Marquis Origo, with 939 hectares and 47 votes. Data from A. Origo, "Assemblea Consorziale," *Bollettino del Consorzio di Trasformazione Fondiaria della Val d'Orcia* 4 (31, May 1933): 2–7.

[57] Ibid.: 3–4.

not have met the requirements for large state subsidies. Only plans that promised massive increases in population density and agricultural productivity could be regarded as truly in the national interest. Ambition had its own rewards.

For a few years the northern half of the valley, where the largest estates were located, assumed the features and noises of a construction site. In describing the scene, a journalist from Florence indulged in a bit of Futurist prose: the valley had become for him "a simultaneity – resplendent on the hills, abutting the trails – of freshly dug roads, sometimes returns to Etruscan and Longobard paths, but more often brand new. A multiplication of dams, trenches, banks, slopes, supports, sewers, greenhouses. Hills broken apart with explosives, reactivated wells. Everywhere the roar of the truck chases away the echoes buried in the clay formations, like the soundtrack to a news report."[58] By the time the Prefect and Bishop came to visit on the twelfth anniversary of the March on Rome in 1934, two major roads were complete, one along the Orcia River and the other linking La Foce to Contignano, for a total of 37 kilometers. New secondary roads crisscrossed the valley for another 25 kilometers. The reclamation of two of the streams flowing into the Orcia (the Formone and the Piaggia) had been accomplished. Some 15 kilometers of banks had been built along the Orcia River and its tributaries. The members of the consortium were also building 43 new farmhouses and restructuring at least as many (Illustration 4). For this work the consortium had employed an average of 500 workers, including many mercury miners from Mount Amiata who had lost their jobs after the closure of the mines in 1932. The consortium leaders hoped that these miners, who had been at the forefront of the post–World War I "Bolshevist" movement, would now be transformed into grateful rural dwellers, "an increase in good Etruscan seed, perfect to protect the gold reserve of our traditional ethnic values in tomorrow's Italy."[59] As it turned out, most of the former miners lost their jobs again when public funds dried up in 1936, and at least one commentator remarked that they had never been very good at their tasks anyway.[60]

As the consortium reforested stretches of land, remodeled many hills *a spina* along the lines recommended by Ridolfi and his successors, channeled and dammed streams, built roads and farmhouses, and intervened on the topography of the valley in many other ways, a series of parallel

---

[58] Alberto Luchini, "Bonifica Integrale in Toscana": 3.
[59] Alberto Luchini, "Problemi Toscani": 2.
[60] Vincenzo Bellucci, "Aspetti Tecnici ed Economici della Bonifica della Val d'Orcia" *Bonifica e Colonizzazione* 2 (11, November 1938): 3–29.

Illustration #4 New farmhouse built with the funds of the Reclamation
Consortium of the Orcia Valley, early 1930s.

projects were carried out on the peasants themselves. The landscape created by the reclamation had a disciplinary dimension as well. The consortium hired several guards in charge of making sure that the peasants did
not damage the reclamation works and followed the new rules that came
with them. On March 8, 1935, a guard fined Angelo Tribocchi, age forty-
five, for working the land up to the edge of a major reclamation ditch,
damaging it. Tribocchi had already been fined a few months before for
hunting on his lord's land, and he retorted that this fine he would not pay,
and that the guard could take the jacket off his back, for that was all he
had. A few weeks later Valentino Bensi, age thirty-seven, was issued a ticket
for letting his three goats eat poplar seedlings planted by the consortium.
Those were tickets number 17 and 18, respectively.[61] Clearly the peasants
were in need of some monitoring and prodding. Moreover, it is worth
reiterating that the sharecroppers were responsible for a share of expenses
incurred in the maintenance of several kinds of reclamation works.

More generally, land reclamation was also an opportunity to imagine
and forge a new peasantry. This was what the Fascists called *bonifica*

[61] *Bollettino del Consorzio di Trasformazione Fondiaria della Val d'Orcia* 6 (55, May 1935): 12.

umana, or human reclamation, and this too could be viewed both as a qualitative leap in the socialization and politicization of the peasantry, and as the continuation of the paternalistic benevolence exercised by some landlords since at least the eighteenth century. The very term, *boni-fica umana,* alluded to the ambition of remolding the "human material" of the Italian countryside with the same determination devoted to its topographical features. Some of the qualities attributed to the peasants, such as their attachment to the land and their willingness to sacrifice themselves, were to be retained, but many others had to be overcome, with the expectation that the subjects of this transformation would grow grateful to the government and the upper classes, who had jointly devised and promoted the changes.

Education figured prominently in these visions of paternalistic mod-ernization. Estimates of the extent of illiteracy among the Orcia valley's peasants ranged from 60 to 80 percent, much higher than in other parts of Tuscany. Although the valley already had a couple of sparsely attended rural schools, these were restructured and new ones were added, so that by the mid-1930s four elementary rural schools operated at Le Checche, San Piero in Campo, La Foce, and Conie.[62] The emphasis here is on "rural." Of course Pienza, San Quirico, and the other towns in the valley had their own schools. But there was never any discussion of encour-aging the peasants to send their children to these more urban schools. Geographical distance was certainly a factor, but at least as important was the assumption that rural children needed to be educated as future model peasants. They needed their own schools. The curriculum adopted by the valley's rural schools was the one specially developed for the chil-dren of the newly reclaimed Agro Pontino. Every school had a garden where the children, age six to ten, could learn the rudiments of modern farming.

Moreover, these rural schools were attached to some of the area's great estates. At La Foce, for example, the Origos had financially contributed to the construction of the new school, and they paid the salaries and living expenses of the two teachers. Thus, instruction at these schools taught respect and gratitude for both the government and the landown-ing class. On one day, the pupils would plant a cypress tree and dedicate it to the Duce's brother, Arnaldo, who had died prematurely of a heart attack (Illustration 5). On another, they would all participate in a joint ceremony with the children of the other rural schools and listen to an inspiring speech by Marquis Origo. Even so, fourth grader Fosca Marri

---

[62] "Scuole Rurali," *Bollettino del Consorzio di Trasformazione Fondiaria della Val d'Orcia* 5 (51, January 1935): 29–30.

Illustration #5 Boy and girls in Fascist uniform in the yard of a rural school in the Orcia valley, after planting a cypress tree commemorating the death of Mussolini's brother, Arnaldo.

commented in her paper after hearing her landlord speak: "Marquis Origo thinks of so many things! If all the Signori did like the Marquis this would be a different world."[63] Children like Fosca would indeed grow up to imagine a different world, but one without Signori.

Some of the interventions associated with the valley's reclamation works must have improved the peasants' quality of life, albeit always within very hierarchical settings. The clinic built in the proximity of La Foce's villa, for example, came to be staffed with a district nurse and visited periodically by a doctor. According to the data provided by the nurse herself, the clinic performed approximately five thousand and five hundred inpatient visits and almost two thousand outpatient calls in its first year and half of activity. One of the rooms was reserved for birthing mothers, and another housed a solarium – sunlight being regarded as crucial to children's proper growth. The nurse also organized summer trips to the regime's "sun colonies" on the seashore, noticing that those children (the boys among them – that is) also got to see a train at least

---

[63] "Scuole Rurali," *Bollettino del Consorzio di Trasformazione Fondiaria della Val d'Orcia* 6 (55, May 1935): 19.

once before leaving for military service. The clinic operated in coordination with the rural schools, so that the nurse could keep a file on each of the enrolled children, monitoring their growth. It was customary for pregnant women to propitiate lactation by visiting some caves in the valley's wildest reaches, where rock formations resembled human breasts (the so-called *pocce lattaie*). The nurse remarked that she had to struggle mightily against these kinds of superstitions and impart the rudiments of modern childcare. She felt like a missionary of sorts, committed to improving "this corner of Tuscany that is still so primitive in the face of the great progress of these years."[64]

By the same token, there is no reason to doubt that the newly built farmhouses were more spacious than those to which many peasants were accustomed. Improvements, however, came with strict limitations. In an arresting passage from Antonio Origo's report to the Georgofili Academy about the progress attained on his estate, the Marquis recalled the horror he felt upon visiting the peasants' houses shortly after his move to La Foce: "I cannot talk of the farmhouses, all of them, other than as decaying hovels, in which families with 12 or 18 members lived in the most squalid poverty, piled up in two or three rooms. In one of those houses I once saw the old head of the household take his last breaths in the same bed, under the same blankets, as his young daughter-in-law was about to give birth."[65] The newly built houses would make these kinds of horrors unnecessary, Origo argued. These houses came in four different sizes. The largest model was meant for a family of up to nine adults, four youngsters, and five children, and it included seven bedrooms; the smallest one was meant for a family of up to five adults, three youngsters, and three children, and it included four bedrooms. All four models featured a latrine without plumbing, located at the end of an upstairs hallway. The cattle were housed in the stable downstairs, as was customary all over Tuscany.[66] Thus, perhaps not to incite jealousies, the brand new houses remained quite faithful to tradition. Modern hygiene for peasants did not come with a modern bathroom or a separate facility for the animals they tended. As we will see in the next chapter, after the war these houses became the subject of vocal protests against conditions the peasants had come to regard as unsanitary.

Overall, a precise assessment of what was actually accomplished in the luster of sustained activity that followed the Mussolini Law is far from

---

[64] R. Guidetti, "L'Assistente Sanitaria in Zona di Bonifica," *Bollettino del Consorzio di Trasformazione Fondiaria della Val d'Orcia* 6 (60–61, October–November 1935): 14–15.

[65] Antonio Origo, "Verso la Bonifica Integrale di un'Azienda nella Val d'Orcia: Risultati di Dodici Anni di Lavoro," *Atti della Regia Accademia dei Georgofili* 3 (January–March 1937): 19.

[66] Archivio del Consorzio di Bonifica della Val d'Orcia, folder 3538, year 1929. Cubature dei Locali delle Case Coloniche.

easy. The reclamation promoters wavered between triumphal rhetoric and thinly disguised frustration both at the government, often late in disbursing the funds, and even more at the bulk of the consortium members, who were happy to receive public subsidies but then failed to follow through with the expected improvements on their land. Marquis Origo was indeed somewhat unique in his ability to rely on his wife's extensive wealth. Many other landlords, including some of the large-scale ones, balked at the idea of contributing two thirds of the reclamation expenses on their estates in such uncertain times. This reluctance was far from irrational, since the agricultural redemption of clay soils could only succeed after many years of painstaking work, once the organic content in the soil had reached a sustainable threshold. Approached with a short-term attitude, temporary improvements risked making the situation worse, leading to complete erosion and the loss of the area's cultivability for generations. Of course the regime imagined itself as eternal and all-powerful, but many Tuscan landlords must have known better. Indeed, some reclaimed areas were "lost" in the mid-1940s, and it took the consortium another major reclamation effort in the 1950s and 1960s to stabilize them once and for all.

Nevertheless, the valley, like many other areas around the country, began to change shape with unprecedented rapidity under the Fascist regime. In the long run, this was bound to be a process replete with ironies. In the context of the reclamation efforts the Origos built what is today the single most iconic country road in all of Tuscany, photographed and filmed ad nauseam, to connect the San Bernardino farm to the main road. With its winding path and cypress trees, it was also meant to grace the view from the villa as if it had been there since the times of the Sienese Primitive painters – almost an extension of the formal garden designed for Iris by famed British architect Cecil Pinsent (Illustration 6). Other forms of landscape redemption did not carry the day. Since the 1990s, a conservationist movement has been afoot to protect the few biancane that have escaped the redemptive attention of the reclamation consortium since the 1930s. Many of these clay formations now reside in a strictly regulated natural reserve at the center of the valley.[67] The graceful and the horrid, the deceptively traditional and the traditionally unappreciated, are thus made to coexist almost side by side, in the name of landscape preservation.

---

[67] This is the Riserva Naturale di Lucciola Bella, in the municipality of Pienza. See Michela Marignani et al., "Planning Restoration in a Cultural Landscape in Italy Using an Object-Based Approach and Historical Analysis," *Landscape and Urban Planning* 84 (2008): 28–37.

Illustration #6 Iconic cypress-lined road near La Foce estate, designed by Cecil Pinsent for the Origos and built in part with the funds of the Reclamation Consortium of the Orcia Valley in the 1930s.

Fascist Redemption in Practice: The Chianti

If slushy or desiccated mud was the hallmark of the Orcia valley and other clay areas, stones informed the hard lives peasants led in the hills between Florence and Siena, including the already famous wine-producing region of the Chianti.[68] Soil on these hills is looser and more permeable than farther south, but it is also filled with sedimentary rocks of all shapes and sizes, which have to be removed for the precious woody plants, the vine and the olive tree, to thrive. These stones testify to an older geological origin than the Sienese clays. They too sedimented at the bottom of an ancient ocean, in the Jurassic period, but they solidified and fragmented in their slow journey east, at the time of the formation of the Appennine mountain range and the Italian peninsula itself in the Cretaceous period, more than 100 million years prior to the emergence of the Orcia valley. Geologists think of these hills as the ramparts of the Appennines, from which they are separated by the upper valley of the Arno River, and three main tributaries to the

[68] The delimitation of the Chianti region has long been a contentious matter because of its association with wine branding. Even the Fascist regime failed to adjudicate this issue, as we will see in Chapter 3. The discussion that follows holds for much of area between Florence and Siena. To this day, many people in Tuscany denote the entire region as "Chianti," to the chagrin of some wine producers and traders.

Arno (the Elsa, the Pesa, and the Greve) carve them in almost parallel succession from west to east.[69]

Human settlement in the Chianti was predicated on the painstaking sorting out of different kinds of stones, used for the construction of rural and urban buildings, but also for the buttressing of the terraces on top of which agriculture could take place. Peasants here had to be builders as well, skilled at erecting and maintaining the dry stone walls (*muretti a secco*) that prevented the terraces from collapsing. The Fascist redeemers could not help noticing that this had been a reclaimed landscape for centuries, and it was in these hills that mezzadria revealed most clearly its ability to reshape the land through the labor of generations of peasant families, each in charge of its topographically diverse and agriculturally self-reliant farm. As agronomist Vittorio Montanari put it in the late 1920s, "we cannot help admiring these good and intelligent rural folks, who shaped the steepest slopes with terraces so ingeniously executed that they testify luminously to what can be accomplished with determination, passion, and attachment to the land."[70] As we will see in Chapter 3, the neglect and active destruction of these terraces in the 1960s and 1970s signaled the end of tradition and the dawn of a novel kind of agriculture.

This was also the area where the considerable capital of generations of Florentine and Sienese aristocrats (or aspiring aristocrats) had been invested. Thus, settlement was far denser than in the Orcia valley. Farms were much smaller – typically 8 to 12 hectares – and property was less concentrated than farther south, with only 20 percent of the agricultural land belonging to estates larger than 100 hectares in the 1920s. Land distribution was also very uneven, with many small estates belonging to the middling bourgeoisie closer to the cities (every well-off Florentine shopkeeper had a podere or two in the Chianti) and some vast aristocratic estates occupying areas deeper into the countryside. Baron Ricasoli, for example, owned 40 percent of the agricultural land in the municipality of Gaiole, in the Sienese portion of the Chianti. If wheat dominated the Sienese clays, albeit always within the context of mixed cultivations typical of mezzadria, wine reigned supreme in the hills between Florence and Siena. More than 60 percent of the revenue of a typical farm came from wine. But here too mixed cultivations were the norm, and every sharecropping family grew grains and fodder crops in the stripes of land between the rows of vines, which usually rested on olive trees or field

---

[69] For a *longue durée* perspective, see Francesco Pardi, "Le Trasformazioni del Paesaggio Storico nelle Colline Toscane," in Simone Neri Serneri (ed.), *Storia del Territorio e Storia dell'Ambiente* (Milan, Franco Angeli, 2002): 51–78.

[70] Viscardo Montanari, *Agricoltura Senese*: 27.

maples. Wheat yields in these stripes of land were extremely low, almost always less than a ton per hectare, but the subsistence needs of the family took precedence over considerations of productivity and specialization.[71] Finally, unlike the Orcia valley, these were (and are) heavily forested hills, with oak and chestnut woods occupying roughly half of the territory. These forests, however, were tightly integrated in the sharecropping economy, and they provided fodder for the pigs and sheep, chestnuts for human consumption, and wood for fuel and construction.

As we have seen, these hills had been the target of reforming ambitions since at least the eighteenth century. As moving and admirable as the terraced fields may have seemed to generations of observers, the systematizations recommended by Cosimo Ridolfi in the early nineteenth century, for example, would have done away with them altogether, concentrating cultivations on newly created and more gently sloping terrain. By the same token, generations of agronomists and landlords had debated the virtues and drawbacks of mixed and specialized vineyards. The latter, however, had always been exceedingly rare, since they defied the logic of sharecropping. Only a minuscule portion of the territory was occupied by orderly and tightly arranged rows of vines – arguably the most distinctive trait of today's landscape in the Chianti region.

Overall, the hills of central Tuscany had not been dealt very good cards to play in the Fascist reclamation game.[72] The regime's agricultural obsession, wheat, was hopelessly unproductive on these hills, and most of it was meant for peasant subsistence. High-quality wine was an export good that hardly fit with the general retrenchment from free trade. Finally, human settlement was, if anything, too dense for the area's productive capabilities. Despite these drawbacks, no one could deny that the Chianti was in dire need of redemptive attention. Like many other wine-producing areas around Europe, the Chianti was experiencing its worst agricultural crisis in centuries. The phylloxera, a tiny aphid indigenous to the American continent, was attacking the vines' roots, leading to their decay and ultimate death. The phylloxera infestation started in France in the early 1860s and reached northern Italy at the end of the 1870s. It took decades, however, for the infestation to spread through the Italian peninsula. Even though the first report dates back to the late 1880s, it

---

[71] Data from Archivio di Stato di Siena, Gabinetto Prefettura, Filza 44, 1935, Folder Ministero dell'Agricoltura. Report to the Prefect for the Minister for Agriculture on the agricultural situation in the province.

[72] This was the assessment of the Sienese Provincial Council for the Economy as early as 1928: Archivio di Stato di Siena, Gabinetto Prefettura, Filza 3, 1931, Folder Ministero Agricoltura e Foreste, "Relazione Statistica del Consiglio Provinciale dell'Economia per il 1928."

Illustration #7 Peasants at the Brolio estate, in the Chianti, digging ditches for new vineyards in 1932.

was only in the 1900s that the Chianti region began to seriously suffer the effects of the infestation. By the 1890s it had become clear that the only effective defense against the bug was the grafting of local varietals onto resistant American rootstock, an operation that required a considerable amount of financial and organizational resources, not to mention a dedicated and skilled work force (Illustration 7).[73]

By the Fascist period, an infrastructure of institutions and know-how, centered on the provincial agricultural extensions (*cattedre ambulanti*), was in place to assist in the replacement of local vine varietals with grafted ones. Well before the era of official Fascist reclamation began, mandatory "anti-phylloxera" consortia had been formed in many provinces to coordinate the effort. The Sienese consortium, for example, sold three hundred thousand new plants in 1930 alone, and at production cost. Credit was available for landlords who committed themselves to the extensive and labor-intensive process of uprooting the old vineyards and installing new

[73] Mario Bandini, *Aspetti Economici dell'Invasione Filosserica in Toscana* (Rome: Treves, 1932).

ones. Nevertheless, the general sense in the region was that the bug was winning the war, also because many landlords were strapped for cash, discouraged by the falling prices for wine, and often simply in denial about the need for action. This was especially true of the many smaller estates that sold wine only locally and without any brand. These producers' reluctance to act of course endangered their neighbors as well, and the mandatory nature of the "anti-phylloxera" consortia was mostly theoretical, given the paucity of funds for monitoring the territory, enforcing the mandate, and providing resources for the poorer members.

In this context of mounting challenges, it was only natural for the largest and best-connected landlords to try to jump on the reclamation bandwagon in the wake of the Mussolini Law. In the course of the 1930s two reclamation consortia were established in the hills between Florence and Siena, one for the basin of the Pesa River and the other for the basins on of the Greve and Ema Rivers (the Ema being a small tributary to the Greve that runs through the southern neighborhoods of Florence). The very fact that these consortia were centered on river basins testifies to the delicate (and perhaps somewhat deceptive) game the organizers were playing with the national government. The real emergency was about wine production, which had very little to do with river management, but the promoters knew that they had to make grander claims in the context of an increasingly competitive arena where dozens of rural areas vied for attention and recognition. Thus, their pitch included the specter of impending urbanization and land neglect, which would have led to uncontrolled erosion and silting, which in turn would have jeopardized the regimen of the Arno and increased the risk of floods for the region's most populated areas.

Count Lorenzo Guicciardini presided over the Pesa River consortium, which was constituted in 1930 but only recognized by the national government in 1935, too late to benefit from the relatively short season of public generosity.[74] The tortuous character of the pitch Guicciardini had to make to the public authorities explains this delay. The organizers tried first to have the area, with almost 34,000 hectares and a population of more than forty thousand, recognized as a first-category reclamation area like the Orcia valley, but that attempt failed immediately. Thus, they reduced their expectations and began to campaign for the lower categories of subvention in the hierarchy of public interest, asking for 28 million lire of public funds to be complemented by 128 millions in private investments.

---

[74] The following discussion is based on the documents held by the National Archives in Rome: Archivio Centrale dello Stato, Ministero Agricoltura e Foreste, Dipartimento Generale Bonifica e Colonizzazione – Toscana, folder 23, Consorzio Val di Pesa.

Two thirds of the private expenses involved the installation of new vines, an endeavor that fell outside the purview of the reclamation works the state would pay for. Bread was one thing; wine another. In addition to money for roads, water mains, and electric lines, the promoters asked for 7 million lire of public funds to reduce the slope of 3,200 hectares of cultivated land, justified as a measure of erosion management but clearly meant to prepare the terrain for the new vineyards. The provincial inspector saw through this scheme immediately and advised the national government to reject the request. In the end, the approved plan called for very limited state contributions, mostly for works of river management and road construction. The destiny of the consortium for the Greve and Ema Rivers, presided by Marquis Viviani della Robbia, was even less fortunate.[75] The government denied its recognition several times, arguing that there were already too many reclamation consortia around Italy, until it was incorporated into the Pesa River consortium in 1938. Very little actual work was carried out before the breakout of the war.

In sum, unlike the Orcia valley, the Chianti and surrounding hills had to wait till the postwar decades to see major changes to their physical layout. The two consortia in the area never got off the ground. Their stories, however, are worth considering for two reasons. First, the experience of the Chianti in the 1930s demonstrates the peculiar logic of integral reclamation under fascism. Although wine making was a potentially lucrative industry, and one with an international reputation and market, the regime regarded its protection as secondary to far more ambitious schemes of rural settlement based on Italy's future vocation as a grain-producing country, however implausible that vocation may sound today. For all its compromises and limitations, Fascist agricultural redemption did add a novel layer of imaginings and aspirations to the older "liberal" approaches. Purely economic considerations did take a back seat, at least in some cases.

Second, the inability of the leading landowners in the Chianti to rally the national government in the 1930s convinced some of them that the region's regeneration had to involve a gradual transition away from mezzadria. Many agricultural experts noticed that mixed agriculture, one of the cornerstones of the sharecropping system, was a hindrance to a more rational viticulture. The aphid could be turned into an agent of modernity. The necessity to graft the new vineyards on American rootstock represented an opportunity to move beyond traditional arrangements. Only

---

[75] Archivio Centrale dello Stato, Ministero Agricoltura e Foreste, Dipartimento Generale Bonifica e Colonizzazione – Toscana, folder 50, Quarto Raggruppamento – Consorzio Greve e Ema.

social considerations relating to the destiny of the sharecroppers made these experts hesitate in their recommendations. The peasants' renewed militancy in the late 1940s and early 1950s, and the ensuing mass exodus from the farms, made these scruples irrelevant. As we will see in Chapter 3, the more innovative and best connected landlords in the Chianti wasted no time in the 1950s and 1960s in radically reinventing viticulture and its landscape, taking advantage of newly available public funds, originating from both Rome and Brussels. Reversing the previous trend, the Chianti now had an easier time than more isolated and marginal areas like the Orcia valley in sketching the vision of an internationally integrated and prosperous future in which public authorities could invest with confidence. The story of how, despite these extensive transformations, the Chianti managed to remain the quintessential Tuscan landscape will be the subject of later chapters.

In conclusion, the relationship between the Fascist regime and rural Tuscany was as complex as it was contradictory. On the one hand, Fascist ruralism could be understood as the continuation of centuries-old attitudes and projects pioneered by Tuscan elites to "improve" agriculture and rural life while strengthening the foundations of the social order. In this vein, the Fascist reclamation policies could be interpreted as a re-edition of the reforms of the late eighteenth and early nineteenth centuries. On the other hand, fascism had risen to power in overt opposition to an unprecedented wave of peasant unrest and mobilization. This legacy of violence, which the regime itself touted as revolutionary, tinged Fascist ruralism with the dark tones of class revenge and repression. In this vein, the reclamation projects of the late 1920s and 1930s appeared as ways of rewarding the loyalty of the landlords and strengthening their paternalistic hold on their lands and the peasants who worked for them. Rural fascism was both the heir to a modernizing tradition that bore the signs of the Enlightenment and a movement that struggled against the tide of history, resisting the hollow lures of modernity.

In some ways, the Tuscan countryside, like many other parts of rural Italy, became modern under fascism. Illiteracy, for example, was drastically reduced in the 1930s, as were infant mortality and general morbidity. The regime promoted the construction of new houses and the hatching of novel plans for the cultivation of traditional crops. Roads were built and rivers were regimented. And yet, this was accomplished in the name of a modernity that was battled and defeated after World War II. The regime imagined the vast majority of the population of rural Tuscany as raw matter to be redeemed and remolded in the shape of an imagined tradition of obedience and harmony. "History" was a process to be both joined and resisted.

This contradictory relationship with modernity, in its spatial and temporal dimensions, was arguably the most enduring legacy of fascism. After the demise of the regime, rural Tuscans rose up against those who wanted them to remain passive matter. But they also confronted the seemingly unstoppable tide of processes that would sentence them to irrelevance. The Italian Communist Party, which came to organize Tuscany's rural and working classes in the postwar decades, had no less complex of a relationship with modernity than the Fascist regime. It, too, combined utopian and coolly realistic visions, and saw itself both as a force of progress and as a force battling the tide of "History." Now mobilized within the institutions and discourses of the radical Left, rural Tuscans asked with urgency whether it would be possible to become modern peasants, and do so in a dignified and active way. They now knew they could change, and that their landscape would change with them. They were ready to join History, as Mussolini had promised them, but they would try to do so on their own terms.

2 Newer Beginnings: The Landscape of Social Strife (1945–1956)

According to Eric Hobsbawm, "The most dramatic and far reaching social change of the second half of this [the 20th] century, and the one that cut us off for ever from the world of the past, is the death of the peasantry."[1] Hobsbawm refrains from qualifying this momentous change as an event or a process, although the term "death" does suggest a threshold beyond which there is no return. Whatever the case, this kind of language evokes a temporal narrative historians are familiar with. Societies transition from one stage to the next, crossing thresholds that "cut people off from the past." One can imagine a timeline charting the decade, maybe even the year, in which the percentage of people employed in agriculture in different countries reached, say, 15 percent of the labor force. Within Europe, for example, Britain would be at the beginning of the chart; and Romania and Bulgaria would perhaps "not yet" be there. The death of the peasantry is here both a descriptive and a prescriptive rupture of modernity. This is also a narrative in which time is master; space is almost irrelevant. The places where modernity has not come are by definition marginal ones that will "transition" in due time.

When viewed from the ground up, this conception of historical time as a single and irreversible process appears as only one of the many temporalities describing and motivating social change. Tuscan peasants, as actors in the whirlwind of rapid transformations, both anticipated their death and fought for their survival. Their "horizon of expectation" changed radically in the wake of the war, creating tensions and incongruities with their everyday experiences that were anything but singular.[2] They imagined and anticipated modernities that their surroundings belied and yet also made possible. Peasants began to live in multiple worlds, each with its own sense of time. On the one hand, "historical

---

[1] E. Hobsbawm, *The Age of Extremes: A History of the World, 1914–1991* (New York: Vintage, 1996): 289.

[2] Michael Pickering, "Experience as Horizon: Koselleck, Expectation, and Historical Time," *Cultural Studies* 18 (2004): 271–289.

time" accelerated tremendously. An entire civilization founded on share-cropping began to die, all but disappearing in less than two decades. On the other hand, for over a decade Tuscan peasants imagined and expe-rienced different ways of being on the land – of surviving as peasants. They forged imaginary ties to the Soviet Union, to the people who had opposed the rise of fascism decades before, to the towns that beckoned and rejected them at once, and to themselves as a class. The places where they lived began to tell multiple and contradictory stories. The main con-tention of this chapter is that it was to make sense of, and contribute to, these changes that they embraced as their own the mythopoeic and orga-nizational resources of the Italian Communist Party (PCI).[3]

The profound connection between the PCI and rural Tuscans began during the Resistance, but it was cemented through the struggles of the late 1940s and early 1950s. The history of these struggles has been told many times and in beautiful detail, especially by historians politically and socially close to the peasant movement itself.[4] For all its merits, this litera-ture presents two striking features. First, the concrete relationships between peasants and their territory are by and large relegated to the background. Following many observers at the time, historians have viewed the postwar confrontation between Tuscan peasants and their landlords as a somewhat deterritorialized instant of class struggle, itself part of a universal narrative of capitalist (or even semifeudal) oppression and resistance.

Second, the abstract issue of land ownership dominates these narra-tives, rather than more concrete rights of access, use, and indeed percep-tion of the land as an emplaced experience.[5] This is also a reflection of

---

[3] Since the end of World War II, central and southern Tuscany has disproportionately voted for the parties of the Left. Already in the elections of April 1948, disastrous for the Left at the national level, the electoral district of Arezzo, Siena, and Grosseto gave the Popular Democratic Front (the coalition of Communists and Socialists) more than 55 percent of the vote. This was the single best result for the Left in the entire country. Until its split in 1991, the Communist Party rarely received less than an absolute majority of the vote in the province of Siena and in much of the province of Florence. Northern Tuscany, by contrast, voted overwhelmingly for the Christian Democrats. These regional variations are usually explained (somewhat reductively) on the basis of the historical presence of sharecropping (as opposed to small-scale land ownership) in the different provinces. For an overview of Tuscany's political situation in the postwar decades, see Mario G. Rossi, "Il Secondo Dopoguerra: Verso un Nuovo Assetto Politico-Sociale," in Giorgio Mori (ed.), *Storia d'Italia: Le Regioni dall'Unità a Oggi. La Toscana* (Turin: Einaudi, 1986): 675–707.

[4] For the province of Siena, on which this chapter focuses, see Alessandro Orlandini and Giorgio Venturini, *Padrone Arrivedello a Battitura: Lotte Mezzadrili nel Senese nel Secondo Dopoguerra* (Milan: Feltrinelli, 1980); and Emo Bonifazi, *Lotte Contadine in Val d'Orcia* (Siena: Nuovo Corriere Senese, 1979). The summa of the postwar reflection on these themes is perhaps reflected in the two volumes, *I Mezzadri e la Democrazia in Italia: Annali dell'Istituto Attilio Cervi* 8 (Bologna: Il Mulino, 1986) and 9 (Bologna: Il Mulino, 1987).

[5] The obvious exception is Emilio Sereni, *Storia del Paesaggio Agrario* (Bari: Laterza, 1961) a unique work that reconstructs the long-term changes in the Italian rural landscape

the Communists' complex and contradictory relationship with land ownership. Although the leftist parties (the Socialists and the Communists) no longer preached the virtues of land collectivization, as they had done earlier in the century, they were at best ambivalent toward the prospect of creating a class of small-scale farmers, at least in part because of its historical implausibility. The land was to be conquered rather than bought, as a slogan put it at the time, but what could have been the concrete makeup of a "modern" way of being on the land remained unclear. Tuscan peasants were themselves ambivalent toward the prospect of remaining on the land even as owners, especially without the resources necessary to transform their way of life. They understood their condition as anachronistic, but no one could articulate what it would take to get their lives in sync with "history."

Rather than from abstract "ideological" affinities or promises, the bond between Tuscan peasants and the Communist organizations emerged from the very phenomenology of the struggle itself. Through their ties to the PCI, peasants taught themselves new ways of being on the land and anticipate possible futures in the present, however nebulous those futures may have been. Even as peasants, they began to think of themselves as modern. In this sense, they reinvented their landscape, shaping a place for themselves and making that place tell new stories. When I embarked on this project, I confronted the paradox of a contemporary rural landscape without peasants (and without any reference to the conditions of its own production), coupled with histories of peasants without landscape (or without any systematic attention to the peasants' spatial and perceptual worlds). This chapter is an attempt to remedy this epistemological (and political) gap.

Overview: The Tuscan Countryside between Revolt and Reform

One thing that rural Tuscany needed after World War II, almost everyone agreed, was to join the "modern" era. As we have seen, much of this language dated back to the prewar period. Fascism made relentless use of the rhetoric of modernization during its countless reclamation schemes. The modernity trumpeted by the Fascists now sounded hollow and deceptive, but that realization only made more urgent the desire for real and profound change. The Resistance and the ensuing Liberation

---

largely on the basis of its artistic depictions over the centuries. Even here, however, the landscape is passive matter, molded by socioeconomic relations, and a stage for social struggles.

were hailed as historic turning points even before they were over, and this charged the following decade with potent promises of deliverance.[6] From the perspective of the politically active peasants, the Tuscan hills would now become the stage for an epochal confrontation between the forces of progress (the Marxist parties and their social base) and those of reaction (the landlords and their lackeys, with the police and judiciary on the front line of counterrevolution).

In the decade after Liberation (and indeed for many years afterward), Tuscany's Medieval and early modern past was something to be overcome, not valorized. Thus, in line with orthodox Marxist theory, the Left understood Tuscan agriculture as replete with vestigial feudal and semifeudal traits, which had been solidified during the "refeudalization" process of the sixteenth century and preserved for generations to the benefit of the landlords.[7] For the Left, paramount among these residual feudal traits was the very cornerstone of Tuscany's rural identity, the mezzadria contract, which the Fascists had tried to salvage by underscoring its collaborative and entrepreneurial (and therefore potentially modern) qualities. What simultaneously galvanized and dismayed Tuscany's rural Left in the wake of Liberation was the strident gap (itself not easily explained with the tools of orthodox Marxism) between the incessant pace of political and cultural change, which had brought the Marxist parties to positions of power both locally and (until the Spring of 1947) nationally, and the near immobility of the "economic structure" in the countryside, where mezzadria still ruled.

In the face of political mobilization, the texture of everyday life had to change as well, and it was at this level of everyday experiences that the Left engaged the imagination of Tuscan peasants. The future of rural living would bring private pleasures to be conquered through collective action. In the spring of 1954 the main sharecroppers' union (Federterra) polled some young sharecroppers from Certaldo, twenty miles southwest of Florence, asking them if they were happy with agricultural work, what they would rather do instead, and what they thought was most necessary to make life on the farms bearable. The answers were remarkably similar, suggesting the imparting of previous instructions but also a high level of consensus. Here is Franca: "Working the land summer and winter, with

---

[6] This is a point forcefully made in Giovanni Contini, "Mezzadri e Democrazia," in Attilio Esposto (ed.), *Democrazia e Contadini in Italia nel XX Secolo*, vol. 1 (Rome: Robin, 2006): 35–72.

[7] The concept of refeudalization gained academic currency in the 1960s with the publication of Ruggiero Romano, "Tra XVI e XVII secolo. Una Crisi Economica: 1619–1622," *Rivista Storica Italiana* 74 (1962): 480–531; see also Giorgio Giorgetti, *Contadini e Proprietari* (Turin: Einaudi, 1974), 182–192. The notion that mezzadria was a semifeudal trait, however, has a much older genealogy, dating back to the eighteenth century.

the heat and cold, we don't even make enough to go to the movies ... They should mechanize agriculture to work less, with less effort, so we can make more money and have more fun." Here is Vasco: "Our science has given us machines to produce more and with less effort. But our landlords won't buy them.... Our landlords should bring in machines to reduce the work of the peasants and hygienic houses, too." For Lisena, the only way "for me to get attached to my work again is for my land-lord to build a decent house with electricity and drinkable water."[8] These young peasants felt disconnected from their lives and their environment. They demanded that the speed of change keep pace with the audacity of their imagination.

This desire for change faced deeply entrenched patterns of property and land use. The picture painted by official statistical data was indeed one of relative immobility. The census data, collected at the height of social unrest in 1951, revealed how little had changed since the interwar period in terms of the structure of property and the basic patterns of cul-tivation and soil use. For the province of Siena, the data on the distribu-tion of property still showed the coexistence of very small landholdings, with 61 percent of owners claiming less than 2 percent of the produc-tive land, and large and very large estates, with less than 1 percent of landlords owning 41 percent of the productive land. Approximately two-thirds of the land was run under the mezzadria system and divided into more than fourteen thousand farms (poderi), most of which belonged to approximately one thousand and two hundred estates (fattorie). There were still significant micro-regional differences, especially between the north of the province (including the Chianti), where land ownership was somewhat less concentrated, and the south (including the Orcia valley), where vast extensively cultivated estates were common. But the general picture suggested that the bitter struggles Sienese peasants had been car-rying out since Liberation were yet to have a real impact.[9]

Land use patterns were fully compatible with the preponderance of mezzadria. Arable land without trees (for the most part, wheat fields) occupied 29 percent of the province's agricultural land. Another 26 percent of the land combined arable land and trees (mostly vines). Permanent pastures occupied less than 7 percent of the land, and forests (including six thousand hectares of chestnut tree groves) approximately a third. Specialized vineyards (i.e., vineyards not interspersed with arable

---

[8] Archivio CGIL Toscana, Federterra, box 185, folder "Perché i Giovani Abbbandonano la Terra. Certaldo, Marzo-Aprile 1954."

[9] "Distribuzione della Proprietà Terriera della Provincia di Siena," Archivio Storico del Movimento Operaio Senese (ASMOS), Fondo PCI, Box VA8, untitled folder.

land) made up a puny 0.2 percent (or 725 hectares), and olive groves, even less. In the Florentine section of Chianti, broadly defined, half of the productive land in 1949 was devoted to arable land with or without trees; 9 percent to pastures; 37 percent to forests (including chestnut trees); and only 1.4 percent to specialized vineyards.[10] Clearly, the landscape of mixed cultivation typical of mezzadria was still pervasive. The productive crisis that was going to bring Tuscan agriculture to its knees by the late 1960s had already begun: in the province of Siena, wheat production decreased by 24 percent between 1938 and 1951; olive oil production dropped by 16 percent in the same period; and the production of wine was less than half of what it had been in the early 1930s. Cattle, still important as draft animals and for fertilization, decreased by 13 percent from the late 1930s to the early 1950s.[11]

As these data suggest, Tuscan agriculture was becoming dangerously undercapitalized. The dreams of modernization nurtured by Tuscan peasants and their leftist leaders had to confront the extreme reluctance of landlords to invest in their farms, which they perceived as increasingly under siege and whose future was uncertain at best. Indeed, many of the early conquests of the peasant movement after Liberation consisted of government-mandated injunctions to the landlords to invest a certain share of their revenue in land improvements. This was the case with the so-called De Gasperi "judgment" (lodo), signed by the national government in March 1946, which provisionally settled the issue of the damages and expenses incurred by the sharecroppers during the war, to be refunded by the landlords, and forced the land owners to invest a share of their revenue in repairs. The following year a national agreement between the main sharecroppers' union and the landowners' association, known as the "sharecropping truce" (tregua mezzadrile), confirmed the obligation for landlords to employ 4 percent of their revenue to hire local unemployed laborers for works of agricultural improvement, made them responsible for justifying evictions, and for the first time officially broke the principle of equal crop sharing by awarding 53 percent of production to the peasant family. Afterward the Tuscan mezzadri launched several campaigns of strikes and demonstrations to raise their share to 60 percent, but without success.[12]

---

[10] Here, by the Florentine section of Chianti, I mean the municipalities of Bagno a Ripoli, Barberino Val d'Elsa, Greve in Chianti, San Casciano Val di Pesa, and Tavarnelle Val di Pesa. Archivio della CGIL Toscana, Federterra, box 40, folder Occupazione Agricola 1948–1949.

[11] "Distribuzione della Proprietà Terriera della Provincia di Siena."

[12] The De Gasperi judgment became law in May 1947. The "sharecropping truce" was turned into law in August 1948. For an overview, see Zeffiro Ciuffoletti, "Le Lotte

The investment of a small share of steadily shrinking revenue did very little to modernize Tuscan agriculture, even in the less than uncommon cases in which these provisions were scrupulously applied. In general, the landlords resisted even these relatively mild injunctions by shrewdly manipulating the accounting books, whose drafting became more contentious than ever. Nevertheless, these injunctions to invest in improvement and maintenance challenged one of the cornerstones of mezzadria in its spatial and even esthetic dimensions. Peasant families had been expected for centuries to deliver enormous efforts to take care of the physical layout (the ditches, mounds, stone walls, etc.) on which the delicate balance of soil and water typical of hillside agriculture rested. The Fascist reclamations had done nothing to change the division of labor, further intensifying the amount of work expected of the sharecroppers. Now this previously unpaid labor became the landlords' responsibility and a means of reducing local unemployment. Increasing shares of the landlords' revenue, which the peasants and their leaders viewed as illegitimate rent, was to be redistributed to the community.

The peasants' struggle to force the landlords to invest in the improvement of their farms belonged to a more general campaign to increase the managerial power of the peasant family (or at least of its older male members). One of the most enduring and contentious institutional innovations produced by the Resistance movement was the establishment of elected estate committees (commissioni di fattoria), which acted as de facto representatives of the leftist unions at the company level.[13] In some cases, the landlords refused to recognize the legitimacy of these organizations for years, viewing them as the natural institutional home to the most "ideological" (and therefore "corrupted") members of peasant society. In the decade after Liberation, these committees collected data and opinions, and delivered them to the unions and other organizations in charge of devising a general strategy for the ongoing struggles. On the basis of the information gathered by the estate committees, the unions drafted detailed "work plans" (piani di lavoro), which exposed the decline of Tuscan agriculture and set long-term goals to reverse it. For the province of Siena, for example, these plans revealed that at the beginning of the 1950s more than ten thousand farms (or over 70 percent of

---

Mezzadrili nella Toscana del Secondo Dopoguerra," in Pier Luigi Ballini et al. (eds.), *La Toscana nel Secondo Dopoguerra* (Milan: Franco Angeli, 1991): 213–227.

[13] In the province of Siena the estate committees were recognized by the landlords' association in April 1945, but on the condition that only the heads of the sharecropping households would participate in them. Day laborers were to be excluded. See Archivio di Stato di Siena, Gabinetto di Prefettura, box 55 (year 1945), folder Organizzazioni Sindacali, subfolder Rapporti tra Proprietari e Coloni.

the total) did not have a separate building for the production and storage of manure; four thousand and five hundred rural houses did not have electricity; and three thousand and five hundred rural houses lacked running water. The plans called for the modernization of the peasants' dwellings and for the purchase of at least one thousand and two hundred tractors, made all the more urgent by the decreasing availability of cattle (less than 4 percent of the land was worked with tractors). The use of artificial fertilizers had also decreased dramatically since the late 1930s: for wheat production, 20,330 tons were used in 1951, as opposed to 38,100 tons in 1938. Organized peasants also demanded the planting of almost 2 million vines and more than ten thousand olive trees a year over the following decade.[14]

The unwillingness of the landlords to invest in agricultural and infrastructural improvements prompted the peasants and their leaders to engage in quite creative forms of struggle in the early 1950s. One of the most spectacular, as we will see, consisted in carrying out the improvement works without the landlords' permission or supervision, often in previously uncultivated or poorly cultivated plots, which would be "occupied" by crews of peasants in the face of escalating confrontations with the police. The landlords reacted to these and other attempts at their managerial authority by refusing to settle the farm accounts with their sharecroppers. These settlements became one of the main demands of the Tuscan sharecroppers in the following years.

In sum, in the late 1940s and early 1950s, hardly an element of the mezzadria contract escaped the scrutiny and organized challenges of the sharecroppers. The management of the cattle, which since the late 1930s were jointly owned by the landlords and the peasants, became an intractable matter, with the sharecroppers trying to gain immediate control of the revenue and the landlords arguing for complicated accounting procedures that would presumably have enhanced their supervisory function. When the traditional sale period came, the peasants sold the calves without the owners' permission and, with the cooperation of their union, unilaterally deposited what they believed was the landlords' rightful share in special bank accounts. In response, the landlords sued, alleging embezzlement, and threatened eviction. In the 1950s the landlords knew that they could count on the class solidarity of the judges who practiced in the tribunals of small-town Tuscany. In the vast majority of the more than five hundred cases of embezzlement examined in the province of Siena from 1950 to 1953, the judges ruled in favor of the landlord and mandated

---

[14] "Distribuzione della Proprietà Terriera della Provincia di Siena." This data also appeared in the leftist press. See "I mezzadri senesi vogliono macchine per i loro campi," *L'Unità*, August 3, 1952.

that the peasants repay their debt, which often led to painful repossession procedures. Evictions became extremely contentious as well, with the sharecroppers fighting for guarantees of stability and the landlords viewing the right to evict as their main weapon in a rapidly shrinking arsenal. Some 460 eviction notices were issued in the province of Siena alone, even though maybe only two dozen of them were actually carried out.[15]

The political dimension of these struggles became all the more evident in July 1948, three months after the historic electoral defeat of the Left, when a right-wing student tried to assassinate Palmiro Togliatti, the secretary of the Italian Communist Party. When the news reached Tuscany, a gloomy sense of impending disaster descended on both cities and countryside. The most violent episode took place in the province of Siena, among the mercury miners of Abbadia S. Salvatore on Mount Amiata, not far from the Orcia Valley. Here the miners took over the town, intimidating their social and political opponents. When two policemen were killed in brawls with the demonstrators, a massive intervention by the army ensued, leading to hundreds of arrests and more than one thousand retaliatory dismissals of miners.[16] These dramatic events profoundly resonated with Tuscan sharecroppers, who organized demonstrations of solidarity with the miners. Some 350 peasants, most of them sharecroppers, were arrested in the wake of unauthorized demonstrations in the province of Siena alone. The police shot into the crowd at Colle Val d'Elsa, while light tanks were deployed to disperse the crowd at Castellina in Chianti. When in the following summers, at threshing time, "peace flags" began to appear on haystacks, machinery, trees, and any other tall spots the peasants could find, no one could mistake them for anything else but symbols of defiance. Unbelievably, now the sharecroppers even commented on international issues, such as Italy's membership in NATO and the escalating tensions between the western bloc, to which they reluctantly belonged, and the Soviet Union, that Utopia to which they looked for guidance.[17] For several summers in a row, as we

---

[15] Peris Brogi, "Testimonianza sulle Lotte Contadine degli Anni Cinquanta," ASMOS, fondo Peris Brogi, box XIII 1, folder 3.

[16] Gino Serafini, *I Ribelli della Montagna: Amiata 1948: Anatomia di una Rivolta* (Montepulciano: Editori del Grifo, 1981).

[17] The attachment of Tuscan peasants to the Soviet Union was heartfelt. Communist leaders overtly defended Communist Russia in front of peasant audiences, often risking legal repercussions. The secretary of the Communist youth organization of the province of Siena proclaimed in 1949 before an audience of peasants from Pienza that 250,000 partisans were ready to take arms if the Italian government attacked Russia and Stalin. The Carabinieri promptly reported him and he had to stand trial for attempt on the prestige of the nation (vilipendio) and inducement to commit a crime (istigazione a delinquere). Archivio di Stato di Siena, Gabinetto di Prefettura, box 87 (years 1945–50), Folder

will see, the sharecroppers and the police engaged in a game of cat and mouse, with the Carabinieri seizing the flags and the peasants resorting to all kinds of humorous subterfuges to show their allegiances.

The main consequence of these struggles was to convince the landlords that the days of mezzadria, with its invented traditions of deference and social harmony, were numbered. Starting in the early 1950s, many landlords decided that the time had come to place at least some of their land on the market. With a package of legislative and financial measures, the national government, now firmly in the hands of the Christian Democrats, came to the rescue of the beleaguered landowners (while claiming to be carrying out long-overdue land reforms) by simultaneously encouraging (or forcing) the landlords to sell, giving prospective small-scale farmers loans to gain access to long-term mortgages, and making sure that these measures would be generous enough to sustain (or even inflate) otherwise declining land prices.[18]

The political payoff of this strategy was not only the preservation of the landlords' support, but also the potential creation of a new class of proprietor farmers indebted to the state and loyal to the Christian Democrats and their rural organizations, above all Paolo Bonomi's Confederazione Nazionale Coltivatori Diretti (or Coldiretti for short), to which the majority of Italian small-scale farmers already belonged.[19] The government inaugurated the much-trumpeted land reform with two laws in 1950, one targeting Calabria alone, and the other affecting several areas throughout the peninsula. Nationally, some 700,000 hectares of land were "expropriated" (with generous indemnities) and distributed to approximately 120,000 families, who were supposed to pay rent for thirty years before becoming the legitimate owners of their plots.

In the Tuscan context, one of the two 1950 laws (the so-called stralcio law) tackled the ancient problem of the Maremma, the low-lying and traditionally malarial coastal areas in the central and southern portions of the region, with the goal of promoting small-scale farming of recently reclaimed (but always very vulnerable) land. The choice of the territories to be included in these plans was an extremely contentious issue, fraught with social and political consequences. The southern section of

---

Pienza. For a (less than sympathetic) history of the national context, see Victor Zaslavsky, *Lo Stalinismo e la Sinistra Italiana: Dal Mito dell'Urss alla Fine del Comunismo: 1945–1991* (Milan: Mondadori, 2004).

[18] For an overview of the land reforms of the early 1950s, see Gino Massullo, "La Riforma Agraria," in Piero Bevilacqua (ed.), *Storia dell'Agricoltura Italiana in Età Contemporanea*, vol. 3 (Venice: Marsilio, 1991): 509–542.

[19] For an overview, see Paul Ginsborg, *A History of Contemporary Italy: Society and Politics* (London: Penguin, 1990): 171–173.

the Val d'Orcia, for example, was included in the jurisdiction of the Ente Maremma, the agency in charge of land reform in much of southern Tuscany, on account of this area's notorious restlessness. According to the local lore, one day in the late 1940s the prefect of Siena and Prime Minister Alcide De Gasperi were driving on the Cassia road from Siena to Rome, and as the desolate landscape of the valley rolled before their eyes, the prefect begged De Gasperi to extend the scope of the reform to this area, which had been rocked by insurrectional violence in the aftermath of Togliatti's attempted assassination. The prime minister obliged, even though that meant extending the borders of the Maremma well beyond any traditional understanding of that region.[20]

Over the next few years, the neighboring municipalities of Castiglione, Abbadia S. Salvatore, and Piancastagnaio, whose area stretches from the Orcia river to the peak of Mount Amiata, became the stage of ongoing litigation over whose land should be expropriated and at what level the indemnity prices should be set.[21] In the end, the holdings of two-dozen large-scale landowners were targeted, with plans for major infrastructural works and the creation of brand new model farms to be mortgaged to former sharecroppers. The indemnity prices took into generous account each and every improvement carried out by the landowners in the previous years, so that none of them, after the initial reaction, found much to complain about. This generosity was not repaid in kind. One course of action followed by almost all owners who had been the object of expropriation was the cutting of thousands of commercially valuable trees in this notoriously barren landscape, ignoring the vocal protests of the peasants who relied on the woods for acorns to feed their pigs and for wood.[22] One of the bitter ironies of this process was that the same peasants, lured by the quick cash, ended up doing much of the logging. And then, with an additional twist, in the next few years these peasants manned the crews that carried out extensive state-funded reforestation projects.

Almost simultaneously, the government set up a Fund for the Promotion of Small-Scale Rural Ownership (the Cassa per la Piccola Proprietà Contadina), underwritten by several banks, to offer long-term mortgages to peasants interested in becoming small-scale farmers. The impact of this fund was less spatially concentrated than that of the 1950 land reform laws. In the province of Siena, some 35,000 hectares of land

---

[20] Rino Pecci, *I Solchi della Mia Vita: Memorie di Rino Pecci: Valdorciano Mezzadro* (Siena: Federazione Provinciale DS, 2004): 73.

[21] Archivio di Stato di Siena, Gabinetto di Prefettura, box 219 (1952), folder Riforma Fondiaria. See also Emo Bonifazi, *Lotte Contadine in Val d'Orcia*, 95–99.

[22] Ibid. See also Rino Pecci, *I Solchi della Mia Vita*, 63–73

changed hands thanks to this initiative, greatly contributing to the crisis of sharecropping.[23] As we will see in the next chapter, the rural Left looked on in horror as a quantitatively small, but symbolically highly relevant, share of these farms came to be occupied by peasant families strategically recruited in more conservative regions of Italy, or even by Italian refugees fleeing the conflicts of postcolonial North Africa.

The Communist Party witnessed these changes with a mix of apprehension and skepticism, fearing that the unspoken goal of the reforms was to break the unity of the rural classes and thereby undermining the peasants' support for the organizations of the Left. Even though this change of allegiances did not take place, by the mid-1950s the limited concessions won by the sharecroppers, coupled with credible prospects of gaining access to land ownership by institutional means, sapped the strength of Tuscany's peasant movement. It was at this juncture that the pace of industrial development picked up in many areas of the region, giving the sharecroppers an alternative to rural life. This complex set of circumstances, which included both "push" and "pull" factors, set the stage for the mass flight of peasants from the farms toward the apartment buildings sprouting at the outskirts of towns and cities all over Tuscany and beyond. After the brutal winter of 1956, this flight escalated into an "exodus."

Crossing Boundaries

The most popular slogan of the Italian postwar peasant struggles, written and shouted with minor variations countless times in demonstrations, meetings, and rallies, was "the land belongs to those who work it" (*la terra è di chi la lavora*) (Illustration 8). The slogan argued above all for a contrast between the legal claims inherited by the landlords by virtue of their status and the rights that the peasants (should have) accrued by virtue of their labor and actual presence on the land. This contrast between abstract legal claims and concrete personal and collective rights also informed different understandings of the land itself, which could be viewed alternatively as a disembedded factor of production and as a uniquely situated and experienced place in which actual lives unfolded. The relatively long tenures of Tuscan mezzadria and the traditionally limited geographical mobility of Tuscan peasants made this contrast between abstraction and lived specificity, or between ownership and belonging, particularly poignant.

---

[23] Peris Brogi, "Testimonianza sulle lotte contadine degli anni cinquanta."

Illustration #8 Peasant women nailing a leaflet to a tree along a Tuscan road in the early 1950s. The leaflet reads: "This farm belongs to those who work it."

One important way in which Tuscan peasants articulated this contradiction in their struggles was by crossing (or transgressing) physical and metaphorical boundaries. Ownership and belonging were after all a matter of boundaries, and a novel relationship with the land could only be forged by negotiating boundaries through individual and collective action. Peasants engaged in acts of physical and symbolic trespassing in many different contexts and for a variety of reasons, but always to demonstrate to themselves and society at large the arbitrariness (and therefore potential impermanence) of boundaries which in some cases had been in place for centuries. Therefore, peasants understood these charged movements in space – the openings of locks, the unprecedented presence of union members in estate offices, the land occupations, and so on – as simultaneous shifts in time. By transgressing boundaries, peasants meant to disrupt the scripts imposed on them by "history" and accelerate the pace of change. In other words, by trespassing, Tuscan peasants tried to become the protagonists of their own histories.

It would be hard to overestimate the impact of the war (both of soldiering around the world and of seeing soldiers from around the world roam the countryside) on Tuscan peasants' understanding of their territory. The notion that the war had made previously set boundaries open to negotiation crossed social distinctions to the point of becoming something of a cliché. The war seemed to have "brought the world" to the Tuscan countryside, and the consequences of this intrusion could close old eras and inaugurate new ones. Marquise Iris Origo sensed these changes as they were barely visible at the horizon:

September 15th [1943] … Walking home, we stopped at a farm where a soldier had just returned from Jugoslavia [sic] … At the next farm, one son had just returned from France; another from Russia. Germany, England, Canada, Jugoslavia, France, Russia – the farms of the Val d'Orcia are now linked with them all. Perhaps it is a forecast of the future.[24]

At the opposite end of the social spectrum and sixty years later, Fulvia Massini, born in the late 1930s to a family of sharecroppers just outside the Val d'Orcia, remembered what her parents told her about the climate prevailing in the farm in the immediate aftermath of the war:

When [the young men of the family] came back, they were not the same anymore, they had no longer respect. They no longer brought the first artichoke, the first tomato, the first ripe grapes to the estate, as it was the rule and custom, since they hadn't seen the estate manager use the shovel and till the soil. Antonio (the oldest and my father) was the worst. He had served in Albania as assistant to a military chaplain, and what he had seen and experienced had turned him against the priests and authority in general.[25]

In this passage, Massini recounts how memories of defiance had become part of her family lore: young peasants in the postwar years felt that they were questioning the immutability of several social spaces (class relations, family ties, religion, etc.) at once and fully comprehended how they were all connected. For them, a whole way of life was coming under fire.

This climate of exhilaration affected personal experiences in profound and yet elusive ways. Perceptions of space changed, as peasants steadily dismantled the landscape of deference and submission they had inherited

---

[24] Iris Origo, *War in the Val d'Orcia* (London: J. Cape, 1947), 74.
[25] Fulvia Massini, *Niente di Personale … o Quasi*, Archivio Diaristico Nazionale, Pieve S. Stefano, 9.

from the older generations. The ability to go to new places, break open previously sealed off corners of their territory, and explore the traces of ways of life wildly different from their own all became defining traits of a new and restless generation. The most poignant and symbolically rich rendition of this experience of exhilaration I have found comes from the memoir of Marcello Cioppi, born in 1936 to a family of sharecroppers in the Chianti. Still a boy, Marcello was sent by his financially strapped family to apprentice as an ironsmith. In the same flow of memories, he recounts the strikes and demonstrations of the postwar years and the experiences which his new job opened to him. He spent most of the time learning how to repair the tools of the peasants, but once in a while a wealthy person would call his master for a special job, such as the breaking of locks whose keys had been lost during the war:

I liked it so much to walk into those beautiful homes of the landlords, now as a worker; for now they needed my work.... It was a beautiful adventure to open those rooms in those villas. And then we would open those reinforced trunks. The smell of that old stuff was unique, mixing the smell of moist wood and a coat in naphthalene. Often, when we opened the rooms and the trunks, the lady of the house would become tearful: there were also the memories of the passed.[26]

Cioppi grew up to become first a construction worker in Florence and then, after a terrible accident, a technician for the state-owned telephone company, as well as a union leader. He probably never walked into one of those countryside villas again. But from his prose we can still glean the enthusiasm, pride, and anticipation of great things to come associated by the peasants of his generation with the crossing of that most poignant of boundaries – the threshold of the landlord's house.

One source of wonder and resentment for the peasants about the way of life of the landowning class was the presence of elaborate bathrooms with showers, tubs, and sit-down toilets. Many peasant-produced sources remark on the radically unequal access to "hygienic" amenities between social classes in rural Tuscany, but none more effectively than Rino Pecci's published memoir, a treasure trove of details about the personal experiences and perceptual world of Tuscan peasants in the postwar decades. Pecci, born in 1931 to a family of sharecroppers in the Val d'Orcia, remembers how he had to spend weeks in a Siena hospital in the late 1950s for hand surgery and how relieved he was to find a squat toilet, for he had never used a sit-down toilet in his life. He then recalls that until the 1960s Count Enea Silvio Piccolomini was the only person to have a "modern" bathroom in the municipality of Castiglione d'Orcia,

---

[26] Marcello Cioppi, *La Mamma Ti Sorride col Cuore: Ci Sorride Quando Si Nasce e Quando Si Muore*, Archivio Diaristico Nazionale, Pieve S. Stefano (pages are not numbered).

where Pecci grew up. From there, he goes on to relay a story, which he believes authentic, where another instance of trespassing takes place:

One day in May 1944 Count Silvio, who seldom used his residence in town, showed up unannounced. When he climbed up and made for the bathroom, he found it locked. He asked his servants to open the door, but they replied with embarrassment that the assistant to the estate manager was in there taking a bath. Then the Count didn't budge and waited for the intruder to come out. When he opened the door, the Count said with contempt, "We don't have communism yet." ... Today it is natural to take a bath or a shower, but back then it was a dream, and we all would have liked to dream.[27]

This bathroom story, which took place during the Resistance, has a tragic aftermath: Pecci recounts that the intruder, not yet in his thirties, died a couple of years later while de-mining the Count's lands, his sacrifice narrated as a testament to the injustices of a whole civilization.

These personal experiences of trespassing and boundary crossing formed a continuum with more collective actions, through which peasants redefined their relationships with their territory as a class. Personal and collective subjectivities shaped and were shaped by changing narratives and perceptions of space and time. Even though this dialectical process is difficult to document with precision, Tuscan peasants actively participated in many kinds of collective action precisely because such action promised to open new physical and metaphorical horizons, literally taking them where they had not been before. One such space was the estate office (scrittoio), where the peasants' accounts were kept and updated. Once a year, the estate manager or the owner would convene the head of the sharecropper family to the office and review the financial contributions of the landlord's capital and the peasant family's labor, what these efforts had yielded and at what price the various products had been sold, the extent to which the value of the cattle had appreciated or depreciated, etc. Typically the meeting ended with a settlement: the sharecropper would either be promised some money, to be paid or put aside toward future expenses, or he would incur a debt. This ritual, and the place where it was performed, were supposed to remind both parties that theirs was something of a partnership, however unequal. After the war, however, the unions pushed to have one of their representatives present during the account review, arguing that many sharecroppers were illiterate and easily intimidated. But the presence of a union representative in the estate office also exposed and debunked the myths of partnership on which mezzadria had rested for centuries. This was no longer a ritual between two individuals, but between two classes. Most of these union representatives were sharecroppers themselves,

---

[27] Rino Pecci, *I Solchi della Mia Vita*: 96.

further evidence of the organic relationship between peasant society and the organizations of the Left after Liberation.

One of these peasants-turned-union-representatives was Serafino Soldati, born in 1921 to a family of sharecroppers where the Chianti gives way to the Val di Chiana. He fought in the war, was taken prisoner by the Germans after the 1943 armistice, and spent over a year in a concentration camp. After returning home, he was at a loss. In 1948, the Chamber of Labor of Siena proposed that he take a special accounting course for peasants and become a union representative. After that, Serafino began to haunt the estate offices of the whole area, to the chagrin of the landowners. In his memoir, Soldani remembers that his presence was so resented by the local landowners that his own landlord refused to pay up his debt, taunting him all the while:

I won't give you anything. I know I owe you 200,000 lire but I won't give it to you. Sue me. I don't care: I have my government, my tribunals, my Carabinieri. Today there is De Gasperi, there is Scelba. We are in charge and that's how things are done. When there is Togliatti you'll take away my land and send me to work, but for now we are in charge.[28]

These words, in their theatricality, convey the extent to which territoriality was central to the struggle and how it was remembered decades later. The Communists might have violated the sacredness of his estate office, but the landlord's authority spanned the entire country. Exasperated, Serafino had to move to a different part of Tuscany, at first still working as a sharecropper. In 1956, with the help of the Party, he landed a job at the state-owned railway company, leaving mezzadria behind once and for all.

Instances of individual trespassing and boundary crossing, which in subtle but profound ways must have reshaped the spatial (and temporal) perception of thousands of people, stood side by side with more spectacular acts of defiance, in which Tuscan peasants used collective action to reclaim their territory. These kinds of acts varied in character and impact. In June 1945, for example, many landlords reported to the Carabinieri instances of "white strike" (sciopero bianco), during which the sharecroppers prevented the owners and their representatives to approach the barns in which wheat was being stored, so that traditional partitions could not take place. One can only imagine the anger of the landlords at seeing themselves barred from portions of what was, after all, their property.[29] In other incidents, the physical presence of peasants where they were not supposed to be prevented business from being

---

[28] Serafino Soldati, *La Metamorfosi*, Archivio Diaristico Nazionale, Pieve S. Stefano, 18–19.
[29] Archivio di Stato di Siena, Gabinetto di Prefettura, box 55, folder Organizzazioni Sindacali, subfolder Rapporti fra Proprietari e Coloni.

carried out as usual. This was the case, the Carabinieri of Siena lamented in 1950, with the women of several estates of the province, who every hour or so walked in small groups to the entrance of the company offices chanting slogans, pronouncing threats, and generally acting despondent (petulanti). The police agreed that this conduct was an unacceptable "attempt at the prestige of the state and of the authorities," and promised surprise raids by motorbike, arrests, and formal warnings.[30]

Even more demonstratively, organized peasants would sometimes trespass into the houses of the landlords, intimidating them and demanding with their physical presence that their demands be met. This strategy was implemented in the countryside around Pienza in the summer of 1945, when some three hundred peasants stormed the villa of large-scale landowner Enrico Simonelli. The peasants had unilaterally withheld 60 percent of the wheat, rather than the traditional half, and brought it to the local Consorzio to be sold. But Simonelli personally knew the Consorzio staff and formally warned them not to pay the peasants for the extra 10 percent they had deposited. Now, a few short days later, the peasants showed up at his residence, removed him from the lunch table, and took him to the Consorzio, demanding that he formally withdraw the warning. Simonelli, incensed but also scared, at first complied, but then he denounced the trespassers and "kidnappers" to the police. The incident, which closely resembled others taking place all over Tuscany, even reached the desk of the minister of the Interior, who asked the prefect of Siena for information. The peasants argued that Simonelli, who had been a member of the Fascist Party from 1921 to the end of the war, was a black shirt (squadrista) unwilling to treat the peasants with respect; the landlord compared the peasants' tactics to those of the Fascist squads of the early 1920s. But while harking back to the Fascist period for a comparative reference, everyone was astonished at the sheer novelty of what was going on. Even though the peasants eventually had to give in, they had made their point: no corner of the territory was completely safe for the landowning class, not even their once sacred dining rooms![31]

Whereas these seemingly small (but actually highly significant) acts of trespassing involving houses, offices, and rural constructions were extremely common in postwar Tuscany, classical land occupations were relatively rare.[32] Unlike parts of southern Italy, the Tuscan landscape

---

[30] Archivio di Stato di Siena, Gabinetto di Prefettura, box 192 (1951), folder Vertenza Mezzadrile.

[31] Ibid.

[32] In the province of Siena, the few instances of land occupation took place on Mount Amiata. See Archivio di Stato di Siena, Gabinetto di Prefettura, box 98 (1946), folder Terre Incolte.

lacked vast stretches of completely neglected but potentially productive land, with the partial exception of the Maremma. The spatial organization of mezzadria was such that each farm (and peasant family) was put in charge of portions of territory containing a variety of resources (fields, pastures, forests, etc.) that were exploited with highly variable degrees of intensity. Very little land was publicly owned, and even less had ambiguous or overlapping property claims. Nevertheless, where large-scale property prevailed, episodes of outright peasant occupation did take place, especially under the leadership of the organized landless day laborers (braccianti).

The increasing pressures on the sharecropping system profoundly upset the delicate balance between the settled rural population (i.e., the sharecropping families living on farms and their few long-term collaborators) and the far less stable day laborers who depended on the sharecropping economy for much of their work. An increasing number of day laborers were downwardly mobile sharecroppers, most of them young, who could no longer be fully employed within their family farms. Therefore, after the end of the war and through the 1950s, unemployment and underemployment became for the first time a major social problem in Tuscany's hill country. Hard to measure and monitor,[33] the problem of unemployment drew the attention of a variety of public and semipublic institutions, particularly keen on avoiding the creation of a unified antagonistic front linking sharecroppers and laborers. Parts of rural Tuscany became the terrain for ongoing interventions by multiple and overlapping organizations, largely reliant on state funding, whose mission was to defuse social tensions and help large-scale landowners manage their inevitable decline as smoothly and painlessly as possible. Many of these interventions involved reforestation (or deforestation) projects, road construction and maintenance, reclamation plans, and other measures capable of deeply reshaping the landscape.

Events in the Orcia Valley offer many examples of the ways peasants came to change their understandings and uses of the territory in relation with ongoing state interventions, many of which were justified as measures against unemployment. As previously mentioned, one of the

---

[33] See Camera di Commercio di Siena, "Situazione Economica, Stato dell'Occupazione e Possibilità di Impiego nella Provincia," Archivio della Camera del Lavoro di Siena, Federmezzadri, box IX 1. Estimates of unemployment in the province of Siena, for example, ranged from more than 10 percent to less than a half that figure. The main problem was to capture (or ignore) the underemployment of the sharecroppers and their families, who were barred from seeking alternative occupations (both industrial and agricultural) when under contract: Archivio di Stato di Siena, Gabinetto di Prefettura, box 88 (1945–1949), folder Assunzioni di Coloni presso Aziende Industriali.

strategies adopted by organized unemployed peasants to reshape both the labor market and their territory was to get to work on plots of land without the authorization and supervision of the landlords. In the Val d'Orcia, these so-called reverse strikes (scioperi alla rovescia) targeted first of all large-scale landowners accused of absenteeism. Here crews of peasants would dig ditches for vine growing or for drainage, repair roads within and between estates (strade vicinali), and even restore decaying buildings. An increasing number of these actions, however, were also directed at the provincial and national governments as well as at the Reclamation Consortium (Consorzio di Bonifica), which had been founded during the Fascist period.[34] In these instances, the crews would build or repair public roads, bridges, and works of erosion management. The sources suggest that these acts of trespassing were taken very seriously by the authorities, who responded with a classic carrot-and-stick strategy. In many instances the Carabinieri would not only disrupt the crews' work and remove the peasants from the construction sites, but also arrest and report them. Several trials for trespassing took place through the 1950s, usually ending with acquittals or very lenient sentences.[35] Starting in the late 1940s, however, the government also began to organize ad hoc projects, the so-called Fanfani construction sites (named after the all-powerful Christian Democratic leader from Arezzo, Amintore Fanfani), which employed laborers on a temporary basis for a variety of purposes, ranging from road repairs to reforestation plans.[36]

Organized peasants also began to call on reclamation consortia to provide work for the unemployed, criticizing the "speculative" practices these institutions had followed under fascism. In the Orcia Valley these tensions were exacerbated by the reappointment of Antonio Origo, Iris's Marquis husband, as president of both the Reclamation Consortium and

---

[34] The season of the "reverse strikes" in Orcia Valley seems to have begun in December 1950, when sixty-three workers set out to continue the construction of the road from Vivo d'Orcia to Abbadia S. Salvatore, which had been called off. The workers were tried two years later and acquitted. Archivio di Stato di Siena, Gabinetto di Prefettura, box 140 Disoccupazione (1950–1955), folder Castiglione d'Orcia.

[35] As late as 1957, the parish priest of Castiglione d'Orcia felt compelled to write to the prefect of Siena and several members of government on behalf of fifteen (communist) workers on trial for having continued work for the Reclamation Consortium even after they had been fired. The priest argued that these kinds of trials had been detrimental to social peace. Archivio di Stato di Siena, Gabinetto di Prefettura, box 323 (1957), folder Ministero dell'Agricoltura e Foreste, subfolder Aziende Agrarie.

[36] Archivio di Stato di Siena, Gabinetto di Prefettura, box 88 (1945–1949), folder Cantieri di Lavoro. These construction sites also benefited from ERP (Marshall Plan) funds: Archivio di Stato di Siena, Gabinetto di Prefettura, box 88 (1945–1949), folder Opere di Miglioria a Sollievo della Disoccupazione.

the Agricultural Consortium (Consorzio Agrario) in Siena.[37] Origo was known not only as one of the most intransigent landlords in the province of Siena, but also as one of the most deeply compromised with the Fascist regime. Ongoing campaigns targeted the conduct of the Reclamation Consortium, calling for its democratization and for increasing transparency.[38] The Consortium remained an important actor in the shaping of the territory, but it had to respond to increasing pressures from below. Every major project had to confront the scrutiny of a variety of local organizations and of public opinion more generally, which clamored to weigh in on all kinds of decisions, down to the specific routes of new roads or the location of irrigation projects.[39]

The kind of paternalism that had been typical of the reclamation schemes of the Fascist period was definitely over, but hierarchical benevolence was replaced by ongoing expectations of state intervention. Whenever public funds dried up, organized laborers demanded more. Especially as the emergency posed by the massive unrest of the late 1940s and early 1950s began to subside, laborers felt that unprecedented tactics were called for to draw the attention of the public authorities. Thus, they began to march.[40] The unemployed laborers of the Orcia Valley organized the first "hunger march" in 1957, with the intention of walking the thirty miles from Castiglione d'Orcia to Siena. That year they only reached the Orcia River, where they were stopped by the police. The prefect and other authorities promised, among other measures, the immediate release of state funds to pave the road that linked Castiglione to the Cassia, the ancient Roman road leading from Florence to Rome. That was only the first of a series of marches that took place in the following

[37] Both kinds of consortia were associations of landowners that contributed financial quotas, integrated by state funds. Therefore, they were partially private and partially public institutions. As explained in Chapter 1, reclamation consortia were local institutions founded during the Fascist regime (although some predated it) which dealt with infrastructural work, both on the farms and on public lands. Most agricultural consortia were instead established on a provincial basis at the turn of the century and acted as buyers of agricultural supplies (seeds, fertilizers, machinery, etc.) and sellers of products on behalf of their members. We have an exhaustive institutional history of the agricultural consortium of the province of Siena: Fabio Bertini, *Organizzazione Economica e Politica dell'Agricoltura nel XX Secolo: Cent'Anni di Storia del Consorzio Agrario di Siena (1901–2000)* (Bologna: Il Mulino, 2001).

[38] Pointed critiques of the conduct and administration of the Reclamation Consortium of Orcia Valley began immediately after the end of the war, although they escalated in the 1960s. Archivio di Stato di Siena, Gabinetto di Prefettura, box 88 (1945–1949), folder Consorzi di Bonifica.

[39] Archivio di Stato di Siena, Gabinetto di Prefettura, box 138 Disoccupazione e Cantieri di Lavoro (1945–1949), folder Opere di Bonifica.

[40] R. Pecci, *I Solchi della Mia Vita*: 91–95. See also Emo Bonifazi, *Lotte Contadine in Val d'Orcia*: 91.

years. In January 1959 the laborers managed to reach Siena, where the riot police doused them with high-pressure water along the main stroll under the startled eyes of the city folks. According to Rino Pecci, who participated in the demonstration, the citizens of Siena were generally supportive, but he also told me that the stories of misery and deprivation the laborers shared with the Sienese made them feel like they were coming "from another world."[41] In the end, several cooperatives of laborers were organized to receive public money and put in charge of (not always transparently useful) projects of construction and forest management. This windfall of money, however limited in scope, eased the brunt of unemployment in the area well into the 1970s but also created something of an underclass of workers entirely dependent on the public purse. Rino Pecci, for one, moved on and became first a janitor and then the bus driver at the elementary school of Castiglione, as well as a long-time city councilor and political activist.

The "hunger marches" were only one example of the complex and rapidly changing relationships between postwar Tuscan peasants and the towns where political and socioeconomic power resided. Ultimately, the most visible and symbolically charged boundary Tuscan peasants had to confront was that between town and countryside, a threshold that in Tuscany seemed as old as social life itself, and one that the Fascist regime had recently reinforced through its ruralization policies. This divide has been studied extensively from the perspective of the literate classes,[42] but it is exceedingly difficult to retrieve the peasants' experiences of anger, displacement, and exhilaration as they crossed over into the urban world. It is worth emphasizing that, unlike in other parts of Italy, in Tuscany even minor centers (towns the size of Montepulciano or Pienza) had a distinctively urban character and identity. Everything in the physical layout of Tuscan towns, with their piazzas, main stroll (the corso), public and private palazzi, and of course their walls, spoke of separation from (and command over) the country (the contado). To experience the feeling of empowerment towns confer in the Tuscan landscape, one only needs to cross one of the gates in Pienza's walls, climb up the hill, and stand in the middle of Piazza Pio II, named after Pope Piccolomini, who founded this "ideal city" in the fifteenth century. City life responded to the needs of the urban classes. It was utterly irrelevant that some town neighborhoods were inhabited by day laborers, people who sold their

---

[41] Interview by author, February 2008.
[42] For an insightful overview of twentieth-century literature, see Silvia Ross, *Tuscan Spaces: Literary Constructions of Space* (Toronto: University of Toronto Press, 2010).

arms to anyone who could pay, and who were often far poorer than the sharecroppers who lived on the farms.

At dedicated moments, of course, the country entered the walls of the city to sell its products or pay its homage to particularly important religious sites, but such instances of intermingling were strictly regulated and limited in their scope and duration. Well into the twentieth century informal curfews prevented peasants from going to town after a certain time at night, especially if they were young, male, and potentially threatening. Urban youngsters were in charge of enforcing this rule. Listen to this memory from the countryside around Montalcino, with its mixture of resentment, compassion, and humorous resignation:

One of Armando's uncles was impaled! It was just a prank, if you can believe it. Poor guy, tied with some ropes to two sticks like on the cross. At night he arrived from Montalcino to Pieve Vecchia so lopsided that he could barely walk. At the door of his house he knocked with one of the sticks and his dad went, "The key is there!" "I know, but I can't," was the reply. When his dad saw him, he got so upset: he was tied with these ropes like Christ on the cross![43]

In these tales the peasant was indeed the archetypal "poor christ" (povero cristo) bearing the cross of centuries of urban exploitation and arrogance.

Rino Pecci (and this is still one of the most common memories of traditional country life in Tuscany) remembers that as a rule sharecroppers married each other: it was rare enough for a sharecropper woman to marry into an urban family, no matter how poor, but it was absolutely inconceivable for a peasant man to marry an urban woman.[44] This discrepancy was mostly due to patrilocality, typical of mezzadria: as a rule the young sharecropper would bring his bride into his father's home, and this would have forced the city girl to renounce her urban identity and fall to the status of a peasant (contadina). And yet this politics of separation coexisted with complex acts of participation, familiarity, and reciprocity that linked town and country dwellers in complex ways. For example, it was not uncommon for young peasants to feel an affiliation with a specific town near their farm, and even participate in rituals of rivalry (anything from pranks to full-scale brawls) between the youth of different urban centers.[45] Peasants were not of the town, and yet they were inextricably linked to it.

---

[43] Carlo Cambi (ed.), *Orcia Miseria: Quando Campare Era un Rimedio* (Montepulciano: Le Balze, 2004): 92.

[44] R. Pecci, *I Solchi della Mia Vita*: 44.

[45] The feelings of familiarity expressed by the town dwellers for the life of the country are of course much better documented. Entire urban literary genres were inspired by this kind of familiarity or on familiarity's deferred fruit, nostalgia. In the Tuscan case, in my

Things did not change overnight after Liberation. The archives are full of complaints by town dwellers about the unpleasantness of seeing demonstrating peasants invade their cherished streets and piazzas. Sometimes the rhetoric of these complaints was extremely strong. An anonymous writer from the town of Castellina in Chianti appealed to the prefect of Siena in January 1951 to protect the town dwellers from an impending demonstration of Communist peasants from the surrounding farms to protest the visit of Dwight Eisenhower to Italy: "Let us know that you exist, or we'll take care of it ourselves, for we are sick and tired of putting up with this. We'll do like we did in 1920, and then whatever will be, will be. Just don't say we hadn't warned you!"[46] By raising the specter of the Black Shirts, who had terrorized the Tuscan countryside in the early 1920s to restore order and threatened social boundaries, the writer knew he would be striking a raw nerve.

In the postwar period, however, collective action also allowed peasants to show their newly found pride and generosity by building metaphorical bridges over the city walls. In the late 1940s and early 1950s it became customary for Tuscan sharecroppers, especially the politically active ones, to bring to town baskets full of vegetables, eggs, and other products. Sometimes this gesture would be performed in support of political causes, as was the case in late December 1949, when seventy sharecropping families went to San Quirico d'Orcia with their baskets to be donated to the families of the people detained for having participated in the violent demonstrations in the wake of Togliatti's assassination attempt.[47] More generally, these rituals became an integral part of newly secularized Christmas celebrations: instead of giving poultry, vegetables, and eggs to the landlords and managers, as called for by an ancient tradition (the *regalie*), sharecroppers would now bring the same goods to town and donate them to the poor, or to the sick at the hospitals. There are still a few photographs of these events, showing the peasants in their Sunday best, waiting in line outside a hospital entrance. It would be hard to overestimate the emotional and political impact of these gestures: centuries

---

opinion, one of the most beautiful examples is Piero Calamandrei, *Inventario della Casa di Campagna* (Florence: Le Monnier, 1941).

[46] Archivio di Stato di Siena, Gabinetto di Prefettura, Filza 146 Situazione Politica Comuni della Provincia, Fascicolo Castellina in Chianti. See also the Carabineri's letter to the prefect of Siena, sent on December 9, 1945: "The population of Montepulciano can hardly bear the ongoing invasions of the town by peasants, who threaten, albeit just at the level of speech, to set the town itself on fire," Archivio di Stato dui Siena, Gabinetto di Prefettura, box 98, folder Vertenza Agraria Atti Relativi, sottofascicolo Montepulciano.

[47] Archivio di Stato di Siena, Gabinetto di Prefettura, box 87, anni 1946–1950. Situazione Politica dei Comuni, folder S. Quirico d'Orcia.

Illustration #9 A girl hands out produce to a smartly dressed woman on
a Ciao moped in 1969 or 1970. The sign on the truck reads "Serve your-
selves without ceremonies." Sharecroppers had been donating produce
to urban dwellers in the context of demonstrations since the mid-1940s.

of enforced hierarchical distance and separation were coming to an end,
thanks to the peasants' organizational unity. Finally, peasants would also
become full-fledged *cittadini*, which in Italian (like in other romance languages) means both citizens and city dwellers (Illustration 9).

Staking Out Territory

In July 1953 the Carabinieri filed a report to the prefect of Siena about
the town of Monticchiello, a beautifully preserved Medieval castle six
miles west of Pienza, now famous throughout Italy for organizing one
of the best examples of "teatro povero" (literally, "poor theater") in the
country.[48] At the time, approximately three hundred people lived within

---

[48] I will discuss this example of "teatro povero," founded in the 1960s, more extensively
in Chapter 6. For an overview in English, see Richard Andrews, *A Theatre of Community
Memory: Tuscan Sharecropping and the Teatro povero di Monticchiello* (Exeter: Society for
Italian Studies, 1998).

the town walls and five hundred more lived within walking distance in the farms nearby. The overwhelming majority of them, the policeman noted, were of the "Marxist faith" and gathered every night at the Communist Party offices "to kill time talking politics." These radical peasants, however, did more than just talk. They had established a cooperative store and – herein lay the problem – had managed to locate the first public telephone in town right on the premises of the coop. Obviously, this would not do. The prefect immediately got in touch with the telephone company, which proceeded to install a public service at the local post office within four short weeks, a remarkably speedy affair by the standards of 1950s Italy.[49] This episode accords a rare glimpse into the social life of postwar Tuscan peasants. Not only did they challenge long-established boundaries, they also carved out spheres of action – let us call them territories – that escaped the supervision of the upper classes and of the state authorities. Moreover, they embraced "modernity," which they understood above all as movement and connection, as the opposite of the traditional isolation they had been sentenced to since time immemorial. Once again, the staking out of territory – a spatial move – was intimately connected to the speeding up of time – the construction of an alternative temporality.

In the years after Liberation, Tuscan peasants transformed their patterns of sociability and whatever leisure they managed to eke out at least as extensively as they reshaped their work organization and practices. Especially the young among them felt a burning need for spaces where they could socialize in novel ways, integrating political activity and fun. Of course this process was not unique to Tuscany, but the sharecropping landscape of central Italy, with its scattered settlement, seemed particularly impervious to "modern" leisure activities and nontraditional moments of socialization. Gone were the times when a young peasant could make do with the rotating winter wakes (veglie) in the neighboring farms and the few occurrences in the agricultural calendar, chief among them the threshing of the wheat at the height of summer and the grape harvest in September, when peasants from different farms (and families) gathered to work, eat, and drink. Now, in the brave new world of ongoing political mobilization and unprecedented organizational unity, Tuscan peasants demanded more. By staking out spaces of socialization, they were also reaching out beyond the confines of the peasant world.

In inventing spaces for socialization, however, Tuscan peasants also harked back to the pre-Fascist period of mass mobilization in the countryside, which had given rise to a network of socialist-organized "People's

---

[49] Archivio di Stato di Siena, Gabinetto di Prefettura, box 146, Situazione Politica dei Comuni della Provincia (1951–1955), folder Pienza.

Houses" (Case del Popolo) throughout northern and central Italy. Attacked by the Fascist squads in the early 1920s and then shut down or transformed into "Fascist Houses" (Case del Fascio), these older examples of rural self-organization were very much alive in the memory of postwar Tuscany. Often built by the peasants and town dwellers in their spare time, thanks to donations and collection campaigns, in the postwar years People's Houses became a source of pride as well as concrete spaces for novel kinds of interaction between the rural and the urban worlds.

This pride transpires vividly in the memoirs of former peasants. Marcello Cioppi remembers how he joined a group of young peasants in renting a couple of rooms for political meetings at San Fabiano, a hamlet half way between San Casciano and Greve in Chianti. Then the same young peasants began organizing dance parties and the two rooms became a political, social, and entertainment center for the area: "No one had ever seen anything like that."[50] Fulvia Massini remembers how she used to go to the new People's House in Castellina in Chianti with her father shortly before he died and recounts how that institution had been transformed into a Fascist house during the dictatorship to then become a People's House again after Liberation. In the mid-1950s, however, it had been requisitioned by the state and turned into the Carabinieri's barracks. But the peasants of the Chianti, including her father, were not deterred. They volunteered their work and just built a new and bigger People's House just around the corner.[51] Other towns had to wait a long time before these kinds of litigations could be settled. Franco Guarducci, born to a family of sharecroppers in the Florentine section of the Chianti, remembers that the people of Tavarnelle and surrounding area had to wait till the 1960s to have a safe and secure space to meet and socialize. Here too a mixed group of town and country folks decided to rehab the premises of the dismissed slaughterhouse, volunteering their work and receiving some financial support from several leftist organizations. All that work paid off:

At Christmas [1965] we held the opening gala both for the bar and for the huge dance hall that could easily accommodate one thousand people. We invited the best bands and orchestras with popular singers, and for the first time ever women could sit at the bar without feeling any shame.[52]

---

[50] Marcello Cioppi, *La Mamma Ti Sorride col Cuore*.

[51] Fulvia Massini, *Niente di Personale*: 16. Many People's Houses around Italy were requisitioned by the state in the 1950s, in the wake of ongoing litigations regarding the status of these spaces which, under fascism, had been nationalized and run by the Opera Nazionale Dopolavoro. Of course the political and symbolic valence of these moves was not lost on anyone.

[52] Marcello Guarducci, *Memorie di un Contadino Smesso*, Archivio Diaristico Nazionale, Pieve S. Stefano: 27. This building, the Circolo Ricreativo La Rampa, still stands in Tavarnelle Val di Pesa, one of the municipalities of the Florentine section of the Chianti.

Again, a seemingly mundane space allowed history to accelerate, bringing fashionable music to the rural backwoods and even transforming traditional gender behaviors: in the People's House a peasant woman could
now even sit at the bar!

Although all these memoirs convey the excitement of finally conquer-
ing spaces for leisure and socialization, once again none of them can
compete with the evocative power of Rino Pecci's account of how television came to Rocca d'Orcia, the castle in the municipality of Castiglione
where he lived.[53] Here too a group of locals, including Rino, had obtained
from the city government two rooms to establish a social club with an
unmistakable leftist bent. When, in the mid-1950s, the first television
sets began to appear in the bars and clubs of the Orcia Valley, Rino and
his comrades wanted to install one too, beating even the local priest at
offering the populace access to this new marvel. Rino had just been paid
for a three-month stint as a logger, and three month's worth of wages
was approximately what a TV set went for at the time. He gave the club
the whole amount as a loan and the TV was bought. The problem was
that the ceiling in one of the rooms was too low to make room for the
public. The club members set out to work to lower the floor with pickets
and shovels, but the rock in which the rooms had been carved was so
hard that progress was frustratingly slow. Rino and a couple of the guys,
however, had also worked as quarrymen and in road construction for the
reclamation consortium, and they had some explosives left. Even though
the club was located downstairs from the local primary school, they took
a chance (when school was out, of course), they set the mines, and –
boom – the floor was blown up without any unwanted damage. It goes
without saying that someone in town caught wind of what was going on
and warned the Carabinieri. In the end, Rino and his friends got off easy,
but only after a lot of explaining. How fitting that the same explosives
that were reshaping the landscape of the valley would be used to share
with the locals the irresistible appeal of Italy's version of the *$64,000
Question* (*Lascia o Raddoppia?*).

The pride and initiative showed by Tuscan peasants in building, rehabilitating, and decorating their socialization spaces stand in stark contrast
with the sense of shame, rage, and powerlessness felt by most of them
with regard to their own dwellings – the farms and annexes where they
lived and worked. Since the 1970s, as we will see, these rural constructions have become the object of an almost fetishistic appreciation from
a growing international audience of Sunday farmers, summer residents,
and retirees. But no one could have predicted or even imagined this turn

---

[53] Rino Pecci, *I Solchi della Mia Vita*: 81–85.

of events in the 1950s, when the houses of rural Tuscany were still the most tangible symbol of the sharecropping landscape. Starting shortly after Liberation, Tuscan peasants began to protest their living conditions, drawing attention to the pitiful state of the buildings in which they were forced to live. Two parallel processes seem to have been at work here. First, landowners balked at making major (and sometimes even minor) investments at such politically and economically uncertain times. This unwillingness or inability to invest led of course to a general deterioration of the housing stock, exacerbated by the somewhat startling refusal by peasants to fix the places were they lived, even when this would have been relatively easy. Second, and more subtly, Tuscan peasants began to compare their living conditions to those of other social classes, finding their traditional living arrangements increasingly inadequate. In a characteristically self-serving move, many landlords blamed leftist agitators for stirring up discontent among people whom they had imagined as satisfied and grateful clients just a decade or two before. The sources, however, are unanimous in showing that Tuscan peasants needed little convincing to complain about (and organize around) the state of their dwellings.

The peasants' complaints fell in at least three different categories. First of all, they clamored to have their houses supplied with electricity and running water. The electrification of rural Tuscany had begun under fascism, but at the beginning of the 1950s the completion of the project was still a long way off. Maybe 40 percent of rural houses still lacked electricity a decade after the end of the war – far less near the major urban centers and far more in the more isolated and/or mountainous areas.[54] Of course the scattered settlement pattern typical of mezzadria did nothing to expedite the process. Regular water supply was also a problem, although the majority of Tuscan farms had potable water wells. Often, however, water supply was a euphemism used to request bathrooms with modern plumbing, which were exceedingly uncommon and imbued with powerful symbolic meanings, as we have seen.

The provision of both electricity and running water depended on the somewhat delicate collaboration between the public authorities and (in the case of electricity) the local monopoly, who were in charge of the major infrastructural projects, and the landlords, who had to request the services and financially contribute to their installation in each farm. Therefore, it was not uncommon for the same estate to have some farms supplied with electricity and others, more remote, without. Unsurprisingly, the provision of electricity was often a major terrain of

[54] "Distribuzione della Proprietà Terriera della Provincia di Siena."

Illustration #10 Light is on! Electricity comes to Tuscany's farmhouses.

negotiation between landowners and sharecroppers, who demanded it in exchange for other concessions.[55] Ultimately, modern utilities arrived to the more remote areas of Tuscany well after the peasants had begun to leave en masse, whereas in the more easily connected areas, which received them in the course of the 1950s, they did little to stem the tide of urbanization (Illustration 10).

Second, Tuscan peasants complained about the lack of separation between themselves and their animals (as well as their animals' useful but noxious droppings). The typical Tuscan farmhouse was a two-story building which included the bedrooms upstairs and a large kitchen with a substantial oven for the baking of the bread downstairs. As a rule, these houses

---

[55] Archivio di Stato di Siena, Gabinetto di Prefettura, box 192 (1951), folder Vertenza Mezzadrile.

did not have separate dining or living rooms, which the peasants increasingly resented. The stable for the cattle was also located downstairs, sometimes directly connected to the rest of the house through a narrow hallway that the man in charge of the animals (the bifolco) walked through several times a day. The proximity between humans and cattle testified to the fact that cows and oxen were the farm's most precious and vulnerable asset. The animals also provided a source of heat in the winter. Traditionally, the bifolco shoveled the dung into a small construction attached to the farmhouse, where the animal droppings (including those collected from the pigsty), mixed with straw and other materials, turned into composted manure. The liquid refuse was conveyed into the dung room via an open conduit.

After Liberation, organized sharecroppers began to view this layout as unacceptable and called for, at a minimum, the construction of "rational" annexes for the production of manure (concimaia razionale), removed from the rest of the farmhouse and with sealed conduits and an impermeable floor, so as to avoid the possibility of the sludge seeping into the ground and contaminating the water well. Local and provincial authorities issued detailed ordinances in the name of public health, calling for the construction of these annexes,[56] but well into the 1950s "rational" dung houses remained anything but the rule, since many landlords were unwilling to foot the bill. The fact that some landlords were willing to endanger public health and violate the law to avoid investing in their farms was perceived as further evidence of impending doom for the entire sharecropping economy.

While the risk of disease cannot be dismissed as a motivating factor for the peasants' protests, the sources are primarily concerned with the animals' noxious smells. Smell is the most elusive of senses for the historian to recapture, but it is pretty clear that the olfactory landscape of Tuscan peasants changed quite dramatically in the decade after Liberation. What used to be "natural" (or at least customary) became offensive, and what used to be perceived as an unmediated fact became symbolically charged and controversial. Sharecroppers literally slept upstairs from their cattle, and they had done so for centuries. Now they remarked on the unpleasantness of interspecies proximity in terms that conveyed a genuine sense of disgust.[57] The same was true for the dung room, which had been a

---

[56] The prefect of Siena, for example, issued one of these ordinances in June 1950, calling for the landlords to build separate and hygienic annexes by the end of the following year. The ordinance went largely evaded. In Pienza, for example, more than 150 of these annexes remained to be built in August 1952. Archivio di Stato di Siena, Gabinetto di Prefettura, box 219 (1952), folder Pienza.

[57] See, for example, the testimonies of the sharecroppers in Archivio CGIL Toscana, Federterra, box 93, folder Commissione Case Coloniche 1954.

staple of rural life since the basic architectural features of Tuscan farm-houses were set in the sixteenth and seventeenth centuries.

Even human smells became more perceivable and controversial. Sweat seems to have carried particularly powerful connotations, being connected to the unforgiving (and possibly debasing) character of rural work before extensive mechanization. In July 1957 one of the tenants of an estate in Castiglione d'Orcia wrote to the prefect of Siena complaining that the landowner, a lawyer, intended to renege on the lease. To make matters even worse, the lawyer had walked into the villa that presided over the estate saying with contempt that it smelled like sweat, since the tenants allowed the workers to sleep there. When the workers heard the comment, all hell broke loose, and the tenant told the prefect that he feared the breakout of a full-scale riot.[58] The same kind of comment that twenty years before would have been received as a statement of fact – the people who work the land smell like sweat and therefore need to sleep in separate quarters – had now become a terrible offense. In postwar rural Tuscany modernity was also a sensory experience that measured how profoundly smell perceptions had changed in the span of one generation.

Finally, peasants complained about the houses' general state of disrepair – about major problems such as cracks in the walls and holes in the roof, but also about problems that could have been fixed rather easily, such as how infrequently the interior walls were painted or the outside walls whitewashed. The same people who were willing to volunteer their time (and sometimes resources) to build and decorate meeting rooms and dance halls refused to paint the walls of the houses where they lived, appealing to the fact that traditionally this had been the landlord's responsibility. This unwillingness speaks volumes about the state of class relations in postwar rural Tuscany and about the peasants' disaffection with their life, but it also shows how subtly and powerfully peasants' actions were affected by their perceptions of ownership and territoriality. Despite the omnipresent rhetoric about the Tuscan peasants' traditional attachment to "their" farms, they proved reluctant to lift one finger to beautify houses which belonged to their landlords and from which they could have been evicted.

Traditionally, evictions were indeed a readily available option for landowners. Before World War II, even perceived "incompatibility of personality" was reason enough for the contract to be rescinded. In this case, however, the peasant struggles did lead to major changes shortly after Liberation. Postwar legislation made evictions far more difficult: now the

[58] Archivio di Stato di Siena, Gabinetto di Prefettura, box 323 (1957), folder Ministero Agricoltura e Foreste, subfolder Aziende Agrarie.

landlord had to provide a "just cause" (giusta causa) for his or her decision, meaning that proof of a major breach of contract by the sharecropper was usually required. But what constituted breach of contract in the
social climate of postwar rural Tuscany was far from obvious. Many of
the tactics employed by sharecroppers in their struggles could be interpreted as such, and many civil courts were more than happy to embrace
the landlords' perspectives and give them the force of law. The political use of evictions by many landlords alienated the sharecroppers even
further and paved the way for their realization of how unlikely it was for
mezzadria to be reformed from within.

The case of La Foce, the estate in the Orcia Valley that Antonio and Iris
Origo had tried to turn into a model of rational and humane husbandry,
is particularly revealing of the challenges Tuscan sharecroppers posed to
the owners' managerial (and territorial) authority and of the counter-
measures adopted by large-scale landlords, namely eviction threats. The
wave of unrest that followed the end of the war seems to have caught Iris
by surprise. Only a few months after she had helped dozens of children
leave her estate and reach the relative safety of Montepulciano as the war
front advanced (the most famous episode memorialized in Iris's book,
The War in Val d'Orcia), the Marquise and her husband found themselves
facing a very different kind of conflict, which defied their comprehension
and their humanitarian impulses:

> Strikes were organized at the most crucial moments of the farmer's year, espe-
> cially during the harvest; tenants who had received notice refused to leave; and ill
> feelings ran so high for several years that, if we met two or three of our *contadini*
> together, they would refuse even to greet us. We had become "the Enemies of
> the People," the abusers of the poor. The church was no longer attended, and in
> the school the children's essays stated, a little puzzled, that now all the *padroni*
> [landlords] had become "bad."[59]

It is somewhat curious that in this passage Iris Origo feels compelled
to mention the eviction notices she and her husband issued to several of their sharecroppers, especially because in the next paragraph
she wonders if social conflict might have been the product of a failure
of communication, an inability of both landlords and peasants to listen to each other as they supposedly had done during the war. But of
course evictions signed the end of any possible communication. In their
brutality they reminded the parties of who owned the territory and
could call it home, and who could be irrevocably reduced to replace-
able labor power.

---

[59] Iris Origo, *Images and Shadows: Parts of a Life* (London: John Murray, 1970): 246–247.

Antonio Origo became one of the most unpopular landlords in the province of Siena, but the reasons for the peasants' overt hostility were not quite as mysterious as Iris implied in her memoir. He joined a relatively small but powerful cohort of large-scale landowners who were determined to use the courts to restore order and punish what they perceived as peasant abuses. The civil court of Montepulciano, which had jurisdiction over disputes at La Foce, rarely disappointed him. Ironically, it was Origo's modernizing impulses that made him so intransigent. His entire experience as a gentleman farmer mindful of the common good testified to the necessity of a clear and decisive chain of command. The only way to make a difference was to lead the masses toward a different future, but his peasants no longer allowed him to do this. The challenges came in many forms. The sharecroppers, in a general campaign coordinated by their union, would refuse to transport the harvested wheat to the estate office, as the contract called for, so that Origo was forced to hire extra help; they would slaughter and sell the estate's pigs, pocketing the revenue; they would refuse to pay their share of social security benefits. Origo's response was to keep score of all abuses and hold the peasants responsible for them when the farm accounts were supposed to be settled. When the peasants refused to pay their debts, he would sue them.[60] When that was not enough, he would have eviction notices issued for breach of contract.

As I mentioned at the beginning of the chapter, only a small percentage of the eviction notices issued in the early 1950s were actually carried out.[61] Evictions were viewed as extreme measures whose function was primarily symbolic and demonstrative: evict one peasant to educate one hundred. But the strong collective response elicited by evictions among organized peasants also raised the stakes beyond what public authorities were willing to tolerate in the name of property rights. When Antonio Origo managed to finalize the eviction of sharecropper Serafino Valdambrini and his family in February 1952, the peasants' reaction was powerful. More than one thousand and five hundred people converged at Valdambrini's farm, confronted along the way by almost one hundred

---

[60] See the court sentences from the period 1947 to 1955 preserved in Archivio della Camera del Lavoro di Siena, Federmezzadri, box III b. 7, folders Pienza and Tenuta La Foce.

[61] For the province of Siena, only 4 percent of the 460 eviction notices issued by March 1952 were carried out in the next couple of years. But that means that almost 4 percent of all sharecropping families in the province received a notice. See "Anche la Civile Toscana Oppressa dai Baroni della Terra," *L'Unità*, March 22, 1952. The same source places the number of peasants in the province to have been reported to the police at more than 5,000.

policemen. The standoff went on all day, as the Carabinieri officer present at the scene recalled:

The first military policemen found the area around [Valdambrini's] farm already invaded by numerous peasants who had gathered there since the night before, so that it was necessary to remove them beyond the Cassia road, two kilometers away. In the meantime people kept coming from nearby municipalities and hamlets, and they congregated on top of the surrounding hills, so that it was necessary for the Carabinieri to intervene energetically and force the demonstrators to disperse.[62]

And yet, the officer continued, Origo had done so much for improving the productivity of his estate and the living conditions of his peasants! A leaflet handed out by the sharecroppers' union in the following days begged to differ:

If to carry out an eviction it is necessary to mobilize [so many policemen], we wonder what stage we have reached in the process of pacification and democracy. It was almost like re-living the tragic days of 1944, when war raged on the clay hills of the Val d'Orcia, leaving death and ruins behind.... [The peasants] have made the land of the Val d'Orcia fertile, they defended it with their blood, and they are attached to it.[63]

Clearly the legacies of the reclamation schemes of the 1930s, as well as that of the war, were as powerful as they were contentious. If Origo had expected gratefulness for his activism as a modernizer in the 1930s, his disappointment must have been tremendous.

Overall, a contradictory set of projects emerged from the season of conflicts of the late 1940s and early 1950s. The national government began to understand that the days of mezzadria were numbered, and set out to promote small-scale land ownership through characteristically clientelistic negotiations. This reforming impulse, however, did not entail a challenge to property rights as they were interpreted by large-scale landowners. Property needed to be defended, even at the cost of militarizing the territory. In fact, national authorities began to understand rural Tuscany as something of an extraterritorial enclave, which defied national political trends by stubbornly clinging to radical leftist politics. As we'll see next, the urgency to recapture this territory and make it more compatible with the rest of "Italy" prompted all kinds of initiatives, which combined

---

[62] Archivio di Stato di Siena, Gabinetto di Prefettura, box 219, folder Disdette Coloniche. Sometimes demonstrations lingered on for days after the eviction had been carried out, as was the case at the Lilliano estate, near Castellina in Chianti, in February 1952. See the Carabinieri's report to the prefect on April 22, 1952, Archivio di Stato di Siena, Gabinetto di Prefettura, box 219 (1952), not in any folder.

[63] Ibid.

persuasion and violent repression. But the scenarios envisaged by the organizations of the Left were no less contradictory. On the one hand, the Left saw the creation of a class of farmers as a step in the struggle against monopoly capital and the construction of an Italian path to socialism. On the other hand, this evolutionary strategy coexisted uneasily with more collectivist projects calling for the promotion of cooperatives or even, among some local leaders, with revolutionary dreams of mass expropriation. These contradictions were compounded by the fact that the Left governed most Tuscan provinces and municipalities: there was no consensus over the ways the Communists and Socialists might capitalize on locally based power to increase their appeal and credibility at the national level.

Finally, ordinary peasants, especially the sharecroppers, confronted the contradictions between individualistic strategies and collective action. For a few years, the two seemed to merge and build on each other, creating a sense of class unity they had never experienced before. But this moment of unity was not to last. Moreover, the peasants' attachment to the land coexisted with dreams of modernity that were fundamentally urban in character. As we'll see in the next chapter, through the late 1950s and early 1960s organized peasants made several last-ditch efforts to break their traditional isolation and "modernize" their lives, but once it became clear that they could not muster the resources necessary to transform rural Tuscany, most of them set out to leave the countryside behind.

Farm, Nation, World

By the end of the 1940s, rural Tuscany (together with Emilia-Romagna and sections of Umbria and the Marche) had become an anomaly that flew in the face of the increasingly secure political compromise worked out by the Christian Democrats at the national level. This compromise rested primarily on two pillars, which were shaky at best in the countryside of central Italy: the moral authority of the Catholic Church and the financial as well as military support provided by the United States. In other words, much of the national political balance painstakingly achieved after Liberation by the conservatives relied on the power of two global forces that saw Italy as an important (albeit by no means central) battleground in a worldwide war between opposing "civilizations." The fact that most Tuscan peasants were overtly hostile to the Church and nurtured a complex but nevertheless profound attachment to the global enemy, the Soviet Union, could not sit well with a variety of powerful political and religious authorities, who set out to "reconquer" the Tuscan hills as if they were on a veritable crusade. The Tuscan anomaly had to be normalized, either by winning back the souls of the fallen or by cleansing the territory of those who were irretrievably lost and by replacing them with more amenable subjects.

The case of Colle Val d'Elsa, a town in the northern part of the province of Siena famous for its political radicalism, illustrates the strategies adopted by the centrist forces in their Reconquista. Colle's economy was based not only on the agricultural goods produced by the sharecroppers who lived in the surrounding hills, but also on a few factories specialized in glassmaking. Even more than in other parts of Tuscany, in Colle leftist politics had opened up a terrain for the interaction and collaboration between urban and rural societies – a process which the anti-Marxist forces found extremely threatening. This challenge called for unprecedented measures. In 1951, one of the parish priests of Colle applied his considerable energies to the organization of a "religious mission" aiming at re-Christianizing the local population.[64] On September 24, and for the following two weeks, the Tuscan town and its countryside became the site of a series of meetings, rituals, and ceremonies carried out by eighteen volunteers, both lay and religious, coming from all over Italy. These volunteers not only celebrated twenty-eight special Masses and organized all kinds of public ceremonies, including a Rosary in the main piazza, they also made more than two thousand home visits, bringing with them small gifts and handing out religious literature.

The goal, however, was not simply to instill the fear of God in Colle's recalcitrant population. Rather, the message was one of hope and compassion, even self-critique. The Church had been too detached from the worldly needs of the population and too often willing to compromise with the forces of reaction. The volunteers reminded their audience that Jesus himself was a manual laborer, and that the Church condoned wealth only if harnessed toward the promotion of the common good. In this spirit, on the specially invented Day of Christian Solidarity, Colle's population was invited to donate money and goods for the poor, which led to the collection of 80,000 lire and 200 kilograms of food. The volunteers did not even refrain from delving into the nitty-gritty of political struggle, chastising the right wing of the Christian Democratic party and spreading the message of its left wing, praising more progressive Catholic politicians such as Gronchi, Dossetti, and Fanfani.[65] In the end,

---

[64] The following narrative is based on the reports of the parish priest and of the Carabinieri (the latter largely reliant on the former) in Archivio di Stato di Siena, Gabinetto di Prefettura, box 146 Situazione Politica dei Comuni della Provincia (1951–1955), folder Colle Val d'Elsa.

[65] The operation was conceived and organized by priests and lay people close to Azione Cattolica, whose positions at the time were close to those of the left wing of the DC.

thousands of people were exposed to a somewhat different, maybe even surprising, message from propaganda experts, who commented on how the public facade of anticlericalism paraded by the locals often crumbled behind closed doors. Even though the younger generation seemed less easy to reach, many of Colle's older inhabitants privately confessed to their enduring faith.

The territorial battles over Tuscany's hill country combined propaganda and subterfuge, skillful persuasion and backhanded dealings. The Left was not above questionable strategies. When it came to propaganda, Tuscan Communists could be quite blunt. In the 1950s, political posters and handouts were a mainstay of the urban landscape in small-town Italy, but they had to be reviewed and approved by the provincial police commissioner (questore) before being posted. In June 1952 the commissioner banned a poster submitted by the "peace partisans of Siena" depicting two Korean children being attacked by giant mosquitoes and bearing the script "In Korea and in China, American planes drop bombs with insects carrying typhus, the plague, and cholera."[66] The peace partisans appealed the decision to a provincial court, which sided with the commissioner on grounds that the poster unfairly smeared the reputation of an allied country, constituted a threat to public order, and had the potential to damage international relations.

Quite aside from its lack of fairness, this poster was but one instance of a whole movement that allowed Tuscan peasants to link their farms to the destinies of the nation and the world. In the wake of the 1952 hydrogen bomb test at Bikini, for example, the peace partisans of Montalcino collected eight thousand signatures for the ban of nuclear weapons.[67] The pervasive presence and territorial reach of these "partisans" (the name itself, of course, referred to the legacy of the Resistance) was remarkable. In Osservanza, a hamlet near Montalcino, all twenty-nine local families participated in a peace rally in 1952, after which they penned a petition with the help of the organizers, explicitly linking their concrete experience during World War II to the increasing danger of another world conflict:

The citizens of Osservanza experienced how much damage the war caused to families and things and how many obstacles it raised to the economic and cultural development of the area. Because of that, they unanimously condemn war

---

But clearly the organizers also realized that a simple traditionalist message would have missed the target.

[66] ASMOS, Fondo PCI, box VIII H1 Partigiani della Pace e Movimenti Pacifisti, folder 1952.

[67] Ibid.

and they subscribed to the peace protocols of Stockholm and Berlin and approve of the protocol of Oslo against biological weapons.[68]

The fact that one of the organizers of this rally was Ilia Coppi, a famous Tuscan Communist leader and one of the few women in Parliament at the time, does not undermine the general impression of genuine popular participation and enthusiasm. For the first time, ordinary peasants were asked their opinion about international issues, and they were eager to respond.

This impression of genuine grass-roots enthusiasm for the peace movement is confirmed by what is arguably the best known and most commonly remembered form of protest organized by Tuscan sharecroppers after World War II, the display of "peace flags" from the tops of haystacks, trees, and agricultural machinery at threshing time. Peasants began to expose them in the summer of 1950, which suggests a strong connection with (and awareness of) national and international events, from the establishment of NATO to the breakout of the Korean War and the first Soviet nuclear test in the summer of 1949, all of which were extensively discussed within the international peace movement launched by the Communist-organized World Congress of the Peace Partisans, held in Paris in April 1949.[69] As we have seen, the peace partisans were extremely active in the Tuscan countryside, where they found an exceptionally warm reception. The establishment of American military bases on Italian soil (including one near Livorno, on the Tuscan coast) also figured prominently among the motivations for the peasants' protest. The literature produced by the peace movement abounded with explicit comparisons between the American presence in Italy and the German occupation during World War II.[70]

Despite the increasing international resonance of the peace movement, however, no single and uncontroversial peace symbol seems to have been available to activists at the turn of the 1950s. Indeed, the specific makeup of the Tuscan flags varied significantly: most of them displayed the word "pace" (peace) at the center and were made of sewed-up multicolor pieces of cloth. Even though they were not necessarily striped and included all kinds of seemingly random colors, the flags were often referred to as "rainbow colored" (iridate). Decades later, former

---

[68] Ibid.

[69] For the international dimension of the Peace Partisans movement and its repercussions in Italy, see Ruggero Giacomini, *I Partigiani della Pace* (Milan: Vangelista, 1984).

[70] See the guidelines for discussion at "peace assemblies" sent out by the national leadership of the Communist Party to its local branches, detailing among many other things crimes supposedly committed by American troops stationed on Italian soil. Archivio ASMOS, Fondo PCI, box VIII H1 Partigiani della Pace, folder 1951.

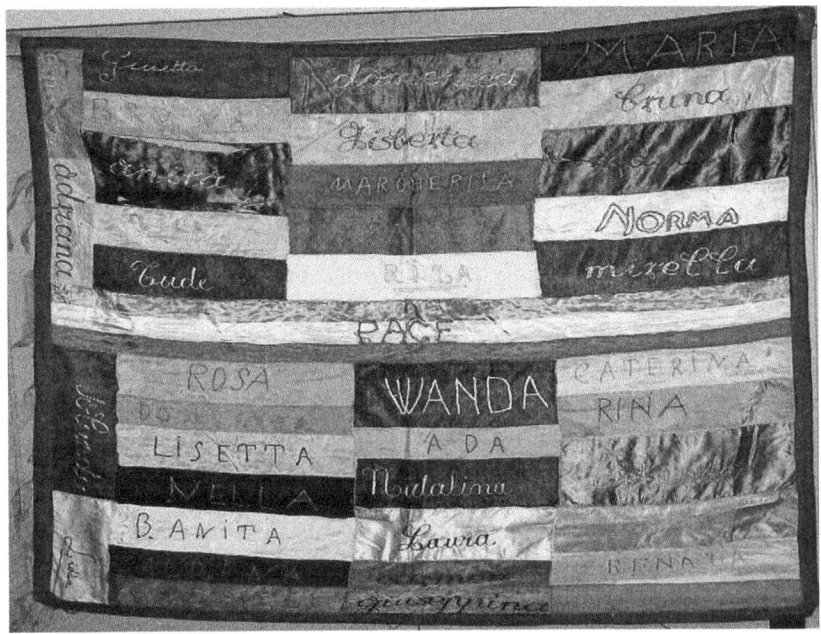

Illustration #11 A peace flag, with the embroidered names of the women who assembled it.

peasant women still had vivid recollections of participating in the sewing of these flags, and some of them recalled how small hammer-and-sickles would be embroidered in some of the cloth pieces. In other cases, women embroidered their names or the names of the farms where they lived (Illustration 11).[71] The timing of the ritual, at the end of the wheat harvest, is easy to explain. This was when sharecroppers from different farms got together to help each other thresh and store the grain. Therefore, this was the year's most important opportunity for collective action. Wheat was also the main subsistence crop for the peasant families and a major source of income for the landlords. Therefore, its harvest

---

[71] See, for example, the following memory from the Val d'Arbia, south of Siena, reported in the form of a dialogue: "'We women got together at night, after dinner, and we sewed the peace flags.' 'Yes, I remember, too!' 'Each of us brought a piece of cloth we had at home – a rectangle, a little triangle – and we embroidered our names in them.' 'We also embroidered some symbols … the hammer and sickle for example.… Then, when we were done, we attached together all these pieces and we made a flag which we would fly at threshing time from the top of the haystack!'" Fiorenza Mannucci, *Un Mi Ci Fa Ripensa'!* (Poggibonsi: Lalli, 2006): 146.

and subsequent division between peasants and landowners signed the most tense moment in the agricultural calendar.

The presence of small, hidden Communist symbols in some of the flags suggests that the idea of sewing up pieces of cloth might also have been an ingenious attempt at circumventing the measures against the display of political symbols, which national or local authorities implemented from time to time and justified as ways to prevent social unrest. If the circumvention of these kinds of bans was indeed the intention of the peasants, it did not work for long. In July 1952 the prefect of Siena explicitly banned the display of multicolor peace flags, and indeed of any flag except the national tricolor, after receiving complaints from landlords and the Carabinieri. To justify this measure, the prefect cited a decree on public safety dating back to 1931, at the height of Mussolini's regime.[72] The reference to the national flag is important. It was not uncommon during the Fascist period to see national flags flying from haystacks at threshing time. As far as I could ascertain, that had been the first time a symbol was used during the wheat harvest. For conservative-minded authorities (as well as for many landlords), to see the national flag replaced with a symbol that defied any traditional understanding of the nation and explicitly gestured toward the political affiliations of the peasants was more than they could bear. Indeed, whereas the landlords viewed the flags as an attempt at their property rights (they were the ones to decide what symbols would be displayed on their farms!), the state authorities viewed them as a challenge to their ambitions of territorial control (Tuscan farms were part of Italy, not some Soviet republic!). These emotionally charged responses produced an extremely strong reaction: the Carabinieri were ordered to respond to every tip by landlords or managers, drive to the farms on motorbikes, seize the flags, and admonish or arrest anyone who put up any resistance. In the summer of 1952 alone, almost six hundred flags were seized, more than five hundred peasants (in most cases the older men in the sharecropping families) were officially reported, and dozens of people were arrested for obstruction and disrespect.[73]

The organized peasant movement saw the prefect's ban and its zealous enforcement by the police as inflammatory provocations. Typically, the police would show up at the farms and order the peasants to take the

---

[72] Archivio di Stato di Siena, Gabinetto di Prefettura, box 219 (1952), folder Ministero Agricoltura e Foreste, subfolder Esposizione Bandiere nell'Aia.

[73] The prefect of Siena kept scrupulous score of every seized flag, compiling tables with data organized by municipality. It is hard not to see this campaign against the flags also as a personal crusade of sorts. The prefect compiled another detailed table in 1953, counting 306 seized flags and 307 peasants reported to the police. See Archivio di Stato di Siena, Gabinetto di Prefettura, box 234 (1953), folder Esposizione Bandiere nell'Aia.

flags down. The peasants would reply with a wall of silence. The youngest or most athletic policeman would then climb up and, whenever possible, grab the flag from the high place where the peasants had put it. At that point, if the police left, another flag would immediately replace the seized one. If even only one of the Carabinieri decided to stay on and preside over the threshing, all work would stop and the head of the peasant household would explain to the police that the threshing would resume only after their departure. In doing so, organized peasants would explicitly refer to article 21 of the post–World War II Constitution, which guaranteed freedom of expression "by writing, speech or other forms of propaganda."[74] The peace flags also measured the distance between the supposedly democratic present and the recent Fascist past: Why were the authorities still justifying their actions on the basis of Fascist decrees? Did fascism really end in 1945? Once again, peasants' actions exposed the contradictions between the recently conquered democratic rights and understandings of the territory based on the alliance between property rights and state control.

Tuscan peasants understood their freedom of expression not only as a right linked to national citizenship but also as a thoroughly local and emplaced prerogative. Therefore, they had no problem juxtaposing their call for peace and international cooperation on the one hand and much more mundane requests on the other. The sharecroppers of Chianciano went on strike to protest the flag seizures, calling the peace flag "the [symbol] which ensures the continuation of fruitful work as well as trust in a future not darkened by military adventures, which damage and compromise the very existence of the nation."[75] But a few lines below, they proceeded to list a litany of requests, from a higher level of mechanization and the end of unjustified evictions to the settlements of the farm accounts and the construction of annexes for the production and storage of manure. For Tuscan peasants there was no contradiction between fighting for freedom of expression and demanding more distance between their bedrooms and animal waste. Indeed, as we have seen, the prefect

---

[74] See, for example, the declaration of the estate committees of the Orcia Valley, penned in Pienza on July 16, 1952: "We declare that these measures are not only provocations but also direct challenges to our republican Constitution … therefore the sharecroppers gathered here are willing to fight to the end, with all their strength, and by all means legally available to them to safeguard and consolidate these rights." Archivio di Stato di Siena, Gabinetto di Prefettura, box 219 (1952), folder Ministero Agricoltura e Foreste, subfolder Esposizione Bandiere nell'Aia.

[75] These strikes, organized in July 1952, had participation rates varying from 50 percent to more than 80 percent in the province of Siena. Archivio di Stato di Siena, Gabinetto di Prefettura, box 219 (1952), folder Ministero Agricoltura e Foreste, subfolder Esposizione Bandiere nell'Aia.

of Siena had issued a decree two years before, ordering the landlords to build separate annexes for the storage of manure, but this injunction had been widely ignored. Why didn't the police drive their motorcycles from farm to farm checking whether these buildings existed and enforcing that decree with the same zeal they used in enforcing the ban on the peace flags? Was there one kind of justice for peasants and a different one for the landowners?[76] These kinds of questions nurtured the very kind of critical political education the authorities wanted to dispel.

The strategies adopted by the peasants to circumvent (and mock) the ban on the peace flags shed additional light on the spatial dimension of the confrontation. The fact that the peace flags created a landscape of defiance, however ephemeral, was not lost on anyone. The police had to rely on tips coming from landlords and managers, who spotted the flags and interpreted them as symbols of their weakening grip on their own territory. The peasants, by contrast, by flying the flags from the tallest spot they could find, claimed and advertised their control over the land. Even external observers could not miss the significance of this territorial game. Enzo Taddei, the reporter sent to the Sienese countryside by the Communist newspaper, *L'Unità*, started many of his articles with an aerial view of what he saw:

From the window of the little hotel one can see the whole valley gently decline and then climb towards the surrounding hills. The town has been asleep for a while, the last steps in the street are no longer audible and the electric lights wait for someone in need to locate his door.... But now I see two boys pass by. They stop, look around, and then one of them climbs up the electric current pole, and when he's on top he fastens a rainbow flag. And the Prefect's order? The crickets chirp, the two boys walk away, and I see them as they turn around to check if the flag is waving.[77]

In this passage Taddei describes one of the strategies adopted by peasants to respond to what they perceived as unacceptable provocations. If the authorities and the landlords did not want to see the peace flags fly on the farms, they surely would have loved to see them decorate trees and utility poles along public streets. Often peasants combined these displays with banners targeting specific landowners or managers by name, or bearing slogans against the war, the government, and the police.

The authorities reacted to these acts of defiance with characteristic zeal. The peak of absurdity was reached when a particularly athletic peasant

---

[76] The Communist press had a field day exposing these contradictions. See "Le Due Ordinanze del Prefetto di Siena," *L'Unità*, local edition, July 14, 1952.

[77] "Una Quercia con la Bandiera Iridata Abbattuta per Ordine del Maresciallo," *L'Unità*, July 27, 1952.

fastened a flag to the top branch of a huge oak tree by the road leading from Montalcino to Buonconvento.[78] Someone called the Carabinieri, and when they showed up several of them took turns trying to reach the flag, to no avail. But the officer in charge of the police detail was not to be mocked by some peasants. He called a local forest guard and had the tree felled right there and then, before an astonished crowd. Even the prefect seems to have been puzzled by this action, and he penned a big question mark next to the report dutifully filed by the police. Upon the prefect's request for clarifications, the police officer replied that the owner of the land where the tree stood had given him permission. Property rights, if not common sense, had been respected! The authorities' zeal had an almost religious quality. The peace flags were not simply an in-your-face reminder of the peasants' unseemly political affiliations. They desecrated the landscape around them and had to be removed, by all means necessary, to restore the natural order. If that was the case, a police officer's lack of restraint could be excused.[79]

If some peasants defied the ban by bringing the peace flags from the farms to public spaces, others brought them closer to their bodies, wearing them. On July 23, 1952, the Carabinieri paid a visit to a farm near Montepulciano and seized the flag that was flying from the haystack. In response, as soon as the police left, the peasants came up with a most ingenious way of expressing their views: each of them attached a stripe of cloth to their hat, so that, when they stood in a row, the viewer could see that they formed a living peace flag – a collective performance of political theater. On another occasion, on a farm in Val di Chiana, a peasant responded to the flag seizure by sporting a brightly colored woman's scarf. Even though it was red with yellow polka dots, its subversive qualities could not go undetected. In both cases the Carabinieri were summoned back, presumably by the landlord or farm manager, and the peasants, probably somewhat amused, witnessed the extremes to which the authorities were willing to go. The cloth stripes and the dotted scarf were dutifully seized.

In the confrontation over the peace flags, many of the processes I have been discussing come together and become instantiated as symbolically powerful actions. By flying these controversial symbols, thousands of Tuscan peasants intended to comment on the ongoing conflicts over different understandings of ownership and territory; they demonstrated

---

[78] This particular flag is described as red in the documents of the authorities and as a multicolor peace flag in the Communist press. *L'Unità* ran a front-page article on the episode in its national edition (see preceding text).

[79] I should say at this point that the Carabinieri are the classic butt of jokes all over Italy, much the same way as Poles used to be in the United States.

their awareness of the links between spatial and temporal moves; and they illustrated the copresence of local, national, and global struggles for justice and democratic self-rule. The extreme reaction of the authorities testifies to the symbolic dimension of the confrontation and to their determination to regain control over the land by normalizing it as part of the "national" territory. And yet, despite all the clamor and passion of these events, none of the visions articulated by the contenders carried the day. Less than a decade later, the peace flags were already being framed and exposed in museums and political headquarters, while the police barely even bothered to control a territory the formerly riotous peasants were emptying in droves, leaving behind a peace and quiet that sounded like nobody's victory.

In the wake of the war, the Tuscan countryside no longer appeared as a silent and marginal space, as it had been for centuries before 1900, or an area to be paternalistically managed from above, as had been the case under fascism. Rather, after 1945 rural Tuscany seemed to matter on its own terms for the first time in its long history, as a major front in the Cold War that was being fought at the national and international levels. By mobilizing around the organizations of the Communist Party, rural Tuscans tried to join the whirlwind of modernity on their own terms, and they did so as peasants. For the first time, national political forces did not descend on the land with hegemonic goals, but organically integrated with local societies, letting a new political class deeply rooted in the territory emerge from within the peasants themselves. For the first time, peasants and sons (sometimes daughters) of peasants became mayors and local administrators of towns across the region. Whatever else they might have been standing for, the Communists (and, to a lesser extent, the Socialists) seemed to be willing to let the peasants speak for themselves, and in front of an audience that crossed national and even international boundaries. In the face of the centralization and hierarchical procedures of the Communist Party, this perception of spontaneous autonomy and organic integration between political and civil society should be taken with a grain of salt; but as a myth, it proved resilient and inspiring at the local level. If myths of harmony and class collaboration had sentenced Tuscan peasants to silence and irrelevance for centuries, now struggle – the shouted, sweated, unashamedly performed rituals of class insubordination – would finally force the powers that be to listen and realize that ordinary peasants could no longer be ignored.

The peasants' hopes for a radically egalitarian transformation of the Tuscan countryside went unfulfilled. This is also the story of a social defeat, albeit punctuated with major accomplishments. This pervasive sense of defeat explains why, in spite of many academic studies of the peasants' struggles, Tuscans have found it hard to keep the memory of these events alive. Followed by the long agony of sharecropping and the mass exodus from the countryside, the struggles of the late 1940s and early 1950s could not but be regarded as a dead end, however heroic. Tuscan peasants, like so many other actors across the world, could only "join history" by rebelling against its tide. For a while at least, they refused to die and imagined implausible but powerfully motivating futures. In that sense, their legacy lives on. Their rebellion, albeit unsuccessful, still haunts the Tuscan hills. It is also thanks to that season of struggles that Tuscany can today be imagined as the site of alternative modernities. The radical sharecroppers' imagined futures did not quite materialize, but their sons and daughters, now empowered by the democratic process, kept imagining. And they kept negotiating their territories and their futures.

3   Left Behind: The Rural Exodus (1957–1970)

Within a couple of decades, the Tuscan peasantry organized and rebelled as a class, to then all but vanish from the land. Tuscan agriculture shed two-thirds of its workforce from the early 1950s to the early 1970s. In the province of Siena, the number of sharecropping families was cut in half between 1951 and 1964, when the sharecropping population was approximately one-third of what it had been at the beginning of the previous decade.[1] This "exodus" was led by young people. In 1951, 22 percent of the Tuscan agricultural workforce was younger than thirty, as opposed to only 9 percent twenty years later.[2] In the same period, agricultural machines increased ninefold in terms of units and eleven-fold in terms of horsepower. The quantity of electricity used in Sienese agriculture more than quadrupled from 1951 to 1966; the consumption of diesel fuel increased sevenfold; and the use of nitrogen-based fertilizers doubled.[3] As the world of the peasantry died, Tuscan agriculture seemed to be joining the modern era.

In historical time, modernity must begin with a rupture, and people of all stripes partook of this narrative and looked back to a dying civilization that, in retrospect, appeared frozen in time. Marquise Maria Bianca de Larderel-Viviani della Robbia was a cultivated and socially active woman who, like Iris Origo, spent much of the interwar period trying to modernize agricultural techniques on her estate in the Florentine Chianti. She also left us a memoir, originally published in 1937 and updated twenty years later. In the first section of the memoir the Marquise depicts her peasants as children trapped in their age-old mores: "It is difficult to persuade the peasants who, closed off in their age-old stubbornness, are now like uncertain children that take their first steps in fear they could fall....

---

[1] ACdLSi, Confederale, Box IX a.3 Convegni Sviluppo Economico, folder Dati Statistici.
[2] Ibid.
[3] Elaboration from the following two sources: *Il Prodotto Netto dell'Agricoltura negli Anni 1951–1958* (Siena: Camera di Commercio di Siena, 1959); and *Il Prodotto Netto dell'Agricoltura nella Provincia di Siena negli Anni 1959–1966* (Siena: Camera di Commercio di Siena, 1969).

All is static in the life of the peasant and has the solemnity of immutable things. He is the man of the earth and the earth never changes."[4] The second part of the memoir, written in the mid-1950s, depicts quite a different scenario. Viviani della Robbia could not hide her dismay at the younger generation of peasants, who replaced the alleged passivity of their parents with overt insubordination, only to then leave the countryside behind: "The young men aspire to become workmen, a grade which seems higher than farming to them and to their sweethearts. Therefore they rent a room in the village and work in the city as day laborers, since they are not capable of any sort of work other than digging in the field, which is all they know."[5] The peasants' recalcitrance had remained the same, but now, puzzlingly, it pointed to the opposite direction, to an uncertain future rather than to the "traditional" past.

This contrast traveled widely. Stuart Hood, a Scottish officer, was taken prisoner in World War II. After being released in the wake of the armistice in September 1943, he spent the next several months in central Tuscany fighting alongside the partisans against the occupying German troops and their Italian collaborators. Like many other insurgents, he had to rely on the support of the local peasants for long periods. In the early 1960s, Hood, now a left-wing activist, a BBC producer, a novelist, and a translator from the Italian, published a memoir that recounted his wartime experiences. Again, in his recollections, a rupture separates tradition from modernity:

[During the war] I was caught by a regression in time. Living with the peasants I saw the last upsurge of peasant life and of an ancient civilization – la civiltà contadinesca. The skills I learned, the crafts I watched, had not changed since Ambrogio Lorenzetti in the fourteenth century painted his great murals in the Town Hall of Sienna.... Today [in the 1960s] the brides no longer bring a dowry of chestnut trees. The girls no longer wear the coarse home-spun stockings. The women no longer fan the charcoal stoves. They have methane gas and are the better for it. The young men cavort with their motor-scooters and the girls sit side-saddle, flouncing their nylon petticoats. I am glad – and glad that I saw what went before.[6]

Hood is here more sanguine and far less paternalistic than Viviani della Robbia, but the contrast between an immutable past and an eventful present is just as stark.

The Resistance and the decade of social strife that followed it constituted a first break from tradition, but it was the exodus from the farms that

[4] Maria Bianca Viviani Della Robbia, *Fattoria nel Chianti* (Florence: Le Monnier, 1993): 26–29. The first edition was published in 1957
[5] Ibid.: 161.
[6] S. Hood, *Pebbles from My Skull* (London: Hutchinson, 1963): 149.

was perceived to usher in a new era. The exodus seemed simultaneously inevitable and perplexing. Observers could not agree on whether Tuscan peasants were being expelled, lured, duped, liberated, or a combination of all those and more. Central Tuscany was hardly the first region in Europe to "transition" to industrial society. The bitter and largely unresolved conflicts that had followed the end of the war were routinely read as signs of coming radical transformations, and it was hard to imagine how the modernization of Tuscan agriculture, which everyone desired, could have been achieved without a wide-ranging process of consolidation, leading to the disappearance of the smaller and less efficient farms. And yet, despite these commonly debated considerations, observers from many different social and political backgrounds spoke and acted as if the exodus was in some way an unexpected crisis. The very language used to describe the phenomenon all over Italy (*esodo, abbandono, emorragia*, and so on) testifies to this sentiment. Many mobilized to stop the outflow of people, or at least counter its consequences. The widely shared temporal narrative of "transition" confronted the desire of going against the grain of history, to oppose the momentum of processes that seemed out of control.

The goal of this chapter is to examine the exodus from the vantage point of the people and places that were "left behind" in the countryside. Rural Tuscans had no choice but to confront the juggernaut of history, trying to make sense of rapid change and shape its features. The temporal narrative of transition coexisted with many spatial perceptions that challenged its determinism and sense of inevitability. By attending equally to senses of time and place, this chapter will examine what happened to the Tuscan rural landscape when the social class that had shaped it and experienced it for generations began to leave en masse. As Don Mitchell has argued, landscape is always in transition, always unstable, and "yet landscape is also a totality. That is, powerful actors ... are continually trying to represent the landscape as a fixed, total, and naturalized entity – as a unitary thing."[7] I intend to show that relatively powerless actors continually try to make sense of their surroundings as well, in the face of rapid change, and they also long for a sense of coherence and totality. As the exodus unfolded, Tuscans of all social classes were losing control over the shape and destiny of the territory they inhabited. A sense of spatial unity and totality is also the projection of a society coherent enough to read itself in space. But this sense of totality was as elusive as ever in postwar Tuscany. The rural landscape was losing legibility as Tuscans were achieving unprecedented levels of prosperity and mobility.

[7] D. Mitchell, *The Lie of the Land* (Minneapolis: Minnesota University Press, 1996), 30.

The old relationships of otherness and familiarity that had linked town and country were no more, but no one seemed able to anticipate what the future might hold.

In the following pages I will focus on two processes that demonstrate how rural Tuscans of different classes and backgrounds perceived and tried to shape their territory in the face of the exodus. First, I will look at the crisis of mixed agriculture (agricoltura promiscua) and its replacement with specialized and highly capitalized cultivations. Tuscan vineyards may now appear as a natural and typical trait of the landscape, but their establishment in the 1960s and 1970s signaled the irreversibility of the exodus, the defeat of the peasant movement, and the triumph of what many understood as capitalist restructuring. This process of restructuring relied primarily on public funds, which greatly exacerbated its problematic character in the eyes of a generation of left-wing Tuscans. Second, I will examine the politics of settlement and show how rural Tuscans of different social and political backgrounds, far from taking the exodus for granted, tried to counter it through a variety of schemes and strategies. Rural settlement became an arena of struggle and the site where widely different imaginings confronted each other. In both these cases, I will propose historical analyses attentive to the politics of space, resisting the hindsight perspective inherent in narratives of transition.

Queen Vine: The Exodus and the Rise of Vine Monocropping in the Chianti

The collapse of sharecropping in central Italy did not take place directly in the wake of (and on account of) the bitter class struggle that had pitted peasants against landowners in the decade after the war. The struggles increased the cost of immobility for the landlords and their political patrons, creating a climate first of anticipation and later of resentment. But Italian sharecroppers did not conquer the land through collective action or even political pressure. By and large, the landlords adopted a stalling strategy, waiting for social tensions to subside and peasant organizational unity to fissure. As a consequence, Tuscany's starkly dualistic structure of property survived the rural exodus and the demise of the sharecropping economy. In 1970, less than 2 percent of the farms had an extension of more than fifty hectares (approximately 125 acres), but made up 35 percent of the land, while 77 percent of Tuscan farms had an extension of less than five hectares but made up only 19 percent of the land. In some provinces this dualism between very small and large landholdings was much starker. In the province of Siena, estates with more than 50 hectares made up 8 percent of the total number of farms but occupied 69 percent of the cultivated territory, while two-thirds of farms were smaller than 5 hectares but occupied less than 5 percent of the agricultural land.[8]

This enduring polarization between very small and large properties was accompanied by profound transformations in the ways farms were run. As sharecropping retreated, two novel forms of agricultural management expanded. By the early 1970s, more than half of the farms were directly cultivated by their owners, with or without family collaborators. This land tenure form, almost nonexistent in much of central Tuscany until the 1950s, had become the rule for small-scale farms, which had traditionally been run under the sharecropping system. Many of the large-scale estates, by contrast, were now cultivated by wage laborers, often with the extensive use of machinery and artificial fertilizers. These new "capitalist" enterprises were particularly common in the most productive areas, that is, in the few plains and in the low-elevation hills where market-oriented agriculture was potentially profitable.

This restructuring, accompanied by depopulation, profoundly changed land use patterns and made them difficult to read. The mixed cultivation of grassy and woody plants, placed in orderly rows and intermittent patches, typical of hillside sharecropping agriculture, relied on relatively high human density and extensive care, not only for the plants themselves but also for the intricate systems of irrigation and drainage that made hillside agriculture possible before extensive mechanization. Starting in the early 1950s, farms were abandoned in a piecemeal fashion, with the visually striking consequence that one patch of territory would show the signs of abandonment while another next to it retained its traditional features. In the meantime, in select portions of the territory, specialized and highly capitalized vineyards began to replace mixed cultivations. In the province of Siena, vine monocropping covered 1,600 hectares in 1929, vis-à-vis 74,000 hectares of mixed cultivations with vines. Forty years later, monocropping had more than doubled its area to 3,700 hectares and mixed cultivations had declined to 46,000 hectares. But even more revealing is that the yield of wine per hectare in mixed cultivations had decreased from 11,200 liters in 1929 to 7,800 liters forty years later, indicating that many of these old vineyards were actually barely tended to.[9]

---

[8] According to census data, medium-size farms in the province of Siena occupied 43.6 percent of agricultural land in 1960 and 21.3 percent in 1970.

[9] These data have been elaborated from those included in "Situazione Attuale e Prospettive della Viticoltura Senese," *Agricoltura Senese* 58 (August 1969): 1–3. This was the journal of the Provincial Inspecting Agency for Agriculture (Ispettorato Provinciale dell'Agricoltura). Official data are less than useful in this case. The national bureau of

The spread of specialized vineyards created a landscape whose monotony felt utterly novel and puzzling to the remaining peasants. In the last page of his 2002 unpublished memoir, former sharecropper Franco Guarducci, born in the early 1930s in the Florentine section of the Chianti, is still trying to make sense of the remarkable recent changes experienced by his native region:

> In our countryside, where I still live, so many changes have taken place. The rural houses, many of which were once barely standing and where the peasants had to share their living space with mice, after being abandoned for a long time, are now villas for the foreigners. They are all restored. The stink of the stables is gone and amazing halls have replaced them. But the animals have disappeared as well, as has the manure that was taken to the fields to fertilize them and retain the rain, which now washes right away. The environment has changed and many birds no longer nest here.... But there are so many vineyards that I am reminded of that prophecy attributed to Brandano, the Sienese hermit from the sixteenth century, who responded to someone asking him: "When will the wine cost dear?" by saying "When the Chianti will be covered with vineyards!"[10]

Guarducci's attention moves from the country houses, once centers of family life and rural settlement, to the disappeared domestic animals and the increasingly rare wild ones, to then focus on the one species that now dominates Chianti's landscape – the seemingly omnipresent vine. But even this element of continuity with the past is deceptive. For mysterious reasons, which belie the landscape and seem to fulfill an ancient apocalyptic prophecy, wine, once cheap, is now obscenely expensive.

The history of the Chianti, now one of Tuscany's most iconic areas, is inextricably linked to the history of its most celebrated (and eponymous) product, which became almost a synonym for Italian wine around the world. But as we have seen in Chapter 1, even more than to vines and wine, Chianti's recent history is linked to the phylloxera aphid. The Chianti kept feeling the brunt of the phylloxera infestation during and after World War II, when the infestation made all the more visible a social and political crisis that had been decades in the making. In these years,

---

statistics (ISTAT) directed surveyors working on the first agricultural census in 1960–61 to fit land uses in a few categories, attributing land plots to the most valuable crop grown on them, thereby completely missing the changes taking place in much of central Italy, where mixed cultivations were traditionally the rule. ISTAT changed the surveying categories for the third agricultural census of 1982, when mixed cultivations were duly recorded. But each cultivation on any plot of land was to be recorded separately. So, for instance, if a company grew wheat and vines on a plot of land, the owner and the surveyor were to estimate how much of the land was devoted to each crop. In practice, mixed cultivations were recorded as if they were not mixed at all!

[10] Franco Guarducci, *Memorie di un Contadino Smesso*, Archivio Diaristico Nazionale, Pieve S. Stefano, 29.

the infestation coincided with (and was made more serious by) the peasants' attack on the sharecropping economy, to which the landlords (and the conservative national government) responded by suspending extensive investments until the early 1960s, when the peasants' mass exodus had blunted the edge of the social crisis. The effects of this socio-natural storm were devastating in all of central Italy, but nowhere were such effects more evident than in the Chianti region, where wine could easily make up more than half of the cash revenue of sharecropping families.

What Guarducci registered in his memoir was, above all, the shift from a subsistence- and rent-based economy (and landscape) to a market-oriented one. Although winemaking had been a central activity in the Chianti for centuries, vines were cultivated in rows interspersed with grassy crops (above all, rotations of cereals and fodder crops) as well as fruit and olive trees, all of which provided for the family's subsistence. This type of mixed cultivation had been praised for centuries. It was believed to have slowed down the spread of phylloxera. The rows of vines could demarcate different fields, thereby facilitating rotations. More generally, the diversity of cultivations made use of steep terrains and therefore hindered erosion. The specialized vineyards that Guarducci saw everywhere around him, by contrast, were very rare in the Chianti, as elsewhere in Tuscany, until well into the 1960s. For at least a decade, it remained unclear (and widely debated) which type of cultivation and landscape should prevail.

In order to understand how vine monocropping gained the upper hand, we need to start with the historical narrative prevalent in the region in the wake of World War II – a narrative in which winemaking took center stage. In the late 1940s, most inhabitants of the Chianti believed themselves to be living in a period of dire economic crisis, which they contrasted with a bygone economic golden age. Chianti's population had doubled between the mid-eighteenth century and Italy's unification in 1861, when it was approximately fifty-seven thousand. It had then doubled again by the late 1930s, before starting its seemingly unstoppable decline after the end of World War II.[11] The Sienese portion of the Chianti, corresponding to the municipalities of Gaiole, Radda, and Castellina, lost almost 40 percent of its population from 1951 to 1968. Here the number of sharecropping families decreased from one thousand and four hundred to three hundred, a fivefold decline in less than two decades.[12] At least in the minds

[11] Romolo Camaiti, *La Popolazione e la Realtà Statistico-Economica del Chianti* (Milan: Giuffré, 1965): 24. By Chianti, Camaiti includes the area of Chianti Classico plus San Casciano, Poggibonsi, and Castelnuovo Berardenga.

[12] "Le Proposte dei Comunisti per lo Sviluppo Economico del Chianti," ASMOS, PCI, box X D 1 Comitato di Coordinamento del Chianti, folder 1969.

of the locals, there was a strong correlation between demographic change and wine production. It looked like the two processes had been linked for centuries in a positive direction, as they were now spiraling down together. Even the Communist leaders of the peasant movement shared in this narrative of rise and fall, although it sat so uneasily with their hostility to traditional sharecropping, which lay at the basis of the social order throughout this supposedly ascendant period.

Pleas for the "rebirth" of the Chianti were already commonplace a few years after Liberation. In 1949 the Communist mayor of Radda, Dino Ciani, opened a town hall meeting in Gaiole by recounting data the audience knew all too well. Since the mid-1920s, the production of wine had decreased by almost 80 percent in the three municipalities of the Sienese Chianti (Radda, Castellina, and Gaiole); pig rearing for industrial use had all but disappeared; and the revenue obtained from the woods had decreased by 90 percent. But it would have been a mistake to attribute this collapse mainly to the consequences of the phylloxera infestation: the worst "phylloxera" (by then a synonym for scourge) had been the practice of selling ordinary wine for Chianti wine in the 1920s and early 1930s, when production boomed and traders proliferated. Then these traders drove each other out of business through shady practices, and only one (the consortium headed by Baron Ricasoli) remained. The wage of excessive competition was the current dearth of technical innovation and investments. What to do? Touting the plan of the leftist union, the mayor depicted a scenario of astounding ambition. Some 12 million vines should be planted in mixed cultivations over four years, giving work to the one thousand and two hundred sharecropping families and four hundred day-laborers living in the area. The landowners should be forced to foot the bill, with substantial state contributions. At the same time, sharecropping contracts should be replaced with perpetual leases (*enfiteusi*), so that the peasants would have a real incentive to improve the land. Ricasoli's commercial monopoly should be broken and all producers in the area should be allowed to sell their wine, while prosecuting frauds and making sure that only wine from the Chianti region could bear that name.[13]

What is most striking about this plan is its mixture of commitment to radical reform and reluctance to abandon tradition. According to Ciani, millions of vines needed to be planted and modern brand protection measures introduced, but by following the traditional patterns of mixed cultivation and by relying on the labor of the sharecropping families

---

[13] ACdLSi, Confederale, Zona IV a. 1 (1949–1953), Chianti, Relazione sulla Crisi Agricola del Chianti nella Conferenza Economica per la Rinascita del Chianti, held in Gaiole on November 20, 1949.

present in the territory. Even more telling is his reference to the forest economy, which in the Chianti (and especially in its Sienese portion) meant, above all, free-ranging pig (and to a lesser extent sheep) pasturing in the oak woods that covered almost half of the territory. This form of animal farming was, after winemaking, an important source of cash revenue for the sharecropping families. As if the phylloxera had not been enough of a scourge, the oak forests were under attack by hordes of oak processionaries, skin-irritating caterpillars that fed on the leaves nightly for weeks on end before turning into moths. Again, this was not a new threat, but the extremely tense social and political climate of the postwar years made old problems much more urgent and intractable. For roughly a decade after Liberation, the restoration of the vineyards and of the woods was understood to be in service of the preservation of the local population on the farms, an absolute priority for the local leftist leaders in the late 1940s and early 1950s. Restoring Chianti's glory meant, above all, holding on to its declining population.

While leftist leaders held on to the idea that the exodus could be stopped by recapitalizing traditional agriculture, albeit under different tenure forms, Chianti's most forward-looking landlords reckoned that specialization of land by function was the only way out of the crisis, and that such specialization required the drastic decline of the rural population, even though this condition was rarely spelled out. A truly modernized agriculture could not support tens of thousands of hungry peasants. Baron Ricasoli, who owned 40 percent of the agricultural land in the municipality of Gaiole,[14] seems to have started planning for the inevitable depopulation very early. Soon after Liberation, he created an outrage by ordering the thinning out of the oak forests on his estate, a move he justified as necessary to combat the caterpillar infestation.[15] Many of his sharecroppers, however, believed that this was blatant evidence of his intention to make pig rearing even harder, thereby forcing them out of their farms. The Baron duly started a process of reforestation, but planting more oak trees made no sense to him. Instead, following the forestry recommendations of the day, he chose conifers. He planted thousands

---

[14] Bettino Ricasoli (1922–2009) was elected mayor of Gaiole in 1951, becoming the only Christian Democratic mayor in the Chianti region. He would remain in charge of the city for the rest of the decade. Some 40 percent of Gaiole's population was directly or indirectly employed by the Ricasoli family, and the leftists never tired of pointing out that only coercion and fear of reprisals explained the town's political anomaly.

[15] "Solo Promesse Ha Fatto a Gaiole il Sindaco D.C. Barone Ricasoli," *L'Unità*, April 17, 1954. In this article, published in the communist daily, appears a photograph of sparsely treed woods surrounding Gaiole, with a caption saying "All that is left are a few little plants still incapable of producing enough fruits for pig rearing, not even at the level needed to complement the activities of the peasant families."

of pine trees, which would grow quickly and could be cut for timber (he also owned a sawmill). But where were these trees to be planted? If specialization was to carry the day, these trees should be planted in plots not suitable to vine growing, no matter their current use. And thus Ricasoli's sharecropper Silvio Mattonesi, who lived on the Campo alla Badia farm, had to make sense of why his landlord would start planting four thousand pine tree saplings around the estate, even in the ditches Mattonesi had dug by hand in the hope that Ricasoli would plant two thousand vines. Major investments in the vineyards, the Baron must have thought, could wait for more propitious times. For peasants like Mattonesi, the writing was on the wall.[16]

For approximately a decade, the rationalization strategies implemented by the largest landlords were actively resisted by the peasants' leftist organizers, whose modernization visions for the Chianti region relied on the expansion of traditional patterns of cultivation to stem the rapidly escalating flight from the farms. After all, traditional patterns, aided by a degree of mechanization, seemed to promise the only kind of rural modernization that would not make peasants redundant. In a conference held in Radda in 1954, Walter Madrucci, the councilor in charge of public works for the province of Siena, opened his speech by noting how "Today ... the physiognomy of the Chianti appears harsh: The character of the landscape, with its barren and fruitless features, conveys immediately a sensation of harshness and hardness that reminds of the grim and difficult lives workers lead here."[17] This depressingly self-reinforcing resonance between people and landscape, so distant from contemporary perceptions of eternal calm and harmony, could be broken by planting vines and oak trees and restoring rural houses, but more extensive infrastructures were necessary as well. Roads were key to improving the population's standard of living, and the province of Siena had only twenty-six kilometers of paved roads! Virgilio Lazzeroni, president of the provincial government, reassured the audience that the National Institute for Labor Accident Insurance (INAIL) had issued the province a 400-million-lire loan for road paving and construction. The president would also try his best to make the toll road (*autostrada*) connecting Milan to Rome pass through the Chianti. The Milan-Rome autostrada ended up bypassing

---

[16] Ignazio Salemi, "Perché a Siena i Mezzadri Abbandonano la Terra," *Federmezzadri* 62 (December 1954): 8–9. One can only imagine the bewilderment felt by Ricasoli's sharecroppers at seeing some (for them useful) woods being thinned out and others (to them useless) come up almost overnight.

[17] ACdLSi, Confederale, Zona IV a. 1 (1949–1953), Chianti, Convegno per lo Studio dei Problemi del Chianti, proceedings of the conference held in Radda on April 12, 1953.

the Chianti hills entirely, but within a decade hundreds of miles of roads had been covered with asphalt.

The paving of the roads, and even the construction of a secondary two-lane highway (*superstrada*) between Florence and Siena around 1960, did nothing to stem the rural exodus. Instead, it became easier for the members of many sharecropping families to commute to jobs in the nearby towns.[18] By the time of this revolution in mobility, most observers had more or less reluctantly accepted the irreversibility of the exodus. Like in other parts of rural Tuscany, the coup de grace to the ailing sharecropping economy, and the turning point in many people's perception of rural Tuscany's demographic destiny, arrived in February 1956. At the beginning of the month, a high-pressure system stationed between northern Russia and Scandinavia started piloting extremely cold continental air toward central and southern Europe. The cold blast went on for three weeks, causing heavy snowfalls and double-digit negative nighttime temperatures in central Tuscany, killing or severely damaging the majority of the region's olive trees. In the Sienese Chianti there were more than 725,000 olive trees when the big freeze of 1956 struck, cultivated in association with other plants over an area of almost 7,000 hectares. As late as 1968, the area of olive tree cultivation had only rebounded to less than 4,700 hectares, 700 of which were in newly established specialized groves, and the number of trees had declined to less than half a million.[19] After the blows suffered by vine growing and pig rearing, olive oil production was the last standing pillar of traditional Tuscan agriculture. Now that had fallen, too.

The few years following the 1956 cold spell saw the ascendancy of a novel awareness of depopulation's ineluctability in the Chianti. What many moderate and conservative social scientists had been implying for years, that the "rebirth" of the area had to build on the exodus rather than on its reversal, made inroads into the worldview of the leftists as well. And whereas the latter had envisaged comprehensive plans in which vine growing and winemaking were but one of the activities to be revitalized, albeit the most important, now even the Marxists came to understand

[18] Archivio della CGIL Toscana, Fondo Federterra, Box 206 Chianti, Folder Convegno sull'Ipotesi di Sviluppo Agroeconomico del Chianti. By the 1960s, this was especially true of the Florentine Chianti, where at least a third of the population that was not employed in agriculture commuted north to Florence and south to Poggibonsi. Data in the pamphlet Comitato per lo Sviluppo Economico del Comprensorio del Chianti Fiorentino, *Dati Sommari sulla Popolazione e le Attivita' Economiche*, S. Casciano, November 18, 1967.

[19] Ente Autonomo per la Bonifica, l'Irrigazione e la Valorizzazione Fondiaria nelle Provincie di Arezzo, Siena, Perugia e Terni, *Contributo per lo Sviluppo dell'Agricoltura del Chianti Senese* (Arezzo: Amminitrazione Provinciale, 1971): 125.

that the rationalization of wine production was the single key to the future, and that such rationalization implied the departure of thousands from the farms and a radical change in land use. Representative of the moderates' opinions was a 1957 report by agricultural economist Enzo Giorgi. He began by coming to terms with the inevitability of the exodus, at least in the more peripheral areas: "The grants and public interventions implemented to contain the exodus from the mountains ... would only constitute costly and useless deferrals of evolutionary or degenerative processes that are natural – that is, linked to an inevitable structural transformation."[20] In making a case for the urgency of state intervention, Giorgi proceeded to argue that public funds should focus on the reconstruction of the vineyards, a process that in the hilly and rocky terrain of the Chianti was more than twice as expensive as in the plains. Revealingly, he made a direct plea that the public investments in the vineyards be given priority over the restoration of the peasants' houses, for wine and wine alone was the area's source of wealth. To allay possible objections, he reminded his audience that the legislative framework for this kind of intervention was already in place: all that was needed was some retooling of the Fascist legislation on land reclamation.[21]

These requests were echoed by the most visible and influential members of local society. Baron Ricasoli himself, as mayor of Gaiole (the only non-Communist town leader in the area), wrote to the prefect of Siena in April 1956 trying to convey the urgency of the situation in the wake of the cold blast.[22] Ricasoli noted that the Chianti was plagued by the gap between the productivity of its land, which was extremely low, and the potentially excellent quality of its typical products, above all wine and olive oil. This situation would militate in favor of "the intensification of the specialized cultivation of vines and olive trees," but none of that had been happening because of the staggeringly high costs of the required restructuring work and the limited profits to be made in the wine trade due to unfair competition from other areas. The destruction of the olive trees, which Ricasoli expected to reduce the next olive harvest by at least 80 percent, would now take the people of the Chianti over the edge.

---

[20] Enzo Giorgi, "Aspetti Particolari dell'Economia Vitinicola Chiantigiana," in *Atti del Convegno Tecnico ed Economico per la Difesa dell'Agricoltura del Chianti* (Radda, Amministrazione Comunale, 1957): 56.

[21] The Fascist-era legislation, as we have seen, only promised state contributions of one-third of the costs of agricultural improvements. But given the extremely high costs associated with vineyard reimplantation in the Chianti region, Giorgi maintained that state contributions should be raised to 50 percent.

[22] Archivio di Stato di Siena, Gabinetto Prefettura, box 323, 1957, folder Ministero dell'Agricoltura e Foreste, subfolder Crisi Economica nel Settore Agricolo Zona del Chianti. Report dated April 18, 1956.

The main advantage associated with olive oil resided in the fact that its production costs were a fraction of those incurred in winemaking, and therefore in recent years, given the pitiful state of the vineyards, oil could make up as much as two-thirds of the profits of a typical Chianti estate. What could be the solution? The state must help local producers rationalize and protect wine production more than ever before, through loans and grants (to be obtained through the reclamation legislation), and through those legislative measures which farmers had been demanding for a generation – above all, the institution of the denomination of origin (*denominazione d'origine*) on the French model. In other words, the most suitable areas would be covered with vineyards, and the profits associated with winemaking could be integrated with an equally rationalized cultivation of olive trees.

Before the 1956 freeze, leftist social scientists rejected outright the idea of resurrecting the old Fascist legislation regarding "integral reclamation." The main reason for their opposition was that that type of public intervention strengthened the class structure of the target area, further empowering the largest and best-connected landlords. Leftist economist Reginaldo Cianferoni, for example, remarked in 1954 that the costs of reconstruction in the Chianti region were so high that the public grants requested through the reclamation legislation would approximate the market value of the farms themselves.[23] Much easier and less costly, Cianferoni argued, was to rely on the work of the sharecropping families in exchange for their access to absolute residential and employment security, through some kind of perpetual lease facilitated by state funds and regulation. But these reforms could not but challenge deeply entrenched class privileges and the existing structure of property, especially considering that large estates (those with more than one hundred hectares) occupied two-thirds of the Chianti's agricultural area. Cianferoni maintained that protection of the Chianti brand and its wine quality were important, too, but only if those provisions did not detract from the necessity of radical changes.

This orthodox position, repeated countless times in meetings and rallies in the decade after Liberation, began to fall apart in the face of the massive exodus of the late 1950s. Already by 1960, even the most vocal Communist leaders acknowledged the inevitability of specialization and rationalization based on the reconstruction of the vineyards. The mayor of San Casciano, Remo Ciapetti, famous through the

---

[23] Archivio della CGIL Toscana, Fondo Federterra, box 206 Chianti, folder Primo Convegno del Chianti Fiorentino, Greve, October 30, 1955. Cianferoni had published the paper he delivered at this conference the previous year.

Chianti for his rhetorical flair and radicalism, welcomed a meeting of technical experts to his town by arguing that "the Chianti region is a seriously sick patient.... We need to perform surgery on it, plunging the scalpel into its structures, into its outdated social relations, such as the sharecropping contract." But then he proceeded to embrace two notions that had been anathema to the Left just a few years before. First, he maintained that the Chianti should become an area of reclamation, even though he did not mention the Fascist-era legislation; and second, he argued that from a technical point of view the restructuring should "avoid the perseverance of mixed cultivations, which does not solve but rather exacerbates the crisis."[24]

The report presented at the meeting by agronomists Marcello Cellerini and Giorgio Marchetti made it clear that "the specialized vineyard will have to become predominant in the process of intensification of tree cultivation, followed by specialized olive groves as recommended by the new cultivation criteria of modern plant technology."[25] The Chianti would have to be divided into three areas, according to elevation. Above 600 meters of altitude, forests should prevail; between 500 and 600 meters of altitude, a mix of forests and pastures for extensive animal husbandry should be preferable; below 500 meters of altitude (corresponding to approximately three-quarters of the region), irrigation should be intensified and a mix of specialized tree-based agriculture and intensive animal husbandry introduced. In this third area, Cellerini and Marchetti recommended the irrigation of almost ten thousand hectares though the establishment of hillside lakes, to be dug at the state's expense.

The social and political implications of this new commitment to specialized agriculture and to the rationalization of the territory by function were not lost on the leftist leaders of the peasant movement or its rank-and-file activists. These plans made the small farming units typical of traditional sharecropping inadequate, both for technical and economic reasons. The new emphasis on intensive animal farming, above all cattle for meat, also revealed a change of heart among leftist activists. The creation of large specialized vineyards would have made much of the land now occupied by mixed cultivation redundant. The production of fodder for cattle rearing seemed like the only alternative to complete abandonment, given the rapidly rising demand for meat, but this new specialization called for extensive investments in irrigation projects to mitigate the severe summer drought typical of central Tuscany. In sum, implicit in

[24] Archivio Federterra, Busta 206 Chianti, Fascicolo Comitato Unitario per la Difesa del Chianti, Gaiole, June 12, 1960.
[25] Ibid.

these new plans was a sense of resignation on the part of people who had vowed to stem the exodus until a few years before. Moreover, by speaking the language of reclamation (*bonifica*), the Tuscan Left was also beginning to divorce the desirability of technological innovation from the necessity of radical social reform.

The meetings and rallies of this period bear the signs of this new sense of resignation. In June 1961, when the Chianti branch of the sharecroppers' union called a meeting at Castelfiorentino, a few miles west of the historic Chianti area, ordinary militants were eager to intervene. One of them was a forty-three-year-old sharecropper by the name of Lupi, who presented the conundrum posed by agricultural specialization in the hills of central Tuscany in stark terms: modernization was indeed desirable and necessary, but "we can't talk about machinery, new cultivations, new technologies and seeds with a horizon of six hectares. The sharecropper exists in the confines of five to six hectares. Can any technician argue that in this context it is possible to set up specialized vineyards?"[26] If this is the situation, Lupi continued, there were only two options: one was to fire the vast majority of peasant families and set up capitalist enterprises, and the other was to give the land to the peasant families who worked it. But these families must unite and coordinate, creating cooperatives and providing collective services. Even though all present paid lip service to the necessity of struggling toward the second scenario, it was painfully clear that the first option – capitalist restructuring – was the one being implemented on the ground. The conference climate was indeed far from triumphant. One person in the audience could not refrain from commiserating with his comrades: "You, who have been the very first, the vanguard of labor and mobilization, I now see you old, sluggish, and bitter – a sign of material and moral suffering."[27] By then it was clear that the Left was losing both the political and the rhetorical battle over the future of the Chianti region and of rural Tuscany more generally.

Despite its electoral success and deep social roots, through the 1960s the Tuscan Left failed to come up with a coherent and credible plan for the future of the region's agriculture, and nowhere was this difficulty more evident than in the Chianti area. At the beginning of the decade the Communist-dominated union, Federterra, still commanded a massive presence among the Chianti sharecroppers: between two-thirds and three-quarters of the sharecropping families of Greve and Barberino, for

---

[26] Archivio della CGIL Toscana, Fondo Federterra, box 187, folder Comuni, document titled Conferenza Agraria Comunale, Castelfiorentino, June 2, 1961.
[27] Ibid.

example, were union members in 1961.[28] The leaders never tired of prefacing their interventions with the absolute necessity of a land reform radical enough to overcome (*superare*) the sharecropping system once and for all. But the details of their agricultural visions betrayed their disorientation and difficulties in making sense of the rapid changes taking place around them. While some of the leftists ventured into outlandish plans calling for the razing of the old scattered farmhouses and their replacement with rural villages, where farmers could close the social and psychological gap between city and countryside,[29] most activists limited themselves to a rearguard critique of public interventions in the countryside, without however questioning their ideal and material foundations, that is, the rationalization of vine growing and animal husbandry to be reached through the specialization of land use by function.

Highly revealing of the leftists' mind-set was their denunciation of the wasteful ways public funds were being deployed. Hillside lakes, even more than specialized vineyards, constituted the targets of ongoing campaigns meant to expose the corrupt relationships between landlords and state officials.[30] These lakes, meant to pave the way for irrigation, fodder cultivation, and cattle rearing, were being dug by the dozens in the Chianti, but in most cases they were not yet part of a larger infrastructure. Conduits for irrigation were nowhere to be seen, nor were the shelters for the cattle or, of course, the animals themselves. In all their incongruity, these small lakes exposed the disorientation and loss of legibility experienced by the people of the Chianti, as the rural exodus advanced, more than graft and corruption. In fact, these lakes were a crucial element of the plans recommended by the Communist Party for the revitalization of the area as well. To point out that many of them were only being used for fishing, as the Leftists did, had the contradictory implication of condoning the general thrust of the restructuring process by calling for

[28] Archivio della CGIL Toscana, Fondo Federterra, Busta 187, Fascicolo Questionario per Convegno Bologna 27 e, October 28, 1961.

[29] See Marcello Cellerini, "Proposte per uno Sviluppo Democratico dell'Agricoltura chiantigiana nel quadro del piano regionale di sviluppo economico," paper presented at the Union Conference of August 4, 1963, in Radda. Archivio della CGIL Toscana, Fondo Federterra, Busta 206 Chianti.

[30] See, for example, Archivio della CGIL Toscana, Fondo Federterra, box 187, folder Indagine aziendale sulle responsabilita' della crisi agricola nella provincia, April-August 1964, containing questionnaires about the use of public funds by the estates of the Chianti. See also Archivio della CGIL Toscana, Fondo Federterra, box 187, folder Informazioni sulle Trasformazioni Avvenute e Finite Male, May 1966. In practice this is a census of the artificial hillside lakes that had been built in the Florentine Chianti and lay underutilized. In the municipality of Greve, for example, there were twenty-one lakes, all underutilized. Three of them were only used for fishing and one to supply a new housing development.

its acceleration: what was wrong with these lakes was that they were not being put to use fast enough. But in fact their very existence signaled the ineluctability of the exodus and capitalist restructuring, processes which, in practice if not in theory, the Tuscan Communists were increasingly bound to accept.

Like in many other areas of Tuscany, the hillside lakes built in the 1950s and 1960s in the Chianti never provided water for fodder crops and thirsty cattle. The majority of the approximately two thousand and four hundred hillside lakes present today in Tuscany are in more or less serious disrepair.[31] The vast majority of the lakes serving an agricultural function irrigate a specialized vineyard or olive grove. In other words, the one feature of the landscape that was originally intended to escape, at least in part, the scope of the vine growing economy by promoting intensive cattle rearing ended up being co-opted by it. The makeup of Chianti's cattle had been changing for a couple of generations by the time hillside lakes were being dug. In the area of Chianti Classico there were approximately 11,300 head of cattle in 1930 and 12,800 in 1955, but while early in the century oxen, used for work in the fields, made up almost 60 percent of the cattle, in 1955 more than 70 percent was made up of cows and their offspring, sold for meat.[32] In the course of the 1960s, even the rearing of cattle for meat all but disappeared. In the Sienese Chianti there were approximately eight thousand and three hundred head of cattle in 1961, but only one thousand and eight hundred in 1969.[33] In sum, cattle rearing was one of the blind alleys that Tuscans ventured into as they tried to reinvent their territory in the years of the rural exodus, and the landscape still bears the signs of this aborted vision.

The implementation of "rational" vine growing, increasingly viewed as the natural vocation of the area, followed a barrage of strict government regulations and a massive injection of public funds. By the 1960s, the legislative protection of wine quality and provenance already had a long and troubled history. Even after the major French producers, led by the makers of champagne, managed to promote a comprehensive law tightly linking quality and provenance in the late 1900s (the law on the *appelation d'origine*),[34] the

---

[31] Alessio Susini, "Laghetti Collinari e Interrimento," retrieved on June 6, 2016, from www.rivistadiagraria.org/articoli/anno-2013/laghetti-collinari-e-interrimento/.

[32] Renzo Giuliani, "Relazione Generale sui Problemi Agrari, Economici e Sociali della Zona del Chianti," in Accademia Economico Agraria dei Georgofili, *Convegno del Chianti. Atti* (Florence, 1957): 9–52.

[33] By Sienese Chianti here I mean the municipalities of Gaiole, Castellina, Radda, and Castelnuovo Berardenga. Ente Autonomo per la Bonifica, l'Irrigazione e la Valorizzazione Fondiaria nelle Provincie di Arezzo, Siena, Perugia e Terni: 141.

[34] Of course, wine regulation in France was far from uncontroversial, but its links with national identity and the social turmoil elicited by lack of regulation (as in the bloody

debate in Italy dragged on for decades, pitting those who saw government regulation as key to defeating unfair competition and promoting sustainable economic growth against those who feared that regulation would lead to the restriction of the market and the undue and arbitrary granting of monopolistic advantages to the most famous and connected producers.

Italian large-scale traders were particularly hostile to regulation, accustomed as they were to traveling the peninsula hunting for deals and cultivating their contacts to then sell wine under many well established denominations in absolute freedom and according to different tastes and income levels. But plenty of low- to mid-quality producers also depended on this kind of flexibility. If Americans expected their Italian red wine to be named Chianti, have some predictable general features, and be priced reasonably, why should such demand go unmet, especially since the Chianti region could not even produce enough wine to satisfy it? The fact that "Chianti" denoted both a (far from well defined) region and a type of wine could be plausibly regarded as irrelevant. The second most famous Italian wine in the international market, Barolo, took its name from a tiny Piedmontese town of less than one thousand people. Should Barolo only be produced there? And how much of the wine produced in the hills between Florence and Siena was not really worthy of the Chianti name, in an era when thousands of estate managers and legions of individual peasants took off their shoes and stomped on grapes every September with only a vague idea of what they were going to obtain at the other end?[35]

These arguments (and the underlying interests) proved powerful enough to override concerns over fraud and authenticity for many decades. The first comprehensive Italian legislative measures dealing with the regulation of the wine industry were issued in the 1920s and early 1930s, when producers' consortia were given legal status, but only as voluntary organizations. These consortia's brand names and symbols, as well as the quality and provenance of their production, were subject to definition by their members and enforcement by state authorities.[36] In 1924, at the time of the first of these measures, Baron Ricasoli, one

---

strikes of 1911) brought the debate to its closure through the enactment and enforcement of Europe's most restrictive legislation. See Kolleen Guy, *When Champagne Became French: Wine and the Making of a National Identity* (Baltimore: Johns Hopkins University Press, 2003).

[35] For a reconstruction of these debates, see Paola Borrione, *Analisi Economica e Istituzionale di un Distretto Culturale: I Diritti di Proprietà e il Caso delle Langhe* (Laurea Thesis, University of Turin: 1999–2000), chapter 3.

[36] These measures were inaugurated with the Royal Decree 497, issued on March 7, 1924. The matter was then reorganized in a comprehensive law, Law 1199, issued on January 11, 1930, which confirmed the basic approach.

of Italy's most vocal supporters of regulation, joined thirty-one other winemakers in establishing a consortium for the production of so-called Chianti Classico wine, which could only be produced from vines grown in a specific area by consortium members. Nevertheless, nothing prevented other traders from bottling wine coming from other areas and marketing it as Chianti, as long as they did not claim to be members of the consortium and did not use its brand and symbols. This compromise, of course, satisfied no one. The hold of the consortia over their territorial jurisdiction was strong enough to limit the action of the nonaffiliated producers. Ricasoli's sharecroppers, for example, were entitled to half of the wine they produced on their farms but could not develop trading relations of their own without risking legal repercussions.[37] After World War II, as we have seen, the peasant movement routinely accused the baron and his affiliates of monopolistic practices. But these local constraints failed to stem what Ricasoli and others viewed as unfair competition coming from areas farther afield, over which consortia had no control.

In the end, only the momentum created by European integration managed to break the stalemate. By the early 1960s it had become apparent that the impending establishment of an integrated market for wine called for a degree of regulatory coordination across national borders. French producers and traders, no longer able to protect their market with tariffs, put considerable pressure on their government to demand stricter controls over the quality and provenance of Italian wine. The idea that Italian winemakers could play by laxer rules than their French counterparts was indeed a hard sell, and the French government was in a position to make EEC agricultural funds dependent on Italy's willingness to conform. The result of these pressures was the 1963 law on *denominazione d'origine*, which linked provenance, brand, and quality on the French model; established a public record in which vineyards had to be registered, pending approval by a provincial inspector; and instituted a powerful national committee of wine experts to settle disputes and set standards. Producers and traders caught breaking the law now faced not only steep fines but also the possibility of up to three years in jail in the case of large-scale fraud.[38]

---

[37] The leftist leaders of the peasant movement were very ambivalent about state regulation of wine quality and provenance, sometimes supporting it and other times opposing it, according to the type of audience they faced. In general, however, they were strongly opposed to limiting the use of the Chianti brand to the area controlled by Ricasoli's consortium. See Archivio della CGIL Toscana, Fondo Federterra, box 206 Chianti, folder Federazione Fiorentina PCI, "Convegno per la Riforma Agraria e la Rinascita del Chianti," San Casciano, April 20, 1958.

[38] This was Law 930, issued on July 12, 1963. The law established three different tiers of increasingly strict regulatory regimes: the first for denominazione d'origine semplice; the

The impact of this legislation was every bit as powerful as Baron Ricasoli and his allies had hoped, partly because its implementation coincided with the immediate aftermath of the peasants' exodus and the collapse of the sharecropping system. The spread of specialized vineyards was little short of spectacular during the 1960s. In the Sienese portion of the Chianti, for example, specialized vineyards increased from 142 hectares in 1957 to 2,049 in 1970, while mixed vineyards declined by more than 40 percent.[39] The Florentine section experienced very similar changes, with a slight delay. By the middle of the following decade, the area covered by specialized vineyards in the Chianti as a whole reached 5,000 hectares, relegating the mixed vineyards to a largely vestigial role. Two related processes made the restructuring possible. First, public moneys were crucial to the whole operation, coming both from the national government (under the heading of the Green Plans of 1962 and 1967)[40] and from the European Community, through a series of installments (*tranches*) starting in 1964.[41] Some of these funds were grants, while others were offered as loans at very low rates (typically, 3 percent per year for a twenty-year loan). Public funds also softened the impact of the restructuring process by allowing producers to wait for the new vineyards to

second for denominazione d'origine controllata (denoted with the now-famous acronym D.O.C); and the third for denominazione d'origine controllata e garantita (D.O.C.G.). In practice, very few producers applied for the lowest level of regulation, which rapidly fell into disuse.

[39] Ente Autonomo per la Bonifica, l'Irrigazione e la Valorizzazione Fondiaria nelle Provincie di Arezzo, Siena, Perugia e Terni.

[40] The so-called Piani Verdi of the 1960s were a series of two multi-year plans aimed at providing incentives, subsidies, and tax breaks to the more meritorious companies and institutions, so that agricultural incomes would be able to keep pace with the economy at large, costs would decrease, and the international competitiveness of Italian agriculture would be assured. The plans paid lip service to the widely shared commitment to protecting family farms, but the better-connected actors took disproportionate advantage of state aid regardless of their efficiency and actual agenda. The red tape necessary to apply for state funds was enough to discourage small independent farmers, so that the funds were channeled through the plethora of agencies (*enti*) in charge of rural transformation, who proceeded to distribute them to their members.

[41] The Green Plans were combined with European subsidies and finally merged into the EEC-controlled European Agricultural Guidance and Guarantee Fund (EAGGF) in the early 1970s. Like in the rest of the Community, the Guarantee Section of the fund, devoted to various forms of subsidies, financed the vast majority of the interventions, relegating the Guidance Section, meant to favor the restructuring and rationalization of production and commercialization, to an almost symbolic role. It is worth noting, however, that it was primarily through the funds of the Guidance Section of the EAGGF that vine growing was restructured in the late 1960s and through the 1970s. See E. Giorgi, "L'Agricultura Toscana e la Politica Economica del Mercato Comune Europeo," in Chamber of Commerce of Siena, *Convegno Regionale su Aspetti e Riflessi del Mercato Comune Europeo sul Vino e l'Olio della Toscana* (Siena: Amministrazione Provinviale, 1969): 17–28, held by IRPET library.

become productive. Second, the shift toward specialized cultivation, coupled with the new strict rules governing quality, created a temporary drop in the supply of Chianti wine, accompanied by a rapid rise in prices. The average price of 100 kg of wine at the point of production increased from a little more than 12,000 lire in 1964 to 19,000 in 1968, and it kept increasing for several years afterward as well.[42] The joint impact of public funds, newly exacting quality standards, and increasing prices buoyed up a sector that only a few years before had seemed on the verge of collapse.

This process of recapitalization was both cause and effect of the depopulation of the countryside. On the one hand, many observers at the time pointed to the fact that the restructuring process relied on external wage labor, as opposed to the work that the extant sharecropping families could have provided, and that the use of hired labor was by far the more expensive option, only made possible by extensive public subsidies. In a certain sense, the sharecroppers seemed to be paying, through taxation, for their own dispossession. On the other hand, the landlords could easily point to many instances in which peasant families had left without any pressure, or in which they had even rejected offers for negotiation and compromise. In fact, both patterns took place, but in different contexts. On many large estates where the potential for profitable winemaking was high, sharecroppers were indeed expelled through a mix of inaction and direct threats. On the smaller estates, especially those closer to the urban centers, many different kinds of compromises were reached between landlords and peasants, ranging from allowing some family members to work part-time in exchange for free lodging to the selective sale of land to the former sharecroppers. Ironically, sharecropping resisted longer in these smaller estates close to the towns, where mixed cultivation and vegetable orchards were more profitable and where members of the peasant family could easily find nonagricultural jobs, than in the more peripheral areas, which converted to modern and highly capitalized forms of agriculture in a remarkably short time.

On the larger estates, mechanization radically changed not only cultivation techniques but also the very features of the landscape. Terraced hills were either abandoned or bulldozed over to reduce their slope. The backbreaking process of manually digging the ditches where the vine rows would reside was made immeasurably easier by the use of powerful machinery and even explosives. Mechanization also transformed several maintenance tasks, such as the setting up of irrigation works, weeding, and chemical fertilization. In order to make the use of

---

[42] Data from Biblioteca di Agronomia, Collezione Miscellanee, 11.3, n. 43, Franco Scaramuzzi, "Situazione e Prospettive Tecnico-Economiche della Viticoltura del Chianti Classico," dated November 8, 1969, table 10.

Illustration #12 A modern vineyard in the Chianti. The rows of vines are arranged vertically, along the slope lines, to allow mechanization. Contrast with Illustrations 1 and 2.

machinery possible, the distance between the rows of vines and between the single plants increased by approximately 50 percent compared to the old mixed vineyards.[43] The orderly succession of the vine rows was no longer interrupted by patches of wheat or fodder, creating a much more monotonous landscape. The new rows would now vertically follow the hill slopes (*a rittochino*), rather than cutting across them (*a giropoggio*), as had been advised by the "enlightened" agronomists of the late eighteenth and early nineteenth centuries to counter erosion (Illustration 12). The needs of the tractors, which by working downhill incurred far fewer risks of capsizing, overran the old concerns about erosion. Deep drainage systems, coupled with more traditional superficial ones, were supposed to reduce the risks of erosion, although the results proved to be mixed at best.[44] As is often the case, the mechanization of

---

[43] Ibid.: 11–12.
[44] Biblioteca di Agronomia, Collezione Miscellanee, 11.3, n. 192, Mario Tofani, "Indagine sulla meccanizzazione della viticoltura in Toscana," without date but almost certainly dating to 1966.

one task called for the mechanization of others, to the point that the harvesting of the grapes became the only major task to remain performed by hand, despite extensive research and effort to find ways to mechanize that as well.

Over the course of the 1960s, more than 6,000 hectares of previously cultivated land were abandoned in the Chianti, as the territory assumed the features of a vast vineyard interrupted by woods and sparsely used pastures. Arable land without trees declined by 28 percent, and that with trees by 20 percent, leading to a radical decrease in the production of grains and fodder.[45] Cattle decreased by 83 percent, despite the ongoing plans for promoting husbandry over irrigated land; pigs declined by 71 percent, signaling the near extinction of the old forest economy associated with sharecropping; and sheep decreased by 36 percent.[46] Different actors assessed these changes in radically different ways. Leftist observers generally bemoaned them, arguing that the conversion to agricultural specialization had sped up the peasant exodus and stuffed the coffers of the largest landowners and their agents with public funds. These commentators, while acknowledging the irreversibility of the exodus, argued in favor of at least a modicum of land reform and the spread of animal husbandry, to be organized cooperatively.[47] Others viewed the process of specialization as the only realistic alternative to complete abandonment. After a detailed survey of the Sienese Chianti in 1969, the agronomists in charge of an influential report on the future of the area bluntly argued that vine monocropping, suitably integrated by specialized olive groves, had "solved the serious problem of the rural exodus."[48] Land prices dutifully registered these changes. Whereas in the wake of the 1956 freeze it took 200,000 lire to buy a hectare of land suitable for vine growing, by the end of the 1960s it could easily take four times that amount. These different assessments testified to the profound sense of disorientation experienced by local society in the face of changes few seemed to understand, let alone advocate. The vine ruled again supreme on the hills of the Chianti, but its traditional subjects had by and large fled the kingdom.

---

[45] Antonio Fiorentino and Marco Massa, *La Collina Fiorentina tra Speculazione Edilizia e Investimento Multinazionale* (Florence: Edizioni Pappagallo, 1979): 105–110.

[46] Ente Autonomo per la Bonifica, l'Irrigazione e la Valorizzazione Fondiaria, *Contributo per lo Sviluppo dell'Agricoltura del Chianti Senese*: 236.

[47] See, for example, ASMOS, Fondo PCI, Box XD1 Comitato di Coordinamento del Chianti, Folder 1969, "Le Proposte dei Comunisti per lo Sviluppo Economico e Sociale del Chianti, Atti del Convegno Economico sul Chianti tenuto a Gaiole il 18 maggio 1969."

[48] Ente Autonomo per la Bonifica, l'Irrigazione e la Valorizzazione Fondiaria: 267.

Rural Settlement in the Age of the Exodus

In a documentary titled *Mezzadria* and shot in the late 1960s in the Sienese Chianti, filmmaker and critic Sergio Micheli tells the story of the rural exodus as a classic drama of modernity. Produced in cooperation with the Chamber of Labor of Siena and replete with Marxist tropes, this remarkable cultural artifact lingers with a mix of nostalgia and rage on the ruins engendered by rapid change, searching all the while for a coherent narrative to make sense of it. To the rhythmic and eerily dissonant music of Igor Stravinsky's *Rite of Spring*, the opening sequence takes the spectator in front of a seemingly abandoned landlord's villa, cutting next to a deserted peasant house. The camera closes in, climbs the front stairs and follows the crumbling walls, where weeds are growing through the cracks, as the narrator begins to speak in an elegiac tone:

Nature slowly reclaims what human labor took away from her. Weeds attack the ancient stones on which human footsteps no longer resonate. Ghosts' houses, abandoned houses, as if after a war, an epidemic, a disaster. Here was the kingdom of mezzadria, a kingdom whose hours are desperately numbered. A deserted peasant house is a warning sign, the symbol of a tragic condition, a protest that trumps the pathetic sadness of an ancient villa abandoned by the landlords.... Today there is a feeling of death, a sad premonition of the end. The hollow orbits of collapsing windows open up onto dark interiors that only a few years ago resonated with voices. Little by little, one after another, many have left, and those who remain are contemplating their escape.[49]

The documentary proceeds to follow the daily tasks of one large (and nameless) peasant family, commenting on how the pillars of the traditional sharecropping system, including the patriarchal extended family and organized religion, have all but collapsed. The narrative shifts next to the spaces the sharecroppers are moving to, the factories where workers exercise "the option of being exploited more rationally, but also of going on strike without worrying that the grapes may rot as a consequence." Young men and women are shown at their working stations, and clocking in and out of the factory premises, dressed in smart, modern clothes and nodding at the camera with confidence and amusement. Then, rather abruptly, we are brought back to the immediate postwar period, to the sharecroppers' struggles against evictions and for labor rights. Images of mass rallies, handwritten banners, and union meetings are interspersed in rapid succession with images of

---

[49] *Mezzadria*, directed by Sergio Micheli (with Furio Agnorelli, Franco Andreucci e Gian Carlo Calocchi), with script by Tommaso Chiarelli. The documentary is preserved in digital format at ASMOS in Siena and at Mediateca Toscana in Florence. The exact year of production is not reported.

police repression. Finally, the sequence slows down and the camera closes in on the photograph of a large peasant house with a massive staircase in front of it, full of demonstrating peasants: "It was only yesterday that the sharecroppers occupied the fields to oppose evictions. Now the farmhouse is empty." The same house and staircase are shown in their current state of abandonment. The spectator realizes that this might well be the same house shown at the beginning of the documentary. The commentator goes on to state: "Those who remain are still struggling and no longer just to survive. The farmhouse is empty but the struggle carries on." At this point the music changes abruptly to the Amur Partisan song, the famous Soviet choral piece, as the camera swirls through a modern-day rally of sharecroppers. Despite the epic music, resonant with the memories and aspirations of the Resistance, the assembled peasants look old and poorly dressed, their worried expressions a stark contrast to the sunny faces of the factory workers shown a few minutes before. There is no denying, however, that a struggle (though maybe not the mythical one at the "cutting edge" of history) is indeed being carried on.

The most striking feature of this documentary is the coexistence of a simple linear narrative of modernity as transition from the fields to the factories, from the extended to the nuclear family, from frugality to consumerism, and so on, with a more complex and nonlinear interpretative scheme that privileges space over time, and the perception and politics of place over a temporality of evolutionary change. On one level, the documentary leads the viewer from tradition to modernity, and from the dormant fields to the buzzing factories, but then it compels the viewer to go back to the countryside, to the same abandoned farmhouse, to linger on the haunted character of the landscape. Micheli, like many other Tuscans of his generation, was torn between viewing the exodus as the inevitable, even desirable, product of modernization and a more emplaced experience of disorientation and anger.

To many observers, the most unsettling aspect of the Tuscan rural landscape in the age of the peasant exodus was its increasing lack of legibility. Many of these anxieties focused on settlement practices, on what would become of the peasants' houses and their farms. The sharecroppers' changing settlement patterns became the object of detailed quantitative and qualitative analyses for an army of social scientists and public administrators, who calculated aggregation indexes, measuring the percentage of people living in towns and hamlets, as opposed to houses dispersed in the countryside, which had been the signature settlement pattern of the sharecropping system for centuries. These indexes showed extensive and rapid change. Only one-third of the Chianti's inhabitants, for example, lived in scattered houses in 1961, as opposed to two-thirds before the war.[50]

At the same time, measurements showed the large patriarchal families to be dissolving into ever smaller units. The average sharecropping family in the province of Siena had 7.2 members in 1950 vis-à-vis 3.7 in 1969.[51] These families were portrayed alternatively as dispossessed and uncertain of their future, or calculating and capable of sophisticated strategies for social advancement. These radically different assessments sometimes coexisted even in the same report.[52] The search for legible patterns sometimes seemed to pay off, as when it became clear that former sharecroppers were more likely to buy farms in large municipalities, where nonagricultural jobs were plentiful, than in rural ones, even when their heads of household nominally remained farmers. This seemed to suggest that landownership was not valued in itself, but only as a stepping stone toward urban life.[53] These strategies of gradual and calculated familiarization with the urban world, however, sat uneasily next to mountains of data showing the paucity of comforts and dismal isolation of Tuscan peasantry's dwellings decades after Liberation. This data seemed to indicate that sharecroppers had no other choice than to leave their houses behind and migrate.

A vast and diverse literature portrayed the Tuscan countryside as a space bypassed by modernity, and Tuscan peasants as following modernity's calls whenever they could hear them. In a very influential study commissioned by the Georgofili Academy in the mid-1950s, agricultural economist Ugo Sorbi assembled a series of statistics meant to give a sense of the kind of life the sharecroppers of the Chianti were just then beginning to leave behind. In the Chianti there was only one telephone for every 384 people; one physician for every 1,800; one pharmacy for every 4,800; one cinema for every 1,900; one car for every 533 (but interestingly already one motorcycle for every thirty-four); and so on.[54] The difference between city and country was vast in terms of access to services and even basic amenities. The Census Bureau (ISTAT) reported in 1951 that 83 percent of dwellings in the municipality of Siena were connected to the public water supply system, vis-à-vis

---

[50] R. Camaiti, *La Popolazione e la Realtà Statistico-Economica del Chianti*, 79.

[51] "Indagine sul Fenomeno dell'Esodo Mezzadrile," *La Nazione*, October 20, 1971.

[52] Franco Lumachi, "Aspetti Umani dell'Agricoltura Mezzadrile in Toscana," *La Regione* 10 (1964): 92–107. Here the sharecroppers are portrayed as self-confident (*sicuri di sé*) on page 96 and profoundly uncertain, and therefore conformist, on page 100.

[53] Alberto L'Abate, "L'Esodo Rurale," *La Regione* 10 (April 1964): 81–82.

[54] Ugo Sorbi, "Caratteri Strutturali dell'Orientamento Fondiario e Agrario del Chianti," in Accademia Economico-Agraria dei Georgofili, *Atti del Convegno del Chianti* (Florence: Vallecchi, 1957): 262–352.

only 35 percent of most rural municipalities. More than 90 percent of dwellings in Siena had an indoor toilet, vis-à-vis only 34 percent in the municipalities of the Orcia valley. Practically every dwelling had electricity in Siena, vis-à-vis only two-thirds in the countryside as a whole (and far less in the scattered farmhouses).[55] In terms of electricity and plumbing, by the early 1970s the gap between city and country had all but been closed. By then, more than three-quarters of dwellings in the rural municipalities of the province of Siena even had access to natural gas, albeit from tanks, which rang the final death knell for the old forest economy and the use of wood and charcoal. Of course, as soon as some gaps were bridged, others opened up. Almost half of the dwellings in the city of Siena had central heating in 1971, vis-à-vis only 13 percent in the municipalities of the Orcia valley.[56] Overall, however, this catching-up process did little to stem the rural exodus. Approximately 20 percent of the dwellings in the province of Siena were uninhabited in 1981, but if we exclude the three largest and most urbanized municipalities (Siena, Poggibonsi, and Colle Valdelsa), the percentage of abandoned dwellings increases to a whopping 33 percent.[57]

Rural Tuscans fought mightily to bring some of the trappings of modernity to the countryside in the years of the rural exodus, hoping to stem the hemorrhage by providing peasant homes with at least basic amenities. In October 1959 several academics and administrators gathered in Siena to discuss the conditions of rural Tuscany's houses, defined in the keynote speaker's speech title as a "fundamental problem for the rebirth of agriculture." The speaker, an academic architect, proceeded to review the customary litany of data on the substandard conditions of the sharecroppers' houses and argued, with language that harked back to the Fascist period, that the old buildings had to be reclaimed (*bonificate*) and new ones erected with radically different criteria, for example, by providing "buffer spaces" (*ambienti filtro*) in which the farmers could change before entering the house, leaving their dirty tools and clothes behind. Local authorities had to set standards and monitor their implementation, but also "educate the rural classes, for they must commit them to

---

[55] Istituto Centrale di Statistica, *Censimento Generale della Popolazione 1951*, Provincia di Siena, table 10.

[56] By 1971, for example, between 85 and 90 percent of the dwellings in the rural municipalities of the province of Siena had electricity. In the municipalities of the Val d'Orcia, 80 percent of the dwellings had an indoor toilet, up from 34 percent twenty years before. See Istituto Centrale di Statistica, *Censimento Generale della Popolazione 1971*, Provincia di Siena, table 19.

[57] Istituto Centrale di Statistica, *Censimento Generale della Popolazione 1981*, Provincia di Siena, table 29.

the correct use of the buildings and to the respect of the houses in which they live."[58]

This kind of paternalism was expressly critiqued by one of the chief engineers working for the provincial administration of Siena, which had surveyed more than fifteen thousand farmhouses in the province and found only 20 percent of them in good condition. After noting the paradox "of seeing homes still being lit with oil lamps or candles in a countryside crisscrossed by huge high-tension electricity lines," he warned against the preconceived notion that rural people may not need this or the other thing, or that they might not be put in charge of their future without supervision. The ultimate problem, he noted, was that in the sharecropping system people were treated like means of production, with the immoral consequence that animals were often better housed than humans: it was common to find faucets in the animal shelters of many rural houses, but not in their kitchens.[59] Tradition, in other words, had exploited the peasants, whereas modernity was passing them by.

Local administrators did not limit themselves to debating. They set out to impose standards and guidelines for the rehabilitating of the old farmhouses and the construction of new ones. Many local councils, in which the Communists enjoyed large pluralities, issued extensive and detailed regulations as part of their zoning plans, mandating the radical restructuring of the rural housing stock, to be accomplished with a combination of public and private funds.[60] These regulatory documents read like paeans to the virtues of an imagined modernized lifestyle that would restore some dignity to Tuscany's peasants. In their close similarities, these local regulations also betrayed their origins in a region-wide campaign "for the rural home" waged by the Communist Party and its affiliated organizations through the 1950s and beyond (Illustration 13).[61] The implementation of the new standards would have revolutionized centuries-old customs. New rural houses could no longer be built with the animal shelter downstairs from the bedrooms; each room had to have at least one window, at least as large as one-tenth of the floor area; every

---

[58] ASMOS, Fondo Peris Brogi, XIII 1, Fascicolo 4, Sottofascicolo 1959, Report of Prof. Vezzoso, "La Casa Rurale, Problema Fondamentale per la Rinascita dell'Agricoltura." *Convegno per la Casa Rurale: Atti del convegno tenuto a Siena il 31 ottobre 1959.* The quotation is on p. 29.

[59] ASMOS, Fondo Peris Brogi, XIII 1, Fascicolo 4, Sottofascicolo 1959, Report of engineer Vezzosi, "Problemi della Casa Rurale nell'Insediamento Sparso." *Convegno per la Casa Rurale.* The quotation is on p. 36.

[60] ACdLSI, Federmezzadri IX. 1, folder Regolamenti per le case coloniche approvati dai comuni. Regolamento Comunale di Igiene e Sanita' degli Ambienti Rurali, 1958.

[61] ASMOS, Fondo PCI, V A2, folder Lega Mezzadri, Regolamento Comunale "tipo" d'Igiene Rurale.

Illustration #13 Plan for a modern Tuscan farmhouse, early 1960s.

house needed to be supplied with electricity, have a modern toilet, and at least a shower; and so on. Precise rules regulated the construction of annexes for the production of manure and connections to septic tanks. Even the old houses needed be restructured, repainted, and plastered on the outside (a heresy for today's connoisseurs of rustic living); the windows had to be enlarged to at least one-twentieth of the floor area of each room; insulation had to be checked and improved if lacking; and so forth. Even though loans and grants were available for this kind of restructuring, landowners were supposed to foot part of the bill if they did not want to incur sanctions. Some regulations even set a deadline of six years, by which time all rural houses had to be brought up to code.

Unsurprisingly, most of these regulations remained on paper. In many cases, they did not receive the approval of the national Health Department's officials, and even where they did, local administrators lacked the funds and staff to implement them.[62] The landlords also objected to these injunctions and argued that they simply did not have

---

[62] Giuseppe Marzucchi, "Dopo un Anno l'ACIS non Ha Ancora Approvato il Regolamento per l'Igiene delle Case Coloniche," *L'Unità*, s.d., 1957 (in ASMOS, Fondo PCI, V A2, 1957).

the resources necessary for such a massive project. Much of the restructuring that did take place before the 1980s was carried out in a piecemeal fashion and by private owners, drawing mixed reactions. Some observers found the aesthetics of modernization extremely objectionable and set out to organize a campaign for the conservation of the old peasant houses, viewed as examples of vulnerable and valuable "vernacular" architecture. In a 1961 article sent to the bulletin of *Italia Nostra*, the main national organization for landscape and cultural preservation, architect and amateur photographer Lorenzo Gori-Montanelli invited readers to compare two pictures of the same Chianti farmhouse, taken one year apart. The author extolled the house in the earlier image for the elegance and purity of its architectural proportions. The later photograph, which depicted the result of the restructuring carried out by the sharecropper after his purchase of the building, was meant to fill the reader with horror: gone was the tower, gone was the gated courtyard, and the windows were now double in size (Illustration 14).[63] Gori-Montanelli was only one of the many connoisseurs roaming the Tuscan countryside armed with tripods and cameras to document the beauty of the increasingly deserted farmhouses. In contrast to the aesthetic sensibility of Sergio Micheli's documentary (and of most rural Tuscans), the preoccupation of these urban aesthetes was with the possibility that the abandoned farmhouses could be contaminated by modernity. Although Gori-Montanelli's conservationist sensibility, which will be the subject of a later chapter, was still uncommon in the early 1960s, these latent aesthetic conflicts testified to Tuscans' diversity of perceptions and agendas in the face of the rural exodus, as well as their general disorientation.

While the leaders of the peasant movement and many local administrators struggled to modernize rural settlement, and while a few urban connoisseurs voiced their aesthetic concerns, other actors began to view the rural exodus as an opportunity to reshape Tuscany's social and political orientation in a markedly conservative direction. Even though young Tuscan peasants left the farms in droves, they typically did not go very far. Between 1955 and 1960, 437,000 people changed municipality of residence without leaving Tuscany, while 155,000 arrived from other regions, in the presence of modest emigration flows. Most of the people who migrated to Tuscany came from neighboring Emilia-Romagna, Umbria, and Lazio; fewer than eight thousand came from Campania and approximately as many from Sicily, although immigration from the south received most of the attention. Moreover, most migrants did not move

---

[63] Lorenzo Gori-Montanelli, "Difesa dell'Architettura Colonica," *Bollettino di Italia Nostra* 21 (1961): 9–12.

Tavarnelle - Podere Belvedere 1959

Tavarnelle - Podere Belvedere 1960

Illustration #14 The transformation of a Chianti farmhouse purchased by a former sharecropper and restructured for modern farming, 1960s.

to Florence, the regional capital, which would have transformed it into a large city like Milan or Rome: the Tuscan city that grew the most in the 1950s and 1960s was the textile center of Prato, followed by Grosseto, Tuscany's southernmost provincial capital.[64]

While some observers viewed this process of dispersed urbanization as the natural course of history, others set out to counter it. Starting in the early 1950s and for at least a decade, Catholic politicians, large-scale landlords, real estate agents, and a motley crew of wheelers and dealers in the private and public sectors set out to replace the departing sharecroppers with small-scale farmers coming from other parts of the country, especially areas of central and southern Italy where the Christian Democrats were electorally successful. Albeit quantitatively limited, the symbolic and political impact of these schemes was remarkable. The plans spawned a series of scandals that further undermined the credibility of conservative politicians in rural Tuscany and showed the lengths to which they were willing to go in their dreams of territorial control and purification. National and local officials set out to seek desirable settlers as far afield as the former Italian colonies. The connections between these schemes and postcolonial settlement practices contributed to the widely shared belief that the national government, far from attending to the painful problems created by rapid change, entertained a cynical and instrumental attitude toward Tuscany's rural society.

Resettlement plans debuted during the years of bitter social conflict, before the exodus began in earnest. Landowners were afraid that social conflict might discourage impending sales. As early as 1951, the president of the landowners' association pleaded with the prefect of Siena to have an acceptable level of order and discipline restored, lest prospective buyers withdraw their offers. And at last the president presented the clincher:

We also have to add that the failure of these sales to small-scale farmers would prevent that influx of politically desirable people who would be capable of effecting positive changes in the political outlook of our province as a whole.[65]

In other words, the restoration of order was not just a matter of protecting property rights (and values); this was also an opportunity to dilute the disturbingly intense hue of red that colored the Tuscan territory on account of the sharecroppers' political loyalties.

---

[64] Alberto L'Abate, "L'Esodo Rurale," *La Regione* 10 (April 1964): 71–91.
[65] Archivio di Stato di Siena, Gabinetto di Prefettura, box 192 (1951), folder Vertenza Mezzadrile, subfolder Vendita Aziende Agrarie.

The candor with which many officials discussed these political plans for resettlement is somewhat startling. In the early 1950s the estate of Poggio alla Sala, near Montepulciano, went up for sale, and the inspectors of the recently established Fund for the Promotion of Small-Scale Rural Ownership paid a visit to assess the state of the property and the credentials of twenty-four sharecroppers and their families, most of whom were already living on the estate and who had founded a cooperative with the intention of buying the farms. The inspectors also dutifully noted the political affiliations of the prospective buyers – all Communists and Socialists except for one. A debate among several officials ensued as to whether the sale should proceed nonetheless. Even the Bishop of Montepulciano felt compelled to intervene in May 1952, reluctantly recommending letting the sale go through:

> The color of the peasants today is what it is. But what has been done by the healthy section of society with regards to Communist propaganda, to defend [the peasants] from deception? ... It would be preferable to favor more meritorious people, but if the occasion at hand does not leave any room for choice, some good could come out of it nonetheless. What would happen if this operation [the sale] did not take place?[66]

In other words, it would be preferable to find better (i.e., less red) buyers, but preventing the sale from going through would give Communist propaganda an additional boost. The implication of the bishop's recommendation was nevertheless clear: whenever a choice was possible, more conservative and pliant peasants should be favored, even at the cost of importing them from far afield.

When social conflict subsided and the exodus escalated, resettlement plans increased in number and scope, less encumbered by the fading resistance of Tuscan peasants. The details of these plans shed some light on the ways in which the Tuscan countryside became a nexus in a national, and even international, network of actors involved in managing migration flows. They also contribute to further illustrating the profound sense of disorientation felt at the local level in the face of rapid and traumatic changes. One of the most tangible products of these changes was the unprecedented availability of thousands of hectares of agricultural land for sale and purchase. Investigative journalist Francesco Rossi began his report on the social conditions of Tuscan peasants at the turn of the 1960s with the blunt assertion that "Tuscany, with its rich agrarian history, is today a region on sale."[67] The peasant movement viewed this

---

[66] Archivio di Stato di Siena, Gabinetto di Prefettura, box 219 (1952), folder Riforma Fondiaria.

[67] "Contadini della Toscana," report directed by Francesco C. Rossi, *Itinerari* 45–46 (November-December 1960): 411.

process of increasing commercialization with alarm and disdain. One of the movement's leaders wrote in the sharecroppers' union bulletin:

We estimate that the large-scale Sienese landlords intend to sell 160,000 hectares of land. The army of merchants, speculators, and middlemen set in motion in these last four of five years is truly exceptional. Men and women of the worst kind, coming from all parts of Italy, have cast their nets, waiting for prey.[68]

If Tuscany had become a land on sale, its prices were being artificially sustained in a seeming conspiracy to buoy up the dwindling incomes of the large-scale landlords at the expense both of the peasants who aspired to become owners and of the public at large. Through the 1950s, the peasants' leftist unions mounted a series of campaigns to denounce how the subsidies and incentives meant to promote small-scale landownership were being abused. Union leaders argued that these measures, and especially the 1948 law instituting the Fund for the Promotion of Small-Scale Rural Ownership, exacerbated the exodus by expelling Tuscan peasants from their farms:

With this law they want to feed the real estate market to sustain land prices, give the landlords the possibility of getting rid of their least productive plots, and enable fake cooperatives to recruit peasants in the areas where land reform is most urgent, to use them as troops of maneuver against the most progressive part of the peasantry of other regions.[69]

In other words, political calculations and economic speculation came together to organize shady resettlement plans at the expense of ordinary Tuscan peasants, who in some cases were even forced to formally abjure their Communist faith to gain access to the loans and subsidies.[70]

Southern peasants began to move to rural Tuscany in the immediate aftermath of World War II, sometimes after developing contacts as soldiers during the conflict. As the exodus picked up and farms lay abandoned, more southern families decided to invest their savings in a down payment toward the purchase of a Tuscan farm, also lured by government-subsidized mortgages and the possibility of combining agricultural and industrial work. For example, Sorbi reports that some two

---

[68] Alessandro Viciani, "Perché lo Spezzattamento delle Aziende?" *Federmezzadri* 72 (October 1955): 6.

[69] ACdLSi, Camera Confederale del Lavoro, IX a. 9, folder Convegno Prov.le Riforma Agraria, Siena 18–19 maggio 1957. The folder includes the acts of the conference; the quotation is on page 9.

[70] See the letter of a group of sharecroppers from Staggia, in the Municipality of Poggibonsi, to the leaders of the Chambers of Labor of Siena. These sharecroppers had indeed signed such a statement under pressure, although they reassured the union leaders that "they [were] and always will be Communist." ACdLSi, Federmezzadri, III a. 4, folder Scandalo "Zolle d'Oro."

hundred southern families moved to farms in the Chianti in the first half of the 1950s. In his opinion, they contributed to the "definitive degradation of the agricultural order" of the region because of their ignorance of local varietals and techniques as well as their instrumental relationship with agriculture, which they abandoned at the first opportunity.[71] Not all of these families were recruited by unscrupulous intermediaries acting on behalf of conservative politicians, but politically inspired projects and speculative schemes went well beyond the status of isolated cases. Even sources hostile to the political Left concurred in acknowledging the systematic and planned character of many of these migrations.

In April 1956, for example, an anonymous letter reached the Prefecture of Siena informing the authorities that shady middlemen had been going around the countryside for some time, contacting landowners who had put their farms up for sale.[72] These characters claimed that they could rely on the support of Christian Democratic politicians, namely, Amintore Fanfani, as well as high-ranking ecclesiastical officials, all of whom were interested in recruiting Catholic peasants from southern Italy and have them resettle to Tuscany's "red belt." Of course the support of such powerful people guaranteed a speedy transaction at attractive prices. One such intermediary, Domenico Arrigo, had recently moved to Colle Valdelsa and, the letter concluded, he risked giving the Left even more fodder for its destructive propaganda, unless someone stopped him. The prefect instructed the Carabinieri to conduct an investigation, which uncovered his deep criminal record, including two long sentences for homicide, for which he had been amnestied in 1944. He was indeed traveling around Tuscany facilitating the purchase of farms and he had numerous real estate properties of his own across the region. As to his political connections, he seemed to be acting on behalf of an "ecclesiastical association funded by politicians." The goal of this network of people was clear enough:

Arrigo's intermediary activities aim at facilitating the purchase of land in municipalities whose population is predominantly Communist in order to then establish Christian Democratic peasants coming from Sicily, Sardinia, and other regions where the majority of the population is Christian Democratic.[73]

The fact that the police could use such blunt language in their reports testifies to the generalized character of these operations. By then, they had become part and parcel of the Tuscan rural landscape.

---

[71] Ugo Sorbi, "Caratteri Strutturali": 26.
[72] Archivio di Stato di Siena, Gabinetto di Prefettura, box 146 Situazione Politica dei Comuni della Provincia (1951–1955), folder Colle Val d'Elsa.
[73] Ibid.

The fear that the Communists might expose the shady character of these dealings to gain political advantage came true in 1962, when several leftist publications carried extensive coverage of a full-blown scandal, wryly dubbed "golden sods" (*zolle d'oro*).[74] Two series of transactions involving peasants from the province of Macerata, in the Marche region, and from Campania, took center stage for their outrageousness. In the first case, in 1952, two Roman speculators bought an estate of 200 hectares of arable land and 250 of woods in the Elsa valley, ten miles west of Siena. The original price, negotiated with the aristocratic landlord, was approximately sixty million lire. The pair then turned to their political connections, especially within the Christian Democratic-dominated Association of Independent Farmers (Coldiretti). These connections got them in touch with a group of Catholic sharecroppers and small-scale farmers from the Chienti Valley, in the southernmost section of the Marche. The intermediaries managed to convince thirty-three families, with 150 members, to establish a cooperative so they would be able to collectively access government-sponsored loans and buy their Tuscan estate, which in the meantime they had stripped of most tall trees and cattle. The mortgage was duly underwritten, taking advantage of several incentives and subsidies, but the negotiated price escalated to more than eighty-seven million lire, 45 percent higher than the original price. Part of the mark-up was used to bribe a whole slew of appraisers and technicians, one of whom escaped abroad with his loot. It did not take the new settlers long to realize that they would never be able to repay their debts. As soon as they defaulted on their payments, the farmers faced foreclosure and eviction. Their leader, Florindo Caciorgna, turned first to Coldiretti, to the prefect of Siena, to Fanfani, and to several parish priests in the area, but no one seemed to be able to help. Desperate, despite the recommendations he and his fellow settlers had received to never trust "the Tuscans" (that is, the Communists), in 1956 Caciorgna wrote to several leftist union leaders, who proceeded to collect evidence and turn everything over to the authorities and eventually to the press as well.[75]

---

[74] The ensuing narrative is based on the following archival sources: ACdLSi, Federmezzadri, III a. 4, folder Scandalo "Zolle d'Oro"; and ACdLSI Federmezzadri IX. 4, folder Materiale riservato PCI, which also contains a printed pamphlet published in August 1962 by *Siena Democratica* (a periodical of the Sienese Communist Party) and titled "How the Sienese Clay Fields Have Become Golden Sods" (*Come le crete senesi sono diventate zolle d'oro*).

[75] The scandal seems to have broken out after Bruno dal Pozzo, an accountant who had moved from the Veneto to Asciano, released a detailed report about Mattei's transactions in 1959. This report led to the arrest of forty people. The report is held by the Archive of the Chamber of Labor of Siena, but it is not clear whether Dal Pozzo had leftist inclinations and connections.

The second case was quite similar in structure, except for a postcolonial twist. In this case, too, a Roman intermediary, Giorgio Mattei, bought an estate of 1,060 hectares from an aristocratic landlord, this time near Asciano, fifteen miles southeast of Siena. Mattei was an established expert in settlement programs, having played a similar intermediary role in the shipping of Italian settlers to Libya in the late 1930s. His closest collaborator in the Tuscan deals, Italo Montagna, had been the administrator of the Libyan concessions of no less than Count Giuseppe Volpi di Misurata, governor of Tripolitania in the mid-1920s. After looting the Asciano estate of its timber trees and other assets, he found a group of would-be farmers in Campania and, by exploiting the usual Catholic connections and government programs, sold the broken-up estate back to them. This time the profit was an astonishing 270 million lire, gained in part by negotiating a price twice as high as the one he had paid. In a similar operation near Buonconvento, Mattei had been able to see the price of a crumbling estate treble in less than a year. In the face of these scandals, the moderate and conservative press was somewhat at a loss. Anticommunist local newspaper *La Nazione*, for example, ran a series of articles in which the plight of the southern peasants who had moved to the Buonconvento farms was discussed in moving detail.[76] But the journalist presented the farmers as victims of unscrupulous and greedy middlemen, leaving out the political dimension of these transactions.

The conservative press had a hard time papering over the strong political motivations guiding these settlement plans. Landlords and conservative authorities viewed them as opportunities to imagine a different kind of countryside, where order and obedience could be restored. The possibility of welcoming postcolonial refugees seems to have been especially appealing. Six families of refugees from Libya, for example, settled in 1955 at Colle di Malamerenda, a few miles south of Siena on the Cassia road.[77] Upon instructions from two lawyers, they too had formed a cooperative while in a refugee camp in Campania, after losing most of their possessions during the North African conflict. They had paid 200,000 lire to join the coop, but in Tuscany they worked as laborers for a daily wage of 85 lire. These families had probably been promised access to land ownership as well, although too little information remains about them in the archives to assess their situation. By the 1960s, the presence of both postcolonial refugees and resettlement experts was familiar enough that seemingly outlandish proposals could

[76] Piero Magi, "Quei Poveri Diavoli di Contadini," *La Nazione*, May 24, 1962; and "Mostrarono un Podere ma ne Consegnarono un Altro," *La Nazione*, May 26, 1962.
[77] ACdLSI, Federmezzadri IX. 4, folder Profughi di Malamerenda, 1954–1956.

be seriously debated. When the Tunisian government expelled thousands of Italians in 1964, the president of the Reclamation Consortium of the Orcia Valley, Corrado Peruzzi, wrote to the Italian Embassy in Tunis to investigate the possibility of resettling some of the Italian refugees to some of the many abandoned farms in the area.[78] The embassy wrote back with interest and asked for further information. Peruzzi then wrote to the consortium's members and several of them took the proposal quite seriously. Large-scale landowner Franco Anghiben, for example, argued that it was an excellent idea, as long as the refugees would not be offered sharecropping contracts, for which they might not be culturally and technically equipped. However, "if we got into the frame of mind of truly spreading small-scale ownership, I would be in favor of giving up a part of my estate to this purpose!" Even though Anghiben did not mention it explicitly, we can be fairly certain that he expected to be duly rewarded by the state for his patriotic sacrifice. The embassy failed to follow through.

By the time the national government produced a law about the crisis of sharecropping in 1964, the countryside of central Italy had already changed beyond recognition.[79] The law banned the stipulation of new sharecropping contracts, thereby signaling the official end of a system of land tenure that had dominated much of northern and central Italy since the late Middle Ages. But this measure came into force a full decade after new sharecropping contracts had began drastically to decline. The existing contracts were grandfathered into a new regime, which officially acknowledged the entrepreneurial role of the sharecropper, who could in some cases introduce agricultural innovations even without the owner's permission. Furthermore, the landlord could no longer interfere with the family life of the sharecropper, as had been the case for centuries. Finally, the law attributed 58 percent of the revenue to the sharecropper and made evictions even more difficult for the landlord, thereby gesturing toward some of the most pressing demands of the peasant movement. The law, however, did not envisage any system for the existing sharecropping contracts to be transformed over time, eventually leading to peasant ownership of the farms. It was only in the early 1980s that a law finally turned the few remaining sharecropping contracts into potentially perpetual leases.

At least since the eighteenth century, the coherence of the Tuscan landscape had been imputed above all to the social and spatial consequences of the sharecropping contract. Whether they loathed or admired

[78] Archivio Storico della Val d'Orcia, box 182, Possibilità migratorie Val d'Orcia.
[79] This was law number 756, issued on September 15, 1964.

it, generations of Tuscans had marveled at the fundamental resilience of the "civilization" Tuscan mezzadria had created. As we have seen, this system had been under increasing pressure for decades. It had taken fascism's repertoire of violence and blandishments to give it a new lease on life in the interwar period, when demographic growth and declining productivity thwarted the many efforts made to reform the system "from within." Nevertheless, many landlords and their political representatives hoped that these reforms would succeed, preserving mezzadria in at least its basic socio-natural configuration. These hopes were shattered by the wave of social conflict that swept through the region in the decade after Liberation. Some landlords reacted to the challenge by embracing modern specialized agriculture; others began to sell their land to the highest bidder; and yet others remained paralyzed by bitterness and resentment. As for the peasants, their reactions were at least as diverse, although these generally involved their more or less gradual distancing from traditional agriculture and settlement. The question as to whether these peasants were expelled from the land or chose to leave, on which rivers of ink were shed in the 1950s and 1960s, cannot be answered, for it relies on a dichotomy of coercion and choice that is utterly unrealistic. Most peasants experienced both the violence of decisions made for (or even against) them and the exhilaration of new opportunities for social change.

The rural exodus shattered the coherence and legibility of the landscape and of the society that had shaped it. Tuscans viewed the exodus itself as both an inevitable step toward modernity and an incomprehensible process. Beyond disorientation, there was no single and homogenous response to the transformations taking place in the Tuscan countryside. Different actors debated the features that a "modern" rural society should assume, as a minority began to doubt the desirability of modernity itself. The physical and semantic void left behind by the rural exodus needed to be filled in by any means necessary, whether it was through the recapitalization of specialized agriculture, the modernization of the farmhouses, or ambitious resettlement plans. The initial response to disorientation and loss of legibility was a collective *horror vacui*, which led in a number of disparate (and sometimes desperate) directions. In the years of the exodus, widely diverse agendas were premised on the notion that emptiness needed to be filled in. It was only later, in the 1970s, that it became clear that Tuscans could only hope to manage rural emptiness before they could find ways to valorize it.

4   The Uses of Emptiness: Rural Tuscany after the Exodus (1970–1985)

The adventurous tourist can find an unintentional monument to the rural exodus (if such a thing can be imagined to exist) deep in the Orcia valley, in the municipality of Radicofani, spread over the alluvial plain that stretches between the hilltop hamlet of Contignano to the west and the ramparts of Mount Cetona to the east. Just below the remnants of an abandoned abbey built in the eleventh century lie an outlet tower, built on a thirty-meter-long underground tunnel, and an imposing channel spillway jutting out from the river bed. These cement structures were meant to complement an embankment dam that was never erected (Illustration 15). Although access to the site was theoretically banned, I could climb over the spillway and walk right into the channel through which water would have run when the reservoir filled up. Then I descended into what would have become the bottom of an artificial lake and walked upstream to one of several crumbling farmhouses, once destined for submersion. Although the roof had long collapsed, the upstairs windows were still largely intact, their shutters open wide onto an expansive view of the valley and its concrete ruins, resplendent under the February sun.

As I climbed up to go back to my car, I stumbled into other, arguably even more incongruous, artifacts. Some benches had been laid on top of an embankment, facing an exercise station made of wooden parallel bars. A sign next to the station invited me to engage in six different and rather strenuous routines, both depicted and described on a multicolor panel. The sign title announced this as the thirteenth station in something called "Policrosalus" – "multicolor health," I surmised – promoted by the city government. A few steps farther, by the side of the road, two more signs sat next to each other: a tall pole sported a yellow sign bearing the warning *Pericolo!* (Danger!), while a much shorter one supported a red-and-white plaque with a black arrow inviting me to proceed on a *Percorso vita* (Life path). Clearly, at some point someone had indeed regarded this site as worthy of recognition, albeit in a backhanded kind of way. Before condemning the area as unsafe, the local administrators had

Illustration #15 Part of the unfinished dam at San Piero in Campo, in
the Orcia valley.

envisioned the construction site as the centerpiece of a multistation exercise path *en plein air*.[1] How to make historical sense of these rural ruins,
with their incongruous and contradictory meanings? How could these
ruins exist in a valley that had surged to the status of a World Heritage
Site on account of its landscape? And how could I go beyond the facile
indignation that such a question may invite, to understand the incongruity of these artifacts as the product of multiple stories that, on that winter
morning, I failed to decipher?

A clue to these questions lay all around me, although I was not aware
of it when I first visited the site. This was one of the few corners of the
Orcia Valley that looked and felt like working farmland, with no country
hotel or swimming pool in sight. The simple brick-and-mortar buildings that I saw around me, lost in a sea of arable land, sheltered herds
of sheep, and occasionally I could get a glimpse of white wooly animals
grazing behind metal fences. As I realized much later, the recent history

[1] Laura Valdesi, "La Diga Dimenticata che Incombe sull'Abbazia," *La Nazione* (Cronaca
di Siena), January 22, 2011.

of the Orcia Valley, like many other areas in southern Tuscany, can be told as the tale of two animals, one omnipresent and the other relatively rare: after the sharecroppers' exodus, sheep had multiplied, whereas cattle had dwindled. But this had been anything but a foreordained outcome. The unfinished San Piero in Campo dam, which I had visited that morning, was meant to take its place within an extensive network of irrigation infrastructures, private and cooperative farms, pregnant cows, fattening calves, selection centers, and public slaughterhouses, all of which would have "recovered" southern Tuscany's "animal husbandry vocation" (*vocazione zootecnica*).

Whereas in the 1970s the Chianti, not without controversies and detours, found its agricultural niche in the production and trade of wine, the area between Siena and Grosseto was still searching for a way out of a seemingly unstoppable demographic and economic decline. At the same time, thousands of Sardinian shepherds migrated to the region, moved into the farmhouses deserted by the sharecroppers, and began to raise sheep, primarily for milk, encountering both support and hostility from rural Tuscans. Within a few short years, they had reinvented the sheep milk cheese that bore the name of the "ideal town" that Pope Pius II built in the fifteenth century (*pecorino di Pienza*). As mentioned in Chapter 1, Pius II had himself dreamt of stopping the painfully slow flow of the Orcia River and creating a lake down in the valley, to be admired and exploited by the people of Pienza.[2] Without abundant access to water and locally grown fodder, Tuscan bovines did not have much of a chance in an increasingly competitive European meat market. Sheep, by contrast, thrived, although not everyone welcomed them, their keepers, and the way of life they demanded. The multi-station exercise path, assembled in the late 1990s, was an awkward yet poignant attempt at reconciling the twisted and truncated trajectories that make up the region's recent past and that are still embedded in the landscape. After all, in the face of its history, it did take at least a few parallel bars to reimagine the Orcia Valley as a place of leisure and recreation.

In this chapter, I will focus on southern Tuscany and will reconstruct two related processes, one centered on visions of a bovine-rich future that never quite materialized, and the other on rural Tuscans' reckoning with their relatively ovine-rich present. In the 1970s hardly anyone objected to the dream of a generously irrigated and intensively cultivated

---

[2] The lake was never created, although some locals believed for a long time that the body of water had once existed, in an age of plenty ushered in by Pius II (who had been born in the area) and ended shortly after his demise. See Fabio Pellegrini, *L'Utopia Idrualica di Pio II nell'Immaginario Antico e Moderno della Val d'Orcia* (San Quirico d'Orcia, 2006).

future replete with locally produced steaks (*bistecche*) and cuts for boiled beef (*lesso*), dishes Tuscan sharecroppers had dreamt of for generations. Sheep rearing, by contrast, had complex and (to some) unpalatable associations, exacerbated by the perceived otherness of the Sardinian shepherds who were involved in this activity. When some of these shepherds came to be implicated in a slew of kidnappings, tensions flared, contributing to a general reappraisal of the sharecroppers' exodus and its consequences. At a deeper level, this chapter aims at spatializing the history of southern Tuscany in the wake of the rural exodus. In this period, vastly different perspectives, perceptions, and experiences met and collided, shaping this territory in contradictory and open-ended ways, thereby forging an overtly incongruous landscape. Only by foregrounding spatial change does it become possible to appreciate the multiplicity and open-endedness of the trajectories that converged in this region. As Massey reminds us, "the spatial, crucially, is the realm of the configuration of potentially dissonant (or concordant) narratives. Places, rather than being locations of coherence, become the foci of the meeting and the nonmeeting of the previously unrelated and thus integral to the generation of novelty."[3] Like any other landscape, but perhaps with unusual poignancy, southern Tuscany was built by the incongruous encounter of multiple truncated trajectories, which we must follow in space and time.

Visions of Green: Irrigation Plans in Southern Tuscany

According to one estimate, by the early 1970s, Tuscany's departed sharecroppers had "vacated" approximately 800,000 hectares. One-fourth of this land had been completely lost to agriculture, while the rest had been divided between two different kinds of tenure: approximately 60 percent had come to be cultivated directly by its owners, whereas the rest had been purchased by companies that employed wage labor.[4] The crisis of sharecropping raised the issue of abandoned land, which was unanimously understood to have expanded to an unprecedented extent. Well into the 1980s hardly anyone questioned that land "abandonment" was a problem, but estimates and definitions of this phenomenon varied widely. The Communist-controlled regional government, established in 1970–1971, estimated that 40 percent of Tuscany's agricultural land was either abandoned or "insufficiently cultivated" in the

---

[3] D. Massey, *For Space* (London: SAGE, 2005), 71.
[4] Archivio Storico del Movimento Operaio Senese (ASMOS), Fondo Peris Brogi, Box XIII 1, folder 3, subfolder 1971, report by Duccio Tabet, titled "Prime Considerazioni sui Tipi d'Impresa Agricola in Toscana."

mid-1970s.[5] The Georgofili Academy, the mouthpiece of the landlords, criticized this view by arguing that farms should be the units of analysis, rather than "land" as a disembedded entity. Thus, for instance, the unused land that belonged to a successful farm specializing in modern viticulture should not be regarded as "abandoned," even though vineyards might occupy a small portion of the total area. Even more localized studies, conducted by city council members who knew the history of every plot in their jurisdictions, failed to produce clear results, since their estimates were based on comparisons between past use and future possibilities that were anything but uncontroversial. How should land rented out for periodic sheep grazing be regarded, for example?

In spite of these difficulties, the newly empowered regional government pressed ahead: in 1977 it produced a census of abandoned land and instituted a complex bureaucratic machinery for the possible reassignment of land regarded as neglected, although the current owners could also apply for funds if they committed themselves to a cultivation plan. In so doing, the Communists in charge of the administration kept a promise that dated back to the peasant struggles of the 1940s and 1950s, albeit in a context that had changed beyond recognition. Special committees were set up to evaluate applications, and a fund was established to indemnify the previous landlords and provide subsidies and incentives for the prospective farmers, especially young ones and those who created cooperatives.[6] Some data seemed to suggest that a "return to the land" was imminent. Enrollment in the Tuscan high schools that focused on agricultural subjects (istituti tecnici agrari) increased by 22.5 percent between 1974 and 1977, and college-level courses in rural and agrarian matters also increased in popularity.[7] Tuscany's administrators, however, could hardly hide their disappointment when the first round of applications for neglected land came in. Applications for less than 10,000 hectares arrived from the entire region, roughly half of them from the current landowners; many of the applications had to be rejected because of the applicants' lack of qualifications, revealing a wide gap in Tuscan society between ideological imaginings and practical commitments.[8]

[5] Archivio della Camera del Lavoro di Siena (ACdLSi), Confederale, Box IX a. 9, folder IIa Conferenza Regionale sull'Agricoltura, report titled "Individuazione delle Terre Incolte e Insufficientemente Coltivate."

[6] "Sono in Tanti a Chiedere Terra da Coltivare," Agricoltura Toscana 2 (February 1978): 8–10.

[7] "Conferenza Regionale per l'Occupazione Giovanile," Agricoltura Toscana 4/5 (Giugno 1977): 6.

[8] "Con il Primo Decreto di Assegnazione Operante la Legge sulle Terre Incolte," Agricoltura Toscana 9 (September 1980): 12–13.

On one level, these attempts at rejuvenating agriculture through the settlement of young farmers organized in cooperatives show that through the 1970s most administrators and politicians looked at the Tuscan countryside with predominantly productivist eyes. They generally dismissed the idea of foresting the "abandoned" land as a measure of last resort, for example, noticing that woods already covered 40 percent of the region but only contributed 2 percent of the agricultural revenue, and that such contributions kept decreasing rapidly.[9] As late as 1981, leftist union leaders openly acknowledged that the top priority of rural policy was the "expansion of the productive base" (*estensione della base produttiva*): the creation of protected areas and other conservationist measures constituted "a novel and significant step forward in the culture and needs of Tuscan society, but these orientations should not detract our attention from the fact we still need to take care of basic conditions (*condizioni di base*), such as the assistance to agricultural development."[10] On one hand, these leaders regarded production as "basic" – that is, as more fundamental than other considerations. On the other hand, their public pronouncements betrayed the increasing awareness of possible alternatives.

It would be simplistic to chart the Tuscan leftists' trajectory along a linear axis opposing productivism and conservationism, or material and postmaterial values. The 1970s also saw these leaders (as well as a large portion of Tuscan society) engage in subtle debates about the meanings and implications of speculation in rural contexts: increases in production were only legitimate if they did not result in speculative ventures. In other words, productivist arguments were built on a "conservationist" core that opposed, both at the discursive and practical levels, endeavors that preserved the deployed material and cultural resources and those that threatened to deplete them by accepting high risks and seeking excessive gain. Underlying these debates was the paradox of a countryside that seemed to accrue value only insofar as its population dwindled and its traditional activities were abandoned.

In the course of the 1970s, the Tuscans who militated in the organizations of the Left discussed rural speculation around at least two related themes, both of which were inscribed into the landscape. First, they used this notion to bemoan the spread of "monocultures," which they contrasted sharply with the rapidly disappearing mixed agriculture typical of traditional sharecropping. This was the case, above all, with the

---

[9] "La Seconda Conferenza Regionale dell'Agricoltura," *Agricoltura Toscana* 9 (September 1978): 3–16.

[10] ACdLSi, Confederale, Box IX a. 5, Folder Agricoltura CGIL. Document dated November 7, 1981 on the general objectives of the regional government for the period 1982–1984.

proliferation of specialized vineyards in the Chianti and in other wine producing areas. The restructuring of these vineyards was taking place with public funds, originating from national and supranational sources, but the beneficiaries of these funds were by and large people and organizations external to local rural societies. The profile of these outsiders varied greatly, ranging from small-scale industrialists with a passion for winemaking to multinational corporations, which reached agreements with aristocratic landowners for the reinvention and marketing of their brands and production.[11] Specialized vineyards, thus, could appear as speculative ventures because they were often controlled by outside actors who took advantage of public support, and because the obsessive care bestowed on them contrasted with the desertion of the surrounding areas. Accusations of speculative intentions, however, were not limited to viticulture. As we will see later in this chapter, even sheepherding could be perceived as speculative because of its exclusive focus on milk production and its association with Sardinian immigration.

The other activity to be routinely linked with speculation was the construction industry, which, ironically, employed many former sharecroppers. Tuscan leftists viewed building speculation as a constant threat. The regional government estimated that average land values in the region's most desirable areas trebled from 1970 to 1976 (which roughly corresponds to a 50 percent increase in real terms), and it accused local administrations (most of them also controlled by the Communist Party) of giving out building permits all too easily.[12] In this case, too, public funds seemed to promote practices that ran counter to widely shared commitments, such as the revitalization of agriculture. Inaugurating a long series of similar initiatives, in 1979 the national and regional governments, in cooperation with several banks, designated 1.4 billion lire of public funds as collateral for the granting of 14 billion lire in low-interest mortgages, to be used for the restructuring of the rural housing stock or, with strict restrictions, the building of new structures for agricultural purposes.[13] In this case, too, the regional government kept a promise made by the Communist Party in the 1950s and 1960s (see Chapter 3), but again in a radically changed context. These funds allowed work on almost a thousand buildings, but it was an open secret that many of these restructuring initiatives served the needs of the burgeoning tourist industry rather than agriculture. Moreover, the mixture of restrictive

---

[11] A. Fiorentino and M. Massa, *La Collina Fiorentina tra Speculazione* Edilizia (Florence: Edizioni Pappagallo, 1979):148–150.

[12] "La Seconda Conferenza Regionale dell'Agricoltura," *Agricoltura Toscana* 9 (1978): 3–16.

[13] "Edilizia Rurale: Recupero del Patrimonio e Nuove Costruzioni," *Agricoltura Toscana* 3 (June 1980): 25.

regulations and subsidies that was promoted by the regional government contributed to the increase in land values in a few select areas, such as the Florentine Chianti, and did little to stem devaluation in more remote areas.

In sum, the empowerment of local authorities in the allocation of public funds, due to the creation of the regional governments in 1970–1971, enabled Tuscany's leftist administrators to implement measures that had long been on the agenda of the Communist Party, such as the reassignment of under-cultivated land and the restructuring of the housing stock. But these initiatives were only aspects of a larger vision. When the national government issued a new comprehensive law for agricultural support in 1977, the so-called Quadrifoglio (four-leaf clover) Law, Italy's regional administrations were given the chance to set their own priorities and follow their implementation.[14] Almost half of the 217 billion lire reserved for Tuscany was designated to expand irrigation and animal husbandry.[15] Making good on promises dating back to the postwar years, the regional administration set out to revitalize cattle rearing and forage production on irrigated land, viewed as possible paths to prosperity for the region's less prosperous areas.

By now it should be clear how deep the roots of this project of revitalization reached. Cattle rearing promised to preserve the agricultural vocation of vast stretches of territory, stem the spread of land abandonment, and, most importantly, create a legible landscape made up of integrated activities linking functionally differentiated areas. Moreover, this integrated territorial system, built thanks to the vision and resources of newly empowered local administrators, effectively countered the speculative tendencies at work in other parts of Tuscany. This was an activity that did not privilege small parts of the territory and neglect the rest, as was the case with viticulture. The cattle industry promised to be economically self-sustaining, at least in the sense that it responded to the ever-increasing demand for beef among Italians, who imported most of the meat they consumed. Finally, cattle rearing could preserve more people on the land than highly mechanized wheat cultivation, increasingly the most common crop grown in the drier areas of southern Tuscany. Unlike what had happened in the Chianti, where cattle rearing could not be integrated with specialized viticulture, in southern Tuscany wheat

---

[14] This law (Law 784/1977) was willed by long-time Minister of Agriculture, and Christian Democrat heavyweight, Giovanni Marcora. It committed some 7,000 billion lire and led to the construction of thirty-two dams nationwide, among countless other infrastructural works. Marcora's own background was in the construction industry.

[15] "217 Miliardi da Spendere Presto e Bene per la Nostra Agricoltura," *Agricoltura Toscana* 4-5-6 (June 1980): 3–12.

(and other grains) could also fruitfully complement animal husbandry, providing fodder and pastures on land under rotation.

To get a more concrete sense of what these visions entailed, let us focus on the Orcia valley, where a particularly active reclamation consortium had been reshaping the landscape since the 1930s (see Chapter 1). The exodus had hit this area of the province of Siena particularly hard: almost half of its population had left by the mid-1970s. As we have seen, the Orcia valley had also been at the forefront of the postwar conflict over the future of sharecropping. The consortium, now led by Corrado Peruzzi, who had succeeded Antonio Origo, had no doubt as to what kind of infrastructure work the valley needed to stem the demographic bleeding and find a new purpose. Through the 1960s, the consortium worked on drafting a series of plans for dam construction and the irrigation of significant portions of the valley.[16] The details changed over time, with the early plans calling for the construction of smaller dams on several tributaries of the Orcia River, as well as on the creation of hillside lakes. At the end of the 1960s, following the example of the adjacent Paglia valley, where a dam and reservoir had been built at San Casciano dei Bagni, the consortium leadership settled on the idea of erecting a dam on the Orcia itself, at San Pietro in Campo, receiving an enthusiastic endorsement (as well as financial support) from the province's most important bank (the Monte dei Paschi di Siena) and of the newly organized Tuscan Agency for Agrarian and Forestry Development (ETSAF, previously part of the Agency for the Reclamation of the Maremma).[17] All the local political forces, from the Communists to the Christian Democrats, declared their unqualified support for the initiative. The goal was equally uncontroversial: to grow enough forage crops on irrigated land to turn the valley into a "meat factory" through the spread of bovine husbandry, preferably organized in cooperatives.

The emotional impact of these visions on the local population was remarkable. As early as 1964, the consortium's newsletter told the story of a man who had returned to the valley after having left as a boy some sixty years before.[18] His childhood memories were filled with penury and squalor: "We lived on that hill, in a house that was then all shattered,

---

[16] Archivio del Consorzio di Bonifica della Val d'Orcia, Box 1871, "Rilevazione generale dei fabbisogni di opere pubbliche per lo sviluppo della bonifica del comprensorio e formulazione di proposte di programma quadriennale," dated January 17, 1964.

[17] ASMOS, Fondo PCI, Faldone X I1 Comitato di Coordinamanto della Valdorcia, Fasc. 1979. Little pamphlet called Notizie Sanquirichesi (Year VI, n. 11, December 15, 1979). Front title is "La Diga si Farà."

[18] "Il Ritorno di Bista. Quasi una Novella," La Val d'Orcia 3 (June 1964): 1–3. I found this publication in the Archivio Storico del Consorzio di Bonifica della Val d'Orcia, Campiglia d'Orcia.

with bare floors. The stink of the animal waste came through the broken walls. The gaps were so wide that we could see the sheep, whose bleating rattled us." They felt isolated, especially in the winter, and the nearest school was ten kilometers away, so no one attended. Now he had come back, and where his old house stood he had found "a new house, with a bathroom, electricity, running water, a stable for the animals, and a building for the manure that is far enough from the house and does not stink." The house was now next to a paved road, and the farmer who lived there had a FIAT 600 and two mopeds, to go into town whenever he felt like it. The modernity of the dwelling resonated with that of the landscape as a whole: the old Orcia river, whose bed during his childhood was almost one kilometer wide, was now channeled between straight banks, and all around were green fields. And this was only the beginning: the Vellora, one of the tributaries of the Orcia, was to become an artificial lake with 2.9 million cubic meters of water; two other large lakes were to appear near Monticchiello, alongside many more hillside lakes. "The Val d'Orcia will no longer be the sunburnt land of our childhood, but a fertile valley, devoted to the production of meat for the national market." If all of this had been around when he was a boy, his family would surely have never left!

These dreams of regeneration were long-lived in the Orcia valley. A decade later, in 1975, when the plan for the San Piero in Campo dam was firmly in place, the consortium summoned the inhabitants of the valley to an open meeting where a plastic model of the dam would be displayed.[19] The project promised nothing less than dignity and self-reliance for the valley's dwindling population: the new infrastructures would make the valley dwellers "actors and participants in their own future" by recovering a meat-producing past that dated back to Roman times, when the valley supposedly was one of the main suppliers of beef for the imperial city. If sheep, rather than cows, currently provided the most important source of income, that was about to change. The valley would now become "self-sufficient, full of white herds of cows, and not one blade of grass would be left in the field to rot, not one sack of grains would go wasted, not one unemployed man would have to aspire to an industrial job, not one family would have to emigrate, witnessing instead the replacement of the goat with the cow, the mule with the tractor."[20]

There is little doubt that this kind of powerful rhetoric was also meant to defend the record of a particular institution, the reclamation consortium, which had been founded by the Fascist regime and had remained

---

[19] "Questo 'Nostro' Consorzio," *La Val d'Orcia*, May 1, 1975: 1–2.
[20] "Un Programma ... Bianco, dai Rosei Aspetti," *La Val d'Orcia*, December 30, 1975: 3.

under the hegemony of the large-scale landlords after the war. No sooner was the plan for the dam agreed upon than a conflict flared between the consortium and the Communist-led administrations at the regional and local levels. In 1976 the regional government told the consortium leadership that their jurisdiction would no longer extend beyond the use of water for agricultural purposes and made fund disbursements predicated on the creation of another consortium between the four municipal governments affected by the project. By 1977, the reclamation consortium had been all but divested of any authority.[21] Starved for funds and subjected to ongoing criticism, the reclamation consortium was dissolved in 1980, when its functions were devolved to the Comunità Montana (Mountain Community), a layer of public jurisdiction between the municipality and the province created in 1972 to coordinate the social and economic activities of city governments in disadvantaged areas across the country.[22] Thus, the leftist administrators, by propounding the notion that the future of the valley should be in the hands of elected officials rather than landowners, took the opportunity to settle scores that dated back decades. But the conflict was also about the ownership of a project that inspired widespread hope and that could be translated into further political consensus.

These visions of regeneration, which relied on ambitious irrigation plans, were especially compelling when they spoke the language of rupture. At the beginning of the 1970s, only 6.5 percent of Tuscany's agricultural land was irrigated, vis-à-vis a national average of more than 14 percent.[23] Most of the irrigation works that had been accomplished before the 1970s had taken the form of hillside lakes, which fit the spatial makeup of a landscape divided into distinct estates. Each landowner (or small group of landowners) received funds to carry out these small-scale projects on their property. By the mid-1970s, approximately a thousand of these lakes had been created throughout Tuscany, but according to some estimates as few as 5 percent of them were actually used.[24] This waste of public funds proved in a tangible way that the old policy of reclamation (*bonifica*), institutionalized by the Fascist regime in the 1930s, had run its course. The newly empowered (and Communist-led) regional

21 ASMOS, Fondo PCI, Faldone X I1 Comitato di Coordinamanto della Valdorcia, Fasc. 1979. Document by the Consorzio di Bonifica dated May 24, 1979 and addressed to many public institutions and political parties.
22 ASMOS, Fondo PCI, Faldone X I1 Comitato di Coordinamanto della Valdorcia, Fasc. 1981. Minutes of meeting of April 13, 1981.
23 "Regione Toscana e Agricoltura. Gli Interventi sul Territorio," *Agricoltura Toscana* 3 (March 1980): 13–21.
24 Regione Toscana, *Una Politica per l'Irrigazione, Atti del Convegno Regionale*, Siena, March 26, 1975 (held by IRPET library): 103–105.

administration could point to the blatant failure of irrigation as a sign of the more general failure of reclamation policy, which relied on the consensus and participation of the landlords. The collapse of sharecropping, the rural exodus, and the devolution of agricultural policy finally made a novel course possible.

For all their ambitious thrust, these plans were above all defensive: they were meant to stop depopulation, which, in the words of Peris Brogi, the agricultural councilor of the province of Siena, had led to "the destruction of many material and human resources whose recovering will require the effort and work of many generations, supported by remarkable financial resources."[25] In other words, productivism and conservationism coexisted in the same vision. First of all, Tuscany's administrators vowed to quadruple the amount of irrigated land, bringing it from 67,000 hectares to approximately 250,000. This fourfold increase would have been achieved through the construction of dams and reservoirs, viewed as the safest source of water for the region (Tuscans drew less than a quarter of their water from artificial reservoirs, as opposed to rivers and wells). These public works, however, were not only to be relevant to agriculture. They would also have contributed to quenching the growing thirst of the expanding towns and even created a supply of water for industrial use. Their proponents justified them also as flood-management measures. The memory of the devastating floods of November 1966, when Florence and many other Tuscan cities had gone under water, was very much alive. Thus, these multifunctional dams would also have contributed to the integration of town and country, which had never been farther apart in Tuscany's long history.

A major dam on the Tiber would have created a reservoir of more than 100 million square meters and irrigated approximately 60,000 hectares. Another dam of similar size was to be built in the Ombrone basin, at the confluence of the tributaries Farma and Merse, near the border between the provinces of Siena and Grosseto. Smaller dams would be built downstream in the Ombrone valley; another would have been erected north of Siena, on the river Arbia near Petrignano, with a reservoir of 12 million square meters and an irrigated area of 1,500 hectares; and a similar-sized dam would also have been built on the Orcia River, at San Piero in Campo, with a reservoir of 11 million square meters and an irrigated area of 3,400 hectares. The creation of several dozen hillside lakes would have complemented the project.

[25] ASMOS, Fondo Peris Brogi, Box XIII 1, folder 4. Report titled "Problemi dell'Irrigazione."

As far as cattle rearing was concerned, the plan called for an integrated system with three major components. First, cows of reproductive age would be raised in farms that used both stables and open pastures. These farms would be located at higher elevations (over 500 meters above the sea level) – in the areas most affected by depopulation and land neglect. Second, the weaned calves would be purchased by farms at lower elevations, where they would be fattened in stables and fed fodder crops locally grown on irrigated land. Third, when ready to be slaughtered, the calves would be taken to a state-of-the-art public slaughterhouse located at Chiusi, a major transportation hub near the border with Lazio and Umbria, from which beef could easily reach its destination markets.[26] The recommended breed was the traditional draft cattle of central Tuscany, the "Chianina" (named after the Chiana Valley), one of the biggest bovine breeds in the world (adult males can easily weigh more than 1.5 tons), and thus one of the most costly to raise (Illustration 16). The quality of its meat, used for the famous Florentine steak, and rural Tuscans' widespread familiarity with its needs, would have made up for its relatively high cost. Tuscany would thus take pride of place in a larger project meant to make Italy more "meat sufficient," in overt opposition to the European Community's alleged designs to limit Italian agriculture to low-value-added staples or a few specialty items.

The cornerstone of this comprehensive vision was the Chiusi slaughterhouse, whose construction had been in the works since the mid-1960s. This massive structure, with 75,000 cubic meters of built volume stretched over an area of 10 hectares, was erected entirely with state funds.[27] Construction took place between 1978 and 1980, and the product was a plant capable of processing 160 head of cattle and 200 pigs a day, equivalent to a yearly production of 10,000 tons of beef and 20,000 tons of pork. Its operational life, however, was as short as it was controversial. Soon to be regarded as a shamefully oversized monster, it remained active for just a few years before being handed over to the regional government and then to the city of Chiusi as a dismissed area, another rural ruin, itself in need of "reclamation."

The slaughterhouse's demise was only one facet of the plan's overall failure. Of the planned dams, for example, only the one on the Tiber, at Montedoglio, was ever completed.[28] Paradoxically, the plan fell victim

---

[26] ACdLSi, Confederale, Box IX a. 5, folder Agricoltura CGIL. Leaflet by CGIL-CISL-UIL dated July 1975 and titled "Per l'Ammodernamento e lo Sviluppo dell'Agricoltura."

[27] ACdLSi, Confederale, Box IX a. 5, folder Agricoltura CGIL. Correspondence between Emo Bonifazi and the Ministry of Agriculture in January 1970.

[28] This dam, built between 1977 and 1993, captured the attention of all of Italy on December 29, 2010, when it suffered a major breach, leading to the evacuation of almost

Illustration #16 Chianina oxen, the largest cattle breed in the world, 1950s.

to its systemic coherence touted by its proponents. If decisions were to be made at the level of the river basin as a whole, with very high upfront investments, the plan would stand or fall on the basis of the compatibility between its diverse goals (flood control, irrigation, potable water supply, etc.), as well as their feasibility and perceived urgency. The debate over these issues put in direct confrontation visions and actors that had until then looked at each other from a distance. At opposite extremes were the proponents of agriculture in the regional administration and in society at

five hundred people. The ensuing polemic focused on the quality of the cement used, but also on the dam's disproportionate size, now that its agricultural uses were far from clear. See Laura Montanari, "Cede la Diga sul Tevere. Notte di Paura," *La Repubblica (Cronaca di Firenze)*, December 31, 2010.

large, many of whom were of peasant extraction, and the activists in the burgeoning environmentalist movement, most of whom were urban professionals. In Tuscany the debate took place squarely within the Left, and in many cases between different constituencies within the Communist Party itself.

Crucial to the outcome of the controversy was Marco Marcucci, who became the first environmental councilor in the regional government in 1983, and its president in 1990. It was under his influence that a team of experts was charged with drafting a "basin plan" (*piano di bacino*) for the Ombrone River, which covers almost the entirety of southern Tuscany, to assess the feasibility and impact of the dams. The committee was called on to express an opinion on both the larger project on the Farma and Merse Rivers as well as the smaller one on the Orcia, viewed as parts of the same plan, thereby considerably raising the stakes of the decision. The committee was made up of environmentally minded experts, including Giuliano Cannata, one of the founders of Lega Ambiente, Italy's oldest and best organized environmental NGO, and professor of hydrology at the University of Siena. Professor Cannata told me in an interview that this river basin plan was the first in Italy to be based on a rigorously quantitative type of cost-benefit analysis.

Whatever the claims underlying such quantitative rigor, it is hard to imagine how the cultural and political background of the drafters could not inform the panel's final recommendation.[29] The experts began by noticing that the Ombrone basin had one of the lowest population densities in Italy, and that its "resources" lay far more in the diversity of its flora and fauna and in the beauty of its landscape (that is, in the existence of extensive "abandoned" areas) than in its agricultural potential. But even without quantifying the economic value of these "intangibles" and the costs incurred in their depletion, the projects failed on their own terms, in the sense that viable and far less expensive alternatives could be easily envisaged to irrigate the relatively small portion of the basin that had agricultural potential, to manage the risk of floods, and to mitigate the summer droughts. In one particularly striking passage, the report goes as far as to argue that it would have been less costly to supply the coastal population of southern Tuscany, inflated by summer tourists, with tank trucks in the eventuality of a severe drought than to incur the huge sunk costs of the envisaged infrastructures. More generally, the report mercilessly denounced the myth of multiuse dams in the

---

[29] *Piano di Bacino del Fiume Ombrone. Studi Preliminari*, Rome, March 7, 1991. Professor Cannata kindly shared this document with me when I visited him in Rome in December 2011.

Mediterranean context, because the demands for irrigation and potable water both peak in the summer, and warned against the high risk of silting at the dam sites, given the clay soil prevalent in the area, and of the erosion of the coastal beaches, a phenomenon already taking place on a large scale because of ongoing digging in the river beds for construction purposes.

The experts' trenchant findings beg the question of why such momentum had been building behind these projects: how could so many people believe in visions that within a few years would seem little less than outlandish? Cannata used the familiar language of transition to make sense of this shift: "The process through which institutions and organizations change their cultural perceptions of large-scale economic and technological transformations is always rather slow and complex. Often the official motivations and claims of social groups and 'lobbies' (and to a lesser extent even individuals) follow needs that are no longer present or are becoming economically obsolete, and they ignore promising possibilities opened up by the new rapid evolution."[30] In other words, the awareness of the shift from a productivist to a postproductivist (or post material) sensibility permeated society unevenly, reaching a few well-informed individuals first, and then different institutions and organizations depending on their degree of investment in the status quo. In the context of this study, however, it is Cannata's emphasis on perception that matters most. The debate over the dams, which ordinary people could follow in the press and to an extent even participate in, contributed to the emergence of a new appreciation of Tuscany's rural landscape, increasingly understood in its putative systemic coherence. But these new perceptions were both temporal (that is, they were predicated on specific narratives of transition) as well as spatial, in the sense that actors were called on to give new meanings to the places they lived in, perceiving them in novel ways. Quite simply, narratives of change only make sense when they become emplaced, when the places we live in are made to tell particular stories and feel in particular ways, thereby becoming "landscapes."

At one level, the history of the irrigation plan's failure is a story of generational change. The older generation of Tuscans, largely born and raised in sharecropping families, could not envisage a future for rural Tuscany that would not be predominantly agricultural. Their sons and daughters, by contrast, were far more open to the new possibilities

[30] P. G. Cannata, "Le Risultanze e le Proposte," in *Regione Toscana, Studi Preliminari, Piano di Bacino dell'Ombrone*, Vol. VII, Rome, 1991, quote on p. 89. This document was also kindly provided by Professor Cannata.

offered by tourism and the culture industries. This interpretation is strengthened by the fact that many of the infrastructural projects fell victim to the wave of scandals that shook the country in 1992–1993, the so-called Clean Hands (*Mani Pulite*) investigations, which uncovered systematic corruption in the adjudication of public contracts to private companies, especially in the construction industry. This was the case with the dam of San Pietro in Campo, whose works were interrupted when the national wave of scandals hit the management of the Milan-based company in charge of construction at the site.[31] Even Marcucci spent time in jail, accused of receiving bribes for a large project meant to mitigate the floods of the Arno (he was later acquitted). It was in this kind of climate that the report by Professor Cannata and his colleagues was officially released. Actual work on the Farma-Merse project, whose projected costs had increased exponentially through the 1980s, would never get started. In a bitterly ironic twist, the antispeculative thrust that had informed the launching of these projects in the 1970s had given way to the worst kind of speculation, casting a shadow on the honesty of an entire generation of leftist administrators of peasant extraction.

There is no doubt that some actors took advantage of the opportunities offered by these projects in shameless ways, nor were all these unscrupulous actors outsiders with respect to local society. The landowners whose property was to be expropriated, for example, were offered extremely "generous" rates for what was by any standard marginal land. Public authorities also allowed a plethora of small-time construction companies to dig in the river beds and accumulate materials that would later be sold at high profit. These actors' speculative behavior, however, should not lead us to doubt the sincerity of the people who had hatched the infrastructural plans in the wake of the rural exodus. The sources clearly show how deeply they felt about the necessity of ambitious projects, which they viewed as the last chance to turn around the destiny of an increasingly illegible and deserted territory. In many cases, the older rural Tuscans, born and raised in peasant families, were no more "materialistic" than their environmentally minded sons and daughters. They simply perceived their territory in different ways and made the rural landscape tell different stories from those that would soon become hegemonic. To them, the

---

[31] See the series of articles published in *DonChisciotte*, a periodical based in San Quirico and reflecting positions very critical of the old "productivist" paradigm: Antonio di Paolo, "Da Bilancino a S. Piero in Campo," *DonChisciotte* 7, 36 (November 1992): 6; Antonio di Paolo, "Diga: Atto Secondo," *DonChisciotte*, 8, 37 (January 1993): 7; Antonio Di Paolo, "La Diga Crollata," *DonChisciotte*, 8, 38 (May 1993): 7. The estimated costs of the project had risen from 10 to 115 billion lire in fifteen years. Work on the dam had begun in the mid-1980s.

dams and irrigation projects were endowed with powerful symbolic values; these projects represented an opportunity to redress injustices and keep promises that still resonated in the land, even though they belonged to a different temporality.[32]

The livelihoods of thousands of farmers hung in the balance of this shift between different visions and sensibilities. In many parts of southern Tuscany, farmers faced an extremely uncertain and complex situation in the late 1970s and through the 1980s. International wheat prices fluctuated wildly: they were high in the early 1980s, then they dropped in 1987, rose again for a few years, and collapsed in the early 1990s. The regional government, as we have seen, offered incentives to create animal husbandry cooperatives, which demanded far more labor and capital than wheat cultivation, but the long-term viability of these ventures relied on infrastructural projects that in most cases would never see the light of day. The European Community was trying hard to change the Common Agricultural Policy and curb its outrageous costs. Within these supranational reform plans, Tuscany and other "poor" agricultural regions did not seem to hold much of a future in either wheat or meat production. To negotiate this contradictory set of signals and expectations was no easy matter.

In the face of these uncertainties, the number of bovines raised in Tuscany kept declining. There were almost half a million head of cattle in the early 1960s; by the mid-1970s their number had been cut in half; and by 2000 there were little more than one hundred thousand bovines in the entire region. Viewed from the perspective of the would-be animal farmers, this decline had dramatic consequences. Anthropologist Jeff Pratt spent years researching the changing meanings of work among the inhabitants of the lower Orcia valley, straddling the provinces and Siena and Grosseto.[33] He found a social and natural landscape in flux, where families adopted a variety of strategies to cope with rapid change. Already in 1987, only a third of the farms in this area kept cattle. The farmers who had responded to regional incentives by creating cooperatives for cattle rearing faced

---

[32] A document testifying to this sensibility is Ilario Rosati, *L'Agricoltura Senese: Tra Memoria Storica e Politica Corrente* (Montepulciano: Il Grifo, 1985). Rosati was a Communist leader, former mayor of Chiusi, and the vice president of ETSAF. In this book, lengthy discussions of the challenges faced by Sienese agriculture are interspersed with historical documents and memories, thereby envisaging a degree of continuity and coherence between the current projects and Tuscany's leftist tradition. As Rosati and the other members of the "old guard" came under attack (especially over the Farma-Merse project), they tried to defend themselves by harking back to a usable past of democratic achievements and populist emancipation.

[33] J. Pratt, *The Rationality of Rural Life: Economic and Cultural Change in Tuscany* (Chur: Harwood Academic, 1994).

increasingly dire prospects. Pratt tells of the Montenero cooperative, established with a regional loan in 1973 by thirty farmers to fatten 650 calves a year by producing animal feed (mostly green barley and hay) on approximately 300 hectares. But the calves of the Chianina breed, which they had initially adopted, did not fatten fast enough, so they had to import calves from as far away as Poland and France, while they were often forced to purchase slurry in the market because of the low productivity of their arable land. The venture collapsed entirely in 1989, when the regional government withdrew its subsidies.[34] But the farms that placed their prospects with wheat cultivation did not fare much better in the long run, and not only because of the erratic prices: the use of massive amounts of fertilizers and insufficient rotations depleted the soil, producing wheat that tended to fall over. As Pratt shows, many of these farmers felt nostalgic about a traditional agrarian past at which they had barely glimpsed in their childhood. The old sharecroppers were poorer, and yet they were better off, in the sense that they were imagined to have been in better control of their destinies. Ironically (and somewhat tragically), the same projects that had promised to empower rural folks in new ways were now subjecting them (again) to forces that seemed out of control.

The destiny of wheat production in Tuscany was indeed decided very far from the region's hills and valleys. In 1988, the European Community issued a series of provisions meant to reduce the enormous surpluses of agricultural products that could not be placed in the market and were thus stored and ultimately destroyed. Even though the Community had been lowering the target prices for wheat and other products for years in order to reduce the gap with international prices, the average price of European wheat in the early 1990s was still two-thirds higher than that set at the Chicago Board of Trade. The proposed solution was to provide European farmers with incentives to stop producing wheat, thereby reducing the supply of an unsalable product. Farmers received different levels of incentives depending on whether they kept their land fallow for five years, reforested it, put it under rotation of fallow and pasture, and so on. In the Tuscan context, these incentives to "set aside" land clashed with the still very recent policies meant to curb land abandonment and neglect. In the course of barely a decade, land abandonment seemed to have been transformed from a problem into a virtue to be encouraged.

The Tuscan regional government did try to resist European regulations by limiting the permissible form of land set aside to a rotation of fallow and pasture, but this measure was struck down in court. Turning

---

[34] Ibid.: 74–75.

the regional administrators' worst fears into reality, Tuscan farmers responded to European incentives enthusiastically.[35] Among the twenty Italian regions, only Sicily surpassed Tuscany in the amount of land that was taken out of production. By 1991, a full quarter of Tuscany's arable land had been set aside, and approximately half of this land resided in the provinces of Siena and Grosseto. Moreover, the vast majority of Tuscan farmers chose to keep their land fallow for at least five years, thereby taking advantage of the highest level of incentive provided by the Community. The contrast with the disappointing campaigns to repopulate the countryside of a decade earlier could not have been starker. Observers, without much fear of being contradicted, could label those campaigns as "pure demagoguery."[36] And Corrado Barberis, one of Italy's foremost experts on agricultural matters, commented wryly that Tuscan farmers had gone full circle, from exploited sharecroppers to idle rentiers.[37]

The destiny of Tuscan cattle was almost as paradoxical. At the beginning of the 1980s, when hope for the revitalization of animal husbandry was still widespread, commentators observed with relish that the Chianina breed was experiencing something of a renaissance. Bulls and their semen were being exported to all corners of the world, from the United States to Australia, to be crossbred with a wide range of bovine breeds, including zebus, to increase their size and reduce the fat content of their meat.[38] This led to a new emphasis on the genetic purity of the breed, which even in Tuscany itself had been crossbred for decades with northern livestock. By the end of the 1980s, only thirty-four thousand head of Chianina nationwide were regarded as pure enough to be registered in the breed's herd book, established back in the 1930s. But by then this relative rarity had already become an asset. A conservationist ethos, coupled with the existence of customers willing to pay a premium for an authentic Florentine steak (or the "pure" genetic material capable of producing it) radically reorganized the breeding of Chianina cattle.[39] A select network of small-scale breeders took their cattle to the mountains, where for eight months of the year the animals could graze free (and almost for free, too). In 1982 they coordinated with the breeders of four other specialty cattle varieties

---

[35] Stefano Tesi, "Più Terre a Riposo che Campi di Grano," *Toscana Qui*, 12, 2 (February 1992): 3–15.

[36] Leonardo Torrini, "Chianti: Mercato d'Oro, Però...," *Toscana Qui*, 9, 11 (November 1989): 72–75.

[37] Stefano Tesi, "Più Terre a Riposo che Campi di Grano": 10.

[38] Raffaele Giberti, "Ma il Chianino si Sposa all'Estero," *Toscana Qui*, 1, 5 (May 1981): 126–129.

[39] Enrico Nistri, "Hanno Scelto la Libertà," *Toscana Qui*, 12, 1 (January 1992): 68–73.

from central Italy (the Romagnola, the Maremmana, the Marchigiana, and the Podolica) to create the 5R Consortium, in charge of certifying the authenticity of premium beef. Thus, the bovines that only a few years before had inspired dreams of revitalization for thousands of hectares of irrigated land looked down from their mountain peaks onto a landscape their plow-drafting ancestors would hardly have recognized.

A Landscape of Dread and Civility: Debating the Sardinian Shepherds' Migration to Rural Tuscany

Whereas in the 1970s Tuscan bovines inspired dreams of regeneration, ovines elicited a more complex reaction. In the last pages of her memoir, published in 1970, Iris Origo reflects on the many changes her estate and the Orcia valley have experienced since the end of the war, and on how futile it would be to stand remonstrating against the tide of time. But it is a spatial gesture that proves her point. As if guiding the reader's gaze over the valley from the vantage point of her villa, she waxes elegiac: "It is possible that, within a generation, the woods will again spread down toward the Orcia, as they did ten centuries ago – and already, just across the valley, a large colony of Sardinian shepherds are grazing their sheep on what used to be cultivated fields."[40] Origo could not hide her dismay at seeing her valley, so painstakingly reclaimed under her husband's leadership during the Fascist period (see Chapter 1), go to "waste" again. But to underscore the ineluctability of change, welcome or otherwise, she quoted, in Italian, a famous passage from Dante's Paradiso, whose translation reads: "All your things find their death, as do you."[41] Origo could not have been unaware of the context in which these words appear in the Divine Comedy. Dante has just asked his guide and ancestor, Cacciaguerra, to comment on the changes he sees happening in the city of Florence and on how the current city compares to that of his times. Cacciaguerra harshly critiques the corruption and vulgarity of Florence's current urban life, contrasting it with the virtues of the past. The main reason for this decline, he argues, is the increasing impurity of the city's population, now polluted by unscrupulous intruders from the countryside. Lamenting the erosion of previously sacred boundaries, Cacciaguerra proceeds to list some of the now decayed noble families, who were united in purpose and equal in blood, and contrasts their unity with the factionalism that besets Florence in Dante's times.

[40] I. Origo, *Images and Shadows* (London: John Murray, 1970), 249.
[41] "Le vostre cose tutte hanno lor morte / Sì come voi" (Paradiso, XVI, 79–80).

Origo was far from alone in seeing the Sardinian shepherds that were settling in remote corners of the Tuscan countryside as intruders, or at least as incongruous presences, nor was she unique in linking, however implicitly, the spread of sheep grazing to decadence, decay, and even death. But this was a phenomenon of great complexity, which was interpreted in a wide variety of ways both by local actors and external observers.[42] For each statement associating sheep grazing with agricultural and social decay, it is possible to find one making the opposite case, praising the Sardinian shepherds' presence as the vulnerable bulwark that had prevented a large portion of Tuscany's rural land from collapsing into utter desertion. Just a few years after the publication of Origo's memoir, for example, geographer Flora Furati assessed the Sardinian shepherds' presence as an unqualified boon for the province of Siena: "Their ability to work, their entrepreneurship, and their sober and constructive labor have been primary factors in the restructuring of land ownership and in the replacement of cultivations with animal husbandry."[43]

This stark diversity of assessments became a chasm when some Sardinian immigrants, many of them shepherds, were implicated in a series of kidnappings that began in 1975 and terrorized the population for the following two decades. The emptiness that the sharecroppers' exodus had left behind seemed to be filling not only with incomprehensible or seemingly primitive practices but also with the dread of violent crime. Tuscans reacted to this peculiar form of immigration on the basis of perceptual schemes and narrative tropes that had developed in the previous decades of struggle and compromise. And in making sense of these strange and frightening events, Tuscans also made sense, however provisionally, of the ways their recent history had reshaped their surroundings. Tuscan kidnappings bore an unmistakably rural character, and Tuscans came to appreciate the implications of the rural exodus, as well as debate the future of their countryside, by framing these dramatic events.

---

[42] Tuscany had a long tradition of transhumant pastoralism, which linked the coastal areas to the mountains of the interior. The sharecroppers of central Tuscany were used to seeing large herds of sheep pass through twice a year, in November and May, in alternate directions. Both conflicts and commercial transactions were common between the transhumant shepherds, whose residence was in the mountains, and the sharecroppers. Countless toponyms and a whole network of paths still testify to this ancient practice. By the 1960s, however, transhumance had all but disappeared in Tuscany, because of the depopulation of the mountainous areas and the transformation of coastal animal husbandry into a sedentary activity, allowed by the defeat of malaria. Maybe even more importantly for the purpose of this chapter, the very memory of these activities was largely lost to ordinary Tuscans, both urban and rural. See Paolo Marcaccini and Linda Calzolai, *I Percorsi della Transumanza in Toscana* (Florence: Polistampa, 2003).

[43] F. Furati, *Aspetti della Migrazione Pastorale Sarda in Provincia di Siena* (Pubblicazioni dell'Istituto di Geografia, Universita' di Siena, Facolta' di Magistero, Arezzo, 1973): 32.

The first Tuscan kidnapping took place in July 1975 in a villa located deep in the Florentine Chianti, near Greve.[44] The villa had recently been purchased by a wealthy American-Argentinian aristocrat, Alfonso de Sayons, who had hired shepherd Mario Sale, born in the Barbagia town of Mamoiada, as a laborer and, as it turned out later on in the court proceedings, occasional lover. Sale organized his kidnapping, and when de Sayons taunted his masked captors by saying that he knew that Sale was behind the whole thing, they grew scared and killed him. His body was never found. Twenty-five more kidnappings took place in Tuscany between 1975 and 1990. Sardinians, most of them shepherds, turned out to be implicated in twenty of them.[45] Seven of the victims never came back. The bodies of at least three of them were cut into pieces and fed to the pigs, a detail so horrific that it was later referenced by Thomas Harris in his Hannibal Lecter saga.[46] One-quarter of the victims were children, as young as seven. Many of the victims were taken from their country homes, which they (or their parents) had recently purchased thanks to small fortunes made as small-scale entrepreneurs or professionals during Italy's economic miracle. They were held in abandoned farmhouses or in tents; in a few cases, they were simply chained to a tree for weeks on end.

Mario Sale was arrested in March 1977, as he was herding his sheep on the Calvana mountain, between Florence and Prato, and taken to the Siena prison. He escaped with two accomplices a few days later, never to be caught again. Sale was also implicated in the most famous of the Tuscan kidnappings, that of West German teenagers Suzanne and Sabine Kronzucker and their little cousin Martin Wächtler in July 1980. The three kids were taken in front of their relatives from a villa in the Florentine Chianti, where they were spending their summer vacations. The father of the teenage girls, Dieter, was a very well-known journalist who worked for the West German public television network. The fact that foreign tourists, and famous ones at that, had been targeted by the kidnappers triggered a very strong reaction. The Pope made an appeal, and the Cardinal of Florence bent the law by acting as an intermediary between the bandits and the victims' families, receiving a formal warning from the authorities.

---

[44] The following account is largely based on Riccardo Catola, "Quel Pomeriggio del 3 Luglio 1975," *Toscana Qui* 3 (1981): 26–35.

[45] The rural setting and character of these acts were so apparent that when two people, a boy of twelve and a woman, were taken from the center of Florence, everyone noted the anomaly. The culprits, a couple of Florentine hoodlums, were arrested before any ransom was paid, but the woman had already been killed and buried in a wood. The press labeled these incidents as copycat cases.

[46] T. Harris, *Hannibal* (New York: Delacorte Press, 1999).

The police organized massive manhunts in the Tuscan countryside, focusing their attention on the Sardinian pastoral community: they searched hundreds of farmhouses and took people into custody for interrogations, convinced that the kidnappers relied on the complicity of their fellow Sardinians. Special legislation against the Mafia, which had never been applied in Tuscany, was activated so that specific suspects could be expelled from the region and even taken into custody and held without charge for several weeks. The police produced thousands of posters with the faces of suspects, all of Sardinian origin, and made it known that a list of approximately one hundred people would be targeted for preventative expulsion. Most of these suspects were shepherds who risked losing everything they owned.[47] These measures, however, proved fruitless. After being held captive in two separate tents for sixty-eight days, the German kids were released near Sociville, in the Sienese countryside, upon payment of a ransom of 2.3 billion lire. Rumor circulated that, in order to hide the money from the authorities, it had been delivered stuffed in the carcass of a pig.[48] Upon the release of his daughters, Dieter Kronzucker bemoaned: "the sky of Tuscany will no longer have the same color for us." Martin Wächtler, interviewed by the German magazine *Stern* on the thirtieth anniversary of his ordeal, volunteered on his part that he had been back many times, because "the landscape is just wonderful."[49]

As Tracey Heatherington has recently argued, central Sardinia occupied a special place in the political imagination of Italians.[50] It was a land of banditry and irreducible resistance to state authority, a place where patriarchy reigned supreme and yet women, left alone for months on end by their transhumant husbands, could establish forms of matriarchy. Sardinian society was primitive, as unintelligible as its languages, and stubbornly attached to its traditions. The political valence of these tropes, however, was contradictory. Sardinia was at times perceived as utterly different and remote, and at others as intimately familiar and as the possible stage for dreams of regeneration. For the Italian radical Left, for example, it was a land of romantic rebelliousness, vividly portrayed by anthropologist Franco Cagnetta in the early 1950s and then enshrined in

---

[47] Giacomo Mameli, "In Toscana Siamo 15 mila Sardi: Paghiamo per le Colpe di Pochi," *L'Unione Sarda*, August 24, 1980.

[48] I do not know what to make of the almost obsessive references to pigs, both alive and dead, in these stories, except to say that they defined a kind of "rural Gothic" that truly terrified me when I was a kid growing up in the late 1970s in suburban Florence.

[49] "Ich bin immer wieder gerne da, die Landschaft ist einfach wunderschön." www.stern .de/lifestyle/leute/was-macht-eigentlich-martin-waechtler-245772.html

[50] T. Heatherington, *Wild Sardinia: Indigeneity and the Global Dreamtimes of Environmentalism* (Seattle: University of Washington Press, 2010).

a critically acclaimed 1961 neorealist movie directed by Vittorio De Seta, *Banditi a Orgosolo*. Cagnetta famously and controversially argued (and De Seta dramatized) that "every bandit knows that he is nothing but an unlucky shepherd," persecuted by a semicolonial state.[51] Prominent Milanese editor Giangiacomo Feltrinelli, not long before blowing himself up in a botched bombing attack in 1972, contacted Sardinia's most famous bandit, Graziano Mesina, investigating whether he would be willing to become the leader of a full-fledged guerilla movement on the island. Images of Barbagia women successfully protesting prospected military exercises in the common pastures became part of the iconography of the 1968 generation. By contrast, the memoir of shepherd-turned-linguist Gavino Ledda, *Padre Padrone*, published in 1975 and turned into a movie by the Taviani brothers two years later, portrayed the pastoral society of central Sardinia as brutally oppressive and hopelessly out of step with the ferments that were brewing in the rest of Italy.

These widely known images and cultural artifacts affected both the Tuscans' reactions to the kidnappings and the Sardinians' defensive strategies. A plethora of Sardinian experts, for example, relied on the work of Cagnetta, among others, to warn Tuscans against adopting the kind of militaristic measures against the Sardinian community that the Italian state had been deploying for generations on the island, with utterly counterproductive results.[52] Mario Sale himself, after his escape from prison, tapped into this rich imagery, by fashioning himself a hero of Sardinian separatism and penning several political "manifesti" with the pseudonym of Chaka II, after the famous Zulu king of the early nineteenth century. Tuscan journalists repeated ad nauseam that in traditional Sardinian culture shepherds kidnapped their rivals in the context of elaborate vendettas, often in retaliation for animal theft, and that "over there" it was sometimes easier to seize people than sheep, because "people do not bleat."[53] The same commentators who portrayed the kidnappers as an isolated minority that terrorized ordinary shepherds as much as urban Tuscans would then speak of them as the atavistic remnants of a civilization transplanted across the sea and corrupted by the lure of consumer culture. In Tuscany, however, these nationally shared tropes interacted with a deeper and more localized set of concerns, which had to do with the contentious meanings of rurality in the region's future.

---

[51] F. Cagnetta, *Banditi a Orgosolo* (Florence: Guaraldi, 1975): 289. The original research had been published in *Nuovi Argomenti* in 1954 and immediately banned and requisitioned throughout Italy for its subversive character.

[52] Widely cited was also Antonio Pigliaru, *Il Codice della Vendetta Barbaricina* (Milan: Il Maestrale, 1975).

[53] R. Catola, "Quel Pomeriggio del 3 Luglio 1975": 33.

Debates about the role of the Sardinian migrants, even before the kidnappings began, were also about the implications of the rural exodus and about the ways in which Tuscans could come to terms with the emptiness the sharecroppers had left behind. The kidnappings drew the attention of the whole region to the rapid changes that had been taking place in the countryside. What had happened on the hills of Tuscany after the sharecroppers' flight?

When the migration of Sardinian shepherds to continental central Italy (primarily Tuscany, Lazio, Umbria, and Romagna) reached the peak of its visibility in the late 1970s and early 1980s, several informed observers interpreted it as the product of two social crises that also signaled two historic defeats for the Italian political Left in its attempt to shape rural change. First was the crisis of traditional sheep husbandry in Sardinia, which became the victim of its expansion in the face of entrenched social and economic structures. The shepherds who migrated to central Italy came primarily from the mountainous interior of the island, especially from the Barbagia and Ogliastra regions, in the province of Nuoro. These areas had been witnessing remarkable social and ecological changes since the end of the war.[54] Over the previous century, a vulnerable balance between herding, agriculture, and population pressure had developed, based on the limited spread of small-scale landownership, integrated by the widespread reliance on communal lands for both pasture and wheat cultivation. Very few shepherds owned enough land to be self-reliant, although the majority of families owned enclosed plots around the villages for subsistence agriculture. Therefore, most shepherds used the communal open lands in the summer and led their herds to lower elevations in the winter, spending months away from their families. A complex system of norms and institutions presided over the management of the communal lands, which went through rotations of fallow, fodder crops, and wheat, with the whole area opening to grazing after the wheat was harvested. Most families engaged in both agriculture and sheep herding, but in different proportions. A small but important portion of the population concentrated on agriculture, leading a sedentary life in the villages. A larger percentage of the population lived primarily on the revenue of transhumant herding, understanding agriculture as women's primary activity, to be complemented by the men's work for a few summer weeks.

This precarious balance was upset by a complex interaction of internal and external pressures after the end of the war. The international integration of Italian agriculture made wheat cultivation in the Sardinian

---

[54] Benedetto Meloni, *Famiglie di Pastori: Continuità e Mutamento in una Comunità della Sardegna Centrale 1950–1970* (Turin: Rosenberg & Sellier, 1984).

mountains increasingly unprofitable, leading to its gradual abandonment and the subsequent migration of Sardinian peasant farmers to cities in Italy and other European countries. In the meantime, demand for sheep milk cheese (*pecorino*) increased, boosted after the early 1960s by the European Community's subsidies for milk production. Coupled with the increasing availability of previously cultivated land around the mountain villages, demand for cheese led to a remarkable expansion of sheep (and to a lesser extent goat) husbandry. In the early 1960s there were already 2.4 million sheep on an island whose total area is 2.4 million hectares. By the mid-1980s, the number of sheep had increased to just short of 4 million. This expansion put pressure on communal land use precisely at the moment when the opportunities for transhumance began to dwindle, due to a variety of alternative land uses in the lower-elevation areas, especially around Sardinia's expanding towns. The outcome of these processes was a severe shortage of land for pastures. The Christian Democrats, the dominating force in the province of Nuoro, set out to manage local tensions by deploying a mix of patronage and military control, in addition to encouraging emigration. The Left called for sweeping land reforms that would encourage sedentary animal husbandry, but sedentarization spread as agriculture declined, rather than as the consequence of reform and political struggle. The Left understood this process as an expansion of the pastoral economy without its modernization.

The second crisis was that of sharecropping agriculture in central Italy, which, as we have seen in the previous chapter, the Left failed to manage or even fully comprehend. The rural exodus made hundreds of thousands of hectares available for alternative use. In Tuscany alone, cultivated land declined by more than 250,000 hectares between 1963 and 1973. At the same time, pastures increased by more than 200,000 hectares. Especially on the Appennines and in the southern half of the region, this meant the creation of vast areas where sheep could graze. In retrospect, the combined force of these "push and pull" factors made the migration of Sardinian shepherds seem inevitable, generating the myth that they had simply filled a void, an empty social and ecological niche that could be profitably occupied.[55] In reality, migrants actively participated in this process, contributing both to the collapse of sharecropping and to its contentious aftermath. The relatively gradual and protracted nature of the Sardinians' migration is an indication of the fact that the

---

[55] Typical of this interpretation is the following statement: "Sardinians arrived at the threshold of the 1970s, when the most ferocious (*feroce*) urbanization had dissolved a whole social fabric, a culture that had taken shape over centuries with great dignity." Maurizio Naldini, "Se non ci Fossero Bisognerebbe Inventarli," *Toscana Qui* 1 (March 1981): 36–39, quote at p. 37.

availability of land for pasture was actively generated or at least negotiated over many years: this was no sudden invasion.

Sardinian shepherds began to cross the sea with their animals soon after the end of the war, moving first to the Maremma, the recently reclaimed but sparsely populated coastal plains that stretch from the province of Livorno to the northern part of the province of Rome. When, in the early 1950s, the government launched a land reform in this area with the intention of establishing small- and medium-size farms for the local population (see Chapter 2), Sardinian shepherds began to move inland, as the conflicts over the crisis of sharecropping peaked and then gave way to the peasants' exodus from the farms. In Tuscany, the Sardinians settled at first in a wide variety of areas, including the Chianti, often directly recruited by large-scale landlords eager to find alternative uses for their abandoned farms. When the recapitalization of Tuscan vineyards and olive groves gained steam in the late 1960s (see Chapter 3), they began to cluster in the mountains and in the clay hills of southern Tuscany, establishing veritable colonies in the provinces of Siena and Grosseto.

For many Tuscan landowners, sheep husbandry represented an ideal solution to the exodus, at least in the short run: it required little or no investment on their part and promised a reliable flow of cash rent. Moreover, Sardinian shepherds represented the kind of motivated (if not necessarily pliant) labor force that they perceived to have forever lost when their former sharecroppers had turned into rebellious Communists. The contract that most of them engaged in, called *soccida*, required that the shepherd and the landlord contribute half of the flock each and share the revenue in half.[56] The sale of milk and, to a lesser extent, lamb meat allowed many migrants to save considerable amounts of money, which they invested in the purchase of relatively cheap land. Over time, some of them became large-scale landlords in their own turn.

It is not easy to assess how many Sardinian shepherds settled in Tuscany between the early 1950s and the mid-1980s. A team led by anthropologist Pier Giorgio Solinas estimated the number of Sardinian shepherds' families in the province of Siena in the late 1980s at 340, with almost 1,300 members. All of them owned numerous sheep (approximately 300 per breeding business on average), and almost two-thirds of them owned land as well (an average of 73 hectares per family).[57] For

---

[56] Linda De Angelis, "Pastori Senza Terra. La Mezzadria e la Soccida," in P. G. Solinas (ed.), *Pastori Sardi in Provincia di Siena, Vol. III: Economia e Strutture Sociali* (Siena: Edizioni Universitarie, 1990): 159–183.

[57] P. G. Solinas, "Il Flusso Mignatorio nel Tempo. Profilo Quantitativo," in P. G. Solinas (ed.), *Pastori Sardi in Provincia di Siena, Vol. I: Demografia e Economia* (Siena: Edizioni Universitarie, 1988): 7–32.

Tuscany as a whole, an estimate of ten thousand Sardinian shepherds and their families is probably not too far off the mark. We have firmer estimates for Tuscany's sheep population, which followed a remarkable trajectory, increasing by 40 percent between the early 1960s and the late 1970s, when it approached seven hundred thousand head, while cattle decreased by almost exactly the same ratio. In the province of Siena, the number of sheep decreased from little more than one hundred thousand at the end of the 1940s to a low of fifty-three thousand at the end of the 1950s, to then go back up to 140,000 twenty years later, signaling first the flight of the sharecroppers, many of whom had small flocks for family consumption and small-scale cheese making, and then the arrival of the Sardinians and the general restructuring and expansion of the sector.

The migrants moved with their animals, which belonged to a different breed than the Appenninic sheep that had been common in Tuscany for centuries. Bred especially for milk production, the Sardinian sheep is a relatively poor provider of lamb meat and an even poorer producer of wool. By the early 1980s, 40 percent of sheep in Tuscany belonged to the Sardinian variety, which had also crossbred to some extent with the indigenous breed. Even so, it is important to keep in mind that Sardinians never controlled more than 25 or 30 percent of sheep husbandry in Tuscany as a whole, although their share was much higher in certain areas, such as the Mugello valley north of Florence and the hills and mountains between Siena and Grosseto. Moreover, most Sardinians who migrated to central and northern Italy did not do so as shepherds: they sought industrial and service sector jobs in the cities, like other southern immigrants, and like the former "indigenous" peasants.

To sum up, the migration of Sardinian shepherds to Tuscany and central Italy more generally has been a geographically and demographically limited phenomenon. Its symbolic and analytical relevance, however, was great: the ways in which the locals and the migrants made sense of each other are crucial to understanding the historic development of Tuscany's rural landscape, both as a material entity and as a set of contradictory perceptions. The relevance and resonance of the Sardinian shepherds' migration can be fully appreciated if we place it at the intersection of several narrative practices that linked notions of transition to experiences of place. The multiplicity and contradictory character of these emplaced trajectories go a long way toward explaining the sense of incongruity perceived by many observers, who tried to come up with one coherent story capable of "explaining" how this migration fit (or failed to fit) into the history and landscape of rural Tuscany, thereby beginning to define what Tuscany itself should stand for. Whether framing the Sardinians' migration to domesticate and integrate their presence, or othering their activities as barbaric, Tuscans and Sardinians alike constructed at the same time the dreaded or desired features of a newly emerging Tuscan rurality.

The first transition story deployed by Tuscans focused on the peculiar character of a migration that moved from remote mountainous locales to other, arguably almost as isolated, rural spaces. If the Tuscan rural exodus had been about the joining of urban civilization by peasants who had long been excluded from it, how to make sense of migrants who sought not only to remain in the countryside, but also to privilege sheep husbandry over agriculture? This move flew in the face of deeply entrenched understandings of the direction that the "rational" flow of change ought to take. To be sure, this was not the first example of rural migration encountered by Tuscans. As we have seen in the previous chapter, southern peasants had been taking over abandoned Tuscan farms since the early 1950s, sometimes with the active involvement of the anti-Marxist forces, eager to sap the strength of the Communist-led peasant movement. Some evidence suggests that, at least at first, Tuscan peasants did understand the migration of Sardinian shepherds as another form of politically motivated settlement piloted from above. A Sardinian shepherd interviewed by anthropologist Linda de Angelis in the late 1980s recalled that many Tuscan peasants believed that he had been paid by the Christian Democrats to replace them, while another shepherd seemed to be subscribing to this interpretation himself: "Sardinians have been used to counter the emancipation enjoyed by Tuscan sharecroppers. What did the landlords do? They divided [the movement] and put up the bogeyman of the Sardinian. They would say [to the Tuscan sharecroppers]: if you do not work, I bring the Sardinians over and you can go to hell."[58] As important as these perceptions proved in making sense of social change, there is little evidence that the majority of Sardinian migrants were actually involved in these schemes. Moreover, unlike the "anti-Marxist" southern peasants, most Sardinian shepherds did not follow the Tuscans into town at the first opportunity. They by and large remained shepherds into the 1980s and 1990s.

Whereas, at a general level, the incongruity of pastoral migration was obvious to most ordinary Tuscans, a select group of experts set out to normalize their presence by spinning another transition story, one that described Sardinian shepherds as fleeing seminomadic husbandry in their homeland in favor of sedentary life in Tuscany. This narrative was reinforced by the perception that the migrants were leaving purely extensive herding in Sardinia to embrace a mix of agriculture and

---

[58] Linda De Angelis, "Pastori Senza Terra": 166–167.

animal husbandry in Tuscany. In other words, these narratives placed the migrants in a journey toward a peculiar, but still intelligible, type of modernity. It would be hard to overstate most experts' hostility toward transhumance and any form of nomadism, viewed as incompatible with modern and civilized life. Even the observers who were most sympathetic to the migrants spared no words in condemning transhumant herding. Luigi Berlinguer, a Sardinian-born law professor at the University of Siena and Communist regional councilor (and Enrico Berlinguer's cousin), emphasized how the availability of land in Tuscany had allowed Sardinian shepherds to emancipate themselves from the backwardness of traditional herding practices: "Transhumance ... is the negation of the modern agro-pastoral farm and constitutes a decisive cause of all the phenomena of 'asocial behavior' ascribed by so much literature to the Sardinian shepherd."[59] This was a judgment that went well beyond issues of productivity and linked nomadism to potentially criminal behaviors, including, of course, kidnappings.

Most experts took it for granted that access to land ownership and self-reliance were these migrants' ultimate goals, and that sedentary life was the natural consequence of those aspirations.[60] Anthropologists were also unanimous in arguing that Sardinian shepherds were "nomadic out of necessity rather than vocation,"[61] and that clear-cut property rights were crucial to overcoming the kind of competition over resources that was the main reason for banditry and antisocial behaviors in central Sardinia.[62] Yet, many of the same experts also commented on the reluctance of Sardinian shepherds to embrace agriculture in any form, also because of its gendered qualities. As Berlinguer put it, "everyone knows that by tradition the Sardinian shepherd has never wanted to become a farmer."[63] In sum, the Sardinian shepherd who migrated to Tuscany was viewed as a settler and landowner by choice, but as a farmer by force; the new circumstances prompted him to engage in agriculture, thereby opening him to agriculture's civilizing influences. As a Sardinian union leader put it in front of an audience of scholars and farmers in Florence, "the shepherd who used to despise the farmer has become farmer himself, and he manages to grow fodder in very arid soil ... this is a merit that

[59] ASMOS, Fondo Luigi Berlinguer, Box VIII 8, Folder Sardi in Toscana, typescript titled "Pastori Sardi in Toscana": 7.
[60] F. Furati, *Aspetti della Migrazione*: 11.
[61] Giulio Angioni, *I Pascoli Erranti: Antropologia del Pastore in Sardegna* (Naples: Liguori, 1989): 132.
[62] Benedetto Meloni, "Codice della Vendetta Come Codice di Regolazione Comunitario. Comparazione tra Passato e Presente," introduction to A. Pigliaru, *Il Codice della Vendetta Barbaricina*: 7–44.
[63] Luigi Berlinguer, "'Tornate nel Sardistan,'" *L'Unità*, September 5, 1980.

must be ascribed to the shepherds, who here in Tuscany have regenerated an activity that would otherwise have been lost."[64] The crucial point in these arguments was that the new civilizing circumstances were rooted in the spatial and social features of the Tuscan rural landscape, broadly conceived.

There was indeed a seemingly simple "environmental" reason for the newly settled shepherds to engage in agriculture more systematically than they did in Sardinia. Tuscany did not have communal lands, and the migrants came to occupy plots that had been at one point sharecroppers' farms (*poderi*), often combining more than one of them to create a continuous space for pasture and cultivation. These plots were far larger than the enclosed fields that surrounded the Sardinian mountain villages, but they were hardly big enough for the extensive grazing needs of the typical flocks shepherds understood as ideal for a nuclear family with a couple of adult males – that is, anywhere between 250 and 500 sheep. Thus, they had to switch to "intensive" husbandry and grow much of the animal feed they needed in the form of barley, rye, and hay, often processed into sileage. They also grew wheat, which they could easily sell for cash and for which they received several kinds of subsidies. By putting the land under rotations of cereal cultivations, pasture, and fodder, they also avoided its depletion and, even more importantly, the spread of invasive Mediterranean maquis plants, such as thistles, which sheep grazing could not control. The spread of these invasive plants was indeed taking place on a massive scale in central Sardinia as a consequence of the peasant farmers' abandonment of the communal lands.[65] In sum, a virtuous circle seemed to be emerging from the carefully monitored balance between husbandry and agriculture in the newly resettled Tuscan farms.

This picture of ecological and social virtuosity was not so much inaccurate as it was selective. More than one-third of shepherd families did not own any land at all well into the 1980s, and many others did not own enough of it, thereby moving their herds to rented plots, sometimes located quite far from their homes. In other words, this was a perception that domesticated the shepherds' migration while stigmatizing the practices that did not align with it. The fact that some migrant shepherds now lived in the old farmhouses, recently deserted by the sharecroppers, seemed to strengthen this optimistic and ecologically inspiring model, at

---

[64] ASMOS, Fondo PCI, Faldone V A10 Pastorizia, Folder 1980, "Il Contributo dei Coltivatori e Pastori Sardi nella Economia Agricola Toscana," conference organized by the Federazioni Regionali Coltivatori Diretti della Toscana e della Sardegna in Florence on September 27, 1980, 39–40.

[65] B. Meloni, *Famiglie di Pastori*: 120–144.

least for some observers. Berlinguer noted how these houses, "one of the most precious examples of cultural heritage and vernacular architecture in our country," were falling apart when the Sardinian shepherds moved in. The new dwellers restored and adapted them to their needs, breathing new life into them.[66] A journalistic report from the same period makes the same point with uncannily similar language: "[the Sardinian shepherds] have restored life to whole areas that were otherwise deserted. They have rebuilt villages, brought electricity and water to farmhouses, but above all they have been an example, demonstrating that some land had been abandoned too precipitously, sometimes chasing absurd dreams."[67] In other words, far from being an atavistic splinter of barbarism in Tuscany's side, these shepherds were simultaneously being civilized by their new dwelling practices, and civilizing the landscape in return.

As we have seen, the Tuscan farmhouses had become powerful symbols of a whole civilization that, some believed, had died prematurely. They were also symbols of a centuries-old tradition, of a kind of permanence that lay at the opposite end from the nomadism that tainted the new dwellers. Yet, these imaginings, too, emerged from selective perceptions. In Sardinia, shepherds, even those who left their families for months on their transhumance journeys, had houses in densely built towns and villages. Their language had very subtle words that starkly distinguished the "civilized" spaces where social life could be enjoyed from the wilderness and isolation of the remote pastures.[68] Unlike the Tuscan sharecroppers, Sardinian shepherds were both creatures of the town and of the countryside. The scattered settlement of the Tuscan countryside was utterly foreign to them. Michelino Marongiu, a Sardinian shepherd who came to Radicofani in the Orcia valley at the age of forty, told a journalist in 1980 that "here [in Tuscany] it's all different. In Sardinia we walked; here we must stay put." What Marongiu meant here was not to contrast seminomadism with sedentary life as types of civilization, but to oppose the temporary isolation of transhumance to the permanent isolation of scattered

---

[66] ASMOS, Fondo Luigi Berlinguer, Box VIII 8, Folder Sardi in Toscana, typescript titled "Pastori Sardi in Toscana" :3.

[67] Maurizio Naldini, "Se non ci Fossero": 38.

[68] Central Sardinians distinguished between *bidda* (built space), which comes from the Latin *villa*, and *sartu* (from the Latin *saltus*) or *kampu*. This is a distinction based on the density of social relations. On the basis of their agrarian functions, the communal lands (*cummonale*) were subdivided between the *vidazzone*, the arable portion that was cultivated at any given time, the *paberile*, the arable portion that happened to be lying fallow for pasture, and *sartu*, the permanently nonarable portion. The difference between this understanding of the landscape and the Tuscan one, founded on the distinction between *città* (town) and *contado* (countryside), populated by different kinds of people and permanently devoted to different activities, was thus great.

settlement in Tuscany's most remote locations. Sardinian shepherds sent for their immediate family as soon as they could, but these families seemed stranded in a potentially hostile land. The journalist himself understood this condition, noticing that in Tuscany these shepherds "are always alone – the man, the dog, and the sheep. It is difficult to see them in the towns. They usually gather in the formerly abandoned farmhouses, which they have restored."[69] In these emplaced narratives, which tell quite different transition stories from those of the "sympathetic" experts, the Tuscan farmhouses become symbols of loneliness and longing, rather than signposts connecting ways of life and generations.

The experts' emphasis on the integration of husbandry and agriculture served the purpose of underscoring the actual or potential integration of the newcomers into Tuscany's social fabric and landscape. Many of these experts, across decades, noticed how little the shepherds were changing the visual outlook of the Tuscan landscape, despite the radical changes in land use and work patterns they had brought about (Illustration 17).[70] In these narratives, the shift toward pastoralism assumed the traits of a bricolage, in which the shepherds made do with the spatial layout inherited from a recent past and a different civilization. In the words of Solinas, "the farmhouses become folds, shelters for the sheep; the hay lofts become stock rooms for the feed and the products; the paved farm yard (*aia*) becomes an enclosure for sheep milking; the houses abandoned by the sharecroppers become lodgings for the shepherds – the sons or the ranch hands (*servi-pastore*) – who spend the night there in the busiest periods of the year."[71] Of course these changes could be perceived as more or less radical depending on the disposition of the viewer. Moreover, in many cases new buildings had to be erected, nested between the vestiges of sharecropping agriculture. The same commentators also noticed that shepherds reclaimed

---

[69] Carlo Cambi, "Al Sardo in Toscana non Date Pane Amaro," *Il Tirreno*, October 19, 1980.

[70] This is how Furati put it: "The transformations of the landscape do not appear striking and the external appearance of the buildings remains more or less unchanged, but in reality all ties to the past have been severed and every activity on the farm take place as a function of ovine husbandry." F. Furati, *Aspetti della Migrazione*: 32. More than twenty years later, anthropologist Benedetto Meloni made the same point: "It is as if Tuscan's hilly sharecropping landscape, moulded by centuries of peasant labor, organically welcomed the newcomers in its fold," B. Meloni, "Pastori Sardi nella Campagna Toscana," *Meridiana* 25 (1996): 167–202 (quote at p. 167).

[71] P. G. Solinas, "Aziende, Patrimoni e Famiglie. Linee di Antropologia Economica," in Pier Giorgio Solinas (ed.), *Pastori Sardi in Provincia di Siena, Vol. III: Economia e Strutture Sociali*: 14–15.

Illustration #17 Sardinian shepherd immigrated to Tuscany, early 1980s.

vast stretches of abandoned land for pasture while razing vineyards and olive groves to the ground.

Despite these experts' efforts, it was indeed difficult to make the image of the vine-destroying shepherd familiar and unthreatening to rural Tuscans, who viewed vines and olive trees as "civilizing" presences in more than a purely agronomic sense. The seemingly all-encompassing interest the shepherds took in their animals stood in stark contrast with the multiplicity of the Tuscan sharecroppers' skills and concerns. As a Sardinian shepherd living in the Mugello valley put it, Tuscan peasants saw sheep husbandry as a minor side activity at best, whereas for people like him it was "a way of life." Moreover, Tuscan peasants had many disparate skills, which they had applied to a wide variety of tasks, turning their hills into orchards; to them, the Sardinian shepherd appeared to only know one thing, herding and milking, and the landscape could not but reflect that.[72] These perceptions of cognitive and spatial impoverishment suggested yet another transition narrative founded on a sense of declension, and it was an uphill battle for the proponents of pastoralism to counter these notions. Bachisio Bandinu, one of Sardinia's best known writers on rural subjects, tried hard to convey the complexity of the shepherds' way of life, contrasting it with that of the extant Tuscan farmers, now hopelessly contaminated by modernity's illusions: "The Barbagia shepherd who moves to the continent is a man, a family, a flock, a world of objects, a way of working, producing, and having fun; a whole culture with its phantoms and its values."[73] In sum, Sardinian sheep pastoralism was far more than a job; just like traditional hillside farming, it was a way of being in the world that developed over a lifetime and across generations.

Many Tuscans strongly believed that the destructive nature of herding extended from vines and olive trees to any wooded area that stood in the shepherds' way. Suspicions of arson were commonplace, and forest fires were routinely attributed to Sardinian shepherds bent on expanding the areas where they could take their flocks to graze.[74] Tuscany was already the most densely forested region in Italy, in stark opposition to relatively bare Sardinia, and forest fires were indeed on the rise all over Italy. A national law, passed in 1975, barred construction on recently burned land in order to discourage building speculation, but it said nothing about herding, an oversight that was often negatively commented on in the press. Tuscan woods, however, had not only been expanding; they had also drastically changed their functions, in that they were no longer embedded in the sharecropping economy and was used as sources of fuel, construction material, and animal feed. By the 1970s many wooded areas had been neglected for years, which increased the risk of summer fires. Perceived as vulnerable spaces devoid of economic value, Tuscan woods were also increasingly thought of as worthy of preservation for ecological reasons. This mix of practical neglect and discursive valorization could not but contribute to the image of shepherds as unscrupulous

[72] ASMOS, Fondo PCI, Box V A10 Pastorizia, Folder 1980, "Il Contributo dei Coltivatori e Pastori Sardi nella Economia Agricola Toscana," conference organized by the Federazioni Regionali Coltivatori Diretti della Toscana e della Sardegna in Florence on September 27, 1980, 28–30.

[73] Bachisio Bandinu, "Restano 'Diversi'," *L'Unione Sarda*, August 24, 1980.

[74] Carlo Cambi, "Al Sardo in Toscana non Date." See also G. Angioni, *I Pascoli Erranti*: 231–238. Not everyone in Tuscany agreed with this perception, of course. In 1979 a reader sent a letter to a specialized journal lamenting the pitiful state of Tuscan woods. But he also wrote of a Sardinian shepherd that he knew, who had managed against all odds to protect a big oak tree that provided his herd with shade in the summer and acorns in the fall. "Il Taglio del Bosco," *Agricoltura Toscana* 8–9 (September 1979): 26–27.

speculators, incapable of appreciating the beauty and noninstrumental value of their surroundings.

Few issues were more muddled and controversial than the Sardinian shepherds' relationship with the instrumental rationality of monetary gain, a trait that could be viewed as simultaneously atavistic and utterly modern, and that permeated their engagements with the environment in which they lived. Unlike the Tuscan sharecroppers, who had to hope that the yearly settlement of their accounts with their landlords provide them with desperately needed cash, shepherds lived in a cash-based economy even when they did not own the land that they used for grazing. They dealt with the market directly, selling milk (and, to a lesser extent, meat and cheese) to buyers without any intermediation. The fact that in Tuscany they faced a relatively restricted (and collusive) group of private cheese-making companies capable of imposing milk prices did not detract from the general impression that Sardinian shepherds, when successful, could accumulate a kind of wealth that would have been unimaginable to traditional Tuscan peasants. Some of them even lived in the former landlords' villas, rather than in the sharecroppers' farmhouses. The prospect of prosperity bred a complex mix of admiration and resentment. As a Sardinian shepherd living in the Maremma put it, "the fact is that many Sardinians have demonstrated that handsome profits could be gained on the very land the locals had given up on."[75] A Tuscan peasant farmer interviewed by Solinas mimicked the deep ambivalence locals felt: "Some said that these Sardinians were nomads, they wouldn't stay, tomorrow they would find another farm to exploit and off they'd go; how could we trust them. And this priest, who saw things clearly, went: 'That's not true. Look, these are stable people, they don't have any other income, if you give them land, they'll improve it.' 'No, they'll destroy it! The shepherd destroys the vineyards, he destroys the olive trees' ... this was the concept, [people believed that] he only knew sheep."[76] In these narratives, financial success bore the stigma of speculation: traditional Tuscan farmers cared about the land and had been its stewards for centuries; the shepherds who had replaced them, by contrast, worked hard but took from the land what they needed in their pursuit of gain, without any concern for the landscape's integrity.

Detailed studies of the strategies pursued by successful shepherd proprietors seemed to confirm their single-minded concern with their

---

[75] Alberto Pinna, "C'E' un Pastore Sardo in Appennino: E' un Bandito?," *Corriere della Sera*, August 18, 1980.
[76] P. G. Solinas, "Aziende, Patrimoni e Famiglie": 18–19.

flocks.[77] They would typically devote less than a third of their land to cultivations, and only one-third of that to wheat, the only crop not employed in the animal husbandry cycle. The rest of the cultivated land would yield feed crops, so that well over 80 percent of the revenue would be derived from the sale of milk and, to a far lesser extent, lamb meat.[78] The extensive use of machines and fertilizers dramatically increased these farms' productivity, so that the ratio of sheep per hectare of pasture was in Tuscany more than double that prevalent in Sardinia. Some of these successful shepherd proprietors had indeed expanded their land holdings until they had hit the property of another Sardinian, a sign that further expansion would be difficult at best. Through selective breeding and carefully monitored feeding, they had also managed to dramatically increase the milk productivity of each sheep, which could be as high as 150 liters per year. Many of these changes, including the spread of scattered settlement and the integration of forage production in the pastoral economy, were actually taking place in Sardinia as well, as anthropologist Benedetto Meloni observed in the mid-1990s, but these signs of "modernity" seemed to be have been prefigured in Tuscany.[79]

These data could indeed suggest yet another transition story, according to which these shepherds had left subsistence husbandry behind in Sardinia to adopt a modern, market-oriented, capitalist outlook in Tuscany. Some experts worked hard at qualifying the nature of the shepherds' modernity. Solinas, for example, drew on Tim Ingold's distinction between hunters, pastoralists, and ranchers to reject the notion that the Sardinian shepherds had become capitalists after moving to Tuscany.[80] From this perspective, shepherds pushed the limits of land fertility and accumulated as many animals as they could, thereby assuming considerable risk. These speculative tendencies, inherent in pastoralism as a way of life, were heightened by the closed character of the productive systems they adopted in Tuscany, where they grew much of the feed they needed for their sheep. The profit they accrued, however, could not be regarded as capitalist because it lacked, in Marxist terms, the abstract quality that derived from the complete commoditization of the factors of production. Shepherds, for example, only accumulated animals up to the point at which they would have had to hire permanent wage labor from outside

---

[77] By "successful," Solinas meant those with more than 100 hectares of land and more than 300 sheep.

[78] Maurizio Gigli, "Cinque Aziende Pastorali. Dati d'Inchiesta," in P. G. Solinas (ed.), *Pastori Sardi in Provincia di Siena, Vol. I: Demografia ed Economia: Profilo Statistico*: 87–119.

[79] B. Meloni, "Pastori Sardi nella Campagna Toscana": 192–194.

[80] Tim Ingold, *Hunters, Pastoralists and Ranchers: Reindeer Economies and Their Transformations* (Cambridge: Cambridge University Press, 1980).

the family (ranch hands were typically paid with an agreed-upon number of live animals). The sheep were not pure commodities, but rather goods that accrued to the family and enhanced its status. The point here is not to assess the accuracy of this interpretation, although it is hard to see how these shepherds would not qualify as at least tendentially capitalist ranchers in Ingold's model. Solinas' framing exercise is relevant in itself, signaling an attempt at rejecting widely disseminated contrasts between the former Tuscan sharecroppers and the Sardinian shepherds based on notions of instrumentality and commoditization. In his account, the migrants were modern subjects, but their modernity did not bear the stigma of unbridled capitalist exploitation of land and labor.

Sardinian shepherds moved to the Tuscan countryside as the Communist Party reached the peak of its consensus and electoral power in the region. The 1970s was also the period in which agricultural policy and territorial planning were increasingly devolved to the regional governments. The issue of whether these shepherds were actual, or at least potential, capitalists and the degree to which they should be supported were of obvious relevance to Tuscany's leftist administrators as well. Like the academic experts and the general public, these local politicians responded to the challenge by deploying perceptual schemes and narratives that had developed historically. Some members of the Communist Party interpreted the Sardinian shepherds' activities in "orthodox" terms, vowing to protect the tenants who were engaged in soccida contracts from exploitation by the landlords and to strengthen the cooperative cheese factories that had been established in the more heavily pastoral areas.[81] The very presence of these cooperatives could be interpreted as another sign of the civilizing influence of Tuscany over the traditionally individualistic Sardinians. A locally famous story is that of Contignano, a hamlet in the Orcia valley where by the late 1960s the majority of the population was made up of Sardinian immigrants. The hero of the story is the local priest, Don Oscar, who set out to conquer the isolation and mistrust of his parishioners by loading an altar on his truck and celebrating Mass in the houses of the Sardinian shepherds, visiting them one by one.[82] After winning them over, he convinced the shepherds to set up a cooperative for the sale of milk. The cooperative proved so successful that it managed to take up the loans necessary to build a housing project for the (mostly "indigenous") poor and elderly. In this story, the dedication of a progressive priest builds an island of integration and harmony

[81] ASMOS, Fondo PCI, Box V A10 Pastorizia, Folder 1980, press release of the Sienese Communist Party, dated September 22, 1980.
[82] R. Catola: 39.

in a territory where hostility is mounting. But he does so by teaching the Sardinians to trust him and become more like ideal Tuscans, thereby prompting them to transition from short-sighted individualism to cooperation and altruism.

The majority of Tuscany's Communist politicians, however, reckoned that most Sardinian shepherds were (or aspired to become) relatively independent proprietors not likely to be mobilized by collectivist arguments. Indeed, local leftist leaders saw the challenges posed by the shepherds' migration as a second chance at avoiding the mistakes they thought they had made in dealing with the departed sharecroppers' struggles in the postwar years. If ideological orthodoxy had sentenced the Communists to irrelevance in the face of the rural exodus, when they had preached that the land was to be conquered and not bought, the limited repopulation of the Tuscan countryside in the 1970s and 1980s offered the opportunity to change gears and truly matter. Evidence of the Communists' relevance would be provided not only by increasing electoral support from a new constituency, but also by the degree to which policy would be able to shape the rural landscape in predictable and legible ways.

For these complex reasons, and in stark contrast to their positions in the 1950s, the Communist regional leaders showed little ambivalence in supporting the shepherds' access to land ownership. Berlinguer went as far as to argue that "a rationalizing form of capitalism" was necessary to "the radical modernization of the pastoral condition."[83] Emo Bonifazi, the regional councilor in charge of agriculture, also touted the regional government's record of active support of ownership in his keynote speech at a major 1981 conference on Tuscany's animal husbandry sector.[84] Between 1965 and 1980, he argued with pride, 3,340 animal husbandry companies had been subsidized by the national and regional governments. Here Bonifazi revealingly conflated sheep- and cattle-rearing businesses, glossing over the fact that the latter were by and large foundering.

The pride that transpired from Bonifazi's words stemmed from his sense that public authorities this time had made a difference, facilitating the integration and modernization of a major component of Tuscany's rural society. Thus, he could point to the very landscape that Iris Origo contemplated with melancholic puzzlement and call it his own. Those shelters, those roads, those cereal fields, and those sheep

---

[83] ASMOS, Fondo Luigi Berlinguer, Box VIII 8, Folder Sardi in Toscana, typescript titled "Pastori Sardi in Toscana," 7.
[84] "La Conferenza Regionale sulla Pastorizia," *Agricoltura Toscana* 5-6-7 (July 1981): 18–30.

herds constituted the instantiation of a kind of progress that had been deliberately pursued by democratically elected administrators. In light of these considerations, the wave of kidnappings of the late 1970s and early 1980s, which implicated the Sardinian pastoral community in complex but undeniable ways, came as an especially traumatic event for Tuscany's Communist leadership and for the academic experts who had been trying to make sense of the migrants' seemingly incongruous presence. After all, kidnappings could be viewed as the outcome of a traditional culture made barbaric and ruthless by its encounter with the logic of capitalist accumulation. Kidnapping could assume the features of the ultimate form of pastoral speculation. Moreover, the shepherds' isolation hindered the social and political control of the territory. The kidnapping victims disappeared, sometimes forever, into a landscape that revealed its ultimate alterity and seemed to belie the domesticating efforts of experts and politicians alike.

In the face of this cacophony of perspectives and perceptions, local leaders doubled their efforts at putting together coherent narratives that could be politically usable and socially reassuring. To their credit, Tuscan leftist politicians refrained from any kind of populist temptations, made possible by signs of racist reactions on the part of ordinary Tuscans. Graffiti that called for the Sardinians to "go home" surfaced in several areas where immigrants concentrated, and the word "Sardistan" was coined to convey the sense that parts of rural Tuscany were now as foreign and incomprehensible as Sardinia itself.[85] A reader's letter to a local magazine, which had run an article arguing that the Sardinian shepherds had rescued the countryside from complete abandonment, is worth quoting at length: "Our region does not need the Sardinians to solve the problem of the abandonment of the countryside.... How will we be able to return and redevelop our peasant civilization if our countryside will be populated by Sardinians, with their introverted, hostile, and violent character, with their ancestral sense of isolation and reluctance to collaborate with the authorities (*omertà*)?"[86] In October 1981, Luigi Berlinguer received an angry letter from the town of Montepulciano that expressed similar sentiments. After rejecting any accusation of racism, the writer wished for Berlinguer to become the victim of one of the kidnappers that he seemed to make excuses for, adding that "when Tuscany belonged to the Tuscans there were no kidnappings (that was never one of our

[85] Maurizio Boldrini, "Nel Vocabolario Toscano non C'E' Posto per la Parola Sardistan," *L'Unità*, October 12, 1980.
[86] ASMOS, Fondo Luigi Berlinguer, Box VIII 8, Folder Sardi in Toscana, handwritten letter dated October 10, 1981.

staples) and there was much less crime in general."[87] These reactions responded to a sense of dispossession of places that until very recently had been utterly ignored. The countryside was no longer something to flee from or at best exploit for resources; it had become the site of identitarian claims and something to preserve.

In the face of these sentiments, unscrupulously fueled by the conservative press, Tuscany's progressive elites, some of whom were themselves of very recent rural origin, greatly contributed to imagining a gentle, civilized, and harmonious countryside that could accommodate the many trajectories that seemed to be in the process of clashing. The fact that the peak of mobilization was reached in the wake of the three German children's kidnapping is highly revealing of the stakes in this process of projection and reinvention. The bandits were discrediting Tuscany before the world, as tourism loomed as a plausible source of prosperity and renewed dignity for rural areas. The Sardinian regional councilor in charge of agriculture suggested, somewhat opaquely, that the target of the German children's kidnapping may have been the tourism industry itself.[88] More intelligibly, the West German magazine *Der Spiegel* ventured that one of the kidnappers might have acted out of hatred for "high-class tourism" (*Nobel-Tourismus*), since he used to graze his sheep on the very land that had been transformed into the resort where the victims were vacationing.[89] Even Berlinguer commented on the utter incongruity of violent crime in Tuscany's history and landscape: Tuscany had never been the site of atrocities, and, as a legal historian, he reminded his readers that the Grand Duchy of Tuscany had been the first Western political entity to abolish the death penalty in the eighteenth century.[90] It was this tradition of civility and harmony, still visible in Tuscany's stones and fields, that attracted tourists from around the world. The vulnerability of this harmony, just like that of the crumbling farmhouses of the departed sharecroppers, made its imagining all the more precious and urgent.

Tuscany was only the ninth Italian region (out of twenty) for the number of kidnappings perpetrated between 1969 and 1997. Lombardy, with 158 incidents (i.e., six times as many as in Tuscany), came first.[91] Yet,

---

[87] *Toscana Qui* 4 (1981): 4.

[88] Francesco Matteini, "I pastori Sardi Tacciono per Paura: Anche il Silenzio E' Legittima Difesa," *La Città*, September 28, 1980.

[89] "Entführungen. Geschenk von Chaka II," *Der Spiegel*, October 6, 1980, available at www.spiegel.de/spiegel/print/d-14317596.html

[90] ASMOS, Fondo Luigi Berlinguer, Box VIII 8, Folder Sardi in Toscana, typescript titled "Pastori Sardi in Toscana," 22.

[91] Commissione Parlamentare d'Inchiesta sul Fenomeno della Mafia, *Relazione sui Sequestri di Persona a Scopo di Estorsione* (Rome, 1998). Nationally, there were 672 kidnappings between 1969 and 1997, targeting 694 people. Of these, 81 never came back. These data

nowhere in northern and central Italy was this phenomenon as hotly debated as in Tuscany, and the reason for this disproportionate attention was precisely that in Tuscany the issue was framed in civilizational terms, as a problem directly bearing on the heritage and future of the region's countryside.[92] Tuscans reacted to the immigration of Sardinian shepherds and to the wave of kidnappings in a variety of contradictory ways. For some Tuscans, the shepherds were intruders and ruthless speculators who had contributed to the dispossession of traditional Tuscan peasants and were ruining the region's rural society and landscape. For these observers, the kidnappings were only the most extreme manifestation of the newcomers' irreducible barbarity. For many other observers, the migrants had rescued thousands of hectares of marginal land from complete desertion. By becoming sedentary and getting in touch with the social and political traditions of the hosting society, embedded in the very makeup of the landscape, the migrants were transitioning to a benevolent form of modernity. For these observers, kidnappings were an aberration perpetrated by a tiny minority of unscrupulous newcomers who had been corrupted by extraneous elements (they would, for example, emphasize the possible involvement of Sicilian or Calabrian *mafiosi* as organizers and funders). What these two seemingly incompatible positions shared was the increasing idealization of the rural landscape and of the society that had built it. The point here is not that this idealization was directly caused by the Sardinians' presence and activities: similar processes took place all over Mediterranean Europe. My goal has been to show that in the case of Tuscany a variety of actors came to delineate the contours of a newly meaningful countryside partly by dealing with this peculiar form of immigration, with its complex mix of hopefulness and dread.

This chapter has attempted to tell the history of a particular landscape, that of southern Tuscany, from the margins. The stories told in this chapter are most certainly not the ones on which tourists focus when they visit the Orcia valley. Like the unfinished dam of San Piero in Campo, these stories are incongruous; they do not fit in. The point that this chapter conveys is that the truncated trajectories that once represented sources of hope or dread can be crucial to a comprehensive interpretation of

---

do not include the politically motivated kidnappings. In 1991, a law mandated that the belongings of the victims' families be frozen, with harsh penalties for those who tried to negotiate with the kidnappers. This has contributed to a precipitous decline of these criminal acts, although a variety of more complex and localized processes seem to have been at work as well.

[92] Calabria and Sardinia follow Lombardy in this grim ranking. In these southern regions, however, kidnappings were not a new phenomenon in the 1970s. Rather, they had been one of the local manifestations of "banditry" and organized crime for generations.

the relationships between society and place. Interrupted paths are key to writing a truly spatial history. The aspiration of turning southern Tuscany into an irrigated meat factory turned out to be a failure. Sheep rearing concerned a small immigrant population that is now largely invisible both to visitors and most urban Tuscans. Nevertheless, these experiences have shaped what rural Tuscany is today, albeit in indirect ways. Microhistorian Edoardo Grendi famously argued that it is by attending to the "exceptional normal" that the contours of historical processes can come into fuller relief.[93] This chapter has attempted to ground Grendi's methodological insight in space. All territories are fundamentally incongruous and exceptional. They all tell multiple and contradictory stories that only cohere into a linear "history" and legible "landscape" after contentious processes of selective analysis.

Both the failure of cattle rearing and the partial success of sheep husbandry constituted ways of dealing with the rural exodus, which came to be understood by many Tuscans as the end of tradition tout court. The irrigation plans' failure and the consequences of the Sardinians' settlement made Tuscans fully aware of the irreversibility of this process, eliciting a variety of intellectual and emotional responses. For the generation of rural Tuscans who had come of age in the immediate postwar decades, the demise of Tuscany's traditional peasantry was timely and perhaps even desirable, as long as it promised to usher in a type of modernity that would have bridged the gap between urban and rural life by increasing the productivity of the countryside and the comfort of its inhabitants. This is what it meant to dream of hills of green and herds of (mooing) white. As these dreams confronted local and global constraints, many urban Tuscans, including many of the recently urbanized peasants, forgot about the countryside altogether, now viewed as irrelevant or, at best, marginal with respect to the main stages of history.

Over the course of the 1980s, both the rural dwellers' aspirations for modernity and the urban dwellers' indifference gave way to a complex form of nostalgia (or perhaps melancholia) that reunited city and countryside after decades of separation. The encounters between Tuscans and the immigrant Sardinian shepherds create a prism through which the emergence of a novel appreciation of the rural landscape can be charted. Even ordinary people now came to view the landscape in civilizational terms, as the legible, vulnerable, and therefore beautiful product of a coherent "culture." This landscape was to be protected from the assaults of a monster that had populated the nightmares of Tuscans for decades: the speculative tendencies of capitalist modernity, whose

[93] E. Grendi, "Ripensare la Microstoria," *Quaderni Storici* 86 (1994): 539–549.

specter haunts the stories I have told in this chapter. The construction of this mythical coherence, at times inhabited with utter earnestness and at times confronted with subtle irony, was a painstaking process. At the turn of the 1980s rural Tuscany was the site of a cacophony of perspectives and trajectories. Their harmonization required creativity and determination, but also the power to silence and make invisible the experiences and memories that did not fit the new sensibility. The goal of this chapter has been to recapture a historical moment in which different senses of place and time vied for hegemony, resisting the condescension of hindsight.

5   The Farmhouse and the Museum:
       Rural Tuscany as Patrimony

One of the many transition stories circulating today in Tuscany argues that at some point in the 1970s and 1980s the countryside and its landscape became "patrimony," or heritage. For some people, this transition has been a sign of progress, signaling the shift from a productivist and exploitative relationship between people and land to a more enlightened commitment to the preservation of beauty and endangered ways of life. For others, the shift to a patrimonial conception has come with a sense of loss, signaling the end of authenticity and the increasing commodification of place to the benefit of tourists and a small elite of locals. These contradictory perceptions of time and place are of course important in themselves, but the previous chapters have shown that patrimonial sensibilities long predated any commitment to postmaterial policies. The most consequential patrimonial story to have been inscribed in the Tuscan landscape was that of the aristocratic landlords, who for decades rationalized peasant subordination through the construction of myths of harmony. Fascism built on this sensibility with its repertoire of violence and blandishments. The postwar Communists told patrimonial stories of their own, and they placed themselves in a lineage that harkened back to the beginning of the century, when a fledgling socialist movement began to inscribe in the land more confrontational dwelling practices.

In sum, different social subjects and political sensibilities have long shaped Tuscany by "reading" themselves and their own sense of heritage in the landscape. Nevertheless, when the rural exodus came to be understood as irreversible in the course of the 1960s, a partly novel approach to heritage became increasingly common. In the following decades a variety of social actors inscribed rural Tuscany in a patrimonial lineage that focused on temporal continuities and spatial homogeneity, smoothing over many of the specificities of an increasingly removed recent past replete with conflict, coercion, and resistance. The increasingly influential sensibilities of the tourists joined the marketing strategies of the wine producers and other heritage operators in resurrecting the myths of harmony and peace that the landlords had spawned in the nineteenth and early twentieth centuries, making them hegemonic once again. This operation met different kinds of resistance. Like other parts of rural Europe, but perhaps with particular poignancy, the Tuscan countryside refused to be Disneyfied, and Tuscans searched with stubborn earnestness for new sources of authenticity rooted in a less generic past, which they could claim as their own. Paradoxically, resistance produced its own kind of value, making sure that commodification would only go so far. Tuscans' search for authenticity could thus quench the cultural tourists' thirst for distinctiveness and exclusivity. Rural Tuscany would sell itself, but not for cheap.

The conception of patrimony, or heritage, that became hegemonic in the wake of the rural exodus in Tuscany and elsewhere was partly new in that it was increasingly bland and generic.[1] No longer the overt expression of class privilege or a particular political ideology, the patrimonialization of landscape emerged in the name of society as a whole. Landscape became the arena where the social body read itself in space. This enforced coherence dismissed the contradictory histories landscape told and called for the redemption of its incongruous features. This approach to patrimony was first of all about the recognition of a lineage that linked past, present, and future, so that conflicts and discontinuities had to be downplayed or even ignored in the name of long-term continuities. In this sense, the myth (or cult) of patrimony can be understood as a way of exorcising a society's fear of rootlessness and loss of direction.

This generic approach to patrimony also had to be shared within a community of subjects who understood themselves as related through emotive and noninstrumental bonds. Just as patrimony dismissed temporal discontinuities, it also simultaneously reified and transcended social distinctions. Not everyone was equally equipped to appreciate patrimony, thereby making it the target of ongoing protective attention, but traditional social distinctions melted away before patrimony, to the point of imagining sites and forms of knowledge that belonged to (and defined) humanity as a whole, as has been the case with UNESCO's World Heritage institutions since the 1970s. The possibility of recognition across social distinctions up to the universal level of humankind makes stakeholders strive for widespread legibility of "their" patrimony. The artifacts or forms of knowledge that are widely legible across a

---

[1] I prefer to use the term patrimony, rather than heritage, not only because it is closer to the Italian *patrimonio*, but also because it can be easily turned into an adjective (patrimonial). The literature on heritage is vast. Particularly influential for my own thinking has been David Lowenthal's work, especially his *The Heritage Crusade and the Spoils of History* (Cambridge: Cambridge University Press), 1998.

variety of social and cultural boundaries have a better chance of becoming especially valuable patrimony.

Almost anything can become patrimony, and patrimonial practices have indeed expanded to ever-new realms in recent decades. Here I am especially interested in the patrimonialization of artifacts and, to a lesser extent, forms of knowledge that came to be understood as belonging to Tuscany's traditional rural society. Over time, the process of patrimonialization has interacted with other practices, especially those associated with market relations. At one level, patrimony is about use-value and its preservation, whereas market commodities are about exchange-value and consumption, but these distinctions gloss over the ways in which the processes of valorization associated with patrimony and market exchange often coexist and even feed on each other.[2] Different social actors have widely different views as to where and how the boundaries between patrimony and market relations should be drawn, so this becomes an area of tension and conflict in modern societies.

In rural Tuscany, two sites offer especially fruitful vantage points for an investigation into the ways the new and more generic approach to patrimony emerged and how it interacted with other kinds of practices. The first site is the farmhouse, which in the wake of the peasants' exodus became the target both of economic ventures, meant to attract the money of residential tourists, and conservation practices, meant to thwart the threat of speculation. The other site is the museum of "peasant culture," which came to collect some of the artifacts that were expelled from the newly restored farmhouses. The relationship between these two sites was dialectical, rather than merely coincidental. To borrow the language developed by architectural theorist and historian Françoise Choay, who in turn borrowed it from Alois Riegl, the restored farmhouses assumed some of the traits of a historical (or unintentional) monument.[3] Originally built for entirely different purposes, these houses became sites of preservationist anxieties and narcissistic projections. Patrimonial practices turned them into symbols of a generic rurality, capable of speaking to connoisseurs across the globe. The rural museums, by contrast, emerged as intentional monuments to endangered memory, the one that was being erased in the farmhouses, together with the traces of conflictual

---

[2] Christian Barrère, Denis Barthélemy, Martino Nieddu, and Frank-Dominique Vivien, "Au-Delà du Capital, le Patrimoine?" in Christian Barrère, Denis Barthélemy, Martino Nieddu, and Frank-Dominique Vivien (eds.), *Réinventer le Patrimoine: De la culture à l'Economie, une Nouvelle Pensée du Patrimoine* (Paris: L'Harmattan, 2005): 7–21.

[3] F. Choay, *The Invention of the Historic Monument* (Cambridge: Cambridge University Press, 2001). The French title is *L'Allegorie du Patrimoine*, which captures more accurately the main argument of the book.

histories and experiences. Unlike other museums, which turn their collections into historical monuments, the rural museums functioned as monuments in themselves, as sites commemorating the ruptures of history and admonishing a distracted society for its loss of meaning.

Originally, the farmhouse and the museum opposed each other as two poles in a dialectical process. The museums reminded the communities around them of the specific forms of labor, conflict, and loss that the restructured farmhouses (and the heritage industry in which the houses were embedded) ignored or made generic. Over time, however, Tuscany's rural museums have increasingly come to terms with the practices associated with the new approach to patrimony, presenting themselves as sites where past and present contradictions can be provisionally worked out, at least at the level of cultural politics. They have themselves become part of territorially defined patrimony.

The Tuscan Farmhouse from Work Tool to Historical Monument

At least since the 1960s, Tuscan farmhouses have been the object of international appreciation, and Tuscany's rural real estate market has been one of the hottest in the world, with dilapidated houses selling for many hundreds of thousands of Euros in the most sought after areas, such as the Chianti and the Orcia valley. But these houses are also widely understood as part of a national (or even universal) patrimony, worthy of legislative attention and protective monitoring. This section investigates the uneasy relationships between these artifacts' processes of valorization – in the market and in the realm of cultural debate – within a rapidly changing economic and social context. In a remarkably short period, Tuscan farmhouses have changed from sites of backbreaking labor to exclusive places of leisure and relaxation, while their peasant origins have been simultaneously hidden as an embarrassment and celebrated as a source of additional value. What is these houses' beauty made up of, and how can historical analysis lead to a deeper understanding of their roles in networks of social relations that span distant continents and widely different generations?

As architectural historian Michelangelo Sabatino has recently argued, the valorization of vernacular architecture was deeply implicated in many Italian intellectuals' search for appropriately modern styles that would be simultaneously innovative and mindful of the country's great diversity.[4]

[4] M. Sabatino, *Pride in Modesty: Modernist Architecture and the Vernacular Tradition in Italy* (Toronto: University of Toronto Press, 2010).

The farmhouses of central Italy seemed to firmly embody many of the principles on which this form of rooted modernity could be founded. And indeed, well before Tuscany's rural houses began to be abandoned by a restless peasantry, they had become the subject of comprehensive research projects that combined "practical" concerns with aesthetic fascination. The 1934 survey on the habitability of Italy's rural buildings, willed by Mussolini, revealed that at least one quarter of Tuscany's farmhouses were in need of restructuring,[5] and shortly thereafter the government funded several experts to classify rural dwellings according to their architectural features, assumed to be the basis for possible interventions.

In the mid-1930s, Renato Biasutti, professor of Geography at the University of Florence, gathered his collaborators and sent them into the Tuscan countryside, where they inspected and sketched hundreds of buildings. The outcome of these efforts was an influential volume that identified dozens of different types of houses, organized by geographical area.[6] Even though he adopted a strictly synchronic approach, Biasutti opened his treatise with an acknowledgement of these houses' layered history: "Rural life, though periodically subjected to the influence of cities and of the trends and styles prevailing there, is eminently conservative. Thus features that are ancient, less ancient, modern, and ultra-modern are often combined, but always to respond to a pressing unitary function."[7] This pithy statement recognized the double nature of these houses' esthetic qualities. On the one hand, many of their features were products of urban contamination. On the other hand, their esthetic appreciation had to start with the recognition of their functionality to agriculture and rural life. The distinctiveness of these houses emerged from this tension between beauty as functionality, which suggested the existence of a coherent and autonomous rural way of life, and beauty as an esthetic surplus intentionally bestowed on these buildings by ongoing contacts with urban culture.

These two perceptions of beauty also had ethical implications. These houses' seemingly perfect adaptation to an autonomous way of life made them symbols of authenticity and simplicity, values increasingly threatened by modernity. The recognition of urban contaminations, however, made Tuscan rural houses unique products of a collective (and usually anonymous) creative sensibility that linked "high" and "low" culture. The notion that functionality could assimilate and make coherent motifs

---

[5] The results of the survey, organized by municipality, were published in the March 1934 issue of the *Bollettino di Statistica Agraria e Forestale*.

[6] Renato Biasutti, *La Casa Rurale nella Toscana* (Bologna: Zanichelli, 1938).

[7] Ibid.: 3.

that originated in disparate times and places pointed to ways of reconciling the increasing cacophony of modern life. It was no coincidence that during the Fascist period rural houses became a major source of inspiration for rationalist architects. Giuseppe Pagano, for example, argued that "The rural house is a work instrument, the most important living instrument that the peasant's soul builds for itself. And it has all the features of the work instrument: nothing is useless, nothing is superfluous, everything is there out of necessity."[8] The classical esthetic principle of *ne quid nimis* (nothing in excess) promised to create a new architectural lexicon for the spatial articulation of modern challenges.[9]

The coexistence of practical and esthetic appreciation came under strain after the rural exodus, when the functionality of these houses could no longer be viewed as the primary spring of their beauty. In the postwar decades photography became the preferred medium of a small army of increasingly concerned urban intellectuals, aware of witnessing the possible demise of these vulnerable buildings. Unlike the Fascist rationalists, these amateur photographers valued Tuscan farmhouses as vestiges of a dying civilization, although they could still be made to tell relevant stories. In this context, the connections between city and countryside, materialized in so many of the architectural motifs of Tuscany's rural houses, could be explicitly acknowledged and admired as instantiations of a supposedly less instrumental relationship between culture and nature.

Architectural historian Lorenzo Gori-Montanelli, for example, toured the Florentine Chianti and the upper Arno valley in the early 1960s taking black-and-white photographs of farmhouses, many of them already deserted, focusing and commenting on the details that demonstrated the percolation of urban styles to the countryside.[10] In Gori-Montanelli's view, an uninterrupted genealogy linked the villas Michelozzo designed for the Medicis in the outskirts of Florence in the fifteenth century and the large farmhouses of the upper Arno valley, many of which had been built in the eighteenth century according to architectural guidelines codified by the Lorenese court in the newly reclaimed areas of eastern Tuscany. Even many of the houses built in the early twentieth century remained true to this stylistic legacy. The distribution of the built volumes, the complex symmetries of the windows and doors, and the expert positioning of the tower for pigeon raising, to say nothing of the

---

[8] G. Pagano, "Case Rurali," *Casabella* 86 (February 1935): 13.

[9] For Fascist rationalists, the appreciation of the rural houses' esthetic qualities went well beyond the vulgar sentimentality of the Strapaese movement, which viewed rurality as an antidote to the complexities of modernity. For these debates, see Ruth Ben-Ghiat, *Fascist Modernities: Italy* (Berkeley: University of California Press, 2001).

[10] Lorenzo Gori Montanelli, *L'Architettura Rurale in Toscana* (Florence: EDAM, 1964).

buildings' very location with respect to the surrounding topography, all testified to a continuity of taste and knowledge that originated in the cities and morphed in the countryside into functionally elegant solutions to dwelling and productive challenges.

Another amateur photographer, Guido Biffoli (a Florentine teacher by profession), tirelessly roamed the length and width of Tuscany for three decades, taking snapshots of farmhouses and landscapes, and publishing two volumes devoted exclusively to rural houses that featured, in addition to his photographs, essays by prominent intellectuals. In the first of these volumes, published in 1966, Biffoli tried to explain his fascination with Tuscany's farmhouses, arguing that he went around the countryside with an esthetic question in mind: "Why is [these houses'] structure ... not simple, rudimentary, merely adequate to their nature and function?"[11] Could the sense of balance and harmony he felt in front of these buildings be the product of "an innate quality of a race (*stirpe*) that bequeathed it as an endemic instinct?" The implication of this question was that Biffoli's own generation had interrupted this lineage, failing to pick up the baton of harmonious beauty that had been passed on for centuries. And if functionality no longer explained these buildings' beauty, as it did for Pagano in the 1930s, the origins of this esthetic "surplus" that made these houses beautiful must have originated in the cities. It is no coincidence that both Gori-Montanelli and Biffoli never directed their lenses toward the extant peasantry, choosing instead to photograph houses that looked deserted even when they were still lived in, as the presence of drying laundry or agricultural tools leaning on a wall sometimes revealed. These urban photographers' melancholic fascination did not target the world of the peasantry in itself, but rather as one pole in a lost relationship between city and countryside, a relationship imagined to have created a beautifully harmonious unity, in spite of its hierarchical qualities.[12]

The social conflicts that had rocked the Tuscan countryside in the decade after World War II made it impossible to assimilate the extant peasants to this vision of harmony. The excision of people from these photographs constituted an attempt at forging a different genealogical (and patrimonial) story. Yet, the awareness of conflict and its centrality to the history of rural Tuscany crept into the narratives of the intellectuals who contributed to Biffoli's volumes. Prominent journalist Arrigo Benedetti, a native of Lucca, went as far as to argue that "the countryside

---

[11] Guido Biffoli, *La Casa Colonica in Toscana* (Florence: Vallecchi, 1966): 17.

[12] This is in contrast with the photographers who roamed the Tuscan countryside before World War II. The most famous example of that tradition is Arnold Von Borsig, *Die Toscana Landschaft: Kunst Und Leben Im Bild* (Vienna: Anton Schroll: 1939).

was for Tuscans what the frontier was for the Americans: it was necessary to annex it, give it a civic nuance, purify it from the disorder of nature."[13] In other words, the Tuscan countryside was colonized and "governed" by the city, often in coercive ways. Architect Guido Ferrara reminded readers that countless architectural treatises, starting with Leon Battista Alberti's *De Re Aedificatoria*, oozed with condescension for the *villani* (peasants), viewed as incapable of self-government and thus of esthetic judgment.[14] In the 1770s, Ferdinando Morozzi, author of an influential architectural manual, still recommended building only a limited number of bedrooms, so that peasants would have had to sleep two per room and keep an eye on each other's work ethic and sexual conduct.[15] In a passage from his early-nineteenth-century handbook, priest Ignazio Malenotti insisted on similar themes, recommending that the oldest brother of the sharecropping family live with his younger brothers but remain single, so that he would not elicit too much jealousy when the landlord prevented some of the younger brothers from getting married.[16] Class subordination relied on architectural forms and dwelling practices.

This legacy of coercion and conflict created a dissonance that could not be completely ignored and that made sense of the rural exodus. The flight of the peasants and the crisis of traditional agriculture had prompted the increasingly esthetic appreciation of the farmhouses and of the rural landscape more generally. But the urban observers who approached the Tuscan countryside as an esthetic artifact aspired to give beauty an ethical content. Their esthetic gaze had to be an ethical one as well. After all, Gori-Montanelli, Biffoli, and the intellectuals who contributed to their volumes were not conservatives trying to extol the virtues of class subordination. To the contrary, if the protection and preservation of these buildings was to be assured, the farmhouses needed to be set as characters in a narrative that preserved their authenticity and made them relevant to the present. After conflict and coercion had been uneasily bracketed, the rural farmhouses became foils for a pointed critique of the instrumentality and vulgarity of consumer capitalism in the wake of Italy's economic miracle. These buildings' ethical beauty, viewed as originating from the organic unity between city and country, could thus be contrasted with the unethical ugliness of modern urban life, which encroached with increasing force on the countryside itself. As Tuscany's farmhouses became part of a patrimonial legacy, their

[13] G. Biffoli, *La Casa Colonica in Toscana* (1966): 9.
[14] Ibid.: 35–80.
[15] F. Morozzi, *Delle Case de' Contadini* (Florence: Pagani, 1807): 14–16. The first edition was published in 1770.
[16] I. Malenotti, *Il Padrone Contadino* (Florence: Guglielmo Piatti, 1817): 86–87.

symbolic and material roles in an actual history of conflict and resistance became increasingly less relevant.

By the time Biffoli's second volume was published in 1984, the rural exodus had consummated itself and yielded to a reverse movement of urban dwellers discovering the countryside.[17] The qualities of the new ties between city and country filled many esthetically minded and politically progressive intellectuals with dread and concern. Former mayor of Siena and prominent Communist politician Roberto Barzanti, who had made cultural policy his main area of expertise, did not mince words in condemning the new "rampant urban effect" on Tuscany's rural farmhouses, noticing how the rural landscape had become a dependent variable "in a narrowly quantitative vision, directed toward rapacious and immediate profit."[18] The paradox with which Barzanti struggled was that the new rural dwellers were occupying the old farmhouses in search for a respite from the pursuit of profit. The esthetic of leisure, however, was as despicable as that of mere instrumentality: "The rural houses are cynically mangled by the new tourists or sacrificed with indifference to the gods of the mandatory weekend or the omnipresent second home. The spatial relationships, the measures of a distant era, vanish without being reinvented or lived according to different signs."[19] In other words, these houses' loss of functionality could not but have esthetic consequences. Rural artifacts were turning into simulacra, signifiers without the signified, and thus into symbols of a profoundly inauthentic, and thus unethical, relationship between people and their territory.

Biffoli himself began his textual contribution with a story, told as a parable that linked the 1984 volume to the one he had published eighteen years before. He had once visited a sharecroppers' beautiful house and met the family's patriarch, who was anguished by his children's desire to leave. Some years later he had returned to photograph the house, and no one was there; it was slowly turning into a ruin. While researching for the current volume, he had recently driven by the house and noticed a crane towering over it. As he walked closer, he could barely recognize it: "Everything had been falsely embellished and prettified (*imbellettato e impreziosito*). The house, in its authenticity, no longer existed. It was the hallmark of a certain class of people that were laying their hands on the old peasant houses, making them unrecognizable and distorting them with deplorable taste."[20] The three phases many rural houses went

[17] Guido Biffoli, *La Casa Colonica in Toscana* (Florence: Vallecchi, 1984).
[18] Ibid.: 12–13.
[19] Ibid.: 45.
[20] Ibid.: 80.

through (crisis, abandonment, and loss of authenticity) signaled the difficulty of charting a process of estheticization that could be ethically commendable as well. The traditional ties between city and country had been coercive and instrumental, but they had produced harmonious beauty; the new ties were informed by the search for relaxation and beauty, but they often degenerated into vulgarity.

These progressive intellectuals understood that the vulgarity they perceived was also the product of the democratization of leisure, which the political movements and ideologies they espoused had greatly contributed to promoting. Commenting in 1997 on Gori-Montanelli's and Biffoli's collections of photographs, preserved at the Regional Photographic Archive in Prato, geographer Claudio Greppi noticed that the rural farmhouses and the Tuscan countryside more generally had become the victims of a paradox: "Right as the qualities of the Tuscan countryside become social patrimony and are no longer the privilege of a few, the process of construction of the rural landscape seems destined to degenerate into pure commercial consumption."[21] If patrimony is always about the recognition of a lineage, whose heirs were the new country dwellers who appreciated rural life for the leisure and relaxation it provided? Were they (or should they have been) the heirs of the "privileged few" who had enjoyed it for centuries as landlords?

A large section of Tuscan society had reviled aristocratic families for decades, both for their cozy relationships with the Fascist regime and for their unwillingness to make concessions to their sharecroppers after the war, but in the 1980s a new appreciation for their ethos became increasingly common in the press and other media. A 1980 documentary funded by the Communist-led regional government and titled "The New Castle Dwellers" (*I Nuovi Castellani*), for example, featured in-depth interviews with four noblemen who owned extensive estates in the region and who had managed to reinvent their social and economic roles, two of them (Bettino Ricasoli and Niccolò Antinori) as internationally renowned winemakers, and the others (Roberto Guicciardini and Bino Sanminiatelli) in the hospitality and culture industries.[22] The director interviewed Marquis Antinori both in his urban residence in the center of Florence and on his estates in the Chianti and at Bolgheri, on the coast of southern Tuscany. Asked whether he preferred to live in the city or in the countryside, the Marquis answered: "When I go to the country

---

[21] Claudio Greppi, "Case e paesaggi della campagna toscana: se trent'anni vi sembran pochi," *AFT Rivista di Storia e Fotografia* XIII 25 (June 1997): 9–13. Quote on p. 9.

[22] *Gli Ultimi Castellani* (dir. Piero Mechini, 1980). The documentary is preserved at the Mediateca Regionale Toscana in Florence.

I mostly go to decompress, to enjoy the beautiful landscapes, especially in the places where the countryside has not been spoiled, and there are not many of those left." Even though he readily admitted to having become a wine industrialist, with considerable joint investments in multinational corporations, he still practiced *villeggiatura* as his ancestors had done for centuries, standing up for beauty in the face of mounting vulgarity.

The lesson to be drawn from the documentary was that these aristocrats had managed to reinvent rurality by reconciling the pursuit of profit and the preservation of beauty. This appreciation for aristocratic sensibility, however, betrayed the legacy and memory of the countless generations of peasants who had toiled for, and finally rebelled against, their landlords. Leisure alone could hardly provide the authenticity that had been lost with the rural exodus, and beauty without authenticity was bound to become empty and unethical. Starting in the late 1970s, these tensions and paradoxes began to inform public policy, increasingly concerned with the evolving esthetic of rurality both for its ethical and political implications and for its promises to chart new paths to economic prosperity. Once again, rural buildings constituted the focus of these debates.

Tuscan aristocrats could perhaps be believed to possess enough cultural capital (or taste) to reconcile instrumentality and affect in their castle estates, but ordinary people could hardly be trusted to do the same in their newly purchased rural homes. Starting in the late 1970s, the regional government set out to regulate construction in rural areas with the intention of thwarting the speculative temptations associated with the emerging leisure industry. In this early phase, however, Tuscany's leftist administrators believed that the best way to fight speculation was to support agriculture, albeit within relatively strict parameters. Even though esthetic concerns could not be ignored, the implicit assumption was that ugliness was the esthetic consequence of speculation, and that, by contrast, a functioning agriculture based on small- and medium-size farms would have created an authentic (and workable) kind of beauty. This reasoning had a long lineage in Tuscan and Italian societies, and it also stemmed from a deep-seated ambivalence toward tourism both as a viable path to prosperity and as an ethically responsible pursuit. Agriculture needed to be at the core of the patrimonial lineage to be protected.

On the basis of these general principles, the law proposed by the regional government in 1978 mandated that new construction in rural areas be only allowed for agricultural purposes, demonstrated by multiyear farm plans to be approved by the municipal governments.[23] The

---

[23] Archivio del Consiglio della Regione Toscana, Proposta di Legge 294 (to become Regoinal Law 10/79).

proposal set upper limits to the size of the residential and agricultural buildings and lower limits to the plots on which these new farmhouses could sit, according to the main kind of cultivation practiced. A new farmhouse could only be justified when surrounded by at least three hectares of vineyards or fruit tree groves, or four hectares of olive groves, or six hectares of arable fields, and so on. Permits for the construction of new buildings could only be issued to "agricultural entrepreneurs" who drew at least two-thirds of their income from the land and who participated directly in cultivation; corporations were thus excluded. The proposal proceeded to strictly limit changes to existing rural buildings, admissible only for proved agricultural needs. For buildings whose use had been changed from agriculture to residence alone or to other purposes, only conservative restorations would be allowed. Finally, the proposal set strict limitations to the ways estates could be broken up, mandating that in most cases land could only be sold with the agricultural buildings that lay on it.

When the proposed law began to circulate, it drew a slew of critiques from opposite sides of the social and cultural spectrum. Italia Nostra, the conservationist NGO, took issue with the very possibility of new construction, and accused the regional government of failing to acknowledge that "the rural housing stock constitutes above all a precious document of typical architectural forms, often qualitatively valuable in themselves and in relation to the surrounding landscape, and shaped by ways of life, dwelling, and production that are today virtually extinct."[24] Moreover, the proposal only reserved special treatment for the buildings that the authorities in charge of protecting cultural assets (the Soprintendenze ai Beni Culturali) had already singled out. But Italia Nostra noticed that hardly any rural houses, still largely viewed as utilitarian buildings, fell in that category. Finally, to frame protection in terms of subjective criteria neglected the fact that "the traditional rural housing stock as a whole represents all over Tuscany an element that is inextricably integrated in the environment (*ambiente*)." In other words, these rural houses needed to be valorized and protected on esthetic and ecological grounds – as patrimony, not as means to an end.

From the opposite side of the spectrum, the regional industrialists' association strongly objected to the notion that the municipal governments could be entitled to approve the farm plans necessary for new construction and major restructuring of existing buildings, because this could

---

[24] Archivio del Consiglio della Regione Toscana, brief by Italia Nostra dated July 6, 1978 and titled "Considerazioni sulla Proposta di Legge Regionale N. 294 Concernente 'Norme Urbanistiche Transitorie Relative alle Zone Agricole.'"

degenerate into a "form of control that is more political than technical," surreptitiously imposing planning guidelines and undue constraints on property rights.[25] The attack on property rights was even more blatant in the case of the norms regulating the sale of rural estates. Finally, the proposal discriminated against corporations, thereby discouraging much-needed investment in agriculture. In the end, the Regional Council approved a law (Regional Law 10/1979) that attempted to strike a compromise between the preservation of patrimony on esthetic grounds and the respect of property rights in the name of economic development. The law entrusted municipal governments with compiling lists of culturally valuable buildings, for which only conservative measures would be allowed. The provisions about the breakup and sale of rural estates were dropped, although municipal governments could make restructuring concessions predicated on the owner's promise that in the future the building would only be sold with a certain amount of acreage around it. In sum, even though the regional government delegated many crucial decisions to the discretion of local governments, the law identified building speculation as a major threat and enshrined the principle that Tuscany's rural houses could be regarded as patrimonial goods of the collectivity both for esthetic and agricultural reasons.

The 1979 law also had pedagogical goals. In the few years prior to the law's passage, for example, the municipal authorities of Greve in Chianti allowed 800 hectares of former agricultural land to be parceled out into 600 lots, some of which were as small as 100 square meters.[26] The new law not only made these kinds of operations more difficult, but also asked municipal governments to scan their territory and identify culturally valuable buildings and farmhouses, prompting hundreds of administrators to get in touch with local experts (architects, geographers, agronomists, and so on) and look at their surroundings in novel ways. For administrators who were often one generation removed from the countryside and rural life, it was far from obvious that they should appreciate their parents' farmhouses as culturally and esthetically valuable artifacts. And even though in some areas, such as the Chianti, the rural housing market was definitely heating up in the late 1970s and early 1980s, that was not the case in more remote parts of the region. Thus, in many cases the attribution of patrimonial value preceded the economic valorization of rural buildings. The prioritization of noncorporate agriculture as the

---

[25] Archivio del Consiglio della Regione Toscana, brief by the Federazione Regionale fra le Associazioni Industriali della Toscana, dated June 14, 1978.

[26] Antonio Fiorentino and M. Massa, *La Collina Fiorentina* (Florence: Edizioni Pappagallo, 1979): 151. This development, below Panzano, is still widely regarded as a major blight on the landscape.

target of support presented clear risks for the preservation of rural land-scapes, but the commitment to the extant rural population, viewed as stewards of the land, responded to a widespread search for authenticity among the progressive Tuscan elites. Esthetic enjoyment of the country-side could not be the ultimate goal of public policy. The old class con-flicts no longer carried the same force, but patrimonial legacies had to be founded on more than the admiration for the landed aristocrats' gazes and ways of life. The enforcement of "good taste" alone could not save the Tuscan countryside from the ravages of speculation.

The regulation of new construction in the countryside and the provi-sion of incentives for agricultural activities did not address the fate of thousands of existing farmhouses slowly turning into ruins. It was appar-ent that public authorities, local or otherwise, lacked the funds to restore them and treat them as unique historical monuments. In the mid-1980s a wide-ranging research project on the Sienese Chianti, meant to solicit funds from the European Community, calculated that half of the nearly 300 farmhouses in the four municipalities (Radda, Castellina, Gaiole, and Castelnuovo Berardenga) that had been singled out for special pro-tection under the terms of Regional Law 10/1979 were in mediocre or poor condition (Illustration 18). This contrasted with the former land-lords' villas, only 16 percent of which were in mediocre or poor condi-tion. Architect Giovanni Barsacchi estimated that at least 76 billion lire would have been necessary to restore this housing stock, but the EC had only promised 10 billion lire for the whole region for this kind of pur-pose.[27] The four municipalities could hope for 2 billion lire from the EC, which would have been matched by the regional government. Barsacchi proceeded to recommend that the houses in good or average condition still inhabited by working farmers be given priority, in the spirit of the 1979 law. The scarcity of public resources sentenced hundreds of his-torically valuable buildings to become ruins. Most concerned Tuscans realized all too well that there was no viable alternative to letting private individuals restructure the rural houses as they saw fit, within relatively loose parameters. In the face of these data, the spread of questionable taste seemed a relatively small price to pay.

The debate on construction in rural areas closely followed the arrival of hundreds of Italian and foreign residential tourists, who placed them-selves in their own kind of patrimonial lineage. Florence and Siena had

[27] G. Barsacchi, "Recupero del Patrimonio Edilizio Rurale a Scopo Abitativo e Ricettivo," in Comune di Radda, *Studio di Fattibilità di un Programma Speciale di Sviluppo per la Sub-Area Omogenea del Chianti Senese: Documentazione inoltrata alla CEE*, November 1984 (held by IRPET library in Florence): 349–379.

Illustration #18 Tuscan farmhouse in ruins, 1970s.

been on the international tourism map since its origins, dating back to the aristocratic Grand Tour, but that kind of tourism was an urban, or at most suburban, affair.[28] Upper-class foreign tourists created colonies of art connoisseurs who aimed to relive and retrieve the glories of the Renaissance in front of audiences of their peers. Therefore, they needed to live in proximity to each other and near the objects of their appreciation – the museums, basilicas, and palazzi that could quench their thirst for beauty, not to mention the art dealers who catered to them.[29] The villas of the richest among them overlooked the city (usually Florence) both in a physical and metaphorical sense. For them the countryside was at best a notion to contemplate from afar and compare with artistic renditions, rather than a space to be in contact with. The new residential tourists of the postwar period descended on rural Tuscany in the foot-steps of their aristocratic ancestors, but they extended their trails farther,

[28] John Towner, "The Grand Tour: A Key Phase in the History of Tourism," *Annals of Tourism Research* 12 (3) 1985: 297–333; Lynne Withey, *Grand Tours and Cook's Tours: A History of Leisure Travel* (New York: Aurum, 1997). In Italian, see Attilio Brilli, *Il Viaggio in Italia: Storia di una Grande Tradizione Culturale* (Bologna: Il Mulino, 2008).

[29] Bernd Roeck, *Florence 1900: The Quest for Arcadia* (New Haven: Yale University Press, 2009).

aided by newly paved roads and the availability of basic amenities, such as electricity and running water, well beyond the confines of the cities and their outskirts. They began to buy both the landowners' villas and the deserted farmhouses, now barely worth the mortar that kept them together, and to "restore" them. These restorations were carried out not with an eye to the needs of modern farming, but with an appreciation for these buildings' exquisitely outdated features. On the one hand, it was these houses' lack of utilitarian value that marked them as worthy of attention. On the other hand, it was not lost on any of the new residents that the purchase of these houses could be at the very least a bargain, if not the economic opportunity of a lifetime.

The Chianti began to receive a significant influx of foreigners only in the early 1960s, and the rest of rural Tuscany even later. These people fell in love with the emptiness – both literal and metaphorical – around them, which allowed them not only to buy property, but also to project onto the landscape their aspirations and anxieties. Many of these residential tourists were upper middle class British citizens, whose increasing presence and visibility warranted the coinage of a new toponym, Chiantishire. They also formed something of a colony, kept together by emulation and competition, but their objects of desire were no longer the Renaissance artifacts of their urban forebears, now permanently out of reach for financial as well as legal reasons, but the qualities of the houses they bought and of the renovations they carried out. The character and meaning of these architectural interventions were far from uncontroversial. Carlo Cresti, professor of architecture at the University of Florence, argued in 1981 that, by turning stables into dining rooms and barns into bedrooms, the new rural residents were betraying the spirit of Tuscany's farmhouses in the name of "consumerism and the bourgeois pursuit of comfort."[30] One person's quest for Arcadia was another's vulgarly speculative venture.

It is tempting to surmise that, in making this point, Cresti had in mind the words of Raymond Flower, a British businessman, sportsman, and writer, who had bought a Medieval tower near Panzano in Chianti in 1962 and published a 1979 memoir about his Tuscan adventures. Here Flower reported with amusement on how in the Chianti British community "covert (and sometimes covetous) glances were given at each other's houses to see what solutions were being adopted – stables turned into living rooms, stairs moved indoors, barns become studios, and so forth – while tips were eagerly exchanged about builders, carpenters and

---

[30] Carlo Cresti, "Un Catalogo dell'Architettura Colonica," *Toscana Qui* 1, 6 (giugno 1981): 122–123.

plumbers and the prices they charged."[31] The use of local labor seemed to reassure the new owners that their renovations remained faithful to traditional styles, but their bargaining over the laborers' wages betrayed a sensibility far removed from that of their fabulously wealthy ancestors. Flower himself remembered with nostalgia how in the 1960s "for between 6 and 10 million lira (or, say, the equivalent of £3,500–£6,000) you could pick up a solid farmhouse with 20 or 30 acres of arable land and woods. And half of Chianti was for sale."[32] A few of these residential tourists, including Flower, made a small fortune by facilitating the migration of their fellow nationals to second homes in need of renovation. Pieces of Arcadia could be purchased at basement prices, at least for a while.

From the very beginning, however, foreign residential tourists were a diverse bunch. Flower and many others saw in rural Tuscany both an opportunity to make money and a chance to escape the bonds and lures of modernity. Other foreign residents came to Tuscany with a more romantic disposition and joined, in private if not in public, the Italian critics of the emerging leisure and heritage industry, even though they partook of many of the same myths. Rather than talk about these more "radical" tourists in a generic way, as a group, I will focus on one of them, a woman who met Flower and to an extent pitted her experience and sensibility against the values he and other more commercially minded residents stood for. I had the chance to interview her at length, visit the place where she lived, and get to know her family. She offered me the kind of detail and texture that even the most sincere memoirs, let alone scholarly studies, seldom grant. In many ways, including a certain obsession with home renovations (or lack thereof), the life path of Suzanne (a pseudonym) can be placed near the origins of the trajectory that has produced Frances Mayes's best-selling memoir, except that Suzanne developed a less reconciled and more confrontational sensibility – not quite the stuff of middlebrow literature.

Suzanne came to Tuscany in the early 1960s from the United States with her husband, a writer and a collector. Suzanne and Richard (also a pseudonym) first rented some rooms in a villa near Tavarnuzze, from a signora whose husband had been a Fascist leader and whose social life was deeply shaped by the enduring hostility of the Communist townspeople toward her and her children. Suzanne and Richard instinctively sided with the local residents, who were busy donating their labor to

---

[31] Raymond Flower, *Chianti: The Land, the People and the Wine* (London: Croom Helm, 1979): 215.
[32] Ibid.: 214.

build the local Casa del Popolo (see Chapter 2), a "heartwarming" sight. Their relationship with the signora was doomed. The next move was to buy a vicarage a dozen kilometers west of Greve, deep into the Florentine Chianti, and settle there permanently in 1964: "It was a fantastic property, because, well, the countryside was being abandoned.... So the Church was selling property in those days, and we bought a property for what was basically 4 million lire, which was *pochissimo*. I can't imagine now." Even in such an isolated place, social obligations could not be escaped. The American couple was immediately invited to the parties that the local gentry organized in their villas. The notion that these foreigners had moved to rural Tuscany motivated only by their love of beauty seemed outlandish to the local residents: "They wanted to know who these Americans were. There were all kinds of rumors going around: that we had come to open an automobile factory, that we were from the movie business ... the wildest stories." At this juncture they also met Flower, for whom Suzanne felt "a great deal of disdain," because he was systematically buying up property in the area and selling it back to fellow Brits: "You know, he was a very smooth character, and he was always inviting people. He used to come over and we'd converse, you know, but he was obviously ... a businessman, and he was getting a lot of Brits to buy their summer houses, and he was making a lot of money that way."

Suzanne's most cherished and vivid memories did not come from her encounters with the local gentry or fellow foreigners. It was the extant peasant farmers who most fascinated her:

I mustn't forget a very important story. When we lived in S., at the very beginning, there was a family of *contadini* that lived behind us, and their son came down, and he was ... he really looked like an Etruscan, he was just as if he had been there for centuries, very handsome boy, and he was always eager to talk with us and tell us things, and I don't know exactly what it was ... there was something in conversation about someone having been born in a strange way, with certain physical defects, and his face lit up and he said: "oh well, you know that there are some people that are born part horse and part person and sometimes you can hear them going through the fields." He believed this, or he really heard it, or maybe it really happened, because in that place, at that time, talking about centaurs did not seem strange. It was part of what would have been in a newspaper of centuries ago: "the centaurs are going through that part of Tuscany."

Etruscan faces and roaming centaurs were what Suzanne had been searching for. This perception of the continuity of time, and of the presence of the past in the present, made Italy, and rural Tuscany in particular, unique and magical: "You can't imagine, someone coming from America and seeing something totally different, particularly Italy. It was so different from any other place.... It was just still in the past, it seemed as if you were really stepping into the past. That was the feeling I had."

In the late 1970s Suzanne "happily divorced" Richard and moved to another house north of Greve, a former mill deep in a valley. Once again, the words of the last miller made this place deeply meaningful to her:

I think I paid 26–27 million [lire] for this house. Nobody wanted it, because it [did not have a view], because there were still lots of houses in the country, and so if you got to the top of the hill it was better. That brought the price down. Nobody was interested in living here except me. It was known as the Mulino di C., and I met C., he was the last *mugnaio* (miller) who lived here. He told me wonderful stories. Wonderful.... Some are shocking, quite frankly. Part of the house, where my daughter lives now, has a wall that is part of the wall of the *gora* (mill race), and he told me that when he was a kid he slept in that room, and the wall would turn into ice in the winter time. It was humid and very cold, but when this little old man told me this story, his eyes were sparkling with glee. It was a wonderful memory for him. The beauty of this place.... He said this and the other thing, he showed me where there had been a bridge that had been buried, where there was a canal that had been covered up, and he gave me a lot of information about how to go about the restoration.

In the meantime, rural Tuscany was changing all around Suzanne, in ways she found objectionable. Her narrative presents her house as an endangered bastion of authenticity. She kept the façade as she found it, restraining from replastering it or removing the plaster to expose the stonework, admiring instead the signs that time had left on it: "It's the only house that looks like this by now.... Most people think this looks horrible, because it looks dirty, it doesn't look right, but when I arrived all the houses looked like this house does now. Many houses now are beautiful. They're very beautifully stuccoed, so you can see the brick and stonework, but it's just still not the house the way that it used to look in a painting." And Suzanne had indeed photographed and painted the house many times, taking pride in its rusticity. She even regretted having to replace the old floors, still remembering the patterns that revealed where generations of people had walked most frequently.

Suzanne's esthetic sensibility is uncommon in today's Tuscany. When she sold the adjacent barn to a family from Greve, she initially hoped they would share her radically conservationist esthetic, taking solace in knowing that one of the buyer's sons was an architect. But the outcome of the restoration disappointed her sorely: "Basically that house you can find in any periphery of any city. Pick it up and put it there. It has no longer any characteristic. It originally had the brick work on the entire upper floor, that was so beautiful. I never imagined that they would just cover it up like that. It had never occurred to me.... It looks like *una villetta di campagna* (little country villa), you know, this idea that you own a little villetta, and a villetta doesn't show that it was once a barn." The new owners had decided to replaster the exterior, paint it a shade of yellow, and install ornate gutters and roof shingles.[33] Like in countless other cases, seemingly strict conservation laws had been bent. Apparently, the new owners knew members of the municipal government very well.

The jarring contrast between Suzanne's house and the restructured former barn, now separated by a tall hedge, tells a story of evolving esthetic sensibilities and of an ongoing search for workable sources of authenticity. In the course of the 1980s, an uneasy balance between esthetic and ethical considerations began to emerge and then become hegemonic. Once it became clear that neither public authorities nor civil society had the necessary political and economic resources to strictly regulate the renovations of the old farmhouses, a sense of concerned resignation began to dominate public discourse. Over time, the debate moved from whether the proliferation of second homes would destroy the Tuscan countryside to the ways in which the pursuit of leisure and the "respect" of patrimony could be made compatible.

The outcome of this debate was the creation of "generic rurality," an esthetic sensibility shaped by the understanding of rural Tuscany as patrimony. A few concrete examples will illustrate this point. In many parts of Tuscany, including the Chianti, farmhouses were traditionally plastered. As we have seen in Chapter 2, in the 1940s and 1950s Tuscan sharecroppers complained bitterly of their landlords' refusal to repair the plaster that was crumbling off the walls of their houses, exposing the stonework underneath.[34] "Traditional" Tuscan peasants viewed the absence of plaster as a sign of disrepair and neglect, leading to complete abandonment. But plaster also made rural houses more "urban" – or, in other words, more civil. Ordinary well-kept buildings in Florence, for example, would be plastered and repainted on a regular basis. In the 1960s this sensibility was still common. As late as 1966 Arrigo Benedetti explicitly argued that "we must discourage any attempt at exposing stone walls to produce those effects that may be respectable elsewhere – in California, Arizona,

---

[33] As we will see next, and as Suzanne noticed, most recent home renovations in the Chianti have included the removal of the plaster from the façades, in order to expose the stonework and make the houses look more "rural." In the case of this and other barns, however, the preservation of the original, nonplastered, façade perhaps went too far in that direction. Buildings have to look just "rural enough."

[34] Even Malenotti urged the savvy landlord to apply at least a layer of coarse plaster (arricciare) to all external and internal walls of Tuscan farmhouses; *Il Padrone Contadino*: 36. In southern Tuscany, where bricks made of clay were common, plaster was not viewed as equally necessary. After all, plenty of urban buildings had facades of exposed bricks.

and also in other parts of Europe – but that over here only represent concessions to passing fads."[35]

Twenty-five years later, even people familiar with the Tuscan countryside took it for granted that exposed stonework was part of what gave Tuscan farmhouses their distinctive beauty. Journalist and military historian Franco Bandini, after working for many years in Milan as a reporter for the daily *Corriere della Sera*, decided to go back to Tuscany and in 1970 bought a large and dilapidated farmhouse near Colle Val d'Elsa.[36] When he hired a British architect to renovate it, Bandini was pleased to see that he was committed to respecting the structure of the building, documented on the basis of a variety of publications, including Gori-Montanelli's and Biffoli's books. But then, theorizing about the beauty of Tuscan rural houses, Bandini proceeded to notice that one of the distinctive traits of central Tuscany was its rocky soil, so that the peasant, as he plowed, gathered mountains of rocks. These rocks would be used not only for the terracing of the fields (*muretti a secco*), Bandini maintained, but also for the building of the houses, which as a consequence beautifully blended with the surrounding landscape. In the span of one generation, what was dissonantly foreign had become distinctively Tuscan. The new rural dwellers loved exposed stone walls for the same reasons the sharecroppers disliked them: they looked and felt distinctively rural.

Another example deals with the visible differences between the landlords' villas and the former sharecroppers' houses. This distinction was traditionally self-evident and deeply meaningful, but many renovations of second homes tended to "ruralize" the villas and "ennoble" the farmhouses. In the 1960s, this process of homogenization was regarded as a loss of authenticity and as an example of disregard for the legacy of rural society. A generation later, this sensibility had changed. In the early 1990s Reginaldo Cianferoni, the firebrand agricultural economist who in the 1950s defended the sharecroppers from dispossession and traditional agriculture from capitalist restructuring (see Chapter 3), was asked by the municipal government of Castelnuovo Berardenga to draft a study on the relationships between agricultural and territorial planning in the municipality's area. He came up with a host of recommendations. When it came to the numerous second homes dotting the landscape, Cianferoni focused on the areas immediately surrounding these buildings, noticing that "there does not seem to exist a culture and advanced know-how able to manage in a correct and economical way these areas that could have a much better function in the landscape, to the enjoyment of the

---

[35] In G. Biffoli, *La Casa Colonica in Toscana* (1966): 12.
[36] Franco Bandini, "La civiltà del podere," *Toscana Qui* 11, 12 (December 1991): 40–45.

whole community."[37] Sharecroppers left the areas around their houses devoid of trees, aside from a fig tree for a little shade or a few cypress trees. They needed to keep an eye on the land and maximize the sun exposure of garden plots. By contrast, landlords always surrounded their villas with small woods, a signal that their dwellings were places devoted to pleasure and leisure. Now Cianferoni recommended that all owners of second homes plant trees around their buildings, after submitting landscaping plans to the municipal government. Again, in the span of a generation, what constituted a sign of vulgarity and disrespect for tradition had become, at least to one prominent and influential observer, a sign of commitment to landscape beautification. And there is no doubt that since the 1960s ornamental trees (above all, cypresses) have proliferated throughout Tuscany. The spread of cypress trees has been such that their density has aided the transmission of fungal diseases, which call for ongoing chemical treatment.[38]

Trying to convey his enthusiasm for living in a Tuscan farmhouse, Bandini resorted to an explicitly genealogical (and patrimonial) image: in every Tuscan farm one feels the sacred presence of hundreds of generations, "of maybe three or four thousand men, women, and children, in an existential story that has in some secret way penetrated the walls, climbing from the unexplored foundations, permeating the air, the green silences, and the rustling woods of these illustrious places. And it is because of this that we must walk into a Tuscan farmhouse on tiptoes, remembering those who preceded us, and saluting those who will follow us."[39] The passion for exposed stone walls and other rural artifacts, as well as the disregard for the traditional signs of social distinction, dovetailed with this sensibility for experiencing rurality as the haunted creation of a mythical past. These signs came to define the features of a generic rurality whose patrimonial value seemed to reside above all in its bland universality, which glossed over the specificities of an emplaced history made of coercion, conflict, and compromises. Above all, this bland universality masked the emergence of new social distinctions, embedded in an increasingly elitist landscape that reshaped old sites of labor and struggle into exclusive sites of leisure and relaxation.

The tensions between history and heritage came together in shaping agrotourism (*agriturismo*), the practice imported from northern Europe and the Alps of hosting (and sometimes feeding) guests on actually

---

[37] Reginaldo Cianferoni, *Le Aree Agricole nei Piani Regolatori: L'Esperienza di Castelnuovo Berardenga* (Siena, 1993) (found in library of the Museo del Paesaggio in Castelnuovo): 33.

[38] Vittoria Guglielmi, "Al Capezzale del Cipresso," *Toscana Qui* 11, 8–9 (August–September 1991): 76–79.

[39] F. Bandini, "La civiltà del podere": 45.

operating farms.[40] This was the practice that proved most consequential in reinventing the features and functions of thousands of Tuscan farmhouses. Unlike "generic" rural tourism, which could be promoted by anyone living in the countryside, agrotourism was supposed to put urban dwellers in contact with actual farmers. At stake in this practice was not only the rounding up of farmers' incomes and their permanence on the land, but also the integrity of a whole civilization, starting from the farmhouses themselves. In other words, all over Europe this form of tourism was understood as productive of public goods, and thus worthy of subsidies and tax breaks. The scattered settlement typical of sharecropping, the presence of thousands of redundant farmhouses, and the fame of easily reachable attractions such as Florence and Siena, made Tuscany an ideal site for the expansion of rural tourism in its many forms. Nevertheless, the presence of a powerful lobby of hoteliers fearful of subsidized competition, as well as the sheer complexity of regulating a potentially large and diverse sector, delayed a comprehensive regional law until after the national government issued a framework measure in 1985.

The law that was passed by Tuscany's legislature (Regional Law 36/1987) was one of the strictest and most ambitious in Italy, precisely because of the particularly high stakes attributed to the relationships between agriculture and tourism in Tuscan society.[41] This measure eloquently spoke the language of postmaterial values. Its stated goals were, among others, the preservation of the "patrimony" constituted by the rural houses and the diverse customs and products of rural Tuscany; the conservation of the natural environment and requalification of agricultural production away from a purely quantitative logic; and the equalization of the relationships between town and country. Since an agrotourism establishment would pay far lower taxes than a regular hotel or B&B and be entitled to different kinds of subsidies, a whole series of rules were meant to discourage "fake" farmers and "speculators" from taking advantage of the incentives attached to the law. The maximum number of bedrooms was set at fifteen, with no more than thirty beds; only farms with at least two hectares of arable land could open an agro-touristic activity; no new buildings could be raised for agro-touristic purposes; and so on. Most importantly, the farmers in charge of a bona fide agro-touristic business would devote at least half of their labor time to agriculture. Furthermore, at least half of the

[40] Giovanna Bellencin Meneghel, *Agriturismo in Italia* (Bologna: Patron, 1991).
[41] Sandro Angiolini, *Agriturismo in Toscana: Protagonisti, Tendenze, Problemi* (Montepulciano: Edizioni del Grifo, 1989).

revenue had to keep coming from agricultural activities.[42] Each agro touristic farm had to present yearly plans and reports demonstrating that these conditions were met, even though they forced some operators in increasingly renowned areas to cook the books and hide part of their touristic business.

Agrotourism has been a huge success. There were five hundred official agro-touristic establishments in Tuscany in 1988; in 2010 there were more than four thousand. European Union funds, channeled through the regional government, started pouring in to restructure the crumbling farmhouses and make them appealing to international visitors. The historical trajectory of these restorations led to increasingly generic and privatized experiences. In the early years of agrotourism it was not uncommon for the farming family to live in a portion of the house and cook for the guests, who would gather around a table at least once a day. Rather quickly, however, this hospitality model became less common, in favor of providing each group of guests with their own apartments, equipped with private kitchens and bathrooms. This meant that the larger farmhouses needed to be subdivided into smaller living units, carved out of previous barns, storage areas, stables, and the other spaces that typically made up the houses' first floors. Equally radical interventions were needed on the upper floors, which before the restorations were occupied by several small bedrooms often arranged without much concern for privacy. Here kitchens and bathrooms had to be installed from scratch as well, and staircases had to be built to provide access to each independent apartment. External changes, by contrast, would be fairly limited, aside from the stripping down of the extant worn out plaster and the opening of the occasional door or small window.[43] In order to survive and retain their basic visible features, the interior of these houses had to be completely altered.

Without a single common space, such as a kitchen, tourists would now meet, if at all, around the swimming pool, an increasingly expected amenity (Illustration 19). The farming family would often live in a completely different house, or even in a nearby town. The occasional sight of a tractor would be the only reminder of the fact that the surrounding terrain was still the site of agricultural production, and that sight would

---

[42] A new version of the law, issued in 2003, relaxed these requirements by stating that either one of those conditions (as opposed to both) should be met to prove the mainly agricultural status of an agrotouristic business.

[43] The owners of the farmhouses had to submit detailed plans of these restorations to the regional governments in order to receive special grants that originated from Brussels. These plans are preserved at the Archive of the Giunta Regionale in Campi Bisenzio, at the outskirts of Florence. The documents are under Departimento Agricoltura, Serie Agriturismo.

Illustration #19 Swimming pool covered for the winter in the backyard
of an Orcia valley agriturismo.

feel almost incongruous. There is little doubt that some of the reserva-
tions and fears expressed in the run-up to the 1987 regional law have
come true. The municipal council of Monteriggioni, just north of Siena,
articulated these fears most succinctly: "The core of the [agro-tourism]
project held the promise for the farmer to become the bearer of that
peasant culture that has so rapidly vanished ... but in this law the role
of the agro-tourism operator seems close to that of a Club Méditerranée
entertainer."[44] Agrotourism, in other words, did nothing to stem the pervasive loss of authenticity of the Tuscan countryside.

The law and the material practices linked to agrotourism, however,
suggest a more subtle interpretation. By the late twentieth century,
the Tuscan farmhouse had become a historical monument as defined
by Choay, an imagined space where the spirits of the Etruscans, the
Renaissance artists, and the nineteenth-century winemaking landlords

[44] Archivio della Regione Toscana, Vol. Verbale 62/Bis Agriturismo, 4th legislature, floder
Regione Toscana – Consiglio regionale – II Commissione- consultazione del 12/1/1986
su Proposte di legge 12, 16, 24 in materia di attivita' agrituristiche.

could all be imagined to be whispering in one's ear. But it was the spirit of the departed sharecroppers that haunted these houses most assiduously, even in their absence. The sharecroppers' legacy lived on not only in the democratization of leisure, for which they had struggled, but also in the ways in which rural Tuscans framed modernity and made it their own. The regional administration's ongoing commitment to agriculture, the omnipresent fears of speculation, and many Tuscans' admittedly awkward search for authenticity were all indebted to the extinct world of the radical sharecroppers. Tuscany has built its appeal on its uncommon ability to speak to everyone in the name of a generic rurality supposedly shaped by (and connected to) the urban glories of the Renaissance. These myths have fueled a thriving heritage industry. Tuscany's distinctive sense of place, however, comes from recent memories few tourists are aware of. The mythical senses of the continuity of time, embedded in Tuscany's farmhouses, confront the inescapable perception that rural Tuscany is also the product of modernity's ruptures. That perception has been central to the establishment of dozens of museums of peasant culture. It is one of the many paradoxes of rural Tuscany (and rural Europe more generally) that farmhouses have by and large become bland heritage sites, as museums have tried to keep the asperities of historical memory alive.

Monuments to Memory: Rural Museums in Tuscany

Tuscan farmhouses were of course full of tools and furnishings. As peasants abandoned their houses and agricultural life, their objects were often thrown away. Dumpsters were reportedly replete with rural objects in the 1960s and 1970s. A few of these artifacts, such as copper kitchenware, found their way into secondhand stores and then into the houses of the urban middle classes. Fewer still ended up in private collections and museums. Today there are in Tuscany dozens of "museums" devoted to the memorialization of the rural past.[45] The director of several of them told me in jest that "sharecropping died, and as its epitaph, as its tombstone, we have the museums."[46] In other words, rural museums are monuments akin to a tombstone: their value does not reside in the preciousness or uniqueness of their collections, but in their functions as cultural markers speaking to the need to remember and to the dangers of forgetting.

[45] Sandra Becucci, "I Musei Demoantropologici in Toscana," in Commissione Nazionale per i Beni Demoantropologici, *Il Patrimonio Museale Antropologico: Itinerari nelle Regioni Italiane* (Pomezia: Adnkronos Cultura, 2002): 177–190.

[46] Interview by author with Gianfranco Molteni, May 26, 2010.

In today's Tuscany there are two broad kinds of "rural museums," which provide the visitor with significantly different experiences: one is the collection of rural tools and furnishings, assembled in display cases or pinned to the walls; the other is the more elaborate museum with photographs, sound recordings, panels, talking figurines, and so on. The relationship between the two kinds of exhibits, however, is complex and not merely oppositional. It is by telling the history of these exhibits that their relationship can be unraveled. To convey a concrete sense of how the tool collections came about, I will focus on two cases, both located in the Chianti. This selection is not meant to be representative, but the two cases exemplify some social and cultural traits common to other experiences of memorialization that developed between the 1970s and the 1990s. In the case of these museums, too, as with Suzanne's experiences, participant observation and interviews have proved indispensable in reconstructing stories and perceptions that have not left many written records behind, both because of their seemingly mundane character and because of their relatively recent vintage. Participant observation has also allowed me to question the few existing textual sources, which tend to tell rather generic and anodyne stories.

The building that houses the first museum, in San Donato in Poggio, a hamlet in the Florentine Chianti near Tavarnelle, doubles as a tourist office. The museum bears the name of Emilio Ferrari (1915–1990), a Ligurian-born engineer and collector who in the early 1970s moved to a tower along the castle walls. The collection is housed in two rooms – the first devoted to traditional crafts (carpentry, ironsmithing, shoemaking, and so on) and their tools, and the second to the tools of the share-cropping peasants, most of which are pinned to the walls in repetitive patterns (a row of hoes, an arc of sheaths, and so on). A panel at the entrance, crowned by an image of Ferrari's profile, expounds on the origins of the collection, but there are otherwise very few textual aids explaining the meaning of the single objects or their assemblage: they are by and large left to speak for themselves. The town's tourist information officer, Gabriella Macì, put me in contact with the collector's heir, Paolo Pellizzari, Emilio Ferrari's distant "cousin" and an engineer in his early thirties, who accompanied me in my visit. Gabriella, who grew up in San Donato, had fond memories of Emilio Ferrari, who never married and had no children. She remembered him as a tall and lean figure, roaming around the countryside with the locals, looking for objects, and added that "everyone knew him and he loved the town dearly."

The official history of the museum tells a seamless tale of collaboration between Ferrari and the local public authorities, who funded the museum project and catalogued the collection shortly before Ferrari's death in 1990.[47] My somewhat indelicate prodding revealed a more complex and interesting story, completely invisible to the casual visitor. After the museum visit, Paolo, the cousin, took me to the tower, where his mother lived, and showed me a folder with some documents related to the collection. Paolo's mother told me that Emilio Ferrari did not only collect rural objects, but also folk religious art and books, by the tens of thousands. She also mentioned with amused puzzlement some four hundred "copper pots" he had collected over the years. I realized that only a small portion of this kitchenware was now on display at the museum, but I did not inquire further. Finally, Paolo took me across the street, to a more modern two-story house overlooking the valley, which he and his American wife were restructuring with the intention of moving there. The collection, he told me, was originally housed there, and he showed me old pictures of what the two large rooms on the first floor looked like when Ferrari was still alive. The walls were covered with objects from floor to ceiling: there were the hundreds of copper pans.

The documents Paolo shared with me tell fragments of a twisted and largely interrupted trajectory. From a long handwritten letter that Ferrari sent in 1987 to Carlo Contini, another collector of rural artifacts from the Emilian town of Carpi, it appears that he had indeed bought the house principally to hold his collection.[48] Here he also expresses a paramount concern – "the inheritance, or to whom to bequeath these collections so that they will live on in an enlightened spirit." He does not clarify what an enlightened spirit might entail, but his intention at the time was to leave everything, buildings included, to a local bank, so that it might establish a foundation and guarantee public fruition of the collection in perpetuity. The fact that he knew the bank director, himself the owner of recently purchased property in the Chianti, seemed to bode well for the plan. A press release dating to just a few months before Ferrari's death, however, suggests that by then he had begun to place his trust with public authorities instead, probably because they promised to validate the collections on an academic level. His plans for the collection and museum, which he had put together "to illuminate the way of life of agrarian society, from which we all originate," were ambitious. He even intended the collection

---

[47] Associazione Culturale Pro Loco San Donato in Poggio, www.sandonatoinpoggio.it/html/home.php?name=Museo&file=storia.

[48] Contini, who died in 2010, was a physician who collected a wealth of artifacts documenting traditional agricultural practices in the Po plain. The destiny of his collection has remained very uncertain for years. The more precious portion of the collection, made up of ornate carts, is now preserved in the Museo Civico Polironiano in San Benedetto Po. For an obituary, see "Addio al Ricercatore dei Linguaggi Ancestrali," *Voce di Carpi*, July 15, 2010, available at www.voce.it/edicola/index.html?section=articolo&id=367&artid=13802.

to inspire conferences on the relationship between city and countryside. The sources also reveal an extensive web of connections: he had made contacts with the provincial administrators, who had entrusted a team of scholars from the University of Florence with overseeing the collection catalogue. A letter from the provincial government to Paolo's mother, dated April 1992, two years after Ferrari's death, promised the continuation of the endeavor and summoned all interested parties to a meeting to discuss the destiny of the engineer's estate.

The ensuing negotiations and compromises led to a solution that testified first of all to the town's gratitude to Ferrari: the small museum, located on city property, is a tribute to an "outsider" interested in preserving memories that the locals were all too willing to leave behind. The museum, in its materiality, also speaks to the inevitable tensions between inheritance and heritage: the collection was made public in ways its author had clearly not anticipated. Finally, the location of the collection exemplifies in a particularly poignant way the tensions between a kind of tourism that is largely uninterested in Tuscany's recent peasant past and the commitment of some contemporary Tuscans to reminding tourists that what they see around them is the product of a specific history of labor and social struggle. During my own visit to the museum I witnessed two separate tourist couples come in; one asked the tourist officer about accommodations in the area and the other about a local food festival. Neither couple seemed to even notice the tools across Gabriella's desk. It is tempting to surmise that in its layout, with the tools displayed behind a tourist office, the museum exemplifies Erving Goffman's distinction between back and front regions in the presentation of the self (a collective self in this case).[49] The back of the building, where the museum is located, is indeed a site of authenticity, but also a place that both locals and tourists largely ignore. Its value is largely symbolic: it is a monument in the etymological sense of the term, a kind of admonishment against the selective forgetfulness of modern life.

A half-hour drive from San Donato, past the towns of Castellina and Radda, is a thriving winery by the name of Montevertine. This is also the address that several websites and guidebooks give for the Little Museum of the Chianti (Piccolo Museo del Chianti). When I visited it, however, the collection was not open to the public, although the current owner of the winery, Martino Manetti, was kind enough to show me around.

---

[49] E. Goffman, *The Presentation of Self in Everyday Life* (Garden City, NY: Doubleday, 1959). This distinction has been widely deployed in the anthropology of tourism. See, for example, Jeremy Boissevain (ed.), *Coping with Tourists: European Reactions to Mass Tourism* (Providence: Berghahn Books, 1996).

It was housed on the ground floor of an annex to the main farmhouse, announced by the incongruous juxtaposition of a Sicilian painted cart and a stone olive press, both surrounded by tall grass. The collection of tools and utensils developed over several small rooms, divided by function, with a large section appropriately devoted to winemaking (Illustration 20). My guide told me somewhat apologetically that he had been negotiating for years with Radda's municipal government to move the collection to a more suitable and accessible site. The present location, he told me, was not even up to code, and as long as the collection was there he could not restructure the building and make it inhabitable.

The collection was put together by Martino's father, Sergio (1921–2000), over the course of the 1970s. In 1967 he had bought the forty-hectare farm from the Church at a silent auction, paying the astonishingly low sum of 5.9 million lire. His was the only offer. Sergio Manetti had grown up in Poggibonsi, a town half way between Florence and Siena, and a destination for thousands of migrating sharecroppers in the 1950s and 1960s, when the wine and furniture industries created manufacturing jobs and prompted the building of many nondescript apartment

Illustration #20 Display at the Little Museum of the Chianti at Montevertine, near Radda.

towers. Sergio himself, after countless odd jobs, had made a small fortune as a manufacturer of corrugated iron, one of the main components of the industrial buildings springing up along Tuscany's main roads. But he wanted a piece of property in the countryside, where he and Giulio Gambelli, childhood friend and rising star in the exploding field of enology, could take a stab at making good wine. A country home was also a good place to entertain his customers, at least until, shortly before the 1973 oil crisis, the Italian steel giant Falck made him an offer he could not refuse. After shedding his urban concerns, Sergio focused on his passions, wine and collecting. And collect he did – not only rural tools but also books, paintings, walking sticks and, appropriately enough, corkscrews.

Sergio Manetti died in 2000 a renowned high-quality winemaker. He employed his considerable resources to reconstitute the farm's semi-abandoned vineyards and in 1977 he defied the Chianti Classico consortium, to which he belonged, by producing a wine that only used the sangiovese varietal, instead of the varietal mix that Bettino Ricasoli had recommended in the nineteenth century and the consortium enforced in the twentieth. He renounced his consortium membership shortly thereafter. This wine, called Pergole Torte (Twisted Pergolas), soon became legendary among connoisseurs, an ancestor of the "super Tuscans."[50] Sergio's son, Martino, has built on this legacy, managing to turn Montevertine into an international brand. In 2009–2010, the winery exported to the United States one quarter of its select production of approximately eighty thousand bottles. Its exclusive U.S. importer is Neal Rosenthal, featured in the 2005 documentary Mondo Vino as the terroir-conscious alternative to Mondavi's imperial and homogenizing ambitions. I could not refrain from asking Martino, who as a boy had given countless tours of the rural collection, if he saw any links between his father's passion for collecting rural artifacts and his heterodox approach to winemaking. He replied that his father had always wanted to respect, and be true to, tradition, but that he understood this respect as a dialectic (his word) with innovation. Inherent in this reply is the notion that patrimony must be continuously reinvented to remain true to itself.

These two cases of rural collecting share some obvious similarities. Both Ferrari and Manetti were thoroughly urban and "modern" individuals who walked into a rural world that was rapidly changing before their eyes. Relatively few collections were assembled by former peasants,[51] and

[50] Armando Castagno, "Pergole Torte, l'Arte della Coerenza," *Bibenda* 34 (June 2010): 60–68.
[51] The most cited exception is the Museo della Civiltà Contadina in Bentivoglio, near Bologna, founded in 1973 on the basis of artifacts assembled by a cooperative of former

landlords are remarkably absent from this group as well. The emotional investment that motivated most collectors developed from a particular subject position that combined distance from the recent history of rural Tuscany and proximity to the people and places that history had left behind. Both Ferrari and Manetti were meticulous collectors by upbringing and inclination, and the rural objects strewn around them featured that delicate balance between seriality and difference that is distinctive of collectables. As long as the collectors were alive, these objects could also tell unique stories about places and people encountered for preciously fleeting moments on "treasure hunts" through the countryside. On one level, these collections testify to two men's irreducibly personal encounters with the detritus of rapid historical change. But there is no doubt that the collectors envisaged a public function for their artifacts. Both Ferrari and Manetti believed themselves to be engaged in an urgent endeavor of conservation and education. In their present state, however, the collections are monuments to the process of memorialization itself, rather than places where knowledge and affect are actively reproduced.

As Ferrari, Manetti, and many other collectors roamed through the Tuscan countryside on their quest for obsolete objects, a distinctive sensibility toward rurality began to develop among some left-wing intellectuals and politicians. Memorialization could speak the language of elegy and bemoan a lost world, as was the case with many collections of rural artifacts, but it could also make a more overtly political argument, denouncing the ways in which Tuscan peasants were being forgotten and viewing this form of amnesia as a necessary move for the legitimation of capitalist modernity – a move that needed to be resisted. The temporality underlying the first kind of memorialization was that of linear progress, to which the old ways had to be sacrificed, albeit with regret; the second approach understood historical time as a dialectical process and deployed memory as a radical critique of the present. This more radical form of memorialization was also a way of coming to terms with the perceived defeats of both the peasant movement of the postwar years and the revolutionary aspirations of "1968," understood as chapters in the same political tradition. In both cases, these oppositional movements, one rural and the other urban, had failed to achieve hegemony, in Gramscian terms, on the terrain of political struggle, and in both cases the lure of a comfortable but stultifying modernity had prevailed. But the

peasants, and now part of a multifunctional center that includes a library and archive, among other initiatives. See the museum's website at www.museociviltacontadina .provincia.bologna.it/Engine/RAServePG.php. I'm not aware of a comparable institution of peasant origins in Tuscany.

struggle continued on the terrain of cultural production: the post-1968 generation looked back at the sharecroppers' world in search of an alternative past capable of legitimating their aspirations and articulating their feelings of alienation from (and perhaps also guilt about) the present. This patrimonial legacy was not meant to pacify the past, but to critique the present and reimagine the future.

The features of this form of overtly political memorialization came into full display in an itinerant 1973 photographic exhibition called "The Other Chianti" (L'Altro Chianti).[52] Organized by photographer Marcello Stefanini and funded by the provincial government of Siena, the exhibit relied on both archival and current photographs to document the recent history of the Chianti, from the Fascist period and the postwar social conflicts to the rural exodus and its aftermath. The show traveled from Florence, where it was staged in Palazzo Vecchio, to the wine fair of Greve (the main town in the Florentine Chianti), and finally to Siena, where it was held in one of the city's most renowned art galleries. The prestige of these venues reveals the paradox of an "insurgent" sensibility that could count on the support of many leftist administrators, some of whom had been leaders of the postwar peasant movement within the Communist-affiliated organizations and were now in positions of power. The title of the exhibit further highlighted this paradox. In the words of the organizers, the hegemonic Chianti was the one portrayed in "facile oleographs of lyrical-touristic inspiration" (facili oleografie di ispirazione lirico-turistica), all focused on the quality of the wine and the beauty of the scenery (scorci paesistici). Theirs, on the other hand, was "a non-conformist exhibition, organized with the conviction that only a critical, even merciless, reflection can produce a different future."[53] The organizers explicitly opposed their patrimonial practices to those of the residential tourists and the burgeoning heritage industry.

The exhibit opened in Florence in March 1973, with a conference held in the lavishly frescoed Sala dei Duecento in Palazzo Vecchio. Some of Tuscany's most prominent left-wing academics, including historian Giorgio Giorgetti, spoke at length about the exploitative character of traditional sharecropping, focusing on the historical responsibilities of the region's landed aristocracy. Some members of that aristocracy were in attendance. One of them, the matriarch of the Ricasoli dynasty, rose up, vented her frustration with the tone and content of the initiative, and stormed out of the room.[54] When the exhibit moved to Greve in

[52] ASMOS, Fondo Peris Brogi, box XIII 1, folder 4, subfolder 1973, "L'Altro Chianti, Mostra Fotografica a Cura dell'Amministrazione Provinciale di Siena."
[53] "L'Altro Chianti a Firenze," La Nazione, March 25, 1973.
[54] Pico, "Le Vipere del Chianti," Nuovo Corriere Senese, March 29, 1973.

September, the grape harvest was in full swing, and the photographs were shown in conjunction with the town's yearly wine fair (Mostra-Mercato del Vino). On opening night, the exhibit was vandalized: someone broke in and tore down some of the panels, stealing dozens of photographs. The local press and the organizers thought immediately of a politically motivated attack.[55] Although the culprits turned out to be some local youths who just wanted to pull a prank, the incident further increased the exhibit's controversial aura.

Even as the images and arguments put forward by the organizers denounced wine connoisseurship and tourism as fetishes that mystified the Chianti's true history, the area's leftist administrations were busy reinventing the future of the region through the values of wine and scenery. The leftist government of Greve did its best to host the wine fair as usual, but accompanied it with an exhibit that openly criticized the restructuring of the old vineyards with public funds, viewed as a way of collectivizing the costs and privatizing the profits of modernization. Once again, the exhibit was a temporary monument with a ritual function: it exorcized the ambivalence many felt toward the region's recent transformation. The promises of prosperity offered by tourism and the wine industry sat uneasily with the debt of gratitude that many felt toward the disappearing Tuscan sharecroppers. Those peasants were no longer physically there to enjoy the fruits of modernity. In fact, it was their disappearance that was making the new scenarios possible. But they could be conjured up with words and images, so that they could give their reluctant blessing to their left-wing sons and daughters, now in equally reluctant charge of their territory and of their future. Again, it was the process of memorialization itself, in its phenomenology, that built spaces where the meanings of historical change could be articulated.

It did not take long for this sensibility to promote the building of more permanent monuments. When the Chianti exhibit reached Siena in late September 1973, the organizers decided to complement it with the screening of Sergio Micheli's *The End of Mezzadria*, the striking documentary I discussed at length in Chapter 3. In those months Pietro Clemente, a young anthropologist whose recent dissertation dealt with Franz Fanon, had just moved to town from Sardinia to take up a position at the University of Siena. As Clemente told me in an interview, it was the viewing of that documentary, maybe even in conjunction with the exhibit, that convinced him of the necessity to concentrate his intellectual

---

[55] "Chianti tra Letteratura e Ambiguità," *Nuovo Corriere Senese*, September 20, 1973.

and political energies on the dying world of the Tuscan sharecroppers, inaugurating a legacy that survives to this day.[56]

In the course of the mid-1970s, a tight collaboration developed between several public administrators, especially Provincial Councilor Peris Brogi (who had also been one of the main organizers of the Chianti exhibit), and a group of anthropologists at the University of Siena.[57] The main fruit of this collaboration was the Documentation Center on Peasant Labor (Centro di Documentazione sul Lavoro Contadino, or CEDLAC), officially established in 1975. The organizers made it clear that this was not going to be an ordinary museum. In Brogi's words, rural Tuscans were faced with two unpalatable options vis-à-vis the sharecroppers' legacy: to resign themselves to seeing a whole "patrimony" (his term) fall into oblivion or to engage in the romantic reminiscing of a lost idyllic world. The emphasis on peasant labor was meant to counter both these tendencies. In the same vein, it was imperative to establish not a museum, understood as a "collection of more or less rare 'pieces,' of curios, but a center for the promotion of broadly conceived research and cultural initiatives."[58]

For the Communist administrators, many of whom were of peasant origins, the Center represented an opportunity not only to validate their own social and cultural background, but also to transfer to the realm of cultural policy the struggle for the revitalization of agriculture that I examined in Chapter 4. For Brogi, rural Tuscany was experiencing "a phase in which speculation [was] under way, and thus [Tuscan society was] beginning to discard the fruits of a long productive process." The Center's mission was to counter the "dilapidation of peasant labor."[59] Embedded in these words was perhaps a sense of impending defeat: if Brogi's generation of administrators were to lose the struggle against "speculation" at the level of concrete agricultural policy, peasant labor would at least be remembered and valorized at the level of cultural production.

The sensibility of the scholars involved in this initiative was no less complex. Pietro Clemente, for example, came to Siena with an explicitly "engaged" (*impegnata*) conception of historical and ethnographic

---

[56] Interview by author with Pietro Clemente, June 1, 2011.

[57] That group included, in addition to Clemente, Paolo De Simonis, Maria Luisa Meoni, Gianfranco Molteni, Massimo Squillacciotti, and Pier Giorgio Solinas, among others.

[58] ASMOS, Fondo PCI, box VA12, folder Varie, subfolder 1975, pamphlet titled "Ipotesi e Proposte per la Costituzione di un Centro Provinciale di Documentazione sul Lavoro Contadino" (Siena, 1975): 3.

[59] Ester Vanni, "Centro di Documentazione sul Lavoro Contadino," *La Nazione*, Cronaca di Firenze, June 15, 1975.

research, which he had developed in Sardinia while participating in the student movement of the late 1960s. With Pier Giorgio Solinas, another anthropologist who had also moved to Siena from Sardinia, he was drawn immediately to the reconstruction of the oral memory of the Resistance in the province's rural areas, where he encountered a generally positive grassroots recollection of the relationships between the peasant population and the anti-Fascist partisans. The scholars brought with them the methodological commitments of the New Left. In Clemente's own words, whereas the Communist Party had a cultural line which it tended to impose on the historical and ethnographic record, for him and his colleagues, "who [were] linked to the student movement of 1968, the idea was the emancipation of the proletarians with their own forces, thus for us it was almost a sacred thing to hear their voices."

These voices, however, were not as forthcoming as Clemente and his colleagues hoped. These scholars' fascination with rural Tuscany's legacy of struggle contrasted with the willingness of rural Tuscans to forget. In Clemente's words, these struggles "had very powerful features, which, I found, were increasingly forgotten by local communities." The same was true for these communities' songs and rituals, which "had fallen into striking disuse." Clemente is now aware of the paradoxical character of his early memorialization efforts: "Collective memory no longer registered these sharecroppers, and thus ours was memory research against the current, even though I realized this after many years. I thought [back then] to be working with the current." After all, so many of the ideals and rituals of the radical movements of the late 1960s and early 1970s seemed to have been foreshadowed by the sharecroppers' struggles. The "red markets" (*mercatini rossi*) of Lotta Continua (one of the largest New Left organizations), for example, seemed to have been foreshadowed in the 1940s and 1950s by the mezzadri, who brought eggs to the hospitals instead of giving them to the landlords, or sold them at a "political" price. These links between past and present were not completely lost on rural Tuscans. Clemente remembered fondly the celebrations of Liberation Day (April 25th) that he helped organize in Tocchi, a hamlet near Monticiano, as an alternative to the official "urban" commemorations held in Siena and elsewhere. But by and large both rural and urban Tuscans wanted to "move on." Most former sharecroppers, now in charge of many local governments, focused on the pragmatic decisions of everyday administration, on building public housing and organizing school bus services, rather than on militant cultural production. Clemente recalled that many of them even refrained from calling themselves former mezzadri, preferring the more generic "peasant farmers" (*contadini*).

For both left-wing administrators like Brogi and radical scholars like Clemente, memory had a distinctive aspirational dimension: it was as much about imagining a future of (possibly unmet or even betrayed) possibilities as about retrieving and preserving a lost world. But how to materialize and emplace such aspirations? What would CEDLAC, as a concrete site and venue, look and feel like? These questions were addressed within a larger debate about the present and future contours of ethnographic museums, a debate to which the Sienese scholars gave prominent national and international contributions. It would be impossible to do justice to these debates in a few paragraphs, but the central trajectory of these discussions reflected a more general shift from a "rationalist" to a more sensorial and emotive approach to memorialization, thereby mirroring the emerging appreciation for "landscape" in society at large.

The Sienese anthropologists, most of whom had come to Siena from other parts of Italy, owed their early approach to museum studies to Alberto Cirese (1921–2011), Italy's foremost Gramscian ethnographer, who had mentored them at the University of Cagliari until 1972 and then at the University of Siena itself, where he taught for a couple of years before moving to Rome. In an influential paper originally delivered in 1967, Cirese argued that ethnographic museums should not try to replicate real-life scenarios, as was becoming common in many northern European venues, but rather speak their own distinctive language – that is, a "metalanguage" capable of exposing the relationships that social actors establish between themselves and the structural forces that shaped their lives.[60] Thus, museums should not be mere collections of objects, nor should they aim for immediate audience fruition and "participation"; instead, they should preserve different kinds of documents (not only objects, but also photographs, videos, sound recordings, et cetera) with the goal of putting these different media in relation with one another. In so doing, ethnographic museums were to become centers for the promotion of research and reflection, inviting the critical engagement of scholars and the general public alike.

In an equally influential paper from the mid-1970s, Cirese added that museums should resist the uncritical encouragement of nostalgia, which must be understood (and thus not merely rejected) as the emotion of ambivalence that industrial society experiences when it assesses the costs its members (but especially the subaltern classes) have paid

---

[60] The original essay was titled "Le Operazioni Museografiche Come Metalinguaggio." The essay is included in Alberto Mario Cirese, *Oggetti, Segni, Musei: Sulle Tradizioni Contadine* (Turin: Einaudi, 1977): 35–56.

for the contradictory benefits of modernity. Referencing a famous passage from Marx's *Capital*, Cirese proceeded to recommend that ethnographic museums expose nostalgia as "the consciousness of the price paid, whose history is written in letters of blood and fire in the annals of humankind."[61] In other words, nostalgia should be neither dismissed nor encouraged, but rationally engaged through a critical analysis of the power relations that structure historical change.

CEDLAC responded to these suggestions not only in its emphasis on peasant labor, rather than on the potentially romantic and unhistorical notions of "civilization" or "culture," but also through its keen attention to different media and types of documents. In the course of the late 1970s and 1980s, the scholars affiliated with the Center and their students fanned out into the countryside snapping thousands of photographs, filming hundreds of videos, and taping hundreds of interviews with rural dwellers. All of that was dutifully catalogued and archived, together with an expanding collection of tools and furnishings. Unlike Gori-Montanelli, Biffoli, and other amateur photographers, these scholars were entirely absorbed by the disappearing world of the sharecroppers, with their gestures, stories, and tools. If Clemente was the main academic force behind these initiatives, Gianfranco Molteni was the main organizational and managerial talent. A native of Milan, he had also studied with Cirese, but he did not pursue a university career, choosing instead to triangulate between academic aspirations and the opportunities (and constraints) posed by the public administrations, which kept footing the bills of these ventures together with Monte dei Paschi, the Sienese bank. The Center's participants soon felt the need for a permanent site, where these collections could be preserved, displayed, and engaged with as Cirese prescribed, but many years went by before Molteni managed to have this need met.

CEDLAC collaborated with several collectors of rural artifacts, and one of these early collaborations took place in Buonconvento, a town thirty kilometers south of Siena on the Cassia Road. Here two collectors, a primary school teacher and a building surveyor, had assembled many objects related to one of the area's main activities, hemp cultivation and production. In 1979 CEDLAC collaborated with the municipal government to stage an exhibit on the "hemp cycle" (ciclo della canapa), viewed as an opportunity to relate family life, class relations, the division of labor

---

[61] The original essay, published in 1975, was titled "Condizione Contadina Tradizionale, Nostalgia, Participazione," included in A. M. Cirese, *Oggetti, Segni, Musei, Oggetti, Segni, Musei*: 3–34 (quote is on p. 26).

by generation and gender, and so on, to the material embodiments of those social structures, that is, the tools and furnishings that mediated the peasants' interactions with each other and their environment.[62] Far from speaking for themselves, these objects were complemented with panels displaying not only textual explanations but also drawings, photographs, family structure graphs, and so on. Even though the commitment to a politically relevant memory constituted an overt motivation for the exhibit, the polemical and militant attitude that had inspired the 1973 Chianti exhibit had given way to a more detached and objective approach.

In the course of the 1980s, Clemente and other CEDLAC participants, including Molteni, grew impatient with the limitations attached to viewing ethnographic museums primarily as research centers and promoters of critical knowledge. Toward the end of the decade, Clemente articulated this growing uneasiness in a series of essays that signaled his intellectual distancing from Cirese. The notion of "museum as metalanguage," Clemente argued, implied a universalist and transparent conception of scientific knowledge, according to which the museum organizers and visitors shared the same rational tools, which they could deploy to expose a previously invisible (and often mystified) truth about social and cultural change. In light of recent critiques of the epistemological underpinnings of structuralism and Marxism, Clemente proposed a more self-reflexive conception of the ethnographic museum as a form of "scenographic" communication. Without foregoing the museum's more traditional functions of preservation and knowledge production, it was time to

accentuate the communicative and perceptual dimension of the message, for today and with today's languages. The guiding notion of this project is what I have called "unitary scenography" of the museum: the museum as "mise-en-scène," central act of didactics, of mass communication, of a discourse that does not single out intellectual engagement but proposes itself as *complete perceptual experience*.[63]

Clemente spelled out the break with Cirese's approach without ambiguity: universities are sites of research; museums are sites of esthetic experience.

---

[62] ASMOS, Fondo PCI, box VA2, folder 1979, catalogue and proposal titled "Il Mestiere del Contadino," or "The peasant trade."

[63] The paper, titled "Il Museo Demologico tra il Ricercatore e l'Utente: Problemi di Comunicazione e di Linguaggio," was originally delivered in 1989. It is included in Pietro Clemente, *Graffiti di Museografia Antropologica Italiana* (Siena: Protagon Editori, 1996): 129–145. The quotation is on page 142, and the emphasis has been added.

This emphasis on museums as sites of perceptual and esthetic experiences led both Clemente and Molteni to rethink their earlier critiques of object collections, which they had dismissed as uncritical and unreflexive. Even though collections of rural artifacts failed at contextualizing their objects in fruitful ways, their reliance on esthetic appreciation and humble openness to different interpretations could provide inspiration for more ambitious museums.[64] From this perspective, nostalgia was no longer a fetishistic ideology to be exposed in order to reveal the conditions for its production, as was the case with the "rationalist" museum. Nostalgia could be viewed instead as an emotion through which the visitor could be engaged in a broad sensorial experience capable of relating the past to future possibilities: in this sense "nostalgia is a more interesting ideology than the socialist praise of present accomplishments and of the penury of the past."[65] Clemente went as far as to compare the ethnographic museum to a seed bank, preserving and enacting the possibility of a more diverse future. He also advocated museums that would become part and parcel of broader "territories," helping their inhabitants and visitors enhance their comprehension and appreciation of their surroundings.

When, in the course of the 1990s, opportunities arose to establish several permanent ethnographic museums, Clemente and Molteni set out to turn these theoretical guidelines into practice. A younger generation of public administrators, who still felt emotionally close to the sharecroppers' world but had never been part of it, encouraged them to make the new museums as technologically (and thus experientially) interesting as possible. European Union funds also became available, adding to the resources offered by the local governments and the Monte dei Paschi bank. The original idea was to have one museum, but the availability of so many abandoned structures and artifact collections led to a proliferation of opportunities. The owners of an old hayloft at Orgia, for example, donated the building to the municipality of Sociville on condition that it become a museum, and at the end of the 1990s Molteni and his collaborators opened a Museum of the Woodlands (Museo del Bosco) there,

---

[64] The Sienese anthropologists, for example, became admirers and promoters of Ettore Guatelli (1921–2000), a teacher of peasant extraction who collected an amazing number of rural artifacts over his lifetime and then turned his home at Ozzano Taro, north of Parma, into a museum (www.museoguatelli.it). Here objects are displayed in repetitive patterns evoking alternative senses of time and space. For a self-presentation of this initiative, see Ettore Guatelli and Paolo Candelari, *Il Museo del Tempo: Amore ed Ingegno tra gli Oggetti della Civiltà Contadina* (Parma: Sagea Editrice, 1988).

[65] "La museografia Locale: Un'Identità Difficile," originally delivered in 1989. It is included in Pietro Clemente, *Graffiti di Museografia Antropologica Italiana*: 165–177. The quote is on p. 176.

documenting the ways in which forests were integrated in the sharecropping economy but also fostered autonomous trades and ways of life.[66]

In the meantime, after a few false starts, Molteni had managed to capitalize on the Sienese scholars' long-established collaboration with the administrators of Buonconvento to locate there the main rural museum in the province, a structure capable of introducing the public to the heritage of sharecropping and housing the research tools that CEDLAC had been producing. In the mid-1990s the municipal government of Buonconvento made a former wine storing facility embedded in the town walls available for the establishment of a Museum of Sienese Sharecropping (Museo della Mezzadria Senese), where the new "scenographic" approach to museography could be implemented.[67] In Molteni's own words, the goal was "to insert, through the concept of scenography, a type of involvement that was not only rational. We employed panels, thereby including the aspect of explanation, but there was the attempt to get visitors involved emotionally, to capture the emotional and sensorial aspects."

In its present form the museum, which opened in 2002, can be viewed as the coronation of the intellectual and political debates over memorialization that have taken place since the 1970s. The initial installation on the ground floor, for example, deploys texts and graphs neatly arranged on panels to convey data on the massive changes Sienese society experienced in the twentieth century, but the visitor learns the basic social arrangements of sharecropping from the voices of iconic mannequins (the landlord, the superintendent, the male head of the peasant household, and his wife), who use the first-person pronoun and speak with realistic Sienese accents. Similarly, a farmhouse has been recreated at the center of the first floor: everyday furnishings are arranged as they would have been in a typical sharecropping farmhouse, but the walls are made up of rusty metal plates and there is no ceiling, to underscore the artificiality of any recreation. Again, voices evoke the tasks and experiences that would have taken place in the different rooms. Even more striking, a little windowless room jutting out of the staircase connecting the two floors only features a row of old shoes of different sizes, meant for peasants of different ages and genders (Illustration 21). The display, which is also on the cover page of the museum's catalogue, is

---

[66] See the catalogue, G. Molteni (ed.), *Il Museo del Bosco, Orgia: Il Catalogo* (Siena: Protagon Editori), 1993.

[67] See the catalogue, G. Molteni, *Buonconvento: Museo della Mezzadria Senese* (Siena: Silvana, 2008).

Illustration #21 Display at the Museum of Sienese Mezzadria, Buonconvento.

indeed eerily evocative (I could not help thinking of similar displays in Holocaust museums), but its meaning is left open.

The Buonconvento museum is today part of a provincial "system" that includes not only the woodlands museum at Orgia, but also a museum devoted to olive oil production near Rapolano Terme, one dealing with truffles at San Giovanni d'Asso, and one about traditional rural theater at Monticchiello, all of which opened in the early to mid-2000s.[68] According to Molteni, the new frontier is "to move from the museums about the past to the museum of modernity.... We are trying to invert the terms, saying: let's try to document the present where the past continues to live on, but as a niche element within the present." Food figures prominently

[68] For the Monticchiello museum, see the website at www.tepotratos.it/index.html.

in this agenda, as an everyday experience in which tradition and innovation are lived in concrete ways but often without a real awareness of the interplay between past and present. The Buonconvento museum has a kitchen that can be used for this type of initiative, and Molteni told me that he has been working for several years on attempts at including nonvisual and nonaural sensations in the museum experience. The exploration of taste is under way, and smell could be next: "Why should the museum deny smell, thus creating an odorless environment. We already have an odorless society ..." The truffle museum, which Molteni directs, is a step in that direction.[69]

Molteni told me that he is struggling to make ethnographic museums relevant in a society where there is no longer any separation between urban and rural culture, and where ties to "traditional" sharecropping are now several generations removed. In the early 2010s the Buonconvento museum received approximately six thousand visitors a year, one-fourth of whom were students on school trips. But that meant that only 12 percent of the operating budget was covered by ticket sales. The other ethnographic museums in the province received less than half that number of visitors. Apparently, the only "minor" museums in the province of Siena (i.e., those without internationally renowned artworks) that did truly well were those equipped with accessible towers, because tourists loved to climb on them and look at the landscape. Since none of the ethnographic museums were so lucky, this increasing attention to taste and smell was also a way of compensating for this handicap.

Molteni's concerns with funding and attendance also testify to the evolving relationship between Tuscany's ethnographic museums and the heritage industry that has grown around them. Many of these museums were established in the early 1970s to counter the way in which rural Tuscany was becoming a generic icon of beauty. The esthetic appreciation of Tuscany seemed to come at the price of removing a recent past of struggle and emancipation to which many were still attached. Originally, the museums were above all monuments to the challenges incurred in the recent transition from rural to urban life. They were attempts at keeping alive the legacy of the Tuscan peasants, as a patrimony that could not be commodified and made inauthentic, unlike the peasants' former houses. Over time, this critical urgency has abated. The current promotion of "complete perceptual experiences," engaging the public's senses and emotions, is informed by a different sensibility, more compatible with the values of the heritage industry, albeit not reducible to it. The growing emphasis on food is telling in this regard, as is the notion of the

[69] See the museum's website at www.museodeltartufo.it/.

"museum of modernity" that explores the past as a niche in the present, in Molteni's phrasing.

The recent changes in the relationships between Tuscans and "their" countryside have led to the search for a coherent memory embedded in the land, a "landscape" to be appreciated emotionally and sensorially. Once again, the growing emphasis on food is revealing here. In the past two decades, food has been increasingly territorialized also through the introduction of a hierarchy of denominations monitored by the European Union.[70] A particular food is regarded as typical because it belongs to a particular territory, and such territorial belonging makes it vulnerable to abuse and thus worth protecting. The emergence of food-themed museums is thus only one element in this process of patrimonialization centered on experiences of place. If generic rurality makes Tuscany resonate across social and cultural boundaries, the creation of territorial distinctiveness founded on the engagement of the senses provides the added value that makes the region unique within a competitive tourist and heritage industry. We must now turn to the processes through which these senses of "landscape" have been constructed and encouraged.

---

[70] The most striking instantiation of this territorializing trend is perhaps the massive Atlas of the Typical Products of the Italian Parks (Atlante dei Prodotti Tipici dei Parchi Italiani), compiled by the Ministry of Environment and Slow Food, which lists some "475 traditional and typical products, 1,585 addresses of producers, 283 of which are signaled with the snail [the symbol of Slow Food]." See www.atlanteparchi.it/home .html.

6   Searching for the *Bel Paesaggio*: Norming
     and Litigating the Landscape

What makes a landscape beautiful and thus worth protecting? This question has been posed at least implicitly by generations of geographers, historians, architects, and politicians of all stripes, in Italy and elsewhere. One concept that recurs in much of the "expert" literature is that of legibility. A beautiful landscape is first of all a legible landscape. Legibility, however, is arguably a problematic category on which to found landscape beauty. After all, no landscape is more coherent and legible than a city planned on a grid, or a geometrical field created by mechanized agriculture.[1] Legibility alone does not guarantee beauty. Planned space has its dialectical opposite in ruined space, exemplified by the cacophonous messiness of the urban slum or of the partially abandoned rural area, both of which emerge from the loss of organic coherence attributed to tradition. The esthetically valuable landscape is appreciated in contrast to both these esthetic dimensions of modernity – planned and ruined space.

The Tuscan landscape, as we have seen, was constructed in the political arena through a series of conflicts and negotiations. It developed from the interaction between many trajectories, some more powerful than others, involving both human and nonhuman actors. Yet, the kind of beauty that has become hegemonic in Tuscany is one whose coherence and legibility seems to have developed as an emergent and organic property. Unlike planned forms, its order is imagined to have emerged somewhat spontaneously from the resonance between the ecological, economic, political, cultural, and even spiritual traits of a timeless "Tuscan society." But this is not the kind of spontaneity that produces modern ruins. The valuable Tuscan landscape is supposed to have retained the orderliness of a particular tradition, however invented. As a coherent system of signs, the beautiful landscape comes to define a particular civilization, which

[1] For a classic discussion of this esthetic of modernity and its failures, see James Scott, *Seeing Like a State: How Certain Schemes to Improve the Human Condition Have Failed* (New Haven: Yale University Press, 1999).

238

reads its positive traits in space in a somewhat narcissistic operation. Placed in its appropriate spatial and temporal narrative, and contrasted with the ruptures of modernity, landscape becomes patrimony.

This kind of appreciation of landscape beauty is built on a dichotomous understanding of modernity. Traditional societies, many scholars argue, did not need elaborate formal norms for the protection of landscape: supposedly everyone, across social divides, shared esthetic and practical codes from which beauty emerged spontaneously. In the words of architectural theorist Paolo Baldeschi, traditional societies did not need plans or statutes, "because men and things were linked by rules of sustainability, without which neither could have survived."[2] The ugly landscapes of modernity, then, are also landscapes of conflict and exploitation. Modern societies need plans and regulations because they are too fractured and greedy. In the Tuscan case, however, this dichotomous view runs into the paradox that the landscape is both painstakingly regulated and imagined to have always already been there as the spontaneous outcome of socio-natural cohesion and coherence.

In a similar vein, geographer Eugenio Turri borrowed from a variety of intellectual traditions to argue that landscape is (or should be) a theater in which human action takes place.[3] Here too the contrast is between a premodern past and a modern present. Before modernity, the two main territorial identities of humanity, as *homo figurans* (who sees and reflects on his or her actions) and *homo faber* (who acts and shapes his or her surroundings), were in balance. Humans were both actors in a landscape, thus shaping it, and spectators in it, thus being able to make sense of what they saw and direct their future actions accordingly. This systemic feedback loop was the basis of sustainability. With modernity, humans (and Italians in particular) have forgotten how to be spectators, concentrating on the instrumental exploitation of nature without the kind of self-referential monitoring that provides change with a discernible direction. In so doing, they have produced ugliness: "Today we face landscapes that are ugly above all because they are illegible in their diachronic development and historical layering."[4] Implicit in this perspective is the possible dawn of a new era, in which new sensibilities, as well as the decreased urgency to meet the basic needs of survival, may restore a new balance between acting and spectating, thereby making landscape beauty possible again, at least in the richer regions of the world.

---

[2] Paolo Baldeschi, *Paesaggio e Territorio* (Florence: Le Lettere, 2011): 110.
[3] Eugenio Turri, *Il Paesaggio Come Teatro: Dal Territorio Vissuto al Territorio Rappresentato* (Venice: Marsilio, 2001).
[4] Ibid.: 22.

These dichotomous imaginings also reveal a deep ambivalence toward democratic control. Left to the vagaries of the democratic process, increasingly captured by interest groups and the logic of market exchange, landscapes lose their integrity. Laws are made and broken in an incessant cycle, as exceptions and post-hoc amnesties (the notorious *condoni*) multiply. As in other realms of social life, Italy stands out both for the number of conservationist laws in the books and for their ongoing violation. In democratic societies landscape should be valued as an experience "from below," shared by the multitude, but the multitude cannot be trusted to even decipher its essential traits, let alone respect them; hence the need for the impartiality of technical experts, the only people who can rise above the fray and protect the common good.[5]

As these claims show, in Tuscany and across Europe landscape has become a normative space where different visions of the polity meet and clash. Landscape has come to mean above all a strictly regulated area where certain things are allowed on esthetic ground and in the name of the common good (that is, of the visions that powerful actors can propose or impose as the common good), while others are not. This normative approach to landscape has been enshrined in legislation, and Tuscany has been at the forefront of these regulatory efforts. Yet, in their everyday lives, people embrace, negotiate, and even subvert these rules all the time, in more or less subtle ways. Potentially elitist conceptions of the landscape elicit forms of resistance and counter-sensibilities. Thus, in this chapter I will first provide an overview of the intellectual and legislative debates on landscape at the national, regional, and local levels, charting a layered normative structure of great complexity. Then I will focus on the two regions of Tuscany that we have visited throughout this book – the Orcia valley and the Chianti – and follow the trajectories through which they have become, in the eyes of local and international observers, almost synonyms of landscape beauty, engendering new values and sources of authenticity. Formal regulation in the legislative arena was crucial to the construction of the linear sense of place and time on which landscape beauty rests in rural Tuscany. Patrimonial beauty arises from the ability to tell one coherent story, easily read in space and shared across cultural boundaries. In light of the tensions and conflicts examined in the previous chapters, the construction of this linear and singular narrative was no easy feat, and it could not fail to elicit new kinds of conflicts and senses of loss.

---

[5] Salvatore Settis, *Paesaggio, Costituzione, Cemento: La Battaglia per l'Ambiente Contro il Degrado Civile* (Turin: Einuadi, 2010).

Norming the Landscape

For analytical purposes, the intellectual and normative debate on landscape in the Italian context can be divided into three phases – the idealistic, the rationalistic, and the holistic – which correspond to partially distinct waves of legislative interventions. In the course of the twentieth century, each of these approaches built on the previous one, rather than displacing it, so that today's landscape-related norms and practices appear as layered structures replete with contradictions. In some ways, the legislative approach to landscape came full circle over the course of the twentieth century. In the idealistic conception, landscape was above all an esthetic experience that reflected the civilizational accomplishments of the nation. The rationalistic approach, by contrast, searched for objective criteria of evaluation and eschewed esthetic judgment, understanding landscape as the product of natural and social processes sedimented over time. Finally, the holistic conception reintroduced perception as crucial to the definition and valorization of landscape, but with an "ecological" ethos that strove to make the perception of people (and not just experts) relevant to the recognition and preservation of sustainable rules of development. Through these shifts, legislation has struggled to square the circle between the protection of the expert-validated beauty of particular places and the more ambitious regulation of society's structural relationships with place. At the same time, an elitist and antidemocratic approach to landscape beauty has uneasily coexisted with a more democratic ethos that values the perceptions of ordinary people and the places they inhabit.

In the first decades of the twentieth century, an idealistic approach dominated the discourses and practices related to landscape. Benedetto Croce was instrumental in developing the notion that the esthetic value of built forms and particular vistas was derived from their ability to instantiate and illustrate different stages in the development of Italian (or even Western) civilization. This ascription of value depended on the knowledge of experts, who could attribute specific places to their correct location in a linear narrative of civilizational evolution. As putatively pristine natural areas became national parks, starting with the Gran Paradiso massif in 1922, the first national law, willed by Croce as Minister of Education, set out to protect "the real estate (*cose immobili*) whose conservation presents great public interest because of its natural beauty or its particular relationship with civic and literary history (*storia civile e letteraria*)."[6] Borrowing much of its language from a similar French measure

---

[6] This was Law 778, issued on June 11, 1922, titled Per la Tutela delle Bellezze Naturali e degli Immobili di Particolare Interesse Storico.

dating to 1906, the law also protected "panoramic beauty" (*bellezze panoramiche*). Since the value of these places was derived above all from their relevance to national history and culture, it was up to the central state to identify the buildings and vistas worthy of protection, although the law did not envisage a precise procedure for this purpose.

The 1922 law inaugurated landscape protection in Italy, even though it did not mention the term itself (*paesaggio*).[7] This was the first law that attributed esthetic value not so much to specific buildings and works of art, already protected by other measures, but to places more generally, making the case that the state had a stake in protecting properly validated perceptual experiences. The Fascist regime took this line of reasoning several steps further with a 1939 law, titled "Protection of Natural Beauty" and drafted by Giuseppe Bottai, then minister of National Education.[8] Places, buildings, vistas, and geological formations could be regarded as worthy of protection because of their "remarkable public interest." The law envisaged a complex procedure for the compilation of lists of valuable places, in which provincial committees of experts and administrators conveyed their findings to the ministry in Rome, which was put in charge of drafting a "national landscape plan" (*piano paesistico nazionale*).[9] It also began to define landscape as the product of the interaction between society and nature. The law's regulations of application specified that the value of a place with typical features worthy of protection was derived from "the spontaneous concordance between the expression of nature and that of human labor."[10] Thus, the 1939 law built on the monumental approach to landscape typical of Crocean idealism, as well as on its reliance on expertise, but it also introduced a more "territorial" conception that valued places also for their traditional or "typical" qualities.

This unresolved tension between natural, artistic, and broadly cultural values, as well as between uniqueness and typicality, informed the drafting of the post–World War II Constitution as well. Article 9 argued that the Italian Republic "protects the landscape as well as the historical and artistic heritage (*patrimonio*) of the Nation." Nevertheless, the massive territorial transformations that accompanied Italy's "economic miracle" in the 1950s and 1960s took place in something of a normative void.

---

[7] Revealingly, the term *paesaggio* was instead used in the laws that established national parks in the Gran Paradiso massif (1922) and in the southern Abruzzo mountains (1923). The implicit assumption of the legislators was that paesaggio was either an artistic term, as in *pittura di paesaggio* (landscape painting), or a term denoting a purely natural environment, as in *paesaggio naturale*. This stark dichotomy will be long-lived in Italian culture.

[8] Law 1497, issued on June 29, 1939, titled Per la Protezione delle Bellezze Naturali.

[9] The law also rejected any possibility of indemnifying the valuable places' owners for their future loss of revenue.

[10] From Article 9 of the Regolamento of Law 1497/1939, issued in 1940.

The national plan envisaged by the 1939 law was never drafted. A few "natural" areas were protected as pristine territories, and valuable places, buildings, and works of art could be singled out for conservation by the provincial Superintendences (*Sovrintendenze*), a bureaucratic structure set up at the beginning of the twentieth century. But the law had little to say about more ordinary interactions between people and place. A variety of associations, starting with Italia Nostra in 1956, emerged to denounce this void and the vulnerabilities it created. As we have seen, even in Tuscany, the region that would come to define Italy's landscape beauty, the esthetic appreciation of landscape was remarkably absent from the debates and conflicts of the postwar decades.

In the meantime, under the influence of Marxism and structuralism, a variety of Italian social scientists, led by geographers, mounted a concerted campaign against the Crocean understanding of landscape, thereby developing the second, rationalistic, approach. Aldo Sestini, for example, introduced the notion that a rational approach to landscape had to start from the realization that landscape is an abstraction, "a complex combination of objects and phenomena linked by functional relationships ... in such a way as to create organic unity."[11] In a similar vein, Lucio Gambi argued that the constitutive elements of landscape might be completely invisible and leave no topographical traces on the land. These "constitutive facts" (*fatti costitutivi*) included not only technologies and relations of production, but also religious beliefs and psychological dispositions. On the basis of this approach, Gambi went as far as to recommend the replacement of the term *paesaggio* with that of "environmental framework" (*quadro ambientale*), in order to distinguish a properly scientific approach from one founded on the subjectivity of esthetic judgment.[12]

One important difference between the idealistic and rationalistic approaches resided in the latter's rejection of a monumental notion of landscape. In need of valorization and protection were not particular places and vistas, but whole webs of relationships (whether vestigial or not) that had shaped entire areas. Typicality was as important as uniqueness. The other main difference lay in the quality of the expert validation required for a landscape to become valuable and authentic. The idealistic approach called for the esthetic judgment of experts in predominantly (though not exclusively) humanistic disciplines, whereas the rationalist one relied on the evaluation of social and natural scientists, committed

[11] A. Sestini, *Il Paesaggio* (Milan: Club Italiano, 1963): 10.
[12] L. Gambi, *Una Geografia per la Storia* (Turin: Einaudi, 1973). The article was originally published in 1961.

to avoiding judgments of taste. The notion of beauty, so prominent in the prewar debate and legislation, fell by the wayside. This search for objectivity was meant to eschew the elitism and arbitrariness associated with esthetic judgment, and it dovetailed with an increasingly influential ecological sensibility. In 1974 a whole new ministry was established to preside over the nation's "Cultural and Environmental Assets" (Ministero dei Beni Culturali e Ambientali). From this perspective, landscape came to be increasingly assimilated to environment or even territory.

The main political outcome of this "escape from the esthetic" was a 1985 law that bore the name of historian Giuseppe Galasso.[13] With this measure entire swaths of territory were declared worthy of special protection, meaning that any transformation of their features necessitated the authorization of several layers of public administration. The law singled out for special protection the coastlines within 300 meters from the foreshore, the areas along rivers and lakes within 150 meters from the water line, mountain areas above 1600 meters of altitude, wooded and forested areas, volcanoes, lagoons, and so on, thereby setting standards that transcended any kind of evaluative judgment. The content of this protective attention, however, was to be decided at the regional level, within landscape plans drafted by each regional council and including detailed analyses of the territory and the identification of its assets and vulnerabilities. Nowhere in the law were the notions of beauty and esthetic appreciation mentioned, under the assumption that the state protected the outcome of sedimented functional relationships of an ecological and/or cultural kind that transcended esthetic validation and even perceptual differences.

By the time of the Galasso Law's approval, territorial planning had been devolved to the regional administrations, established at the beginning of the 1970s. The central state retained monitoring functions and the prerogative of setting general guidelines, but each region could not only produce its own plans but also approve the zoning plans of the municipal governments (*piani regolatori*) and their ad-hoc changes and exceptions (*varianti*). Even more importantly, the very relationships between regional, provincial, and municipal governments could be decided at the regional level, thereby allowing different regions to have varying degrees of centralization. Tuscany soon became a paragon for the empowerment of municipal governments and the devolution of functions from the central to the local level.

---

[13] Law 431, issued on August 8, 1985, titled Disposizioni Urgenti per la Tutela delle Zone di Particolare Interesse Ambientale.

In this spirit, the Tuscan regional government set out to take charge of its territory, paying increasing attention to the "landscape" in the course of the 1980s and 1990s. For all its relevance, the 1979 regional law that regulated building activities in rural areas, discussed in the previous chapter, did not place landscape protection at the center of its purview. But already in 1982 another regional law set the norms for the establishment of parks and protected areas of natural, cultural, and landscape value (*di valore naturale, culturale e paesaggistico*), entrusting the nine Tuscan provinces as well as thirty-three associations between municipalities with a variety of preservation tasks and prerogatives.[14] On the basis of extensive research conducted by a variety of experts from the region's universities, the law identified more than one hundred areas, spread over 235 of the 287 municipalities, and covering one-third of the region's territory. The law also envisaged a complex hierarchy of protective attention, distinguishing five types of areas, from those presenting environmental and landscape interest of an extensive kind, to be subjected to the lowest form of protection, to those presenting unique characteristics in relatively concentrated spaces, to be protected most strictly. In the wake of the 1985 Galasso law, whose general thrust the 1982 Tuscan legislation prefigured, Tuscany's administrators extended the scope of territorial protection even further, so that by the mid-1990s a full half of the region was under some kind of protective regime, even though only 8 percent of the territory was regarded as a "reserve" and subjected to the strictest regulations.[15]

At the same time, the Tuscan administrators set out to move beyond mere conservation and develop a more sophisticated and systemic approach to territorial planning, which integrated previously disconnected dimensions (economic programming, urban planning, agricultural restructuring, landscape protection, and so on). In so doing, Tuscany's political elites embraced the notion of "sustainable development," which gained widespread popularity in the wake of the 1992 United Nations Conference on Environment and Development held in Rio de Janeiro. References to Agenda 21, the blueprint adopted at the conference for the global, national, and local implementation of sustainability, became increasingly common in the debates on landscape protection.

Sustainability was at the core of the third, holistic, approach to landscape. A sustainable landscape was not an immutable one, to be frozen and turned into a museum, but one whose structural rules of

---

[14] Regional Law 25/1982, Norme per la Formazione del Sistema delle Aree Protette dei Parchi e delle Riserve Naturali.

[15] Giunta Regionale Toscana, *Toscana da Proteggere* (Venice: Marsilio, 1994).

development were inherited from the past, consensually rearticulated in the democratic process, and respected for the benefit of future genera- tions. Thus, as large sections of Tuscany acquired value for having been bypassed by modernity, a partially new sensibility emerged that chal- lenged the very notions of conservation and protection. There would no longer be areas worth protecting and others left to the spontaneous speculation of the market. Instead, the entire territory would be system- atically, and yet democratically, investigated at different political levels and in different social venues, so that local populations and other stake- holders would regain control over spatial change. In the words of one of the protagonists of this conceptual and political shift, "There was not a 'beautiful' Tuscany to be protected and an 'ugly' one in which anything was allowed, but rather the necessity of planning the entire regional ter- ritory paying attention to landscape and the environment."[16]

This third "holistic" approach produced its own legislation. In 1995, Tuscany's regional council approved a major law, called "Norms for the Government of the Territory," which set out to integrate different plan- ning functions and different scales of jurisdiction in a coherent frame- work.[17] The regional government, the provincial administrations, and each municipality were to cooperate in the planning effort on an equal footing, instead of having local plans move up the hierarchical ladder for approval. The administrations would produce complementary plans, which became more detailed as the scale decreased, with municipali- ties drafting two kinds of plan – a more strategic one and one for the actual implementation of the agreed upon guidelines. Overall, this new arrangement increased the already wide margins of autonomy granted to municipal governments, under the assumption that it was only at the local level that ordinary people and civil society associations could be consulted. These principles were fundamentally upheld in a new version of the law, issued in 2005.[18]

These regional laws introduced a main conceptual innovation: they defined landscape as an "essential resource of the territory," putting it on an equal footing with water, soil, settlement patterns, historical assets, infrastructures, and so on. Adopting the language of sustainability, the law urged each level of government to found its planning activities on the identification of "structural invariants," that is, the rules of use and streams of benefit that had to be preserved in order for development

---

[16] Marco Gamberini, "La Normazione Toscana e il Paesaggio," in Massimo Morisi and Annick Magnier (eds.), *Governo del Territorio: Il Modello Toscana* (Bologna: Il Mulino, 2003): 127–138 (quote at p. 132).

[17] Regional Law 1/1995, Per il Governo del Territorio.

[18] Regional Law 1/2005, Norme per il Governo del Territorio.

to be sustainable.[19] These structural invariants intersected differently over space, creating the uniqueness of different places. With an additional twist, the laws defined planning as an activity that implemented the "statute" of a territory, composed of its structural invariants. Thus, these invariants were implicitly conceptualized as rights inherent to place, providing localities with their identity, to be preserved over time. The first upshot of this conception was to make landscape and territory potentially coextensive categories: landscape was everywhere structural invariants could be identified. Second, the law introduced a dynamic understanding of landscape, defining it as a coherent set of development rules and their spatial outcomes. In other words, landscape was not so much a representation that could be captured as a process that developed over time.

In its holistic thrust, the 1995 law refused to clearly distinguish between territory, environment, and landscape, deliberately blurring the boundaries between natural and cultural assets. This approach, which was touted as innovative at an international level, should be placed in the context of the long-standing debate examined so far. The law rejected not only the monumental approach to landscape typical of idealism, but also the very distinction between valuable and worthless landscapes implicit in the rationalistic approach, thereby potentially breaking with the very notion of conservation as the imposition of constraints (*vincoli*) on change. Conservation had to be dynamic and active, embedded in social change rather than alternative to it. This radical approach, however, sat uneasily with the proliferation of protective regimes, based on the varying vulnerability and anthropic presence of different areas. Another 1995 law spelled out this hierarchy, ranging from regional parks to the newly instituted category of the Protected Natural Area of Local Interest (Area Naturale Protetta di Interesse Locale, or ANPIL).[20] The latter was a uniquely Tuscan institution targeting heavily populated areas in need of "conservation, restoration, or reconstitution of the original environmental features," but which could be managed by the municipalities themselves, rather than by special agencies set up by the regional government. As we will see, the institution of the ANPIL played a central role in negotiating the protection of the Orcia valley.

On one hand, the holistic conception shared with the rationalistic approach the implicit reliance on expertise and the diffidence toward esthetic perception. The 1995 law on the Government of Territory

---

[19] For a discussion of these "invariants," see P. Baldeschi, *Paesaggio e Territorio*: 73–75.
[20] Regional Law 49/1995, Norme sui Parchi, le Riserve Naturali e le Aree Naturali Protette di Interesse Locale.

aspired to guarantee "the transparency of decisional processes and the citizens' participation in the choices of territorial management." But aside from the establishment of a "guarantor of information" at the provincial level, charged with discussing decisions with the public, the law had little to say about direct participation of ordinary citizens. After all, the recognition of structural invariants depended on expert forms of territorial knowledge, derived from a variety of academic disciplines and methodologies. The ordinary citizen could be completely oblivious to these deep rules of development, and her everyday engagement with place could even be detrimental to their preservation. Indeed, the law completely ignored the diversity of perception typical of any complex society, confiding that consensus would coalesce around the need to preserve the deeper structures of each territory. The perceptual dimension of landscape was at best an epiphenomenon of these structures, and an educated perception would thus conform to such structures over time. Thus, the holistic approach remained potentially elitist and, despite the laws' rhetoric, potentially antidemocratic. If anything, these risks became even greater, since this ambitious approach aimed for the preservation or retrieval of deep and coherent structures that regulated entire ways of life.

On the other hand, however, this dismissal of perception was clearly at odds with a processual and experiential understanding of landscape.[21] If landscape was not to be frozen in time and conceptualized as mere representation, and if the entire territory had the potential to become landscape, people's everyday engagements with landscape had to be recognized as part of what conferred value and identity on places. Indeed, in the course of the 1990s esthetic perception witnessed a comeback in the international arenas where landscape policy was discussed. Under the catchphrase "nowhere is nowhere, and everywhere is somewhere," this reappraisal of perception culminated in the European Convention on Landscape, promoted by the Council of Europe with a conference held in Florence in 2000. The location of the conference recognized not only the role that Tuscany's administrators had played in the policy debates on landscape in the previous decades, but also the prominent place that the Tuscan rural landscape had come to occupy in the imagination and experience of people around Europe and beyond.

The final draft of the convention placed perception at the very core of the notion of landscape, defined as "an area, as perceived by people,

---

[21] For a discussion of the relationships between perception and the Italian legislation, see Paolo D'Angelo, *Filosofia del Paesaggio* (Rome: Quodlibet, 2010) especially chapter 7.

whose character is the result of the action and interaction of natural and/or human factors."[22] The convention also made it clear that, since landscape is important to people's cultures, identities, and quality of life, it could be found in any area where perceptual experiences took place, "in urban areas and in the countryside, in degraded areas as well as in areas of high quality, in areas recognized as being of outstanding beauty as well as everyday areas." The Convention, however, distinguished between three different kinds of policies, to be applied to different kinds of landscape. Protection applied to landscapes of outstanding value; management to ordinary landscapes; and planning (that is, transformative interventions) to degraded landscapes.[23] The drafters assumed that these distinctions would be interpreted and implemented in different countries and regions according to local norms, compatible with the subsidiarity principle.

The Convention defined landscape as a perceptual phenomenon straddling subjective experiences and objective evaluations, and bearing identitarian values, but the text was silent about the actual identity of the perceiving "people" and about the adjudication of different (and possibly conflicting) perceptions. On the one hand, the Convention embraced a radically phenomenological conception of landscape, understood as the experiential engagement of people with place. On the other hand, it clung to more traditional notions of landscape as a unitary representation that could be labeled as outstanding or degraded (that is, as beautiful or ugly). A radically democratic ethos, underlying the idea that "landscape is everywhere," coexisted with the realization that, for practical purposes, some landscapes (and landscape perceptions) were more equal than others.

Italian experts and administrators received the 2000 Convention with a mix of enthusiasm and uneasiness. The latter was already evident in the way key passages were translated from the original English version.[24] To the definition of landscape proposed by the Convention, the Italian translators added the word *determinata* (certain or determined), so that now the definition read that landscape was "a certain portion of territory," rather than simply "an area." The obvious implication was the limitation of the Convention's scope to particular areas, compatible with the older Italian legislation, and the reliance on objective standards in the spatial delineation of what constituted landscape, rather than mere territory.

---

[22] The text of the Convention is available at http://conventions.coe.int/Treaty/en/Treaties/Html/176.htm.

[23] See The World Conservation Union, Landscape Conservation Law. Present Trends and Perspectives in International and Comparative Law: Paris, 2000, available at http://data.iucn.org/dbtw-wpd/edocs/EPLP-039.pdf.

[24] The Italian translation is available at http://conventions.coe.int/Treaty/ita/Treaties/Html/176.htm.

The formal ratification of the Convention by the Italian Parliament took place in 2006, but the Italian government had already set out to integrate the Convention into the existing legislation with a 2004 decree titled "Code of the Cultural Assets and of the Landscape" (Codice dei Beni Culturali e del Paesaggio).[25] Here landscape was defined as "a homogenous portion of territory whose characters derive from nature, human history, or their interrelations." Gone was any reference to perception, replaced by the requirement that, to be regarded as landscape, territory must be homogenous, and presumably according to the objective terms agreed upon by relevant experts. The stakes in this definitional operation were high enough to warrant several successive revisions. In 2008 the Berlusconi government revised the text by defining landscape as "territory expressive of identity, whose character derives from the action of natural and human factors, and by their interrelations."[26] The new version also singled out for special protection the characters of landscape that "constitute material and visible representation of the national identity, as expression of cultural values." The new version replaced the notion of homogeneity with that of identity, drawing a connection between landscape and nation that had not been spelled out as prominently since the times of Croce.

It is worth noting that the reference to landscape as visual representation broke with the much broader experiential thrust of the European Convention, as well as with decades of geographical thinking in the structuralist or rationalistic vein. The Code included large sections of all the previous national laws, protecting "panoramic beauty" in the spirit of the 1939 law, but also embedding much of the 1985 Galasso Law, with its objective references to measurable swaths of territory. Thus, the Code can be interpreted as an awkward summa of the twentieth-century intellectual and legal reflections on landscape. Moreover, if the Code recuperated esthetic perception in the definition of landscape, for example, by mentioning beauty, it did so without yielding to the potentially radical implications of the Convention. In the Italian Code, beauty was an expression of coherence and legibility, derived above all from the resonance of particular places (and their representations) with narratives of national and civilizational development.

To sum up, a landscape is a far more elusive "artifact" than a farmhouse or a church. The arc that the concept of landscape has followed in the twentieth century has led to an increasingly pervasive and diffused definition, morphing from a particular "monumental" vista into a

---

[25] Legislative Decree 42, issued on January 22, 2004.
[26] Legislative Decree 63, issued on March 26, 2008.

system of "structural invariants." At the same time, the debate has long been caught between an understanding of landscape as an object that can be represented (and thus preserved) and a dynamic experience that is embedded in the fabric of social and ecological change. Above all, the previous overview demonstrates how landscape, despite its elusiveness, is implicated in a variety of profound processes, ranging from the tension between democratic control and expertise to the search for a workable definition of the common good and a usable past. These aspirations and contradictions appear in all their poignancy when we move from the legislative and academic halls to the fields and towns of Tuscany.

As the future of entire rural areas hung in the balance between valorization and marginalization, a variety of actors with different ties to (and stakes in) local societies set out to negotiate the increasingly complex norms that regulated landscape. Could these norms be put to work and provide new paths to prosperity? Or should they be battled and subverted as unwelcome constraints? The case of the Orcia valley shows that the recognition of an area as beautiful was not so much the final outcome of the transition from productivism to postproductivism as the beginning of often-painful negotiations over the cultural meanings and political implications of "beauty" itself. In these debates, different senses of place and time confronted each other, and what trajectories and experiences should be read in space remained an open and controversial question, even after the intervention of such a powerful external actor as UNESCO. The case of the Chianti also shows how difficult it was to identify and respect the "structural invariants" (that is, the rules of sustainable development) that made the region cohere into a landscape worth preserving. The very materials that made the Chianti distinctive, such as its vines and olive trees, kept telling different and conflicting stories, which could only cohere provisionally and at some cost. In both cases, to the casual observer, landscape beauty seemed to emerge from the harmonious and legible resonance between people and land. At a closer look, however, the search for a workable definition of beauty fueled conflicts over who had the right and the power to interpret the past and imagine the future, while claiming to be preserving the integrity of place.

Val d'Orcia: The Making of a World Heritage Site

In promotional materials, commercials, and cultural artifacts of all kinds, the Orcia valley and its sceneries are often made to stand for Tuscany as a whole. This is due in part to the status of the valley as a UNESCO World Heritage Site, a recognition obtained in 2004. It is fair to say, however, that beauty was not on many people's mind until the 1980s. The recent history of this area of southern Tuscany makes for a unique and yet paradigmatic case. As we have seen, social conflict was particularly harsh in the valley in the late 1940s and through the 1950s. Likewise, the rural exodus was especially large. The three municipalities at the heart of the valley (Castiglione, Pienza, and San Quirico) lost 22 percent of their population from 1951 to 1967, when almost 60 percent of the men employed in agriculture were over fifty years of age.[27] The population of Castiglione d'Orcia alone was cut in half between 1951 and 1991.[28] As we have seen in Chapter 4, the local administrators pursued many "productivist" schemes meant to stem depopulation by turning the valley into a meat-producing area. By the early 1980s, these schemes were running into serious obstacles, while wheat cultivation faced an uncertain future, dependent both on international prices and the policies of the European Community.

In this fragile context a threat appeared, focusing everyone's attention. The regional government, which had done so much to support the valley in its fading "productivist" phase, seemed to be giving up on it. In the mid-1980s, reckoning that the valley had one of the lowest population densities in Tuscany, it began to float the proposal of locating a massive landfill there, collecting a large portion of the refuse of Siena and Grosseto. Many people inside and outside the valley have mentioned this threat to me as a major turning point and as a rallying cry for the local population and its administrators, although I could not locate official sources that confirmed these perceptions and memories. What is certain is that at this juncture the toponym of "Val d'Orcia" began to change its geographical scope and become more entrenched. Confronted with the possibility of being sentenced to a future of redolent marginality, even places that had never regarded themselves as part of the valley began to claim such affiliation. Such was the case with Montalcino, famous for its powerful wines (Brunello and Rosso), but also a part of the municipality of Pienza, which felt closer to Montepulciano and Chianciano and had long associated the Orcia valley with isolation and backwardness.

This risky and seemingly counterintuitive move was part of a strategy that began to coalesce around a group of scholars and intellectuals, who had more or less close ties to the valley. Foremost among them was Alberto Asor Rosa, one of Italy's foremost Marxist literary critics and public intellectuals, and a resident of Rome, who had bought a second

[27] "Convegno Intercomunale sullo Sviluppo della Valdorcia," ASMOS, PCI, box X-I-1 Comitato Coordinamento della Valdorcia, out of folder.

[28] Data collected by the author in the Commune's archive. The population of the three municipalities is today approximately 7,200 people, or 60 percent of the level reached in the early 1950s.

home near the castle town of Monticchiello, in the municipality of Pienza. These intellectuals promised to be able to raise the profile of the valley, fending off the threat coming from Florence. But they needed a clear commitment from the valley's administrators. By the end of the 1980s, the five municipalities of the area (Montalcino, San Quirico, Castiglione, Pienza, and Radicofani) were ready to present themselves as a unified front, floating the counterproposal of turning the valley into a "natural and artistic park." The preemptive counterattack was thus waged in unmistakably stark terms: not only was the valley to be spared the destiny of becoming one of Tuscany's main landfills, it was also to be singled out as a special territory, replete with sources of patrimonial value.

But the problem soon arose as to what kind of park could be enough of a defense against the landfill plan and yet spare the valley a future of museum-like immobility and hierarchical control. Italy already had several national parks, mostly in the Alps and Appennines, understood as pristine natural areas. As we have seen, Tuscany's legislation, dating back to 1982, envisaged a hierarchy of protected areas. But the local administrators viewed the regulations attached to these norms as too strict. Particularly contentious was the possibility that hunting, an immensely popular activity in southern Tuscany, could be banned. Hunting had been severely limited in the sharecropping economy, under which it was the privilege of the landlord and his friends. For countless former sharecroppers and their descendants, the democratization of hunting was one of the most uncontroversial achievements of modernity. To make things even more threatening to local autonomy, a national law mandated that every "park" had to be governed by a management agency (Ente Parco) staffed by state representatives and experts, and responding to the national and/or regional governments.[29] Thus the local administrators had to navigate the treacherous waters between top-down conservation and the threat of permanent marginalization.

The first move was to turn to the provincial administration in Siena, and obtain the promulgation of a decision (*delibera*) that expressly mentioned the valley as a possible natural, artistic, and cultural park. The language of this document, issued in 1989, was indicative of the stakes and aspirations shared by the local administrators:

The Orcia valley constitutes a territorial, environmental, historical, and cultural unit of rare beauty and singularity. The relationship between human artifacts, historically sedimented over centuries (farms, houses, villages, castles, churches – and cultivations, vineyards, and olive groves), and natural entities (hills, valleys, cliffs, streams, and clay formations), represents a well preserved artistic and

---

[29] Law 394, issued on December 6, 1991 and titled Legge Quadro sulle Aree protette.

landscape ensemble, created in part by fundamental economic choices, already essentially oriented towards agriculture and tourism.[30]

Here, in an official document, was the claim that the valley constituted a unique hybrid of natural and cultural resources whose history was highly legible and whose economy had already entered a postproductivist (or postmodernist) phase.

The language of hybridity, used by the local administrators to protect local autonomy and controversial practices such as hunting, was also embraced by the intellectuals promoting the "park." They easily assimilated the language of hybridity to the increasingly pervasive discourse on sustainability, which underlay the holistic approach to landscape. Prominent Florentine architectural scholar Giorgio Pizziolo, commenting on the provincial decision, eloquently noted that "in a logic of active preservation, the environment is no longer merely a context for human activities but part of a complex system linking man, society, and environment."[31] This more sophisticated understanding of the environment called for "open-ended projects" that would move beyond the mere imposition of constraints and bans (*vincoli*), thereby encouraging the spontaneous vocations of the area – that is, cultural tourism and high-quality agriculture.

This partnership between local administrators and public intellectuals then turned to the organization of two conferences, one held in 1992 at Monticchiello and the other in 1994 at Montalcino, meant to put the valley in a new light and publicize the possibilities inherent in the park project. The second conference, titled "From Projects to Management," included two foreign delegations, one from the French region of Languedoc-Roussillon and the other from the Spanish region of Andalusia, who were invited to showcase their experiences as well as learn from the Tuscan case. The proceedings of the conference read like a manifesto in postproductivist territorial management.[32] In the opening remarks, Michele Logi, the councilor in charge of economic programming for the province of Siena, praised the five municipalities of the valley for ushering in a "new culture," focused on issues of quality of life, environmental preservation, and landscape conservation. The

---

[30] ASMOS, Fondo PDS, Box V Dc – Urbanistica, Istituto Nazionale di Urbanistica, Sezione Toscana, Gruppo Provinciale Area Senese, "Dal piano urbanistico alle riserve naturali: Prospettive di programmazione e di pianificazione integrata del territorio in provincia di Siena."

[31] Ibid.

[32] ASMOS, Fondo PDS, Box V Dc – Urbanistica, "Parco Artistico Naturale e Culturale della Val d'Orcia: dai Progetti alla Gestione" proceedings of the international conference held at Montalcino in December 1994.

centrality of landscape was touted as the paramount achievement of the five towns' institutional partnership. Among the concrete problems solved, according to Logi, were "that of the swimming pools, of their shape and conditions of acceptability, that of the changes to local roads, of the features of the permissible construction materials, and much else." The fruit of this work had been "the designing of rules about what can and cannot be done, and how, in every corner of the Orcia valley." Thus, on the one hand, the beauty of the landscape emerged spontaneously from the resonance between people and land. On the other hand, such beauty had to be carefully constructed, monitored, and protected. As we have seen, this is one of the paradoxes of a holistic approach to landscape.

The organizers of the 1994 conference also announced an unprecedented organizational experiment. The perceived urgency to reinvent the image and reputation of the valley led to the institutionalization of a partnership between public and private actors, a limited liability corporation that included the five municipalities, the Chamber of Commerce of Siena, the Monte dei Paschi (the powerful Sienese bank), and a group of companies in the wine, oil, and tourism sectors. Called Valdorcia srl (Valdorcia Inc.), the company began to engage in a deliberate policy of branding, stamping its logo (the stylized silhouette of a castle circled by cypress trees) on "typical" local products (above all, sheep milk cheese and olive oil) and on a variety of promotional materials. The company also became involved in the organization and promotion of an arts festival to be held every summer, in the campaign for the reopening of a dismissed railway line bordering the valley, and in recovering the memory of the Via Francigena, the Medieval web of trails and roads that led from Rome to the Po plain and beyond passing through some of the valley's most recognizable landmarks. These concerted efforts of place-branding began to pay off handsomely. Tourist presence doubled between 1992 and 1998, when they reached 150,000 units. In the meantime, British director Anthony Minghella set a large section of his immensely popular movie, *The English Patient*, in the valley. When the movie was released in 1996, no one would have believed that this stunning corner of Tuscany had been targeted to host a large landfill only a few years before.

Through all these deliberations and institutional innovations, the valley remained in a legal limbo. It was still a "special" place primarily in the aspirations of its administrators, who called it a "park" but refused to allow any large portion of its territory to fall under the existing regional or national conservation laws. In the words of one of the local administrators, "essentially, we realized that we had been working for a park

that could never have been called a park."[33] In this, they were certainly
at odds with the group of intellectuals they had been cooperating with,
who would have welcomed stricter regulations. But the issue of hunting
alone, with its complex historical meanings, ensured the reluctance of
the majority of the population to accept the inclusion of the valley on the
list of Tuscany's protected areas.

Behind the scenes, major negotiations were taking place to accommodate the normative needs of the Orcia valley and similar areas around
the region, which desired the promotional boost that came with normative protection but were too populous (and fractious) to be regarded
as natural reserves. The introduction of the ANPILs (Protected Natural
Areas of Local Interest) by the regional government in 1995 seemed
tailor-made for places like the Orcia valley: the legislation presented
"dynamic conservation" as a middle way between "the speculative use of
the territory and its museum-like preservation," all the while relinquish-
ing very little local control. Instead of a management agency made up of
national and regional government officials, as would have been the case
with a traditional park, the area came to be coordinated by a committee
entirely staffed by local administrators. The valley officially received the
ANPIL status in 1999, after which local administrators could use the
term "park" with a degree of legitimacy.[34]

When the historic center of Pienza became a UNESCO World
Heritage Site in 1996, the local administrators and their scholarly partners hatched a plan to apply for the same recognition for the entire
valley. This was a major endeavor, which would have taken years of prep-
aration and networking, but the stakes were equally high. A previously
marginal area, which could have joined so many others in the detritus of
modernity, could now become part of humanity's patrimony! The plan
was also ambitious because the valley, with 60,000 hectares of territory
and fourteen thousand people, differed greatly from the kinds of sites
that the UNESCO usually singled out for recognition and protection.
This was neither a relatively small cluster of cultural monuments, such
as a historic center, nor a relatively pristine "natural" area, such as a
national park. But the applicants reckoned that the time might have

---

[33] Proposition d'Inscription dans la Liste des Biens Culturels et Naturels du Patrimoine
Mondial, Nomination 2003, La Val d'Orcia, Document number 4, Quadro Conoscitivo
e Allegati, September 2002 (material obtained from Luca Rossi in S. Quirico).

[34] Lista   aree   protette,   www.regione.toscana.it/regione/multimedia/RT/documents/
1199959125539_ANPIL_lista_aree_protette.pdf. As of 2012, there were fifty-six
ANPILs in Tuscany, for a total area of 93,700 hectares, but the Orcia valley occupied a
whopping two-thirds of the total, revealing the lobbying power that the valley's administrators and stakeholders had waged in their negotiations with the regional government.

come for UNESCO to enshrine the valley as an outstanding example of "cultural landscape," along the lines drawn by the ongoing normative and intellectual reflection on landscape carried out in Italy and elsewhere. But how was the argument to be pitched? The obvious answer was to regard the valley's landscape as a historical product and build the argument around the social and economic formations that had shaped the territory over the centuries. And at first this could only mean one thing: sharecropping.

The skepticism and reluctance exhibited by Tuscany's administrators toward patrimony in the 1970s were now things of the past. To their sons and daughters it was a an exciting prospect to have their family histories validated, albeit indirectly, through an explicit link between beauty and sharecropping. To this purpose, they got in touch with a group of historians of agriculture teaching at the University of Tuscia, in nearby Viterbo, who produced a dossier making the case that the Orcia valley was a landscape created by the sharecropping contract since the late Middle Ages, and one in which the relationships between city and countryside, sedimented over centuries, could still be read with particular clarity. The dossier was rejected at least three times. It turned out that this was not the kind of past that UNESCO deemed worthy of universal recognition. On the verge of giving up for good, the valley's administrators decided to turn to someone who had been successful in the past. Enter Paola Falini, professor of city planning in Rome, who had written the dossier for Assisi, her home town, and had won the UNESCO recognition in 2000.

Professor Falini was given the dossier for the Orcia valley and asked for her opinion. She realized that much work was required, and that the agrarian historians who had drafted the narrative had failed to realize that UNESCO recognized sites whose value was obvious and widely acknowledged: the pyramids at Giza, the Loire castles, the historic center of Florence, and so on. Who had even heard of the Orcia valley? Why should such a place be regarded as humanity's patrimony? UNESCO's gaze was anchored to an idealistic understanding of patrimony and beauty, founded on uniqueness rather than on the illustration of structural relations. From this perspective, places were valuable as instantiations of humanity's civilizational accomplishments. Falini understood this clearly. As she told me in an interview, "After much thought, I found, you know, that eureka moment.... I really care about this, because I think that it is profoundly true, and by now it has been accepted by all. But it was not obvious at first, as is often the case. It was Columbus' egg. Here it is: Let's remember Ambrogio Lorenzetti. Ambrogio Lorenzetti shows good government [*il buon governo*]. And this is the landscape of good government."[35] The present configuration and sharecropping's recent past would only be acknowledged for its ties to the representational practices of a much older era, that of the fourteenth-century Sienese "primitive" painters, presented as the dawn of modern forms and sensibilities. A civilizational genealogy could now be detected, recognized, and valorized.

The opening of the dossier's narrative drew a direct connection between the earliest realistic landscape representation, the birth of a theoretical understanding of landscape, and a new way for city dwellers to "govern" the countryside: "The landscape of the Val d'Orcia was celebrated by painters from the Siennese School, which flourished during the Renaissance. Images of the Val d'Orcia, and particularly depictions of landscapes where people are depicted as living in harmony with nature, have come to be seen as icons of the Renaissance and have profoundly influenced the development of landscape thinking."[36] This was a language the experts of the International Council on Monuments and Sites (ICOMOS, the NGO in charge of evaluating sites on behalf of UNESCO) could understand. Sharecropping was all over Italy and beyond, but the Sienese Primitives were indeed uniquely positioned, both spatially and historically, at the very origin of a linear genealogical trajectory that led to modern appreciations of landscape.

What the ICOMOS experts could not understand was the normative status of the valley. In 2002, for example, they asked Falini and her collaborators for a census of the valley's trees – the type of information that the managers of a natural park were expected to provide. But, as Falini herself put it, "when we use the word 'park' in Tuscany, we do so differently than the rest of the world." It did take some explaining to convince the international experts that the valley would be simultaneously an area of local interest (i.e., an ANPIL) and of universal significance, but nothing would stand in between the local and the universal: the valley was most definitely not a regional or national park. The pitch worked, whether on account of the institutional work the five municipalities had carried out for over a decade or in spite of it. The valley became a World Heritage Site in 2004.

The dossier that was sent to UNESCO included a variety of documents that the local administrators and their intellectual partners had produced over the years in their quest for strategic recognition. These documents eloquently spoke the language of patrimony, thereby flattening spatial differences and temporal discontinuities. The valley was

[35] Interview by author, June 7, 2011.
[36] Val d'Orcia – UNESCO World Heritage Centre, http://whc.unesco.org/en/list/1026

presented again and again as a coherent unit in which history could be easily read off the land: "Built territory par excellence, the Orcia valley testifies to the exceptional stability of spatial, morphological, and functional relationships established during the Renaissance between its different components, as well as the great unity and systemic coherence of the processes that have continued to govern their development in the following epochs."[37] At the same time, the concrete normativity underlying the valley's reinvention revealed very messy negotiations. The building code for the area, submitted to UNESCO, spent three finely printed pages on the regulation of swimming pools, which were popping up all over the valley next to the agriturismi. What could be more incongruous than a swimming pool adjacent to a supposedly operating farm in a territory supposedly unchanged since the time of the Sienese primitives? But the building code demanded, among many other details, that pools be lined with special nonrefracting tiles, deemed less offensive than regular ones, and surrounded by indigenous plants.[38] Palmettos would not be allowed; cypresses would. Incongruity, when inevitable, had to be appropriately framed.

Indeed, by the time the valley was recognized as part of humanity's patrimony, the tourism boom had been in full swing for several years. Given the high number of abandoned farmhouses, agrotourism played a prominent role in this expansion. Agrotouristic farms increased from fewer than 50 in 1992 to 352 in 2006, with the number of visitors approaching 100,000, each of whom stayed for three days and a half on average.[39] At the same time, real estate prices escalated. By the mid-2000s, a ruined rural house in the Orcia valley with some acreage and panoramic views could sell for more than half a million Euros, partly because it could be turned into a lucrative agrotouristic establishment. At the same time, the demographic hemorrhage, which had so consumed the local administrators' attention for decades, stopped. For the first time since the early 1950s, the population of the valley remained almost constant between the 1991 and 2001 census, prompting the local administrators to couch this achievement in the now familiar language of sustainability: "We can state that at the threshold of the third millennium this land has managed to stem the hemorrhage of people and that

[37] Agenda XXI della Val d'Orcia, Piano di Gestione dell'ANPIL, Programma Pluriennale 2003–2006, drafted by the mayors in 2002 (material obtained from Luca Rossi in S. Quirico).

[38] Regolamento Edilizio, drafted by Architect Gianni Neri (material obtained by Luca Rossi in S. Quirico).

[39] Data provided by Luca Rossi at the Parco Artistico Naturale e Culturale della Val d'Orcia, San Quirico d'Orcia.

it bets on a future demographic stability able to guarantee the punctual stewardship of the territory." The dream of reconciling conservation and development seemed to have finally been fulfilled.

But no sooner was the valley recognized as humanity's patrimony than a series of "scandals" erupted, revealing the flimsiness of the partnership between local administrators and intellectuals. The façade of unity that had led to the successful application to UNESCO crumbled, exposing deep social fractures as well as the contradictions attached to the normativity and experiences of landscape. The first casus belli turned out to be a housing development next to the medieval walls of Monticchiello, in the municipality of Pienza and a stone's throw from Alberto Asor Rosa's country home. The town and its immediate outskirts had lost two-thirds of their inhabitants between the early 1950s and the early 1980s, when the municipal government of Pienza began to plan for a brand new residential subdivision. The idea was to build modern residential units that "local young couples" would have found appealing, thereby reversing depopulation. Much like the dam construction and the expansion of wheat cultivation, this was a project meant to counter the area's marginalization and isolation, bringing the trappings of modernity to one of Tuscany's most neglected corners.

Since the late 1960s, Monticchiello had also been the site of Italy's most famous experiment in community theater, the Teatro Povero (literally, poor theater).[40] Every summer, for a couple of weeks, the town's dwellers impersonated themselves in plays that commented on recent social and political events, often starting from the fear of rural communities of losing their identity and ties to their recent peasant past. The first few plays had been staged almost entirely by former peasants and artisans, who soon felt the need for expert guidance, in hope of increasing the visibility and impact of their activities. To that aim, in the early 1970s they had begun to rely on the input of nationally known writers, journalists, and even anthropologists (and including Asor Rosa himself). Thus, the residential expansion of a town that had been reduced to a population of approximately 250 people could be viewed as an opportunity to address some of the anxieties that the local community, in collaboration with a variety of intellectuals, had publicly articulated and put on stage for years.

By the time the municipal government began to take action on the project, in 1997, the local context had changed considerably. Talk of the park and sustainable development was all over town. Even more important, it

[40] For an introduction in English, see Richard Andrews, *A Theatre of Community Memory* (Exeter: Society for Italian Studies, 1998).

turned out that Pienza had exhausted the funds available for public and subsidized housing, so that the project would have been carried out by private developers. The subdivision was to include eleven buildings, and the number of projected apartments had increased from fewer than fifty to ninety-five – a considerable number, given the size of the castle town just behind it. Monticchiello had been included in the list of "beauties" worth protecting according to the 1939 law, and thus changes to its profile could only take place with the blessing of the provincial superintendence to cultural and artistic assets. But the local administrators came up with a crafty strategy. They turned first to the regional government, which rejected the project with the justification that there were plenty of empty dwellings within the town walls and that Monticchiello's population kept decreasing. But the regional government did not say a word about the project's impact on the landscape.

The principle of subsidiarity, enshrined in the 1995 regional law on territorial government, stated that municipalities had the final say on urban planning when artistic or environmental issues were not at stake. The silence of the regional government could thus be used to get landscape concerns out of the way. On those grounds, the municipal government felt authorized to give the project the green light and informed the superintendence of its decision. The superintendent in Siena, instead of stopping everything, suggested changes to the "architectonic language and the construction materials used," thereby de facto condoning the development. In sum, all the authorities framed the issue in such a way that the municipal government could have the final word, and the designation of the valley as an ANPIL in 1999 did nothing to change this state of affairs.[41]

In putting the municipal government in charge of Monticchiello's future, the regional and provincial authorities followed a time-honored practice, which for decades had allowed the expansion of countless Tuscan towns beyond their constraining Medieval walls and the provision of modern housing for former peasants leaving the farms. By the turn of the new millennium, Tuscany was supposed to have transitioned from the longing for modernity to its conservationist critique. But this shift was in practice much less linear and definitive than countless legal and scholarly texts suggested. The recent past seemed to linger on and overlap with the present, refusing to yield to the "centuries-old history" cherished by UNESCO and the scholars promoting the valley, while the locals seemed to inhabit multiple logics and temporalities, with messy

---

[41] This narrative is based on Giovanni Losavio, "Perché Deve Essere Irreversibile?" *Italia Nostra* 422 (2006): 6–10, and on conversations with a variety of people in the area.

and yet practically consequential results. These contradictions revealed that the purity and coherence of the landscape were at best aspirations, by no means shared by all.

The depth of the fracture developing between local administrators and their once-allied public intellectuals came in full focus in August 2006, when Asor Rosa published an alarming article prominently placed in *La Repubblica*, one of Italy's most widely read newspapers.[42] Here he denounced the project as an "ecomostro," a journalistic and somewhat sensationalist term meaning "environmental monstrosity" and usually reserved for massive touristic developments or large-scale factories in coastal areas. Asor Rosa also defined the ANPIL as a "simulacrum" of protection, because of its almost exclusive reliance on local control. The article was the beginning of a campaign that polarized the valley for the next few years, shattering dreams of concord as the tourist boom reached its peak.

Suspicions of self-interest on the part of Asor Rosa and his friends began to circulate immediately. Some argued that these were "radical-chic" snobs who wanted to keep the valley in a state of idyllic immobility so their second homes would remain undisturbed. Even worse, some locals ventured that Asor Rosa was acting up because he had been bypassed by the recently installed center-left government in its search for the new Minister of Cultural Assets, a post that ended up in the hands of one of his archenemies.[43] But the "snobs" opposed developers, such as a married couple whose husband was originally from Sicily, who were already widely suspected by many in the valley of speculative intentions, having bought extensive plots of land and a variety of touristic establishments. If patrimony was to rely on a shared genealogical narrative impermeable to the instrumentality of exchange value, there was little of that in sight in the Orcia valley in the aftermath of the UNESCO recognition. The press began to quip that the poison of gossip and suspicion was embittering the sweetness of the landscape.

Tensions escalated when Asor Rosa and his allies convened a conference in October 2006, inviting the elite of Italian environmentalism, including the national leadership of Italia Nostra, the main Italian NGO concerned with landscape protection. Only a couple of local administrators showed up, keeping a low profile. The main conclusion of the debate was unequivocal: "It is necessary to reaffirm the determined and determining (and ultimately decisive) function of central [state] power, on the

---

[42] A. Asor Rosa, "Il Cemento Assale la Val d'Orcia," *La Repubblica*, August 24, 2006.
[43] Stefano Arosio, "L'Arrivo degli Speculatori. Gli Orchi della Val d'Orcia," *L'Espresso*, September 28, 2006.

basis of the principle that cultural assets are neither Tuscan nor Roman nor Venetian, but Italian, and as such, European."[44] In response, every mailbox in the valley received an anonymous leaflet blasting Asor Rosa as "the true 'eco-monster' of the Orcia valley." Someone proposed a play for the following year's community theater production titled "The Ego-monster," referring to the literary scholar's narcissistic obsession with landscape purity.

The man most visibly associated with the development project was Marco del Ciondolo, the leftist mayor of Pienza and a bona fide Monticchiellese, devoted to the town's community theater since its inception.[45] Indeed, "landscape as theater" was more than an analytically useful metaphor in the Orcia valley of the mid-2000s. The controversy over the housing development hinged on different ways of delimiting the debate's spatial stage and narrative horizon. Journalist Stefano Chiarini argued in an astute article in the Communist daily *Il Manifesto* that the norms regulating the valley's territorial management "possess internal rigidities that make them inadequate to the changed conditions."[46] What constituted defiance of the market in the 1980s, when the purpose of the housing project was to counter depopulation, could become the epitome of market speculation two decades later. In more academic jargon, norms acted according to a different temporality than other dimensions of historical change, in a place that had seen drastic transformations since the end of World War II. Chiarini pointed to the skeleton of the San Piero in Campo dam (see Chapter 4) as evidence of these disruptions. To people who ignored the recent history of the valley, Del Ciondolo could appear as a holdover from a bygone "modernist" era, while in reality he was attempting to reconcile the multiple and contradictory logics that had been shaping the valley for decades. It was the landscape itself, in the materiality of its multiple trajectories, that belied the totalitarian coherence imagined and demanded by Asor Rosa and certified by UNESCO.

While Mayor Del Ciondolo was mired in the Monticchiello controversy, Marileno Franci, mayor of nearby San Quirico, was cautioning Monsanto against using the omnipresent image of a cypress grove in the municipality's area for its advertising campaigns, going as far as to threaten to sue the multinational company.[47] After all, an area that was explicitly OMG-free (but at a time when OMGs were basically banned in

---

[44] A. Asor Rosa, "Lo scandalo Monticchiello," *Italia Nostra* 422 (2006): 4–5

[45] M. Del Ciondolo, "'Scandalo' nella Val d'Orcia," *Il Manifesto*, January 11, 2007.

[46] S. Chiarini, "La disfida di Monticchiello: Così cambia la Val d'Orcia," *Il Manifesto*, January 5, 2007.

[47] "La Val d'Orcia contro la Monsanto: Giù le mani dai nostri cipressi," *La Repubblica*, December 29, 2006.

the entire EU) could not be viewed as complicit in Monsanto's activities. The company relented, but the town of San Quirico ended up issuing a "copyright ordinance" against the commercial use of "its" landscape, a most unusual move that received international attention, including that of baffled tourists. Even though this measure had some precedents outside of Italy, the extension of the notion of copyright to landscape puzzled many observers, above all because it raised the issues of "ownership" that the 2006 conference organized by Asor Rosa had so summarily dismissed. In a parallel move, Mayor Del Ciondolo cautioned the Monticchiello developers from using the logo of the natural and artistic park, as well as the mention of UNESCO, in their advertising campaigns. The developers only refrained from using the logo and kept advertising that their apartments' windows opened up on a universally recognized landscape. The "environmentalist" front praised Franci for standing up to Monsanto, but kept lambasting Del Ciondolo for condoning the spoiling of landscape and yet defending its image.

In the meantime, the director of UNESCO's World Heritage Center, an Italian, as well as the Minister of Cultural Assets felt compelled to intervene in the debate, declaring their dismay at seeing the Orcia valley under threat. The Monticchiello housing project was only one of the looming blights that concerned them. UNESCO's recognition had brought to the fore the issue of a clay quarry in the municipality of San Quirico, established in the wake of World War I by a group of veterans and employing up to one hundred workers. The clay was used to manufacture terracotta tiles, one of the most typical specialties of Siena and its province, and a material widely used to restructure the abandoned farm houses and make them appealing to tourists. By the mid-2000s, however, the company was no longer in local hands. It had been purchased in 2000 by a northern Italian corporation, which had allegedly begun to use the furnaces to burn garbage and industrial refuse, in violation of environmental norms (a practice that is all too common throughout Italy). The quarry was also running out of material to excavate and applied to the municipal government for an expansion of its activities, buying eighteen hectares of land on the other side of the hill, allegedly at a price three times as high as the market rate.[48] This expansion risked creating a crater visible from much of the valley, adding another blight on the landscape. When the news began to circulate, in late 2006, the project began to draw national and international attention, further discrediting the valley's local administrators. Now Marileno Franci, the mayor of San

---

[48] Mario Pirani, "Quando la Repubblica Tutelava il Paesaggio," *La Repubblica*, January 22, 2007.

Quirico and the man who was standing up to Monsanto, came under fire as well.

This time it was not only another article by Asor Rosa that drew attention to the quarry expansion.[49] In 2005 Alistair Tidey, the heir to one of Ireland's largest fortunes and a businessman in his own right, had bought one of the valley's (and all of Tuscany's) most iconic restructured farmhouses, Il Belvedere, for 2.7 million Euros. The villa (for there was nothing farm-like to it anymore) stood on the other side of the hill from the quarry. Tidey found out about the possible expansion of the quarry only after the deal, and mounted a panicked campaign to make sure that the view from his villa would not become a belvedere in name only. The British daily *The Independent* ran a long article on the subject, openly sympathizing with Mr. Tidey's plight.[50] The journalist noted that in Tuscany the locals could not be trusted to preserve the landscape, because "this is a land ruled since the end of the war by communists and then post-communists – the same people. The industrial workers and their workplaces are their vote bank, the source of their values." These words echoed those of one of Tidey's friends: "The local people have been red for 60 years. Eighty-five percent still vote red. They've got the worker mentality: before the tourism came this was a solidly working class area, and the last thing they want is for the brick plant to close." And Tidey echoed Asor Rosa in criticizing Tuscany's excessive decentralization, arguing that "perhaps it takes a foreigner, or at least someone from outside the valley, to see that the unique beauty of the Val d'Orcia is the area's *one* fabulous asset and resource" (emphasis added). Again, another "outsider" was trying to make the valley tell one story.

What the journalist failed to report was that Tidey was one of the main investors in Heuston Hospitality, a multinational corporation that had opened a large resort in the Piedmontese Alps just in time for the Turin Winter Olympics, and was making plans to build two large luxury hotels in the Sienese Chianti, barely fifty kilometers to the north.[51] Therefore, when Mayor Franci retorted that Tidey intended to open a resort in the Orcia valley as well, the accusation had some plausibility. But above all, Franci's reaction was to underscore that the valley had not been put in a time capsule and catapulted from the early Renaissance to the present. Whatever its beauty, the valley had been shaped and experienced

---

[49] A. Asor Rosa, "Una Cava Minaccia la Val d'Orcia," *La Repubblica*, January 4, 2007.

[50] Peter Popham, "Stealing Beauty: The Fight for the Soul of the Tuscan Landscape," *The Independent*, January 30, 2007. The article was also translated into Italian and published in *Italia Nostra*, the conservationist association's bulletin.

[51] Pragelato Resort, www.portfolioitalia.com/pragelatopress.html.

by generations of people who had toiled there: "The time has come to worry not only about environmental issues but also about the people who live, work, and feel they belong in this territory, which has become humanity's patrimony thanks to their hard work."[52] Implicit in these words was a critique of the customary explanation for rural Tuscany's beauty as a fortunate (and unintended) consequence of its depopulation and failed modernization. The landscape had to make sense first of all to the people who lived in it, as the European Convention on Landscape maintained.

Franci's radically democratic (and perhaps populist) rhetoric recurred in the arguments of the local administrators and their allies. Andrea Filpa, the architect (and architecture professor) who drafted the zoning plan of Pienza, put it most succinctly: "A certain kind of culture that I hesitate to call environmentalist, because it should not be confused with real environmentalism, is actually a centralist and authoritarian culture. In the end, it is better to have a few more bricks than a little less democracy."[53] Again, the debate on landscape beauty brought to the fore the tension between democratic and technocratic control. But no amount of prodemocracy argument could dispel the suspicion that the administrators were motivated by far baser interests, such as the need for larger tax bases and electoral consensus. For those who knew where to look, suspicion could indeed be read off the land at least as easily as harmony and beauty, because the landscape accrued different kinds of value from many contradictory sources, in spite of the linear logic of patrimonial narratives.

Suspicion can sometimes be resolved through deliberate acts of disclosure, but this is not what happened in the Orcia valley. Negotiated compromises created situations the contending parties could live with, but only at the cost of deferring the possibility of a final reckoning into the future. Only eight of the eleven buildings were erected at Monticchiello. Two landscape architects, including Paola Falini, were consulted to reduce their visual impact. A clause of the 2004 Code was brought to bear, so that the national government could legitimately overrule (at least in part) the municipality's decision and save face. That called for the official designation of Monticchiello as a *rocca*, a hill-and-castle ensemble that the state could then protect as a unit.[54]

---

[52] Quoted in M. Pirani, "Quando la Repubblica Tutelava il Paesaggio."
[53] Quoted in Federico Scarpelli, *La Memoria del Territorio* (Ospedaletto: Pacini, 2007): 206.
[54] Maurizio Bolognini, "Monticchiello Diventa 'Rocca.' Bloccate Tre Nuove Villette," *La Repubblica* (Florence edition), January 23, 2007.

When I visited the site, I was surprised by the prosaic quality of the apartment buildings (Illustration 22). Externally, they blandly paid homage to the vernacular styles adopted by countless southern Tuscan farmhouses, although car garages now occupied the spaces where the stable for the oxen would have stood. It was unclear to me if they were more offensive or less offensive than some of the 1960s residential buildings just around the corner, with their unassuming utilitarian styles. Inside, they included seventy-nine small apartments, instead of the thirty-six that had originally been planned. Some locals had indeed bought them, but they were not the prolific young couples that the administrators had hoped to attract in the 1980s. Many of the apartments were clearly second homes, like so many larger houses in the surrounding countryside. Other units were still vacant. As the apartment buildings went up, the developers sued Asor Rosa, Italia Nostra, and a couple of news outlets for defamation and economic and moral damages, to the tune of one million Euros, arguing that the controversy had led to a flurry of cancellations. In July 2011, the Tribunal of Rome sided with the defendants, arguing that they had simply expressed their concerns about the landscape, rather

Illustration #22 View of Monticchiello, with the controversial new development on the left and the Medieval castle on the right.

than deliberately and specifically tried to hurt the developers' reputation. The developers were to refund the defendants almost 60,000 Euros in legal fees.[55]

As to the clay quarry, the regional government felt compelled to intervene, using a planning instrument specifically dedicated to the regulation of mining activities. After lengthy consultations and negotiations, it was decided that the quarried area would gradually shrink from thirty to seven hectares, that any additional excavation would only take place in small increments, and that the activities would remain on one side of the hill, sparing the view from the Irish businessman's villa and from the town of Pienza farther up. Also, mining would be restricted to the production of traditional terracotta tiles, rather than common bricks, which according to the environmentalists made up the majority of the company's production. The loss of work would be compensated for by regional funds for the recuperation of the exposed ground. Thus, the quarry workers would be employed, at least for a while, for the beautification of the landscape. Alistair Tidey may not have had the chance to celebrate for long. In the wake of the financial crisis, the Irish businessman decided to put Il Belvedere on sale. In the summer of 2011 it commanded a price of 6 million Euros. Part of the sales pitch was of course the status of the valley as a UNESCO World Heritage Site. And in spite of the Monticchiello subdivision and the barely averted sight of the quarry, optimism was in the air: "There's no prospect of that view being spoilt. The surrounding Val d'Orcia area has been declared a Unesco World Heritage site. This means there's as much chance of apartment blocks going up as there is of a high-rise being built on the Acropolis."[56]

There was also an attempt to update legal norms in the wake of these controversies. The regional government promised to activate on a regular basis an emergency clause in the 2005 version of the regional law on territorial government, which appointed a committee of local, provincial, and regional administrators as the final decision-making body in planning affairs. Even more important, local governments would no longer be able to "bank" zoning changes indefinitely after a decision had been reached. Municipalities only had a window of five years to act on these changes before they became void. By that standard, for example, the Monticchiello subdivision would have had to be built by the mid-1990s or not at all. Some environmentalists argued that Monticchiello had to

---

[55] The sentence is available at www.casolenostra.org/uploads/sentenza_monticchiello.pdf.

[56] Christopher Middleton, "Perfect Views for Sale," *The Telegraph*, August 12, 2011, available at www.telegraph.co.uk/property/luxuryhomes/8695904/Perfect-views-for-sale.html.

be spoiled so that similar tragedies would not be repeated. Perhaps more reasonably, the regional government reckoned that in the supposedly immutable and harmonious hills of rural Tuscany a workable level of consensus could be sustained at most for a luster.

Chianti: A Landscape Above All

While the Orcia valley was reinventing itself as a beautiful landscape, the Chianti's reputation as a tourist destination had been surging for years. Here too, however, conflicts emerged over the relationships between agriculture and tourism, and over the histories that would matter in the present and those that would no longer be relevant. These issues mattered as both cultural and practical concerns. Some "locals," for example, felt increasingly neglected and could no longer afford the escalating real estate prices prevailing in the area. In the meantime, what made the Chianti hills beautiful remained a matter of debate. On the one hand, the Chianti was touted as the quintessential sharecropping landscape, even though sharecropping had since disappeared. In terms of both the rationalistic and holistic approaches to landscape, the structural rules of development that had shaped the Chianti had long ceased to be operational. On the other hand, everyone agreed (or at least paid lip service to the notion) that the area should not become a museum or a postcard representation. Indeed, it remained a lived and dwelt landscape, where agriculture was still practiced and people made vulnerable livelihoods and developed complex senses of themselves. How could the Chianti's beauty encompass all these experiences and trajectories and remain true to its multiple histories?

As the intellectual and political debate about landscape protection unfolded, agricultural practices all over Italy changed dramatically, thereby reshaping the appearance of the rural territory. In the Chianti, these changing practices affected above all the two kinds of trees that had always sustained the rural population, the olive tree and the vine, and those two trees found themselves as characters of increasingly complex stories. It is something of a cliché to argue that trees can tell stories. Dendrochronology, the scientific practice of analyzing growth rings in cut trunks, is arguably the most obvious and rigorous way in which modern societies make trees "speak." But less invasive kinds of observation can also tell complex and often compelling narratives about climate, the evolution of cultivation techniques, the availability of labor and energy sources, and indeed a whole range of interactions between humans and their environment. Many species of trees live much longer than human beings, and it is therefore tempting to see them as witnesses to environmental and social change, if not as some of its agents.

Around the Mediterranean no tree species is more endowed with the ability to narrate than the olive tree, with its panoply of religious associations and its traditionally crucial functions as a provider of bodily energy (edible fats) and light (oil for lamps). In the hilly areas of the Mediterranean basin, the planting of olive trees "colonized" and "civilized" the landscape, hindering erosion and consolidating other interventions, such as terracing, that were preliminary to the cultivation of other crops. In a sense, in these lands, the olive tree was a condition of possibility for settlement, and thus for the narration of stories. History and myth met in the knotty trunk of the olive tree.

As we have seen, the perception of landscape, enshrined by the 2000 European Convention, has been a contentious and yet inescapable component of any normative approach to the relationships between people and place. On the one hand, many felt that norms could not ignore how ordinary people related to the land they inhabited. On the other hand, the distance between these ordinary senses and the "structural invariants" detected by experts could be wide. Olive trees constitute a perfect case to examine this gap, and I can perhaps rely on my own experience to illustrate it. Like many Tuscan children, I grew up thinking of the olive tree as the tree par excellence. That was the tree that I drew at school when drawings needed trees, as they often do. The olive tree had a short trunk, three main branches, and a canopy that extended upward and outward, flattening somewhat at the top. This was also the tree shape used by the Military Geographical Institute (IGM) in its official maps to denote olive groves. It was a personal and public icon. Yet, when I was drawing olive trees at school in the 1970s, their shape and distribution had already started to change, and quite dramatically, although I was oblivious to these eventful stories.

I got to measure the gap between my mental image of olive trees and their material presence in the Tuscan hills on a sunny winter afternoon, when I drove through the Chianti at the very beginning of my research for this book. Behind the wheel was an agronomist whom I had met for completely different reasons and who had kindly agreed to show me around as I pondered the feasibility of my project. Facing a hill evenly divided between a barren specialized vineyard and a verdant olive grove (vines are deciduous and olive trees are evergreen), he made me notice for the first time that the vast majority of the olive trees in central Tuscany did not look like the iconic symbol of "tree-ness" I had cherished since childhood. His perception of olive trees was quite different from mine, and my own perception would no longer be the same after hearing the stories he had to tell.

A recent event and several processes had reshaped central Tuscany's olive trees and their distribution since the end of sharecropping. The event was the big freeze of January 1985, when the temperature for a few nights plunged below –20C (–5F). Inner Tuscany (as opposed to the Tyrrhenian shoreline) is at the very limit of the area where olive trees are reliably productive. In some areas the altitude limit for cultivation is as low as 400 meters and some inner valleys are almost devoid of olive trees. The stress posed on the trees is said to enhance the taste of the oil, always far less abundant than in more southern climes such as those of Puglia or Sicily. As we have seen in Chapter 3, another cold spell had decimated Tuscany's olive trees in February 1956, accelerating the rural exodus, although the physical damage had then been somewhat more limited than in 1985, when the cold killed the above-ground portion of hundreds of thousands of trees, sparing only their roots (Illustration 23). In the following months a debate developed as to whether this catastrophic

Illustration #23 Olive trees near Fiesole in 1986, severely damaged by the previous year's deep freeze.

event should be seized as an opportunity for the radical restructuring of cultivation practices, widely regarded as too traditional, or whether the surviving trees should be allowed to shoot back without radical interventions. Some forty thousand farms applied for relief from the regional government and the European Community. But a complete overhaul of the industry proved too expensive. In the end, a combination of the two approaches prevailed. In many marginal areas, prone to periodic deep freezes or situated on steep slopes, trees disappeared or were left to their own devices. In more suitable areas, experts recommended that farmers cut the trees to the ground and choose the strongest three or four shoots to rebuild a canopy and eventually, after four to six years, olive production. Thus, two decades after the big freeze, when I was made to see (rather than merely look at) them, many Tuscan olive trees did not have a single trunk, but three or four.

In fact, a process of major restructuring had already taken place decades before, in the wake of the 1956 freeze. Like the vines, by the 1980s olive trees were no longer an element in the mixed agriculture of the sharecropping system, in which they had been cultivated in association with a variety of other trees (vines and fruit trees) and grassy plants (cereals and fodder crops), rather than in specialized groves. Olive trees and vineyards had been unscrambled, so to speak, in the 1960s and 1970s, so that many hillsides, like the one I faced that winter afternoon in the company of my agronomist friend, were split between the two cultivations – a specialized vineyard on one side and an olive grove on the other.

The shape of the canopy could tell yet another set of stories. Left alone, olive trees grow in the shape of elongated bushes, without a distinct trunk and canopy. In central Italy, sharecroppers pruned their trees routinely and extensively, giving them the iconic shape. Such extensive pruning was justified by at least two considerations. First, olive trees furnished prized wood, used both as a source of heat and as carving material. Second, they should not produce too much shade, so as to allow the growth of the grassy plants (mostly cereals and fodder crops) that were cultivated at their feet. After the end of sharecropping, these considerations became obsolete, and agronomists began recommending more limited pruning, also on account of the increasing scarcity of labor and traditional expertise.[57] The new canopies no longer flattened at the top; rather, they looked like a single or multiple cones (*a monocono* or

---

[57] For an overview, see Fiammetta Nizzi Griffi, *La Potatura dell'Olivo in Toscana: Riflessioni Tecniche* (Florence: ARSIA, 2002). See also Nino Breviglieri, *Interventi sulla Nuova Olivicoltura* (Florence: Cencetti, 1959); and Alessandro Morettini, *L'Olivicoltura* (Rome: Reda, 1972).

policono), without the flattened top. These new shapes allowed for higher tree density and lent themselves to mechanized harvesting by vigorous shaking, a practice that remained relatively rare in Tuscany (as it still does). Some experts even recommended the "natural" bushy shape, thinned out just enough to refine (*ingentilire*) the branches and make them productive. Already common before the big freeze, these canopies became normative after the mid-1980s.

These more or less subtle changes and economic considerations, however, did not dominate the public debate on the consequences of the 1985 cold spell. Unlike what had happened in 1956, when the focus was very much on the social implications of the freeze, aesthetic concerns took center stage in the winter of 1985 and the following months. Especially in the Chianti, the destruction of the olive trees came to be widely perceived as an attack on the integrity of the landscape, understood as a coherent picture to be admired and represented. Already before the freeze, in the early 1980s, observers started reinventing the Chianti as a place where beauty had always transcended mere instrumentality. In the words of a journalist, "the landscape of the Chianti ... is a spiritual landscape that belongs more to the thought of man than to the land, because man in working, regulating, modulating, and decorating the land, has also looked inside of himself."[58] Olive trees were the main ornament of the landscape, and their loss constituted a blow to a whole civilizational lineage – to a patrimony. Thus, in the wake of the freeze, it became customary to compare the Chianti to a fresco in need of restoration.[59]

It goes without saying that this "aesthetic" sensibility disguised to the larger public the major changes that had already transformed olivoculture in the previous decades. Indeed, the 1985 freeze was in many areas, including the Chianti, an opportunity for the expansion of specialized groves organized by modern agronomic criteria. In the Sienese Chianti, for example, 40 percent of olive trees were already located in specialized groves on the eve of the freeze.[60] In its wake, that share was bound to almost double and olive groves were to become denser and with trees of novel shapes, as we have seen. But even in more informed circles, among people whose job was to comment on rural change and make policy

---

[58] Giorgio Batini, "Chianti: Un Giardino alla Contadina," *Toscana Qui* 1, 10 (October 1981): 49.

[59] Giorgio Batini, "L'Olivo un Anno Dopo," *Toscana Qui* 6, 2 (February 1986): 38–47.

[60] R. Cianferoni, "L'Agricoltura nel Chianti Senese," in Comune di Radda, *Studio di Fattibilità di un Programma Speciale di Sviluppo per la Sub-Area Omogenea del Chianti Senese: Documentazione inoltrata alla CEE*, November 1984 (available at IRPET library): 145.

recommendations, "landscape beauty" became a major concern. When discussing the destiny of olive and vine growing, the extant activities of Tuscan agriculture, people of a more "practical" bent would feel compelled to discuss the aesthetic implications of what they believed were rational solutions.

Three years after the big freeze, for example, agronomist Giuseppe Fontanazza sang the praises of the new intensive olivoculture, which promised to treble yields from 1,500 to 4,500 kilograms of olives per hectare and cut labor requirements by more than half. But then he added: "We know that some people object to these innovations because of the aesthetic impact they would exert." But for him change in the countryside had to aim for "functional beauty" (*bellezza funzionale*), as opposed to mere contemplation.[61] Olive trees, thus, spoke to at least three kinds of beauty: a patrimonial beauty that conceived of the Chianti as a scene from a Renaissance painting; a locally rooted and nostalgic beauty that bemoaned the lost world of the sharecroppers; and a functional beauty that claimed to integrate esthetic and practical concerns. Which of these perceptions of beauty should carry the day and be enshrined in preservation norms has remained an open and contentious issue.

While the 1985 cold spell drew attention to the destiny of Tuscany's olive trees, the relatively novel features of the region's other major agricultural activity, viticulture, came to be perceived as increasingly familiar, even timeless. As we have seen in Chapter 3, the restructuring of Chianti's vineyards had taken place in the 1960s and 1970s with the spread of monoculture, accompanied by increasingly strict legislation to enforce wine quality. In 1984, a new law introduced an even more stringent category of wine than DOC, called DOCG (Denominazione di Origine Controllata e Garantita), with which many Chianti producers vowed to comply. The new norms called for even lower tree density in the vineyards and lower grape production per hectare (a maximum of 7,500 kilograms). This legislation presided over the definitive enshrinement of Chianti as a high-quality brand on the international market. A few observers kept complaining about the impact of the vineyards on the landscape, bemoaning their monotony and noticing that, especially in the winter, they looked very much like cemeteries, but this had become a rearguard action.[62]

---

[61] G. Fontanazza, "Rinnovamento della Olivicoltura nel Rispetto dell'Ambiente e del Paesaggio Agrario," in Italo Moretti (ed.), *Il Paesaggio del Chianti: Problemi e Prospettive* (Florence: Associazione Intercomunale 10, 1988): 95.

[62] Pier Francesco Galigani, "Evoluzione del Paesaggio e Meccanizzazione Agricola," in Accademia dei Georgofili, *Agricoltura e Paesaggio* (Florence: n. p., 1991): 27–34.

More common were statements downplaying the novelty of special-ized vineyards and modern viticulture, to the point of detecting dubious genealogies linking contemporary vineyards to those depicted in the art of the late Middle Ages and early Renaissance, such as the frescoes of Ambrogio Lorenzetti and Beato Angelico.[63] After all, there was nothing natural about the terraces of the sharecropping system, which had been bulldozed to make room for the new vineyards. Thus, terraces that had been built in, say, the eighteenth century according to the recommen-dations of Landeschi (see Chapter 1) could legitimately be torn down in the twentieth. The social and spatial makeup of sharecropping, in other words, was a parenthesis, albeit one that lasted half a millennium. Modern wine producers, with their rows of vines flung straight down the hillsides, fashioned themselves as the heirs of the genteel intellects of the early Renaissance. In this spirit, many Tuscan municipalities began to offer tax incentives to replace the cement poles that supported the vines of the Chianti and other wine producing areas with more traditional-looking ones, preferably made of chestnut wood. The larger and more prestigious companies complied relatively quickly, so that today cement poles can only be seen in small vineyards tended to by Sunday farmers or former sharecroppers. Appropriately framed in these ways, the spe-cialized vineyards could thus reinforce the myths of continuity on which patrimonial lineages rested.

As with the olive trees, the search for the sustainable rules of devel-opment (or "structural invariants") that were to shape the present and future features of the Tuscan vineyards was anything but straightforward. Could the relatively new and unmistakably modern specialized vineyards be assimilated to a holistic approach to landscape, cognizant of ecologi-cal, cultural, and esthetic considerations, and thus made compatible with rapidly evolving preservation laws? Some observers criticized the attempts at normalizing modern vineyards through awkward genealogies linking them to late Medieval representations. Painstaking studies argued that average erosion in Chianti's modern vineyards was thirty tons of soil per hectare, vis-a-vis a level of sustainable erosion of 7–10 tons (that is, the level at which soil erosion and replenishment cancel each other out). According to the same studies, the mixed vineyards of traditional share-cropping, often placed on terraced terrain, had an erosion level of 4–5 tons per hectare.[64] The control of erosion had been the foremost preoc-cupation of the enlightened reformers of the late eighteenth and early

[63] Pier Luigi Pisani, "La Vite nel Paesaggio del Chianti," in Italo Moretti (ed.), *Il Paesaggio del Chianti*: 99–123.

[64] Camillo Zanchi, "Carta dell'Uso Sostenibile del Suolo del Chianti," in Fabio Lucchesi (ed.), *La Carta del Chianti* (Bagno a Ripoli: Passigli, 2010): 34–53.

nineteenth centuries, as we have seen in Chapter 1, and those were the kinds of structural invariants that some experts wanted to see restored on Tuscany's hills.

In the spirit of (re)establishing sustainable rules, several experiments have been conducted throughout the Chianti to build terraces and cultivate vineyards on them. These are wider terraces than the ones typical of the sharecropping past, which were often abandoned or even dynamited in the 1960s and 1970s. Their larger width allows a degree of mechanization, above all for the initial implantation of the vines. These terraces are always presented as operations of "restoration," even where terraces may not have existed before. One of the earliest experiments of this kind took place at Lamole, in the municipality of Greve, in the early 2000s. Here fifteen hectares of top-quality vineyards were terraced through the collaboration of private and public actors, also thanks to municipal and regional funds. Revealingly, however, the workers hired to build the stone walls and draining ditches that harked back to tradition were Albanian immigrants.[65] The cost for the terracing alone was 12–13,000 Euros per hectare, a less than forbidding amount in what is today a highly capitalized industry where the establishment of a high-quality vineyard can cost as much as 100,000 Euros per hectare. Nevertheless, these postmodern landscapes, which combine high-quality production, a nod to tradition, and an environmental sensibility (not to mention the use of immigrant labor force), are still rare even in most highly prized corners of the Chianti. Overall, between 80 and 90 percent of the Chianti vineyards remain cultivated *a rittochino*, with the rows of vines running directly down the hillsides. These kinds of experiments add another possibility, another imagining, to the ongoing reinvention of Tuscany's rural landscape.

However awkwardly, vineyards and olive groves could be properly framed and assimilated to a "postproductivist paradigm" built around norms of landscape beauty. In increasingly prized and renowned areas such as the Chianti, other material features and activities offered more resistance to this process of reinvention. Countless petty legal fights and controversies erupted around places that had attracted little or no attention until a few years before. Unsightly motorcycle tracks, built in the 1970s to provide rural dwellers with leisure opportunities, became the subject of bitter fights.[66] When jobs were at stake, controversies would

---

[65] Paolo Baldeschi, "Nelle Contrade di Lamole un Esempio Innovativo di Tutela del Paesaggio," *Paesaggio Urbano* (July–August 2004): 15–21.

[66] This is what happened in a village near Gaiole. See Nicola Della Santa, "Tra Pievi e Castelli una Pista di Motocross," *Toscana Qui* 2, 7 (June 1982): 27–29. But these kinds of incidents were (and remain) very common.

fester for years, engendering suspicion and resentment. The Chianti, like the Orcia valley and the rest of rural Tuscany, is dotted with quarries for the extraction of construction materials. Many of these unsightly sites date back decades, long before the end of sharecropping and the restructuring of the vineyards and olive groves. Now they have become examples of degradation and defacement (*scempio*), dividing local societies between supporters of jobs and defenders of the landscape, each mobilizing different bureaucratic hierarchies (the Superintendence for Cultural Assets versus the Mining Authority; the provincial government against the regional one; and so on).[67] Even when they remain operational, quarries appear as ruins, as monuments to a more barbaric era coming to a close and separated by a temporal and social rupture that made dialogue difficult.

Locals marvel at how rapidly things have changed in their own lifetime. Ruptures have become narratives, around which local identities emerged. Take the story of Luciana, a small hill that used to grace the outskirts of San Casciano, in the Florentine Chianti.[68] In 1969 dynamite obliterated the hill to supply a nearby cement factory, built at the turn of the twentieth century. A dozen sharecropping families had been relocated from the site and compensated with the offer of manufacturing jobs at the factory and modern housing in the plant's proximity. Interviewed forty years later, some of the relocated people sounded apologetic: "Today the Chianti is fashionable, but it's a recent thing. The appreciation for the landscape belongs to the past few years. But we should have thought of it earlier!" Even Remo Ciapetti, the former Communist mayor who had presided over the excavation, noticed that back then "there was no environmental consciousness, but a compulsion to rebuild and produce." As with the Monticchiello development, what had been touted a few decades earlier as an accomplishment in the face of depopulation had become a source of shame.

These now-incongruous "ruins," however, have remained sources of livelihood, at least for a few. The cement factory closed for a few months in 2009, amid claims of pollution and excessive noise. It then reopened, after protests from the workers and their union representatives. Plans have been afoot to transform the plant into a power station fueled by natural gas, with the furnaces doubling as garbage incinerators. A broad grassroots movement has opposed this prospect and has organized vocal

[67] Italo Moretti, "Radda Minacciata da una Cava di Pietrisco," *Toscana Qui* 6, 3 (March 1986): 52–53.
[68] Silvana Nutini, "Luciana, Ricordo di una Collina Scomparsa," *Chianti* 11 (June 2004): 18–19.

demonstrations against it.[69] The necessity to restore the integrity of the landscape, in a corner of the Chianti touted as a potential paradise (*paradiso*), has become a major rallying cry in this case as well, in spite of the long-standing presence of the factory in the area.

In sum, in the Chianti it has been far from easy to find and enforce the kinds of shared rules of spatial development on which the holistic approach to landscape rests, with its barrage of legislative and planning interventions. In fact, the very existence of the region has come under scrutiny in recent years. In the early 2000s the regional government proposed the creation of an officially recognized "rural district" for the Chianti, which would have facilitated planning coordination and the application for funding at the European level.[70] The prestigious association of wine producers, the Consorzio del Chianti Classico, wanted the district to coincide with the area of production of Chianti Classico wine, thereby consolidating the coextension of viticulture and local identities. The mayors of the eight municipalities, by contrast, wanted to include the entire area under their jurisdiction, implying that there was more to the Chianti region than wine. Like in the Orcia valley, the harmonious landscape beauty that was presented to the tourists rested on quite contentious foundations.

The divide between these two camps was both social and political. The Consorzio was led by aristocratic landlords who generally leaned conservative. The mayors were often the leftist descendants of sharecroppers. The Consorzio emphasized the values of heritage and landscape preservation. The mayors, by contrast, stressed the values of social justice and equality, noticing that modern vineyards were far from environmentally sustainable. They also pointed to a more complex history, not limited to art and wine, and bemoaned the astonishing increases in land prices (a hectare of vineyard in the mid-2000s went for 150,000 Euro, ten times what it cost a decade before), as well as the use of immigrant labor and pesticides by the Consorzio producers. This controversy dealt with the meanings of the past and with possible imaginings of the future – that is, it spoke to different senses of time and to conflicting ways these senses of time shaped sense of place. In the end, the people of the Chianti could agree neither on the boundaries of their area nor on the stories that defined them. The idea of creating an official rural district had to be quietly abandoned.

---

[69] www.chiantisenzainceneritore.it/larea-di-testi

[70] Gianluca Brunori and Adanella Rossi, "Processi Post-Rurali e Comunicazione. Il Distretto Rurale del Chianti," in Gianluca Brunori, Francesca Cosi, and Paolo Pieroni (eds.), *Sviluppo Rurale e Comunicazione* (Pisa: Pisa University Press, 2004): 83–114.

Starting in the early 1980s, an increasingly complex architecture of preservation norms and territorial plans began to confront an equally complex and contradictory set of practices. Indeed, every corner of Tuscany has become the subject of different kinds of planning, acting at multiple and overlapping levels of authority. Agricultural planning, landscape planning, and urban planning supposedly all come together as instruments of territorial management (Governo del Territorio). There is a Plan of Territorial Orientation (Piano di Indirizzo Territoriale) at the regional level; there are Plans of Territorial Coordination at the provincial level; and there are Structural Plans at the municipal level. Then there are mandates for the protection of specific places as instances of national heritage, and these fall under the jurisdiction of the central state (the Minister of Cultural Assets), which administers them through the provincial Sovrintendenze. Finally, there are specific projects of rural development that, after being discussed and vetted at all these levels, gain the funding of the European Union, usually under the aegis of the reformed Common Agricultural Policy.

As already mentioned, the new emphasis on rules of development that informs the holistic approaches to landscape claims to have overcome the old forms of planning, which singled out a few places for protection and left the rest of the territory to the ravages of the market. One challenge of this holistic outlook, however, is where to draw the boundary between the descriptive and the normative. Which of the socially embedded and historically produced processes that have shaped the Tuscan landscape in recent years (the pointy olive trees, the rows of vines straight down the hill slopes, the dynamited hillsides, the modern housing for former peasants, and so on) should be condoned, and which rejected or at least mitigated? Another, perhaps more intractable, challenge of holistic regulation regimes lies in their potentially authoritarian thrust. According to architectural scholar Giulio Giovannoni, the Tuscan landscape is above all the product of a "politics of purification" bent on fighting the inevitable messiness and incongruities of everyday life. Thus, while the rural hills and the city centers are frozen in time and lose any vitality, the peripheries and suburbs become sites of resistance and creativity.[71]

While some scholars warn against the elitism of purification, others argue that the maddeningly complex architecture of landscape planning described above is the result of a design meant to defang conservation and allow profit-driven debasement.[72] From the relatively long-term

---

[71] Giulio Giovannoni, "Everyday Tuscany and the Politics of Landscape Purification." Paper presented at the Contemporary Urban Issues Conference, Istanbul, 13–15 November 2014.
[72] See especially S. Settis, *Paesaggio, Costituzione, Cemento*.

perspective of this book, this cynical interpretation seems simplistic. Normative complexity reflects the wide diversity of perceptions and experiences that shape all modern landscapes, as well as the desire of all societies to be able to "read themselves" in the landscapes they produce. This is a desire that modernity at once generates and denies, and it does so with perhaps unique force in rural Tuscany. The search for shared rules to be preserved and/or inscribed in the landscape is rarely a simple and conflict-free process. In Tuscany that search is both genuine and poignant, even though it generates myths that silence certain perceptions and valorize others. Everyday Tuscany keeps emerging from the tensions between visions of purity and the ever-changing needs of a complex society.

Conclusion

The Tuscan rural landscape has told many contradictory stories in the past century. In light of its messy recent history, it may seem preposterous that so many contemporary observers and visitors approach Tuscany as a land where time has somehow stopped, preserving old vistas and ways of life. Indeed, this book has shown that Tuscany's landscape was not simply preserved but constructed through conflicts, negotiations, and compromises. The illusion of preservation is itself the product of a remarkable amount of material and cultural work, performed by a variety of actors and institutions. Before the Orcia valley could become a UNESCO World Heritage Site, its histories had to be pruned and simplified. Many people – some of them locals, others outsiders, but perhaps all of them a hybrid of the two – studiously directed their own gazes and those of others in highly selective ways, ignoring some sites and trajectories (the Fascist reclamation projects, the unfinished dam, the Sardinian shepherds) and valorizing others (the Sienese Primitives' frescoes, Pius II's sensibility for orderly beauty, Iris Origo's good taste and compassion). Similarly, the vineyards of the Chianti are imagined to have always been there, despite their relatively novel appearance and function, while the wind that caresses its olive trees is perceived to be whispering mysterious Etruscan words, even though those trees have been shaped and reshaped by recent freezes and the requirements of industrial production. Above all, the labor of generations of sharecroppers, with their histories of adaptation and struggle, has been romanticized or ignored, but seldom recognized and placed at center stage.

All landscapes change, but the changes that intervene in landscapes that project an aura of immutability are bound to appear particularly striking. Historians relish the opportunity to demonstrate that what seems immutable is actually eventful and forged in conflict. At one level, this study exposes the tropes promoted by the "heritage industry" in a region where those tropes are particularly salient and consequential, and it accomplishes that goal by contrasting the bland clichés of heritage with more complex histories full of conflicts and compromises. The tourists who rent a "villa" in the Orcia valley for a few days should perhaps know that they are actually staying in a former farmhouse built under fascism that became the stage of a Communist-inspired peasant rebellion before turning into a ruin and being gutted and restructured thanks to European funds. Arguably, that knowledge would make their sojourn more interesting, and I genuinely hope that this book might "enlighten" a few visitors and lovers of Tuscany by making them aware of the region's recent past – a past that has actually shaped the landscape they come to admire at least as consequentially as the arts and sensibilities of the early Renaissance.

At a deeper level, however, this book has tried to go beyond the somewhat facile contrast between (actual) history and (invented) heritage. Not all perceptions of timelessness and immutability are self-interested or even naïve. Some of the people who have thought of Tuscany as "outside of time," like my Tuscan-American friend Suzanne or even Frances Mayes, have been motivated by a genuine desire to find some form of authenticity, lost to other dimensions of their lives, and they have been able to apply a dose of irony and self-criticism to that poignant endeavor. By searching for more authentic selves in their relationship with place, many individuals have reshaped their surroundings and made themselves "at home." In these deeply personal stories, self-invention becomes history. Thousands of renovated houses materialize and emplace that connection for everyone to see. And if these endeavors bear the mark of narcissism, as they arguably do, many "locals" have approached the landscape in similar ways as well, trying to read themselves and their stories in place, and they have done that for decades, if not centuries. Simply put, however invented, heritage is one of the forces that shape landscape in both cultural and material ways, thereby "making history."

Indeed, perceptions of timelessness have not been limited to the residential tourists of the late twentieth century, or even to the eighteenth-century aristocrats on their Grand Tour. Generations of Tuscan landlords thought of mezzadria as a somewhat eternal order rooted in Tuscany's soil and soul. Undoubtedly, their perceptions were self-serving, and they resorted to violence when "their" sharecroppers began to believe in other possibilities, as was the case in the aftermath of World War I. Nevertheless, the romanticization of sharecropping as an antidote to the tensions of modernity must be placed at the root of the myths of harmony and calm that have circulated on the Tuscan hills in the past two centuries. This act of romanticization was locally generated "history," understood both as a historical occurrence in itself and as a narrative making sense of the past, but it was also "heritage," in the sense that it proposed a linear genealogy for a desired outcome, namely, the peasants' enduring submission.

It is a crucial argument of this book that a territory becomes "landscape" when its inhabitants produce stories about it, thereby constructing meaningful ways of dwelling there. Landscape is about both senses of place and senses of time. This process of production is a historical occurrence but, especially in modern times, it also involves a search for coherence and totality, which are central ingredients of heritage. In claiming it as their own and making sense of it, historical actors make the landscape tell patrimonial stories. Thus, we can define landscape, as discussed in this study, as the arena where history and heritage meet and clash, with the crucial caveat that both history and heritage are not singular trajectories. Different social subjects read their territory differently, inhabit different landscapes, and often clash with each other over the meanings of place and how those meanings shape access to material resources. Of course different subjects rarely have equal power in determining the outcome of this struggle. As we have seen, in some ways the contemporary appreciation of Tuscany signals the enduring hegemony of the values and sensibilities of the region's large-scale landlords, with their myths of harmony and uninterrupted beauty. At least at first sight, their patrimonial story has carried the day. And yet, this hegemony is still undermined and resisted by many countersensibilities, with their own genealogical stories. In sum, the previous chapters show that history and heritage should be understood as poles in a dialectical process that, at least in Tuscany, has remained unresolved.

Arguably, heritage had long been a factor of spatial production in Tuscany by the time the Black Shirts imposed their reactionary revolution, but the Fascist regime brought that process to new heights. If fascism ushered rural Tuscany into a complex and contradictory form of modernity, it was not just because it built roads, dynamited clay mounds, and spread literacy. In cooperation with the large-scale landlords, the regime understood the Tuscan countryside as a coherent "landscape" under threat by unpalatable processes and tensions. Fascism built on the conservative and paternalistic attitudes of the Tuscan landed aristocracy to shape a landscape that was simultaneously nostalgic and utopian. Perceptions of anachronism were already common in the 1920s. Rural Tuscany was already "out of time." Its enforced traditions of deference and patronage, embedded in the mezzadria system, made this region both a model to be imitated and a society on a possibly doomed trajectory. Class collaboration, gender and generational deference, and organic unity between people and land came to be seen as both eternal traits embedded in the soil and endangered features to be protected and projected into a distant future.

The utopian temporality of the regime, which extended mezzadria and its social order indefinitely, contrasted with the threats of class struggle, gender conflict, urbanization, and environmental and economic exhaustion. The tension between history and heritage was at the very core of the regime's approach to its rural territories, and Tuscany figured prominently in the panoply of Fascist ruralism. When Mussolini claimed that fascism's greatest success was to have incorporated the peasant masses into the nation's "History," his statement betrayed the awareness that there were many histories competing in Italy's fields and villages – many interpretations of the past and many possible futures. In a fundamental sense, the regime was running out of time and tried hard to forge coherent landscapes in which it could read itself in space, before other trajectories caught up with it.

Fascism's reactionary modernism was defeated in a war that seemed to "bring the world" to the Tuscan hills, and Tuscany's peasants responded eagerly to the world's challenges and enticements. The current leftist identity of Tuscany owes much to the struggles the sharecroppers waged in the aftermath of World War II. Tuscan peasants rose up in the name of a more dignified modernity. For the first time in their own conception of historical time, peasants entered "History" on their own terms, as they stood up for themselves and reshaped their relationships with the land. Their aspirations had strong gender and generational dimensions, with women and the young particularly vocal in rejecting "tradition," as they understood it. Tuscan peasants began comparing their living practices with those of other social classes, and unfavorably so, just as their landlords decided to stop investing in their farms despite a series of government mandates. Through the 1950s and 1960s, the organizations of the Left, often staffed by sharecroppers and their descendants, articulated their own visions of redemption, calling for radical land reform and a kind of recapitalization of agriculture that would not make the extant peasants redundant. Some of those visions did come to fruition, albeit primarily thanks to subsidies originating first from Rome and then from Brussels and Florence. But overall the leftist peasants, newly empowered by democratic representation, faced an increasingly uphill battle. They soon realized that their visions were themselves becoming anachronistic. Their horizon of expectation was itself out of step with "History."

The postwar Communists shared with the Fascists a complex and contradictory relationship with modernity. They both promoted and criticized it, and these contradictions were nowhere more strident than in the countryside, especially in a region like Tuscany that was saturated with special meanings for both movements. The paternalism and coerciveness of the Fascists stood in stark contrast with the embedded character of grassroots Communist politics. Nevertheless, both the Fascists and the Communists combined nostalgia and utopianism, as well as the intransigence of people who wanted to go against the grain of "History" and the pragmatism (perhaps even opportunism) of people who wanted to make a difference on the ground and acquire power and consensus in the process. Much like the Fascists, the postwar Communists failed to reshape the landscape in their own image, also because of the contradictory character of that image. Nevertheless, they managed to embed in society and in the land a different sensibility from that of the aristocratic landlords. Myths of peace and harmony would no longer go unchallenged. The Tuscan landscape refused to be pacified once and for all.

At least for a while, that insurgent sensibility spoke the language of resistance to capitalist speculation. The peasant insurgency of the late 1940s and early 1950s had shattered the landscape of submission imagined by the Fascists and their aristocratic fellow travelers, and the Communists tried to reshape rural Tuscany into a more egalitarian and modern territory, but their landscape of defiance also proved ephemeral and incomplete. The rural exodus emptied the countryside and made it increasingly illegible. The emptiness left behind by the collapse of mezzadria seemed to be yielding to the neglect of the bulk of the territory and the unrestrained commodification of few areas and resources. The newly restructured vineyards appeared to many as a speculative landscape, forged with public funds but enriching the usual few. The influx of southern farmers and Sardinian shepherds seemed a prelude to the exploitation of the land for short-term gain. Most consequentially, the needs of a burgeoning tourist sector threatened to extinguish any source of authenticity and create an elitist landscape bent on restoring the social distinctions that the peasant insurgency of the postwar years had challenged. The legacy of those struggles constituted a patrimonial legacy to which left-wing Tuscans meant to stay true. To be sure, tourism and high-quality agriculture also promised new paths to prosperity, but would such prosperity be sustainable? And how equally would its fruits be shared?

The contemporary Tuscan landscape has been forged in the crucible of these threats and enticements. The normative approach to landscape, which regulates dwelling practices in the name of esthetic coherence and hegemonic understandings of the common good, is something of a compromise between conflicting trajectories and sensibilities. Since the deeper meanings of landscape remain contentious, its appearance provides a rhetorical and political terrain where a workable level of consensus can be reached. "Speculation" (now usually divorced from its capitalist connotations) is a threat against which diverse coalitions can be forged. In this arena, commonalities between the leftist heirs of the sharecroppers, who control the democratic process, and the large-scale landlords, who still own the bulk of the land, can emerge, at least provisionally. The generic character of this compromise dovetails with the sensibilities of the international visitors and residential tourists as well, who are eager to see Tuscany as a place that has been spared the ravages of commodification and where the tensions of modernity have been kept at bay. These groups read different patrimonial stories in the Tuscan hills, while defining the contours of a blandly generic "rurality" that is almost devoid of meaning. Nevertheless, they all actively shape the land in the name of its preservation. In doing so, they follow in the footsteps of generations of concerned reformers, from Ridolfi to Serpieri, and from the postwar Communist administrators to the founders of Italia Nostra, the conservationist NGO.

These compromises are as vulnerable as the landscape they claim to protect. The complex framing practices on which landscape preservation relies produce a variety of contradictory outcomes. Regulations valorize some activities and resources by manufacturing scarcity, especially in the production of wine and in the construction industry. At the same time, the Tuscan countryside, like most other rural territories in Europe, receives a variety of subsidies from the European Union. Thus, in some ways rural Tuscans have become postmodern rentiers, expert in the discursive subtleties of many regulatory arenas. The fruits of these processes of valorization are by no means equally distributed, but the agriturismo boom of the last couple of decades has significantly contributed to the democratization of both rents and subsidies. In more intangible but equally consequential ways, the normative landscape, with its increasingly holistic thrust, also provides senses of pride and identity that can be widely shared. For decades, the Communist Party and its successors have provided arenas in which different interests and sensibilities could interact and work out compromises. The trope of the left-wing aristocratic landlord rubbing shoulders with the grandson of sharecroppers while organizing the local post-Communist festival is not entirely preposterous, even though it signals above all the enviable ability of the Tuscan landed elites to reinvent themselves to keep constraining social change. The protection of landscape beauty, and territorial management more generally, are now the main activities where that kind of social integration takes place. As we have seen, even the museums of peasant culture have toned down their insurgent sensibilities in the name of landscape appreciation.

Because of its generic blandness, however, the new patrimonial sensibility tends to produce flimsy compromises, rather than deeply shared commitments. The largely invented tradition of enlightened "government of the territory" dating back to the Middle Ages is too weak and generic to provide concrete guidelines. Thus, conflicts over the meanings and implications of beauty keep emerging, fueled by novel resentments and senses of loss. The Monticchiello affair and countless other petty squabbles over the production and interpretation of space testify to the enduring contentiousness of landscape. Generic patrimonial beauty is the latest version of the signature combination of nostalgia and utopia that has forged rural Tuscany since at least fascism. This new version produces its own totalitarian impulses in its search for purity and the restoration of an imagined lost legibility. Those impulses are met by ongoing acts of resistance, waged in the name of other patrimonial lineages and visions of the future, as suspicions of guile and speculative intentions ebb and wane in the shadow of a celebrated sun. Through all of this, the Tuscan landscape is still being constructed, and thoroughly so, by the tensions between commodification and the search for the common good; between exchange and use value; and between the perception of "History" as a juggernaut that cannot be resisted and emplaced senses of time that belie the existence of a single path to modernity. In that sense, the Tuscan hills remind us that history, with a small "h," should always be declined in the plural, and that the "true" beauty of the Tuscan landscape lies perhaps in its open, unresolved, and thoroughly modern character.

Index

Abbadia S. Salvatore, 72, 74, 83n34
Acerbo, Giacomo, 27
Agnew, John, 11n19
agriculture, 5, 7
    extensions (cattedre ambulanti), 59
    mechanization, 105, 110, 114,
        130–132, 186, 273
    mixed (agricoltura promiscua),
        34–35, 42, 57–58, 61, 68–69,
        113–115n9, 116–118, 123, 129–130
    and patrimony, 204–207
    specialization, 58, 114, 122–124, 129,
        132, 154–155
Agro Pontino, 44, 52
    reclamation of, 27–28, 28n14, 31, 42
agro-tourism, 19, 215–216, 259–260, 286.
    See also tourism
    and interventions on farmhouses, 217
    legislation regulating, 216–217, 217n42,
        217n43
    and patrimony, 216, 218–219
    swimming pools, 217, 259
Aitchison, Cara, 14n25
Alberese, 23
Alberti, Leon Battista, 201
Amiata (Mount), 5, 14, 45, 49, 50, 72,
    74, 81n32
Andrews, Richard, 88n48, 260n40
Andriulli, Giuseppe, 45n47
Angelis, Linda de, 176n56, 178, 178n58
Angheben, Franco, 49n56, 147
Angioni, Giulio, 179n61, 184n74
animal husbandry, 123
    cattle, 18, 69, 71, 93–95, 123,
        125–126, 132, 151–152, 156–158,
        161, 166–169, 177, 188, 252.
        See also irrigation
    Chiusi Slaughterhouse, 161

pigs, 74, 118, 132. *See also* woods
sheep, 18, 132, 151–153, 155, 170n42,
    174–177, 180, 183, 185–188,
    255. *See also* Sardinian shepherds,
    transhumance
Antinori, Niccolò, 203–204
architecture. *See also* farmhouses
    rural versus urban, 213–214
    treaties and manuals, 201
    vernacular, 139, 180–181,
        197–198, 267
aristocracy, 18, 169, 194, 226
    and Fascism, 42, 52–53, 203, 283
    and land ownership, 32, 39, 48,
        57, 155
    resilence of, 203–204
Arno valley, 38, 56, 199
Arosio, Stefano, 262n43
Arrigo, Domenico, 144
Asciano, 145n75, 146
Asor Rosa, Alberto, 252–253, 260,
    262–263, 262n42, 263n44, 264, 265,
    265n49, 267
authenticity, 1–2, 17, 127, 168–169
    as aspiration, 212–213, 213n33, 282
    and the experience of landscape, 6, 8,
        22, 31, 194, 195, 206–207, 282
    farmhouses, 198–199, 201–203,
        212–213, 213n33, 214–215
    and labor, 204, 206–207
    and tourism, 218–219

Baccinetti, Vera, 47n50
badlands (crete), 45–46
    preservation of, 55
    reclamation of, 44–45
Baldeschi, Paolo, 239, 239n2, 247n19,
    276n65

289